PROFESSIONAL 2

ORGANISATIONAL MANAGEMENT

First edition June 1992
Second edition January 1993

ISBN 0 7517 2007 0 (previous edition 0 86277 611 2)

British Library Cataloguing-in-Publication Data

A catalogue record for this book
is available from the British Library

Published by

BPP Publishing Limited
Aldine House, Aldine Place
London W12 8AW

We are grateful to the Association of Accounting Technicians, the Chartered
Institute of Certified Accountants, the Chartered Institute of Management
Accountants and the Chartered Institute of Bankers for permission to reproduce
past examination questions. The suggested solutions have been prepared by BPP
Publishing Limited.

BPP Publishing Limited would also like to thank Jeff Webb, who teaches this
subject at Nottingham Business School, for researching and writing this Text.

BPP Publishing Limited
1993

(ii)

CONTENTS

	Page
PREFACE	(v)
INTRODUCTION	(vii)
Syllabus – Examination skills – Study checklist	

PART A: THE NATURE AND PRINCIPLES OF MANAGEMENT

1	The principles of management. Management in different organisations	3
2	Theories and approaches to management	26
3	Developments in public and private sector management	35

PART B: ORGANISATION THEORY AND STRUCTURE

4	Analysing and developing organisations	53
5	Types of organisational structure	63
6	Organisational culture	94
7	Relationships within and between organisations	116

PART C: THE ORGANISATION IN ITS ENVIRONMENT

8	The goals and objectives of organisations	133
9	The nature of the organisation's environment	147
10	Managing in turbulence	163

PART D: MANAGEMENT PROCESSES

11	Policy, politics and the decision making process	179
12	Strategic management	204
13	Managing financial and human resources	215
14	Audit as a management tool	244
15	Option choice and quality management	259
16	Creativity, innovation and control	274
17	Renewal and change management	299

PART E: ACCOUNTABILITY

18	Accountability and accountable management	323
19	Political, professional and managerial accountability	336
20	Ethics and the consumer in the public service	349

ILLUSTRATIVE QUESTIONS	373
SUGGESTED SOLUTIONS	378
INDEX	411
FURTHER READING	415

CONTENTS

PREFACE .... (v)

INTRODUCTION .... (vi)
Syllabus   Examination skills — Study checklist

PART A: THE NATURE AND PRINCIPLES OF MANAGEMENT

1   The principles of management. Management in different organisations
2   Theories and approaches to management
3   Developments in public and private sector management

PART B: ORGANISATION THEORY AND STRUCTURE

4   Managing and developing the structure
5   ...
6   ...

PART C: MANAGEMENT PROCESS

11 ...
12 ...
13 ...
14 ...
15 ...
16 ...

PART E: ACCOUNTABILITY

18 Accountability and accountable management
19 ...
20 ...

ILLUSTRATIVE QUESTIONS

ANSWERS TO SOLUTIONS

INDEX

FURTHER READING

PREFACE

The past decade has been a period of major change in all parts of the public sector, presenting new challenges to financial professionals in the sector. The Chartered Institute of Public Finance and Accountancy (CIPFA) has responded by introducing a new syllabus. This demanding syllabus is designed to ensure that new members of CIPFA are not only specialists in public service accountancy practice, but are also generalists trained to manage others and to communicate usefully with other managers and specialists.

BPP Publishing has unparalleled experience in producing learning material for those studying for the examinations of a number of professional bodies in the financial field. With the cooperation of CIPFA and the active assistance of professional educators in the field of public sector accounting, we are pleased that we can now offer a range of study material to those aspiring to membership of CIPFA.

This Study Text is designed to assist students in their preparation for the Professional 2 paper *Organisational Management*. It provides comprehensive coverage of the syllabus (reproduced on pages (vii) to (viii)) in the light of recent developments in the subject.

BPP's Study Texts are noted for their clarity of explanation. They are revised and updated each year. BPP's study material, at once comprehensive and up to date, is thus the ideal investment that the aspiring accountant can make for examination success.

The January 1993 edition of this Study Text

The Text has been improved in the following ways.

(a) Some recent examples of management developments in the public sector have been added to the body of the Text.

(b) The question bank at the end now includes a few more case studies.

(c) Each chapter typically contains short exercises, to test understanding and to stimulate thought.

BPP Publishing
January 1993

Should you wish to test your knowledge of this subject by tackling questions in objective test format, turn to page 415 for more details. If you wish to send in your comments on this Text, please turn to page 416.

INTRODUCTION

SYLLABUS

Aims

(a) To provide for students a knowledge and understanding of the theories and principles of management and the contribution they make to the process of management in the various types of organisations.

(b) To develop students' understanding of the variety of forms and structures of organisations and the relationship between structure and objectives.

(c) To develop in students an appreciation of the political and environmental constraints upon management and their influence on the way organisations are managed.

(*Note*. The numbers in square brackets refer to chapters of this Study Text.)

Content

15% The nature and principles of management

Management principles [1]. Developments in thinking in Management [2, 3]. Various approaches and theories in Management, eg classical, scientific, systems, human relations [2]. Commercial, general, service and professional management [throughout]. Developments in public and private sector management [3]. Comparative analysis of management arrangements in different types of organisations [1].

20% Organisation - theory and structure

Types of organisational structure [4, 5]. Centralised/decentralised, bureaucratic/adaptive structures [7]. Matrix organisation [5]. Contingency theory, adapting organisation to environment [4, 5].

Organisational structure and performance [5]. Recognising structural problems [4]. Analysing and developing organisations [4]. Organisational structure and objectives [5, 6]. Style, image and culture of organisations [6]. Power, authority, conflict and interests [11, 20]. Chain of command, reporting lines and span of control [5]. Relationships within organisations [7]. Inter-organisational relationships; using influence [7]. Organisations as enablers and facilitators [7]. Developing partnerships between organisations [7].

15% The organisation in its environment

Importance of environment for the design of organisations and their goals and objectives [8]. Stable and changing environments [9, 10]. The effects of competition, privatisation, commercialism and consumerism on organisations [9, 10]. Information technology and its impact on organisations [9, 10]. Managing complexity and uncertainty [10].

35% Management processes

Understanding management processes: selling objectives, planning, co-ordinating, communicating, controlling, reviewing [13, 16]. The policy and decision-making processes [11]. Politics and political decision- making [11]. Strategic planning, executive action and operational effectiveness [12]. Use of cost and performance measures in evaluation [13]. Marketing as a management process [9, 12].

The role, contribution and structure of the finance function and its relationships with service departments [13]. The role of the finance specialists [13].

Audit's contribution to management [14]. Audit Committees [14]. Relationships between internal audit and other internal review agencies [14]. Audit, the auditor, efficiency and effectiveness and good management practice [14]. Internal audit as an internal consultancy process [14].

Problem-solving [16]. Problems as opportunities [16]. Quality circles and quality improvement [15]. Generating and analysing options and selecting appropriate solutions [15]. Implementation, target setting and monitoring [17].

The importance of creativity and innovation in managing organisations [16]. Organising for and supporting creativity and innovation [16]. Characteristics of innovative organisations [16]. Creativity, innovation and excellence in management [6, 16]. Creativity as a control concept [16]. The balance between innovation and stability in achieving objectives [16].

Management of change [17]. Models for introducing and using change [17]. Organisational ineffectiveness and organisational barriers to change. Organisational development and renewal [17].

15% Accountability

The definition of accountability and the role of accountable management [18]. Freedom, responsiveness, accountability and responsibility [18]. Differences between political, professional and managerial accountability [18]. Accountability in public service organisations [19]. The role of the general public, consumers of services, the media, pressure and client groups, parent bodies [20]. Standards, values and ethics in accountability [20]. The role of internal and external audit in maintaining accountability [14].

Interpretation of aims

The primary aims of the syllabus are to give students the following.

(a)   An understanding of the principles of organisation and management.

(b)   An appreciation of how organisational structures, management processes and environmental factors influence policy formulation, decision-making and success.

(c)   An awareness and understanding of the importance of innovation and creativity for and in organisations, how these might be organised and supported, their implications for organisational success and the development of individuals.

(d)   An awareness of the importance of change in organisations, how it might be introduced and managed and its relationship with organisational effectiveness, development and renewal.

(e)   An appreciation of the various approaches to enhancing and securing accountability in organisations and their relevance to management and organisational effectiveness.

INTRODUCTION

EXAMINATION SKILLS

The examination paper will usually require you to answer 4 questions in three hours: this means that it will be essential for you to plan your timing and your answers carefully. Planning involves:

(a)   reading quickly through the question to get the general feel of it;

(b)   going through the question more slowly a second time, jotting down in note form what you see as being the main points on which you will need to elaborate;

(c)   numbering the points in your answer plan so as to get them into a logical sequence

Finally, *read the question carefully, answer the question set* and *don't forget to state the obvious.*

Answering case scenario questions

You may be required to produce a report or notes on particular situations.

(a)   it does not simply require a *description* of a topic;

(b)   it requires knowledge and understanding of the *application* of an idea to a particular situation or problem;

(c)   it often involves more than one topic and an understanding of the *relationship* of several topics within a given problem.

Scenario questions test your ability to apply your knowledge in a practical way. They also test your approach to problem solving. The examiner wishes to see you have benefited by your studies in applying a coherent and practical analysis to a problem; that you are aware of the *range* of causes and possible solutions to any given problem; and that you would be certain you had *identified* the causes of the problem before selecting any solution. The systematic approach to problem solving involves several stages in a carefully ordered sequence.

1   Define the problem.
2   Identify the factors likely to be causing the problem.
3   Collect and analyse the relevant facts.
4   Identify the range of alternative courses of action likely to solve the problem.
5   Examine the consequences of taking each action.
6   Select and implement the best course of action.
7   Follow up to ensure your actions have solved the problem.

Approach to case study questions

First of all   Read the case slowly and carefully. Ensure you have identified all the people, actions and issues involved in the case.

Be sure you know precisely what the question directs you to do in relation to the case: ask yourself the following questions.

(a)   What is going wrong?
What is your analysis of the situation?

(b)   How would you help...?
What other approaches could be tried?

INTRODUCTION

Be sure you know the difference between these directions, but note that they frequently occur together, in which case your answer must cover *both* parts of the question.

Then
:   Re-read the case and make an *answer plan* relating the question to the factors you see in the case.

Step 1
:   Start your answer with a clear definition of the problem. Ensure you have identified the problem and not simply its symptoms.

Step 2
:   Identify and list the factors likely to be causing the problem. (There will often be 4-6 possible causes, so don't be satisfied with identifying a single cause).

Step 3
:   Demonstrate in your discussion how you would collect the relevant facts *before* attempting to solve the problem, for example checking the records, interviewing appropriate staff. Analyse the facts and identify the actual cause(s) of the problem.

Step 4
:   Show, by writing down a list, that you are aware of the range of possible courses of action and the consequences of each.

Step 5
:   Demonstrate in your answer that you would only select the appropriate course of action *after* analysing the relevant facts and information. Refer to any constraints which would affect your selection, such as limited resources and time, company rules and policies.

Step 6
:   Show how you would implement your plan of action, say by counselling staff concerned, making arrangements for transfers, training and job changes.

Step 7
:   Always show how you would follow up or check back to ensure your actions have in fact solved the problem.

> It is useful to remember that your *answer* should contain *seven steps* starting with a definition of the problem and finishing with the checks to ensure you have solved the problem. The two initial steps of reading and re-reading, and constructing the answer plan are also very important.

Practice in case study questions

Read the following case very carefully. Follow the problem-solving approach outlined in the previous section and prepare an answer in 45 minutes. When you have completed your answer compare this with the illustrative answer given on the next page. Identify any gaps or steps you left out. Re-examine the case to discover any clues or evidence you ignored in analysing the case. Ensure you understand *why* the factors identified might be causes of this particular problem.

The following exchanges were overheard in an office of an organisation:

Manager:
:   I asked for this report on Friday - what delayed you?

Supervisor:
:   I was trying to clear up the end-of-quarter returns.

Manager:
:   But it's already the fourth of the month.

Supervisor:
:   Yes, but I had two clerks away on holiday at the same time.

Manager:
:   How did that happen?

INTRODUCTION

Supervisor:	Well they asked me separately – a few weeks apart – and I hadn't realised what the consequences would be.
Manager:	I'm afraid it is not good enough. I am constantly having to complain about work which is produced at the last moment – or later. It is often badly prepared and faulty. What are you going to do about it?
Supervisor:	I don't know. I never have the time to think ahead.

How would you help this supervisor?

Illustrative answer

Step 1	What is wrong?
The problem	(a) The supervisor's reports are late and they are often badly prepared. (b) The supervisor has failed to anticipate and plan for the effects of two staff being on holiday. (c) These situations are not rare occurrences since the manager is 'constantly' complaining. (d) The manager does not appear to have any plan to correct this situation. (e) The supervisor appears to be hard working but is this enough for effective management?
Step 2 *Causes*	The question directs us to show *how* we would help this particular supervisor. To do this rationally we must define what the problem is and be sure we know what its causes are. Possible causes might include the following. (a) The supervisor just isn't very competent. (b) Perhaps there is a lack of procedures (for instance holiday forms) to help the supervisor plan properly. (c) The supervisor might be overworked. (d) The manager's help and advice might be either non-existent or not much good.
Step 3 *Analysis*	Information needs to be gathered on the qualifications and training of the supervisor, the extent and effectiveness of formal procedures in the organisation, the amount of work loaded onto the supervisor and the training of the manager. This appears to be problem of a failure to *plan*. The problem might be aggravated by:

- inability of the supervisor to *delegate*; and
- the failure of the manager to provide help.

The likely factors actually causing the problem would include the following.

(a) The supervisor does not know how to plan or does not see the need for planning.
(b) The supervisor is overworked or fails to delegate and therefore has not got the time to plan and organise.
(c) The supervisor may have been badly selected and does not possess the qualities of effective management.
(d) The manager has given the supervisor no coaching to help him overcome his difficulties.
(e) The manager does not give enough information or time to allow the supervisor to plan.

Step 4
Courses of action

The appropriate help would depend on a complete analysis of the facts related to this problem which could only be made after interviewing both the manager and the supervisor, checking the records for evidence of the kinds of mistakes and their effects on the performance of the supervisor's section, with careful distinction between facts and opinions.

The nature of the help given to solve this problem would depend on causes disclosed by the evidence but could include the following.

(a)   The *manager* should be counselled:

    (i)   to ensure subordinates understand their jobs and their wider significance on performance;

    (ii)   to provide the resources and information necessary for effective planning;

    (iii)   to provide feed-back on their performance and be prepared to coach, train or counsel to ensure they plan effectively;

    (iv)   to provide a good example by his or her own approach to planning and reward those who follow his example.

(b)   The *supervisor* should be counselled:

    (i)   to see the need for planning and delegation within the wider framework of the effective management of the section;

    (ii)   to accept the need for further training in planning if this is considered necessary;

    (iii)   to accept the manager's help, to follow the manager's example and to discuss with his or her own subordinates the appropriate approaches to delegation.

Steps 5
and 6
Select and implement course of action

The best course of action might be a combination of these alternatives into a plan which is adequately discussed and communicated to both people to ensure they know their part in the plan. The extent to which the supervisor can be retrained depends on how able he or she is and how much time is still available.

Step 7
Follow up

Allow a suitable amount of time for the plan to take effect. Follow up. Has the problem been solved? It might be necessary to consider:

(a)   further training and counselling;

(b)   transfer of the supervisor to other duties;

(c)   dismissal in the unlikely case of wilful dereliction of duties.

INTRODUCTION

STUDY CHECKLIST

This checklist is designed to help you chart your progress through this Study Text and thus through the Institute's syllabus. You can record the dates on which you complete your study of each chapter, and attempt the corresponding illustrative questions. You will thus ensure that you are on track to complete your study in good time to allow for revision before the exam.

	Text chapters Ch Nos/Date Comp	Illustrative questions Ques Nos/Date Comp

The nature and principles of management

The principles of management. Management in different organisations — 1 | 1

Theories and approaches to management — 2 | 2

Developments in public and private sector management — 3 | 3

Organisation theory and structure

Analysing and developing organisations — 4 | 4

Types of organisational structure — 5 | 5

Organisational culture — 6 | 6

Relationships within and between organisations — 7 | 7

The organisation in its environment

The goals and objectives of organisations — 8 | 8

The nature of the organisation's environment — 9 | 9

Managing in turbulence — 10 | 10

Management processes

Policy, politics and the decision making process — 11 | 11

Strategic management — 12 | 12

Managing financial and human resources — 13 | 13

Audit as a management tool — 14 | 14

	Text chapters		Illustrative questions	
	Ch Nos/Date Comp		Ques Nos/Date Comp	
Option choice and quality management	15		15	
Creativity, innovation and control	16		16	
Renewal and change management	17		17,18	

Accountability

Accountability and accountable management	18		19	
Political, professional and managerial accountability	19		20	
Ethics and the consumer in the public service	20		21	

PART A
THE NATURE AND PRINCIPLES
OF MANAGEMENT

Chapter 1

THE PRINCIPLES OF MANAGEMENT.
MANAGEMENT IN DIFFERENT ORGANISATIONS

This chapter covers the following topics.

1. An introduction: the 'organisational fitness test'
2. An overview of management
3. Management philosophy and practice
4. Management in different organisations

---

1.   AN INTRODUCTION: THE 'ORGANISATIONAL FITNESS TEST'

1.1   Below you will find an *organisational fitness test* and an *organisational fitness chart*. Fill them in, and you will describe, honestly, your view as to how your organisation actually functions.

1.2   You can then compare your results with those of your fellow students.

1.3   Why do an exercise at the beginning of a book, before you have even started studying anything? There are two reasons.

(a)   Management can seem quite an abstract, theoretical subject, and the test is a way of encouraging you to think of the management problems in your *own* work environment. This should make the subject come to life for you.

(b)   It is a way of emphasising the practical aspect of this paper.

Using this list of topics enables us to make sense of the elements of the management process and to see the relationships between elements of the organisation and management approaches used in the organisation.

Exercise: Organisational fitness test

(Please do not turn to pages 13 to 15 until you have responded to all the statements on pages 5 to 12.)

The Organisational Fitness Test consists of 120 statements to do with how your organisation is managed.

You are asked to respond to each of these statements, in terms of the extent to which it describes the organisation in which you work.

You are advised to choose, for the purposes of this Test, that immediate part of the organisation (department, section or unit) in which your post is located. Write the title of this part of the organisation in the box below and be sure you address all your responses to it, except where this is impracticable. (You may have to address a few of the statements to a larger part of the organisation or to the organisation as a whole.)

You should select *one* of the four responses provided alongside each statement in terms of the extent to which the statement applies in the part of the organisation you have named above.

Example

	Applies completely	Applies to a large extent	Applies to a small extent	Does not apply
(22) The organisation resists change	4	3	2	1

If you think this statement an entirely accurate description of your part of the organisation, encircle response number 4, as shown above. If, on the other hand, your organisation is very open and responsive to change, encircle response number 1. Alternatively, you may select response number 2 or 3, depending upon your perception of the situation.

Try to avoid hedging your bets by selecting either 2 or 3, when 1 or 4 might be more accurate.

Try to respond to each statement as objectively as you can, especially where it may relate directly to your own managerial responsibilities, and strengths or weaknesses. However, you should avoid spending a lot of time agonising over the correct response in every case.

Remember to respond in terms of the way things are, rather than the way you would like them to be. The more frank and open your responses, the more useful this activity is likely to be to you.

If you have difficulty selecting a response (although it is essential that you *do* select one), or if you wish to qualify or add to your response, use the space for comments following each statement.

The statements are arranged in sets of twelve. These sets alternate between positive statements (for example (7) People here work hard) and negative ones (for example (14) Work is not well coordinated). The system of numbering the responses changes accordingly (from 1, 2, 3, 4 to 4, 3, 2, 1). This pattern has been adopted to avoid the use of leading statements of either an entirely positive or an entirely negative kind, which can skew the results of the exercise.

When you have responded to all the statements record your responses on the scoring sheets and transfer your scores to the Fitness Profile, but *do not turn to these sheets until you have completed your response.*

		Applies completely	Applies to a large extent	Applies to a small extent	Does not apply
(1)	The organisation has clear goals and objectives	1	2	3	4
(2)	All major tasks get completed in good time	1	2	3	4
(3)	All staff have up to date job descriptions	1	2	3	4
(4)	The style of leadership assists in achieving our goals	1	2	3	4
(5)	Meetings are productive	1	2	3	4
(6)	The organisation has good relations with councillors	1	2	3	4
(7)	People here work hard	1	2	3	4
(8)	Senior managers are committed to teamwork	1	2	3	4
(9)	Staff feel involved in decision making	1	2	3	4
(10)	Staff are cost conscious	1	2	3	4
(11)	The organisation has a staff development plan	1	2	3	4
(12)	People here are willing to take reasonable risks	1	2	3	4
(13)	Working procedures are not clearly understood by all staff	4	2	2	1
(14)	Work is not well co-ordinated	4	3	2	1
(15)	The leader spends too much time out of the organisation	4	3	2	1
(16)	I do not get all the information I need to do my job properly	4	3	2	1
(17)	The organisation lacks political influence where it is needed	4	3	2	1

	Applies completely	Applies to a large extent	Applies to a small extent	Does not apply
(18) Promotion prospects in the organisation are poor	4	3	2	1
(19) Staff tend to work on their own, as individuals	4	3	2	1
(20) There is too much competitiveness between staff	4	3	2	1
(21) We are poorly resourced compared to other similar organisations	4	3	2	1
(22) The organisation resists change good time	4	3	2	1
(23) Opportunities for staff development are severely affected by expenditure cuts	4	3	2	1
(24) I do not agree with the goals of my organisation	4	3	2	1
(25) All staff are clear about the organisation's structure	1	2	3	4
(26) Managers are concerned for the feelings of their staff	1	2	3	4
(27) Decisions reached at meetings are recorded and acted upon	1	2	3	4
(28) The organisation continually seeks to satisfy its clients' real needs	1	2	3	4
(29) People here feel a sense of challenge in what they do	1	2	3	4
(30) Senior managers work as a team	1	2	3	4
(31) People have a sense of loyalty to the organisation	1	2	3	4
(32) There is a systematic and rigorous approach to the recruitment and selection of new staff (if any)	1	2	3	4
(33) The organisation has clear policies for redeployment of staff	1	2	3	4
(34) Staff training is effective	1	2	3	4

	Applies completely	Applies to a large extent	Applies to a small extent	Does not apply
(35) Our goals are both challenging and realistic	1	2	3	4
(36) Responsibilities are delegated effectively	1	2	3	4
(37) Leaders are indecisive	4	3	2	1
(38) People here do not really listen to each other	4	3	2	1
(39) We have poor working relations with other departments in the local authority	4	3	2	1
(40) I do not receive fair pay for the work I do	4	3	2	1
(41) Inter-organisational working teams either do not exist or are ineffective	4	3	2	1
(42) This is an impersonal place in which to work	4	3	2	1
(43) The organisation has insufficient staff	4	3	2	1
(44) Staff are unwilling to try out new ideas	4	3	2	1
(45) There is no effective system of staff appraisal	4	3	2	1
(46) Insufficient effort goes into planning for this organisation's future	4	3	2	1
(47) Tasks are not allocated to the most appropriate members of staff	4	3	2	1
(48) Staff are not clear about their roles and responsibilities	4	3	2	1
(49) Staff are aware of what each other is doing	1	2	3	4
(50) The organisation has good relations with the media	1	2	3	4

		Applies completely	Applies to a large extent	Applies to a small extent	Does not apply
(51)	People are willing to take on new responsibilities	1	2	3	4
(52)	There is a strong team spirit within the organisation	1	2	3	4
(53)	People are willing both to give and to take constructive criticism	1	2	3	4
(54)	The organisation has sufficient up to date equipment	1	2	3	4
(55)	Innovations here are carefully thought through before they are introduced	1	2	3	4
(56)	There is an established programme for the training and development of managers	1	2	3	4
(57)	Everyone is committed to achieving the organisation's objectives	1	2	3	4
(58)	We monitor our output regularly	1	2	3	4
(59)	Staff know where their contribution fits in	1	2	3	4
(60)	Managers here help people to give of their best	1	2	3	4
(61)	The organisation lacks a good, positive image externally	4	3	2	1
(62)	Staff here do not have high standards of performance	4	3	2	1
(63)	There are poor relationships within work groups	4	3	2	1
(64)	We have to stick closely to the rules of the organisation	4	3	2	1
(65)	The organisation is suffering badly from expenditure cuts	4	3	2	1
(66)	Change is initiated only from above	4	3	2	1
(67)	No effective steps are taken to brief, induct and integrate new staff	4	3	2	1

	Applies completely	Applies to a large extent	Applies to a small extent	Does not apply
(68) Our contribution to the community has not been thought through	4	3	2	1
(69) Poor work performance is allowed to continue	4	3	2	1
(70) There are demarcation disputes between sections	4	3	2	1
(71) Managers receive little understanding and support from below	4	3	2	1
(72) Leaders are out of touch with what is going on in the organisation	4	3	2	1
(73) People receive recognition for work well done	1	2	3	4
(74) Teams in the organisation are productive	1	2	3	4
(75) There is openness and trust between members of staff	1	2	3	4
(76) The quality of staff is high	1	2	3	4
(77) I have the freedom to do my job differently	1	2	3	4
(78) The organisation provides ample opportunities for training, retraining and updating	1	2	3	4
(79) We are all clear about our priorities	1	2	3	4
(80) Deadlines are prescribed and met	1	2	3	4
(81) The structure of the organisation assists in achieving our goals	1	2	3	4
(82) Leaders socialise with staff	1	2	3	4
(83) There is good communication between different sections in the organisation	1	2	3	4
(84) We make clients, visitors and members of the public feel welcome	1	2	3	4

		Applies completely	Applies to a large extent	Applies to a small extent	Does not apply
(85)	Team members give each other little or no feedback on their work	4	3	2	1
(86)	People here are defensive	4	3	2	1
(87)	We do not make good use of external resources	4	3	2	1
(88)	Other, similar organisations seem to cope better with change than we do	4	3	2	1
(89)	The organisation provides little or no advice and support for staff preparing for retirement or voluntary redundancy	4	3	2	1
(90)	Our most important work receives insufficient time and effort	4	3	2	1
(91)	It is difficult for staff from different parts of the organisation to work well together	4	3	2	1
(92)	Some parts of the organisation are better staffed than others	4	3	2	1
(93)	Leaders fail to involve other staff in decision making	4	3	2	1
(94)	Staff are uninformed about decisions taken and the reasons for them	4	3	2	1
(95)	We have poor public relations	4	3	2	1
(96)	Staff feel they lack job security	4	3	2	1
(97)	There are good working relationships between professional staff and support (for example administrative, clerical, technical and manual) staff	1	2	3	4
(98)	The organisation has good accommodation	1	2	3	4
(99)	Leaders are receptive to new ideas	1	2	3	4
(100)	Staff are encouraged to develop their potential	1	2	3	4

	Applies completely	Applies to a large extent	Applies to a small extent	Does not apply
(101) I can see how my personal goals relate to the goals of the organisation	1	2	3	4
(102) The work of the organisation is well planned and controlled	1	2	3	4
(103) All the parts of the organisation pull together	1	2	3	4
(104) Leaders put in their fair share of work	1	2	3	4
(105) There is good communication between the organisation and the outside world	1	2	3	4
(106) The organisation rates high in the eyes of the profession(s)	1	2	3	4
(107) Existing staff stand a good chance of being appointed to vacant posts	1	2	3	4
(108) members of teams feel able to discuss their personal feelings	1	2	3	4
(109) The organisations severely needs 'new blood'	4	3	2	1
(110) Innovations do not succeed in this organisation	4	3	2	1
(111) Staff would like to move to jobs with other organisations, but are unable to	4	3	2	1
(112) There are unresolved conflicts between the goals of the organisation	4	3	2	1
(113) There is no clear system for allocating tasks to staff	4	3	2	1
(114) The structure of the organisation is top heavy	4	3	2	1
(115) Leaders are too much aware of their status	4	3	2	1

	Applies completely	Applies to a large extent	Applies to a small extent	Does not apply
(116) There is poor communication between the different levels in the organisation	4	3	2	1
(117) The organisation is unconcerned about the social impact of its work	4	3	2	1
(118) Staff regard their jobs strictly in terms of '9 to 5'	4	3	2	1
(119) People here do not like working in teams	4	3	2	1
(120) People here suffer high levels of stress	4	3	2	1

OFT scoring sheets

The purpose of the following tables is to enable you to collate and compare your responses to the statements on the preceding pages.

Take the number (1 to 4) of the response you have encircled against each statement and enter it into the appropriate table (A to L) below. You will need to do this carefully, as statement numbers do not always follows consecutively.

Then add up the response numbers in each table to obtain a score. Plot your scores on the fitness profile on page 15.

A: Goals

Statement number	Your response
1	
24	
35	
46	
57	
68	
79	
90	
101	
112	
Score	

B: Tasks

Statement number	Your response
2	
13	
36	
47	
58	
69	
80	
91	
102	
113	
Score	

C: Structure

Statement number	Your response
3	
14	
25	
48	
59	
70	
81	
92	
103	
114	
Score	

D: Leadership

Statement number	Your response
4	
15	
26	
37	
60	
71	
82	
93	
104	
115	
Score	

E: Communication

Statement number	Your response
5	
16	
27	
38	
49	
72	
83	
94	
105	
116	
Score	

F: External relations

Statement number	Your response
6	
17	
28	
39	
50	
61	
84	
95	
106	
117	
Score	

G: Rewards

Statement number	Your response
7	
18	
29	
40	
51	
62	
73	
96	
107	
118	
Score	_____

H: Teamwork

Statement number	Your response
8	
19	
30	
41	
52	
63	
74	
85	
108	
119	
Score	_____

I: Climate

Statement number	Your response
9	
20	
31	
42	
53	
64	
75	
86	
97	
120	
Score	_____

J: Resources

Statement number	Your response
10	
21	
32	
43	
54	
65	
76	
87	
98	
109	
Score	_____

K: Change

Statement number	Your response
12	
22	
33	
44	
55	
66	
77	
88	
99	
110	
Score	_____

L: Development

Statement number	Your response
11	
23	
34	
45	
56	
67	
78	
89	
100	
111	
Score	_____

ORGANISATIONAL FITNESS PROFILE

Dimensions of the organisation		Your score	FITNESS	UNFITNESS	POOR HEALTH	SEVERE ILLNESS	TERMINAL CONDITION
A	Goals	☐	10	20	30	40	
B	Tasks	☐	10	20	30	40	
C	Structure	☐	10	20	30	40	
D	Leadership	☐	10	20	30	40	
E	Communication	☐	10	20	30	40	
F	External relations	☐	10	20	30	40	
G	Rewards	☐	10	20	30	40	
H	Teams	☐	10	20	30	40	
I	Climate	☐	10	20	30	40	
J	Resources	☐	10	20	30	40	
K	Change	☐	10	20	30	40	
L	Development	☐					
	Total score	☐	120 180 240 300 360 420 480				

2.   AN OVERVIEW OF MANAGEMENT

2.1   The syllabus and the examination paper for this subject are concerned with the application of theories of *management* in practical, real-life situations. A good definition of the nature of management is given by Drucker.

'There are *five* basic operations in the work of the manager. Together they result in the integration of resources into a viable, growing organism. A manager in the first place *sets objectives* ... Second a manager *organises*. He or she analyses the activities, decisions and relations needed. He classifies the work. He divides it into manageable activities and further divides it into manageable jobs. He groups these units and jobs into an organisation structure. He or she also selects people for the management of these units and for the job to be done. Next a manager *motivates and communicates*. He or she makes a team out of the people that are responsible for various jobs ... The fourth basic element ... is *measurement*. The manager establishes targets and yardsticks ... He or she sees to it that each person has measurements available which are focused on the performance of the whole organisation and which, at the same time, focus on the work of the individual. The manager analyses, appraises and interprets performance ... Finally, a manager *develops people*, including himself or herself.'

2.2   Management exists at a variety of levels, from the *strategic management* of the organisation in relation to the external environment in which the organisation operates, to the *operational management* of daily work tasks.

2.3   The objective of all levels of management is operational efficiency and success in achieving the organisation's objectives. This involves planning and co-ordinating the work of the organisation and, particularly in public sector organisations, communicating with the public, with elected or nominated members, with subdivision of the organisation, and with a wide range of other organisations. Communicating, convincing, cajoling, and even coercion are all part of the management process.

2.4   Many writers maintain that management is thus an *art* rather than a science. A science of management, on the other hand, would be concerned with identifying *principles and rules* which can be learnt and used in *any* management situation and which generate the desired outcome.

2.5   Both approaches perhaps rest on certain assumptions about the way people behave and how they should be treated. Douglas McGregor offers two theories of how *managers* see *people*.

(a)   Theory X: the average human being as having an inherent dislike of work and will avoid it if they can.

(b)   Theory Y: the expenditure of physical and mental effort in work is as natural as play or rest.

(c)   Studies of Japanese organisations have created Theory Z type organisations, in which a manager adopts a spirit of cooperation, a consensus approach to decision making, with people valued for the work they do.

2.6 Much management literature is thus concerned with how to *manage people* (eg motivation theory and human resource management). In the public and service sectors, human resources are seen as a major *asset*, and efforts are now being put into staff development, measuring staff performance, and establishing performance related pay schemes.

2.7 The *organisational fitness test* which you have jut completed is based on the principles of Likert *(New Patterns of Management, 1961)* which advocates a participatory *team based* approach to management.

   (a) The agreement and acceptance of the goals of the organisation by everyone in the organisation is seen as the basis for good management.

   (b) Leadership is important in establishing *clear goals*, especially in multifunctional organisations which are task driven and depend upon technically qualified staff working together.

   (c) The control processes involved in such organisations are concerned with resource use and the quantitative and qualitative measurement of the performance of the organisation.

   (d) The decision making process depends on *expert* and *position* power and the influence of a wide range of interests and political choice in the public sector. Note that:

      (i)   *expert power* is possessed by an individual who has specialised knowledge (eg of planning regulations, environmental health) and is usually symbolised by some sort of professional qualification;

      (ii) *position power* is possessed by an individual by virtue of his or her position in the organisation hierarchy;

      (iii) *personal power* comes from someone's force of personality or charm;

      (iv) *physical power* comes from superior force;

      (v)   *resource power* (including access to authority) comes from controlling resources;

      (vi) *negative power* is the power which comes from the ability to disrupt operations.

2.8 Likert *(New Patterns of Management, 1961)* developed from research a four fold model of management systems.

   Likert identifies a *four fold* model of the management system.

   System 1: exploitive authoritative
   top down management decisions are imposed from above
   motivation is based on threats (of punishment)
   little team work and poor communications

   System 2: benevolent authoritative
   condescending form of management
   motivation based on rewards (eg pay increases
   limited team work

System 3:   *Consultative*
diffuse responsibility and sharing with subordinates
motivation based on rewards and some involvement
fair degree of team work

System 4:   *Participative groups*
trust and confidence in subordinates
motivation is related to achievement of agreed goals
high degree of team work and communication

2.9   The System 4 model is advocated as providing the most *productive* management approach both in the public and private sectors. Is it then a general management principle?

(a)   This has been reflected in the management philosophy introduced to government departments since the Financial Management Initiative was outlined in 1982. The management of the Civil Service has been based upon setting clear objectives and targets, improving line management responsibility, and a concern with results.

(b)   In the Likert model, motivation is based on the achievement of agreed goals through team work and communication, and the rewarding of effort in achieving goals. The System 4 model is perhaps akin to Japanese management practice.

The public sector has introduced a wide range of performance indicators. The setting of performance targets reflects the Likert model. Performance related pay has also been introduced into parts of the public sector.

Organisation variables

2.10   Likert suggests a table of organisational variables which can help in understanding the principles of management in all *organisations*. These organisational variables are as follows.

(a)   Leadership process (who follows whom?).
(b)   Motivational forces (why work hard?).
(c)   Communication process (how do you know?).
(d)   Interaction influence process (how can you tell?).
(e)   Decision making process (how are things decided upon and choices made?).
(f)   Goal setting or ordering (how can you direct the organisation's activities?).
(g)   Control process (how do you make sure everything is going according to plan).

Staff motivation

2.11   Much of the management literature of the day has been influenced by the Likert thesis. Broadly speaking, this states that the best way to get things done is through:

(a)   supportive relationships;
(b)   pursuing group methods of decision making; and
(c)   creating expectations of high performance for all staff. This requires that all the processes identified above require attention and that they are all interrelated.

Other authors have expressed the same principles in different ways; perhaps with a particular emphasis on one or two of the factors (eg: identifying *leadership* as the issue to be addressed; human relations; creating a learning organisation).

2.12 A *mission statement* which perhaps covers all aspects suggested in paragraph 2.10. The objectives of the mission statement can be used to measure the performance of the organisation both internally and externally. *Performance* targets can be established to meet both customers' needs, and to promote the efficiency of the workforce and the resources used to achieve the targets.

2.13 The System 4 model also requires balancing the needs and objects of individuals with those of the organisation, through:

(a) understanding work problems and helping people to do the job;
(b) seeking employees' opinions;
(c) giving credit and recognition;
(d) maintaining good incomes.

2.14 It is often the job of *middle management* to communicate the objects of the organisation to the staff and to manage both the day to day work of the section or unit and to develop the ability of the section and the staff to improve performance and meet future challenges.

2.15 In common with service industries in the private sector, the efficiency and effectiveness with which services are delivered by the public sector is very much a consequence of the *motivation* and commitment of the individuals providing the service (unlike, say, a robot-controlled production line).

A 'people-centred' management approach, in which trust, openness, cooperation and support are the predominant features, and which human resources issues are seen as investments, rather than expenses, is thus relevant to the public sector.

Subgroups within the organisation

2.16 Implementing this philosophy might imply in practice, a team-based approach, but this must be coordinated with the needs of the overall organisation. Likert describes a link pin structure, so that teams are linked by overlapping membership.

2.17 Furthermore, teams are coordinated through the existence of clear goals and objectives. This is implemented in systems of:

    (a)   personal accountability (ie the buck stops *here*);
    (b)   detailed introduction of performance measures (for each individual);
    (c)   detailed cost measurements.

2.18 In short, many recent changes in the public sector have included:

    (a)   reinforcement of hierarchical systems of control by establishing objectives;

    (b)   giving work units more power to arrange operations to determine how these objectives should be achieved.

2.19 This can be shown in the Financial Management Systems and Processes introduced into the Civil Service and all government departments.

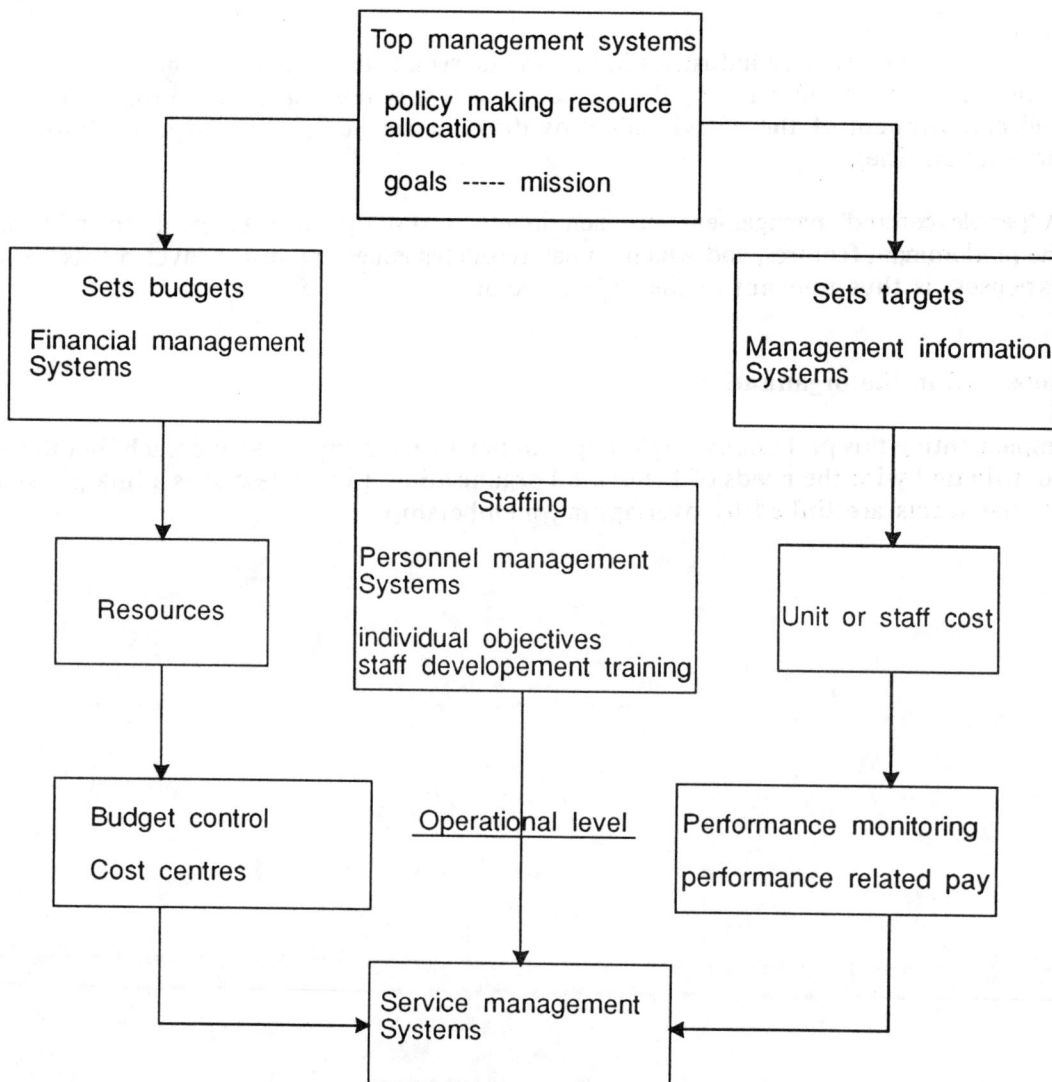

2.20 Changes in management approaches and structures in the civil service have been supported by the introduction of:

(a) new information technology systems;
(b) more analytical and evaluative accounting systems.

The assumption is that computer information systems will free middle managers to improve working practices, develop staff competencies and meet customers' requirements, while enabling greater analysis and review at the centre.

2.21 In the private sector one role of middle management was to train and develop staff in the organisation. This also fits in with management theories that emphasises human resource management, team work and the development of individuals in the organisation.

2.22 Staff development and training become an important element of the System 4 type of management which is reflected in *Organisation Development*:

'... organisation development is a human resource technology; that is it is concerned with marshalling the capabilities of people meeting their own as well as organisational objectives. It is a process, a process of planning and implementing change in such a manager that enterprises have increased capacity for survival and growth.'
E Schein *(Organisational Development: French, Bell and Zawacki 1983)*

3. MANAGEMENT PHILOSOPHY AND PRACTICE

Mechanistic vs participatory

3.1 These are both linked to what definition of management is used and how this relates to the views on motivation of people.

(a) If a mechanistic control view is taken then:

(i) *management philosophy* will be concerned with having clear rules and procedures;
(ii) the issues of *practice* are concerned with the procedures for exercising control.

(b) If an open 'participatory' view is taken then:

(i) the philosophy will be about establishing a learning organisational structure (listening, involving people at all levels);

(ii) the practice will be about setting up teams, delegation and the communication between teams.

Internal vs external

3.2 Depending on the manager's level and functions, he or she may be concerned with:

(a) the external environment in which the organisation operates (and so will be seeking changes in the organisation which will maintain or improve its position or secure its survival); or

(b) the internal environment of the organisation (and so seeing that particular functions are performed, eg control over finance).

Technique vs culture

3.3 Another definition of management is given by T Watson: *Management, Organisation and Employment Strategy.*

(a) 'Management can be taken to refer to the work that any individual contributes to the steering of the organisation as a whole.'

(b) Managing is organising: pulling things together and along in a general direction to bring about long-term organisational survival.'

3.4 Two strands emerge from Watson's view of management. One is concerned with structures, plans and techniques and the other with culture, ethos and meaning. Over the last ten years a private sector culture has become dominant in public sector management thinking and has influenced the structure, the planning and technique of public sector management practices. More importantly, attempts have been made to change the management philosophy, the *culture* and ethos of the public sector. (The notion of different cultures will be taken up in Part B on Organisation Theory and Structure: Chapter 6.)

The public sector

3.5 The 'failure' of the public sector to deliver, from political perspectives of both left and right, has led to:

(a) the introduction of financial and cost controls over the public sector;
(b) a search for improved management *of* and *in* the public sector.

The appearance of models of good management practice from studies of the private sector in America and Europe and the taking up of these ideas by the Government and the Audit Commission has been seen as the panacea for poor public sector management.

3.6 *Private sector management* ideas have been implanted in the public sector by managers and staff who have been swapped between the civil service and major companies. Private sector advisers have also been appointed to advise the Prime Minister and the Cabinet, and to draw up plans to reform the civil service and the health authorities. Representatives of the private sector have been appointed on to governing bodies in health and education to add the business culture to the public sector.

3.7 *Cost control.* General changes in the management systems in the public and service sectors over the last few years have emphasised control over the cost of services and providing services at least cost. This has required having targets or performance criteria to measure activities which do not have a profit or returns on investment basis of measurement.

3.8 *Quality enhancement.* Having identified cost savings and improvements in ways of providing services, the next stage is concerned with quality and consumer satisfaction. This has been reflected in movements to establish 'Charters' for standards of service, obtaining 'quality' standards for the service provided. Future developments may well include adding a system of quality control through such bodies as the Audit commission.

Summary

3.9 A simple summary of *changes* in the management of the public sector since 1982 is given below.

Aspects of management	Old systems stable environment	New systems dynamic environment
Objectives	Meeting needs, social equity, provide a service	Value for money, economy, efficiency effectiveness. Commercial, competitive advantage, consumer satisfaction
Key tasks	Administration	Business (market based) decisions, demonstrating low cost with high productivity, achieving performance targets
	Professional advice to political decision makers	
	Provider of services	Facilitator of service provision, enabler
Structure	Centralised and bureaucratic	Decentralised and flexible, open to competition
Decision making	Rules and regulations	Personal initiative
Power	Seniority, general skills, and wide experience	Expertise, specialisation training in management
	Status and position power	Job content and teamwork
	Weak consumers	Strong customer voice
Rewards	Based on position, criticism of poor work	Based on performance and achievements
Service quality	Internally defined professional administrative view	Externally defined 'best practice' set standards
Strategy	Service role based	Corporate and political task based
Staff	Loyal and security of employment set roles	Short-term contract, personal competencies

3.10 An example of changes in a public sector institution is given by changes in the Civil Service College.   (*Economist* 31 October 1992)

(a) The college has been reorganised as a business, with a strategic plan of its own.

(b) Performance is measured against targets, and 'consultants have been brought in to advise on how to reward it in pay'.

(c) 'Market-testing' (trying out courses and altering them in line with customer needs) is enbraced with enthusiasm.

4. MANAGEMENT IN DIFFERENT ORGANISATIONS

4.1 The management of organisations will vary according to a variety of factors. Here are some examples.

(a) *Size*. In a small organisation the management tasks may not be differentiated from operational tasks of the organisation. In a long established and large organisation a whole management structure has become the norm with its own history and force in the organisation. Survival may be the main issue for a small business, whereas maintaining market share and developing new products may be the driving force behind large businesses.

(b) *Type of business*. International business will have a different management approach than, say, medium sized businesses meeting a very local market. The power they have to determine and the nature of the 'market' in which they operate is bound to be different. The ability to generate internal resources, to finance new products, to train and develop staff and to develop new markets is expected to be found in the larger organisations. For the public sector it may be providing a service which is free at the point of consumption and has to be managed efficiently and effectively within resource limitations and rules laid down at a higher level of policy making.

4.2 Private and public sector organisations also can be distinguished on the following grounds.

(a) The aims of the public sector are to provide a service which is for the benefit or potential benefit of the community or the public as a whole, not the individual consumer. For example, defence against foreign aggression is not a consumer good, purchased by some people rather than others. The welfare state acts as a safety net on which all in theory should be able to rely if circumstances dictate.

(b) The people who pay (taxpayers) may not be the people who consume the service (school children), although this is often the case in the private sector too (parents purchase computer games for their children to 'consume').

(c) The measure of success of the public service cannot be measured on the basis of profit, market leadership, share value or return on capital.

(d) The public sector is *politically* accountable and a two tier level of decision making is clearly defined.

(e) The idea of 'public service' as a moral ideal is not really found in the private sector.

(f) Uniform policies on grading, payment and levels of reporting are common.

(g) It is sometimes difficult to measure performance and compare operations against performance standards in the public sector.

(h) Bureaucratic procedures are laid down to provide for accountability.

(i) The Audit Commission, ministries' inspectors and appeals procedure are put in place to safeguard the consumer and the taxpayer. This does have some private sector equivalents, particularly for the privatised utilities.

5. CONCLUSION

5.1 Organisations can only achieve their goals by the coordinated effort of their members and it is the task of management to get work done through other people. Management is concerned with being responsible for the attainment of the objectives of the organisation and setting those objectives in the light of environmental goals.

5.2 Management can be regarded as:

(a) occurring within a structured organisation;
(b) aiming to achieve certain objectives;
(c) operating through the efforts of many people;
(d) using systems and procedures to organise tasks.

5.3 Drucker sees 'management' as denoting a *function* as well as the *people* who carry it out, a social position and authority, and also a discipline and field of study.

TEST YOUR KNOWLEDGE
The numbers in brackets refer to paragraphs of this chapter

1 Describe six types of power. (2.7)

2 Describe the changes in public sector management since 1982. (3.9)

3 What are the main distinctions between public sector and private sector organisations? (4.3)

4 What are the variables in Likert's model for the public sector? (2.10)

Now try question 1 at the end of the text

Chapter 2

THEORIES AND APPROACHES TO MANAGEMENT

This chapter covers the following topics.

1. Classical theories of management
2. Scientific management
3. The human relations school
4. The systems approach to management
5. Contingency approaches to management

---

1. CLASSICAL THEORIES OF MANAGEMENT

1.1 The notion of management as a skill in its own right and the development of 'management' as a separate group of people, occurred in the nineteenth century.

1.2 The *classical theories* are exemplified by Henri Fayol who identified *five elements* of management.

(a) *Planning* (examining the future, developing a plan of action).

(b) *Organising* (providing the materials and resources to carry out the activities of the organisation).

(c) *Command* (getting optimum returns from all employees in the interests of the whole organisation).

(d) *Co-ordination* (harmonising the activities of the organisation to achieve success).

(e) *Control* (measuring achievement against the plan, establish instructions and principles of command).

1.3 Fayol also recognised fourteen *functions* of management.

(a) *Division of work:* the objective is to produce more and better work from the same effort through specialisation of tasks.

(b) *Authority and responsibility:* wherever authority is exercised, responsibility arises. The application of sanctions is seen as essential to good management.

(c) *Discipline:* the system has to be seen to be fair and applied judiciously.

(d) *Unity of command:* for any action a subordinate should receive orders from one boss only. Dual command was seen as a source of conflict.

(e) *Unity of direction:* there should be one head and one plan for any group activities with the same objective for the organisation.

(f) *Subordination of individual interests to general interests:* the interests of the organisation should dominate individual and group interests.

(g) *Remuneration of personnel:* employees and employers should both be satisfied as far as possible. Well directed effort and achieving performance standards can be rewarded.

(h) *Centralisation:* the degree of centralisation is a question of proportion in achieving overall efficiency.

(i) *Scalar chains:* the chain of superiors from the ultimate authority to the lowest ranks. Some measure of initiative is still required at all levels in the organisation.

(j) *Order:* all things should have a place and everything should be in its place in material order to reduce loss. Social order requires an appointed place for every employee which means a good organisation and good selection of staff.

(k) *Equity:* equality of treatment should operate at all levels in the organisation.

(l) *Stability of tenure of personnel:* generally organisations are better off with stable managerial personnel.

(m) *Initiative:* is a source of strength for the organisation and should be encouraged and developed.

(n) *Esprit de corps:* harmony and units are the strength of the organisation. Verbal communication should be used in preference to written communication whenever possible.

The 'classical civil servant'

1.4   The implication of Fayol's approach is that the *same* management principles can be applied in any situation. Fayol, in drawing up this list of characteristics, emphasised personal flexibility with managers having both administrative and generalist skills. Fayol's description of a fairly rigid hierarchy, with clear spans of control and reporting procedures, stability and a social order with everyone knowing their position, could be a description of the Civil Service.

1.5   The *civil servant* is seen as a generalist administrator who can be moved from department to department, from education to health and still successfully manage the activity. This generalist administrator approach has been under challenge in the civil service since the Fulton report in 1968, but is still maintained in the higher echelons of the policy makers and advisers to ministers. It demonstrates, in practice, the actual distribution between 'management' as a skill in its own right, and the technical mastery of subject matter that is being managed.

2.   SCIENTIFIC MANAGEMENT

2.1   Frederick Taylor is described as the father of scientific management. Scientific management rigidly divided doing work from the management of that work.

2.2   Taylor proposed four principles of scientific management.

(a)   *A development of a true science of work.* All aspects of work should be investigated and laws developed for managers to deal with problems and that managers should not rely on 'seats-of-the-pants' judgements.

(b)   *Scientific selection and progressive development of workmen.* Workmen's skills should be investigated and training provided to bring the best out in the workers and allocate workers to tasks to which they were most suited.

(c)   *Bringing together of the science and scientifically trained people:* the use of scientific principles to decide what should be done and using properly trained workmen should maximise productivity.

(d)   *Constant and intimate co-operation between management and workers.* This is the most important aspect of management and includes rewarding effort and understanding the attitudes of workers.

2.3   The application of Taylor's ideas coincided with introduction of production line methods of mass production. These production methods applied scientific techniques to increasing output, and used workers as cogs in the production line. There were good rewards for workers who could develop the right skills and apply themselves to the limited tasks they had to perform. The problems associated with the approach were hostility from the unions who predicted job losses and felt that workers were being dehumanised. The rules were strict and the pace of work was dominated by the speed of the production line.

2.4   Direction, control and adherence to rules became the hallmark of the scientific management approach. Time and motion studies, the organising of working procedures to maximise output and profitability, were its tools. The alliance of management and workers was limited to rewards and working conditions and profitability for the enterprise. Increasing productivity and increasing profits were the measures of success.

2.5   As importantly, planning was divorced from doing, with workers having less autonomy to plan and control their work.

3.   THE HUMAN RELATIONS SCHOOL

3.1   The human relations approach examined the social system of the work environment. The attitude of workers should not be ignored and attention should be given to human psychology. A sociological perspective on management was developed which added a *behavioural* aspect to scientific management. This was because it was felt that there were limits to the capacity of scientific management to achieve results.

3.2   Elton Mayo's experiments in the 1930s in the Hawthorne Plant of Western Electric Company, now known as the Hawthorne experiments, found a feeling of group solidarity and that workers were motivated by the psychology of the group, and through their relationships with supervisors. Mayo believed that the economic motive stressed by Taylor was unimportant compared with the emotional and personal sentiments of workers in improving productivity and efficiency. Team working, organising work and setting targets by negotiation with management were key factors in establishing motivation and production efficiency.

3.3   Following on the early research work of Mayo, a systems and contingency approach to motivation of workers has been developed by such writers as Kurt Lewin (1938) and Frederick Herzberg (1966). Motivation of the individual depends on the system in which they operate, the environment and work group. Different people react to the same environment in different ways. Motivation may vary from day to day according to the person's moods, as well as the 'hygiene' and 'motivator' factors in the work situation.

3.4   Herzberg (1966) identifies those factors which cause job dissatisfaction (hygiene factors) and those which cause job satisfaction (motivator factors).

(a)   Dissatisfaction or hygiene factors included:

(i)   company policy and administrators;
(ii)   salary;
(iii)   the quality of supervision;
(iv)   interpersonal relations;
(v)   working conditions;
(vi)   job security.

(b)   Satisfaction or motivator factors included:

(i)   status;
(ii)   advancement;
(iii)   gaining recognition;
(iv)   being given responsibility;
(v)   challenging work;
(vi)   achievement;
(vii)   growth in the job.

3.5   These satisfaction or motivator factors are the most effective in motivating workers to achieve a higher performance. The dissatisfaction or environment or hygiene factors are essential because they prevent conflict but they will not produce positive motivational effects for long. A lack of motivation means workers concentrate on the hygiene factors such as pay and working conditions.

4.   THE SYSTEMS APPROACH TO MANAGEMENT

4.1   'Management by objectives'. The phrase is attributed to Drucker (1954) and attempts to link *organisation goals* to *individual performance*. It has been taken up by the organisation development writers and is part of a behavioural approach to management.

4.2   The participation of individual managers in agreeing the objectives for their units and the criteria for measuring performance review and appraising of results. The concern is shifted to the *measure* of performance, rather than the subordinates following procedural instructions to undertake their work.

4.3   This approach implies a rational model of policy making and implementation, which contains elements of strategic planning, short-term tactical plans, and these are translated into operating procedures for each division of the organisation having a mechanism for reporting back on the achievement of the objectives and the costs involved.

4.4   Introduced into the Department of the Environment by Michael Heseltine (1980) management information systems for ministers (MINIS) has been extended to other government departments as a series of management information and review systems. The White Paper *Financial Management in Government Departments September 1982*, sets out the principles behind this approach.

4.5   This approach process requires that *clear* objectives can be set which achieve the goals of the organisation or in some cases the policy being introduced.

(a)   These objectives have to be capable of being measured in terms of the input required to achieve them and the outputs expected. This may be expressed as 'man days' of work necessary to perform a particular task.

(b)   The other problem is that of breaking collective performance of the organisation into individual tasks. The political priorities of policy makers and objective setters may differ from those who have to carry out the task.

4.6   The *advantages* of MBO are that it:

(a)   provides for a critical review of the goals of the organisation;

(b)   clarifies the strategic objectives;

(c)   identifies problems in the tactical implementation of the objectives;

(d)   improves the management control procedures;

(e)   identifies the contribution of individuals in achieving the objectives and meeting the performance standards set;

(f)   provides for improved control and early responses to problems in the operation of the organisation;

(g)   provides appraisal systems which are fairer as it is clear how people are being assessed;

(h)   improves motivation as individual performances are monitored.

4.7   The *disadvantages* are that:

(a)   it needs clear goals and objectives which may be difficult in the public sector as *policies* are not 'self contained';

(b) there is the potential problem of good management of a bad policy;

(c) it requires commitment by top management in setting objectives and reviewing the outputs;

(d) a meaningful relationship between work tasks and objectives is hard to establish;

(e) the objectives should be achievable and capable of measurement, which is not always possible;

(f) participation and teak working has to be maintained;

(g) there is a problem of paperwork and filling in work returns and analysis of work done;

(h) a standard *performance level* to achieve an objective may be *meaningless*;

(i) an incompetent manager can appear effective because the unit achieves its objectives, outside the control of the manager (ie despite, rather than because of).

4.8 Many of the management initiatives in central and local government are based on the principles of management by objectives. The setting of clear objectives for running a service and working within performance guidelines can provide the framework in which policy can be implemented.

4.9 The next step in the introduction of these ideas is concerned with grading of staff and using staff appraisals to evaluate performance and to have a system of performance related pay.

Systems approach

4.10 The systems approach requires co-operation and the ability of individuals to communicate and work together to achieve a common purpose, or set of purposes. Two types of systems have been identified.

(a) A *closed system* is isolated from the external environment and is likely to decay.

(b) An *open system* is concerned with interacting with the external environment. The open system is dynamic and is able to adjust and evolve in relation to the external environment. Managers require more freedom to act and exercise discretion in achieving objectives by varying inputs and the use of resources to achieve the best results in relation to the shifting environment in which they operate.

4.11 Trist has suggested that organisations have a set of subsystems which include the structure of the organisation, the technological system which covers the work to be done and the machines and tools and resources used, and the social system which includes the people in organisation and the way they think and react with each other.

4.12 The emerging *holistic* view of organisations and the interdependence between the sub systems has become a basic principle of management thinking, together with the concern to provide the organisation with *a mission* to guide it in the ever dynamic and changing environment in which it operates. Management theories have moved from seeking certainty, by attempting to establish scientific principles and rules to guide managers, to an uncertain world of 'it all depends', and questions of 'what if this happens', and the need to communicate and manage change.

5. CONTINGENCY APPROACHES TO MANAGEMENT

5.1 The contingency approach states that the ideal type of management structure will vary according to the situation or circumstances of each particular individual organisation. There is no *universally* correct answer to a given management problem. The *contingent* factors can be identified, and so the criteria by which one can assess the most efficient organisation for the circumstance.

5.2 Contingency theory states that management structures are likely to be a compromise between pressure for *uniformity* and pressures *of diversity*.

   (a) The *pressures for uniformity* are concerned with standardisation, rules and procedures which reduce waste. Centralised control and checking is possible with uniform systems and staff who are skilled in particular parts of the task.

   (b) The *pressure for diversity* arises from the need for local solutions. The customer is satisfied with different technologies, and individuals identify with smaller work groups. Decentralisation of authority can provide for diverse responses to issues as they arise. The power of small decentralised units can be also limited as they are only a small part of the whole and have little call on resources or impact on the output of the organisation.

Environment

5.3 A main factor in determining the optimal structure of an organisation is the nature of the *environment* in which it operates and the stage it is at in its own development. The environment can be:

   (a) political;
   (b) economic;
   (c) social;
   (d) technological.

5.4 In *stable environments* the move is towards uniformity with the top managers being able to direct activity and keep in touch with the external environment. This is the case for a well established organisation which has a clear market or niche position from which few threats are likely to emerge.

5.5 In *unstable environments*, more diversity is seen, as the organisation has to have more contacts with the external environment and to allow lower order managers to respond quickly to the ever changing situation. The private and the public sector have both been coping with an unstable environment and have gone through a number of structural changes to create responsive organisations which are close to the customer.

5.6 The contingency theory probably fails to demonstrate that management is a science. 'Management is no more of a science than is medicine: both are practices ... Just as medicine feeds of biology, chemistry, physics, on a host of other natural sciences, so management feeds of economics, psychology mathematics, political theory, history and philosophy.' *Drucker (1987)*

Exercise

Here are two departments.

(a) Department X processes certain benefit claims. It employs 39 people including at its head, a Chief Supervisor, who has two supervisors reporting to him. Each of these supervisors in turn directs three under-supervisors. An under-supervisor is in charge of five staff. The documents are dealt with in turn by Section A, B, C, D and E each of which performs a particular clerical procedure. The system was implemented one year ago by the Chief Supervisor who mentioned 'economies of scale caused by division of labour' which would result. In the old system, forms were only processed by one individual.

(b) Department Y has 40 people, including a chief supervisor, and three supervisors each supervising a team of twelve individuals. They also process benefit claims, but each team is responsible for a whole claim, sharing out the longer and shorter work. Each team has a series of performance targets related to estimated workload, and past performance.

Required

Compare and contrast the management practices of each department.

Solution

Hints. Department X appears to have been reorganised on scientific management principles. Department Y appears to have adopted some of the techniques of MBO.

---

6. CONCLUSION

6.1 Management thinking has undergone several mutations since the subject was first discussed.

6.2 Scientific management concentrated on the work process. Later theories examined the social factors in the work environment, to include studies of the way people are motivated.

6.3 Some thinkers made a distinction between:

(a) processes; and
(b) results.

TEST YOUR KNOWLEDGE

The numbers in brackets refer to paragraphs of this chapter

1 List Fayol's fourteen management functions. (1.3)

2 What were the principles of scientific management? (2.2)

3 Distinguish between hygiene and motivator factors. (3.4)

4 What is management by objective? (4.1)

5 What two factors must be reconciled in the contingency approach? (5.2)

Now try question 2 at the end of the text

Chapter 3

DEVELOPMENTS IN PUBLIC AND PRIVATE SECTOR MANAGEMENT

This chapter covers the following topics.

1. What do managers do?
2. From crisis management to strategic management
3. The 7 'S's
4. The 7 'C's
5. Management competencies

---

1. WHAT DO MANAGERS DO?

1.1 Managers make decisions for the organisation. A variety of management positions are possible. The appropriate style of management depends upon the situation or opportunities which arise, in a particular time and place and with those particular actors involved.

1.2 Managers have to deal with *uncertainty* and turbulence in the external environment or the market. They must resolve uncertainty and steer a pathway through the environmental turbulence to maintain the organisation's and their own survival. They need a knowledge and understanding of the external environment, and relationships with others working in that environment.

1.3 Managers have to make best use of the inputs they receive to achieve organisational goals, whatever these are. They must inevitably consider the complexity of the organisation they control.

1.4 We have briefly examined some of the *theories* of what management is - but what about the *empirical studies* as to what management actually does?

Networking

1.5 Managers spend between 50% and 80% of their time talking to people. The decisions they make and the data they receive are transmitted mainly through people, not via formal reports or on computer screens.

1.6   Kotler (1982) defines the core behaviours of managers as:

(a)   setting *agendas* for action;
(b)   establishing and maintaining networks to implement those agendas.

Agendas are lists of things to be done, short or long term, details of action or just vague ideas. These come about by generating possibilities, questioning plans and policies, gathering information and calculating ways and means of implementing proposals, strategies and agreements. The agenda items are implemented through a network of contacts built up by the manager.

1.7   Management in practice may be different from the theory and studies of 'what managers do with their time' is perhaps the starting point. Mintzberg in looking at what managers did challenged the views of the management science school. Mintzberg identifies ten roles for the manager.

(a)   *Interpersonal roles*

(i)   *Figurehead:* to represent the unit formally.
(ii)   *Liaison:* to deal with peers and outsiders to swap information.
(iii) *Leader:* to staff the unit and motivate its members.

(b)   *Information roles*

(i)   *Monitor:* to gather and store information useful to the unit.
(ii)   *Disseminator:* to pass on to subordinates information not otherwise available.
(iii) *Spokesperson:* to pass information out from the unit.

(c)   *Decision roles*

(i)   *Entrepreneur:* to initiate change.
(ii)   *Disturbance handler:* to take charge when the unit is threatened.
(iii) *Resource allocator:* to decide where and how unit resources will be deployed.
(iv)   *Negotiator:* to deal with outsiders whose consent and cooperation is required by the unit.

1.8   A similar list can be produced for the role of the *leader* of a local authority, to which can be added:

(a)   maintaining party or faction unity;
(b)   achievement of party or faction aims;
(c)   coordination of party or faction behaviour in various committees;
(d)   securing reelection.

1.9   The studies of managers' behaviour (R Stewart *The Reality of Management*) suggests that the belief that the manager is a reflective and systematic planner is a myth. Managerial work is disjointed and discontinuous. Much of management is crisis management, not strategic management.

1.10 The research also demonstrated that rather than relying on aggregate information and reports, the manager gained most of the information from *verbal communications*. This more informal source provided an up to the minute perspective, was easier to understand and to interrogate and weight against other feelings about what was happening.

> 'The manager is ... forced to do many tasks superficially. Brevity, fragmentation and verbal communication characterise his work.'

The telephone, the corridor chat, the business lunch, attending a conference, are the work of the manager.

2. FROM CRISIS MANAGEMENT TO STRATEGIC MANAGEMENT

2.1 Coping on a day to day basis is ultimately made easier if a longer-term view is available. Some advance planning can be helpful. *Strategic management* is concerned with making decisions about *objectives* and resource allocation, motivating the organisation to implement them and making sure the *desired results* are achieved.

(a) In the private sector the desired results cover profit levels, changes in market position, new product development and keeping up with competitors. Increasing productivity and even slimming the company down to maintain a viable business may be required to provide a measure of value of money to investors and financial backers.

(b) The private sector approach is being introduced to the public sector. Examples are as follows.

 (i) The NHS internal market requires a split between the purchaser and provider, to create the effect of marketing trading.

 (ii) Compulsory competitive tendering has had a similar affect on local authorities.

 (iii) Exam-results tables for schools are supposed to indicate the 'quality of the service'.

 (iv) The DVLA has targets for the time it takes to process licence applications.

2.2 At the same time, these experiments are invariably flawed. At best they will produce a controlled simulation of free market conditions. This is for several reasons.

(a) They still rely largely on external funding (ie government financing), with its inevitable restrictions.

(b) Pricing cannot be on a market basis.

(c) They are controlled by professional personnel whose objectives are directed more towards quality of service delivery rather than resource efficiency.

2.3 The importing of a managerial rather than administrative culture into the public sector has resulted in a number of changes in how public sector organisations operate.

(a) They will have chief executives.

(b) Mission statements are introduced.

(c) Output as well as input measures are developed.

(d) A marketing and public relations strategy is adopted.

(e) They identify their markets and their *competitors*, perhaps the most radical change. After all, the notion of hospitals competing against each other goes against decades of NHS management.

(f) Meeting consumer preferences is the top priority.

(g) It is desirable to have known costs, and unit costs so that a price can be developed for everything.

Executive agencies

2.4 The creation of executive agencies was supposed to inject a certain private sector approach into public sector central government management, by developing a *management strategy* for the public sector.

(a) It is sometimes asserted that in the Civil Service, the prestige positions are those related to the *creation* of policy. The *execution* of policy has become a less prestigious task.

(b) *Executive agencies,* which are separate units, enable a career structure to be based on purely management skills.

2.5 The executive agencies are thus a new approach to public sector management, given that they are arenas in which the *management* of service delivery gets prime attention.

(a) The objectives measure the use of resources in providing the service and meeting the policy goals and testing management performance against the strategy. A similar type of objective could be established for private companies under the control of a holding company.

(b) The strategies discussed concern managing the organisation, not about the actual policy or service. The general managers in the health service, administrators in educational institutions, managers of a supermarket could all work under the same type of strategic guidance.

2.6 There are currently (December 1992) about 75 Executive Agencies dealing with areas as diverse as the payment of social security benefits (*Benefits Agency*), and driving licence processing. Agencies are semi-autonomous bodies, not under the *direct* control of central government. Each has a Chief Executive. There is some autonomy in decision making.

2.7 An example of 'new style' Executive Agency in the Driver and Vehicle Licensing Agency (DVLA). Here are examples of private sector practices introduced in this agency.

3: DEVELOPMENTS IN PUBLIC AND PRIVATE SECTOR MANAGEMENT

(a) All staff go on 'customer care' programmes.

(b) Staff are personally responsible for their work, so that mistakes are dealt with by the person directly concerned rather than sent to a Complaints Department.

(c) Decision-taking is devolved to line managers.

(d) There are clear performance targets for service delivery.

(e) The agency now has a marketing department (eg selling vehicle licence numbers, selling information about a car's history to dealers).

(f) There is more flexibility and autonomy in staffing (eg more part timers at peak levels).

That being said, the agency is still partly controlled by the Department of Transport, and is subject to Treasury financial controls.

The 'old' civil service

2.8 The public sector has been dominated by professional and administrative ways of working and have had little management training to be able to cope with these new management approaches which originated in the private sector. Professionalism in the public sector has meant long periods of training 'on the job', progressing up the career ladder as a competent *professional*, and eventually arriving at a management position without any management training.

2.9 Managers in the public sector are seen as agents of the state, putting into effect government policy which might often mean a cost cutting exercise and managing on a reduced or controlled allocation of resources. This seems to imply more central control despite fragmentation of activities into budget or cost centres. It does not encourage team working and can undermine goal achievement with units or sections fighting for scarce resources.

Possible new cultures

2.10 On the other hand, research into the operation of social services shows autonomous managers who work to professional ethics and practice and are neither 'policy puppets' nor 'budget maximisers'. These managers might find it difficult to operate under central control. They operate outside standardised norms and the work they do is related to clients' needs. Problems arise in *imposing* performance measurement, and expecting work to be completed within notional deadlines just because it *can* be done that way. They work in a *task* culture, solving problems, operating in a number of vertical and horizontal networks, which is advocated by current management thinkers such as R M Kanter in *When Giants Learn to Dance*.

2.11 A culture is a set of share values, assumptions, beliefs and practices into how work is to be organised. It is the culture of the public sector which needs to be changed and to adapt to the market-led approaches of the political ideology of the day. *Handy* identifies four *gods of management* that are reflected in the philosophy, culture and structure of organisations. Each person has a preferred god and so fits more happily into one organisation than another. The gods are as follows.

(a) *Zeus* is a dynamic entrepreneur who rules with snap decisions (a *club culture*), is the central figure in a spider's web.

(b) *Apollo* is the god of the *role culture*. Everything and everybody are in their proper places. In short, this is a bureaucracy.

(c) *Athena* is the goddess of the *task culture*. Expertise is the basis of power and influence, and operated in a matrix structure (ie there are a number of overlapping sources of authority in the organisation).

(d) *Dionysus* is the god of the *existential culture*. Management is based on personal relations *without a defined boss*. Examples are professionally based organisation, or some research and computing companies.

2.12 These cultures may operate together but it is the Athena and the Dionysus which are currently advocated as the most relevant to coping with *change* and the turbulence being experienced by both the public and private sectors. A concern with the creative organisation, ways of using intuition in organisations and improving communications and networks are seen to be the ways forward.

Which god is worshipped in your office?

3.   THE 7 'S's

3.1 Peters and Waterman highlighted eight attributes characterising excellent companies. 'Excellent' is defined as follows.

(a) *Bias for action:* 'a can do' approach which delivers the goods.

(b) *Closeness to the customer:* listen to your customers.

(c) *Autonomy and entrepreneurship:* allow managers as much freedom as possible.

(d) *Productivity through people:* a company's major asset is its workforce.

(e) *Hands on value driven:* management by walking about; top managers to run the reception desk to see how it operates.

(f) *Stick to the knitting:* do what you do best and do not stray into unknown territory.

(g) *Simple form, lean staff:* no complex hierarchies or patterns of reporting.

(h) *Simultaneous loose/tight properties:* tight central control with clear goals which allows the rest to get on with the business.

The interactions can be demonstrated in the following diagram.

7'S' Framework

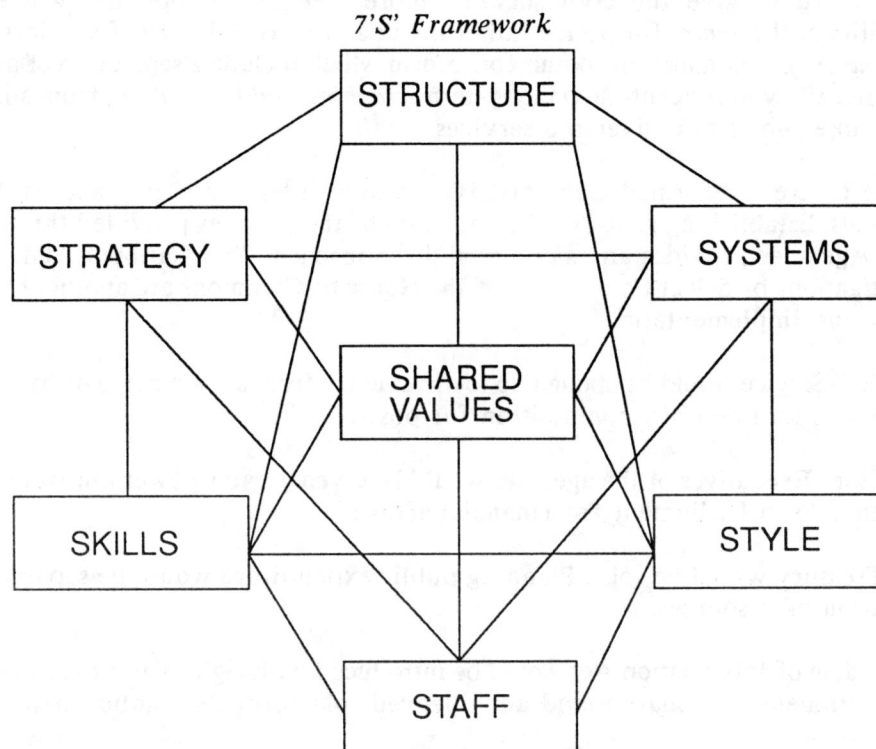

This emphasises that both the traditional 'hardware' of organisations (strategy and structure) and the 'software' (style and staff) must be managed equally to be successful.

3.2 The elements all focus on *shared values*. This is the vision or mission for the organisation, which is recognised both internally and externally.

A *mission statement* is a clear articulation of the organisation's agreed values and goals.

(a) *Structure* is how the tasks are divided up.

(b) *Strategy and budget* are concerned with making the organisation work and allocating resources.

(c) *Systems* are how the organisation communicates.

(d) *Style* is of the image and presentation of the organisation.

(e) *Staff* and *skills* are concerned with staff development and how staff are treated.

3.3 All of these have been taken up by the *Audit Commission* and *Local Government Training Board* in identifying 'Good Management Practice'. A number of local authorities have:

(a) produced mission statements and action plans;
(b) related budgets to objectives;
(c) decentralised decision making;
(d) created a house style or image;
(e) introduced short-term contracts, performance related pay, staff appraisal and development.

3.4   At central Government level changes in management are also taking place with further reforms being advocated to give the civil servants more freedom to operate, while increasing accountability at the *centre* for policy rather than day to day delivery of services. Ponting in *Changing the old guard* makes proposals for reform which include a separation of a small policy elite in Whitehall, who concentrate on long-term *planning and legislation*, from administrative agencies whose job is to deliver the services.

(a)   At the centre a reformed Cabinet Office would integrate policy and evaluate policy proposals. Establishing goals for the operation of the services provided through the Next Steps Agencies provides an example of this approach. The National Audit Office and investigations by Select Committees of the House of Commons are another check on both policy and implementation.

(b)   The Civil Service would be opened up to direct entry from a wide range of backgrounds and at the top, and be open competition for posts.

(c)   The Chief Executives of the agencies would be given greater power but would be directly accountable to Parliament for financial affairs.

(d)   The Treasury would be split. Planning public expenditure would be separated from the allocation of resources.

(e)   A Freedom of Information Act would be introduced with rights for citizens to have access to government information and an enhanced role form the Ombudsman.

(f)   There would be protection for civil servants who disclose abuses of power by the executive.

(g)   An inspectorate of administration to monitor the performance of administrative agencies and recommend improvements in the management and delivery of public services.

3.5   The use of outside experts to advise the Cabinet on management reforms has resulted in a 'New Public Management' emerging, which is concerned with change and asking fundamental questions. The reforms introduced by Griffiths, Rayner, Ibbs, and now put in practice by Kemp have changed the nature of the way in which the civil service is working.

3.6   Having established a change in culture and ways of working, creating new structures and reporting systems, giving more freedom and flexibility to unit managers is only the start of the changes. These changes now have to become the new culture and they themselves would be the basis for future working and staff development. Moving people across the public-private sector divide may be one way to merge the cultures. Blurring the edges between what is public and what is private, working more in partnership across the public, private and voluntary sectors may become more common. For organisations to survive, they will have to be more aware of change and how to manage and avoid crisis management and breakdowns.

4. THE 7 'C's

4.1 The renewal factor by R H Waterman identifies planning as practised by renewers and those organisations who are able to identify and manage change.

This is shown in the 7 'C' framework.

7 'C' Framework

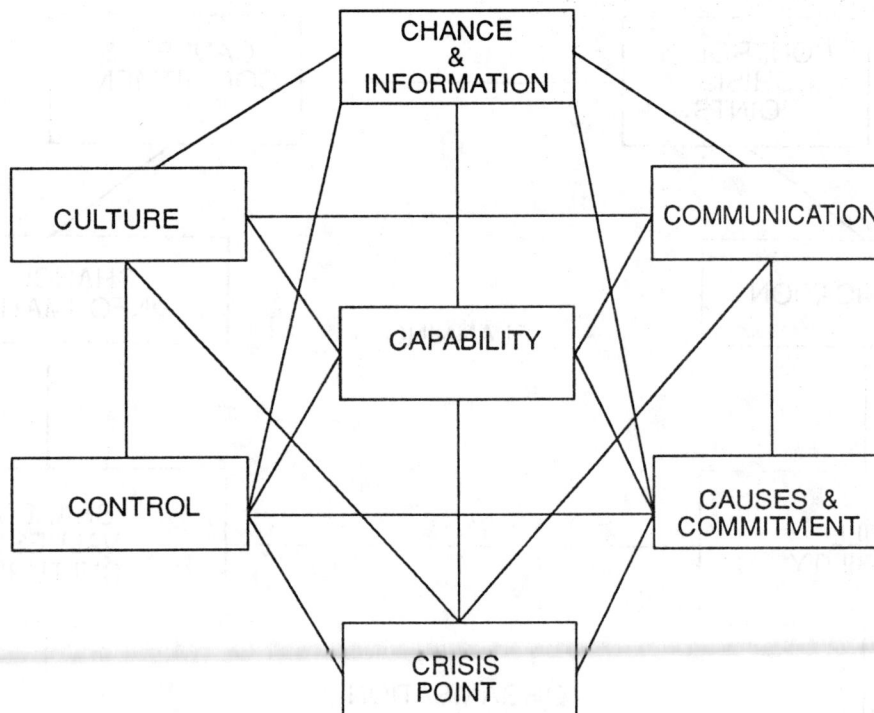

4.2 (a) *Capability* is the need to all work together to create an effective organisation, the ability to react to problems and to work through to solutions.

(b) *Chance and information*. This includes being aware of the organisational environment and recognising opportunities in it.

(c) *Culture* is the shared values of the organisation.

(d) *Control* is concerned with forecasting/measuring change.

(e) *Crisis points*. These need to be forecast to avoid breakdowns in operation, the what if questions.

(f) *Causes and commitment* are concerned with 'issue brokers' who consider wider issues and seek out solutions to problems.

(g) *Communication* is the division and integration of tasks.

4.3 Link the two models (7Ss and 7Cs) together as a way of reviewing the operation of the organisation which can manage to survive and prosper.

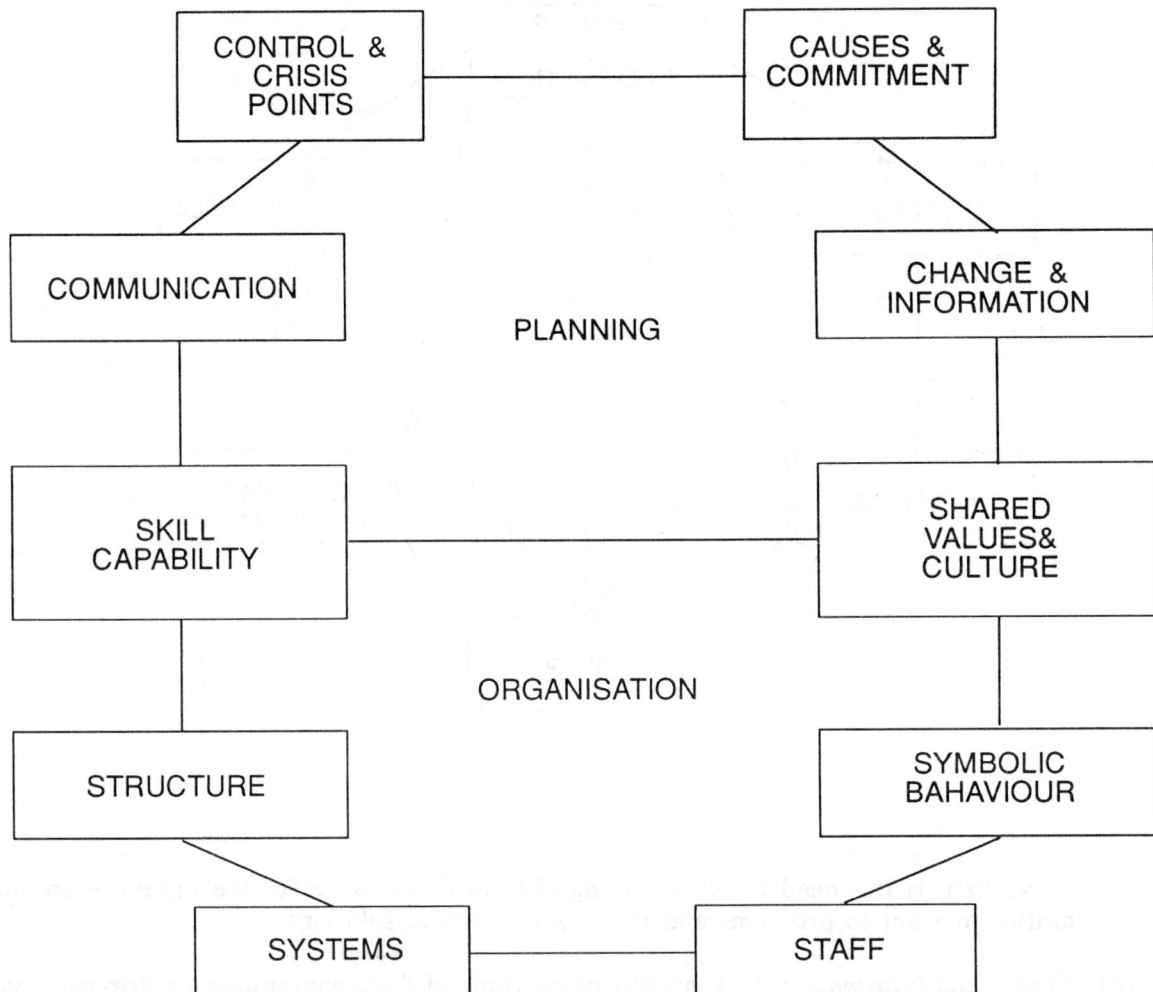

4.4 Common themes appear to be:

(a) delivery to the customer;

(b) to provide open and reactive communications systems;

(c) to introduce a style that is willing to face problems;

(d) to develop a structure to cope with change and instability, puts a lot of effort into training and developing staff;

(e) to create a 'learning' organisation.

5.   MANAGEMENT COMPETENCIES

5.1   The type of managers required in these organisations in the public or private sectors will need special skills and attitudes to be able to cope with managing in unstable situations. The American Management Association has identified the characteristics of the modern manager. These are demonstrated by Hayes in a series of films on management.

5.2   An extensive survey of successful managers identified eighteen competencies grouped under four headings:

   (a)   intellectual;
   (b)   entrepreneurial;
   (c)   socio-emotional;
   (d)   interpersonal.

5.3   These notions of competencies have been taken up by 'Management Charter Initiative' in the UK and work based management competencies are now being tested. For local government these competencies would be expected to cover the following.

   (a)   *Dealing with people*

        (i)   Those for whom one has responsibility
        (ii)   Peers (those working at the same level)
        (iii)   Those to whom one reports
        (iv)   Clients, customers and citizens.

   (b)   *Managing activities*

        (i)   Financial activities
        (ii)   System control
        (iii)   Human management techniques
        (iv)   Functional activities.

   (c)   *Sensitivity to the environment*

        (i)   The political world
        (ii)   Customer expectations/needs
        (iii)   Legal considerations
        (iv)   Organisational, social, economic and technological change.

   (d)   *Personal effectiveness*

        (i)   Communication
        (ii)   Numeracy
        (iii)   People orientation
        (iv)   Results orientation
        (v)   Self awareness/developing orientation.

Many of these competencies are about feelings, judgement and performance and will depend on individual and organisational *values*. They can lead to conflict as well as cooperation. The ability to deal with conflict and make it a positive factor in management is as important as dealing with apathy. The motivational factor in management again becomes important. The purpose and organisational culture of the public sector, and the underlying political and value positions of the stakeholders, mean that *equity* and a *collective view* of providing a service are core issues which have to be an integral part of public sector management.

5.4 Two opposing views have been held on the purpose of public sector management.

(a) The public sector is an agent of the capitalist state managing social problems to maintain the basic structure of capitalist power.

(b) From the right, public sector managers are responsible for inefficiency and wastefulness in the provision of services and these services should not be provided by the public sector anyway.

Limitations of private sector models

5.5 The introduction of private sector management into the public sector is seen as increasing efficiency and decreasing costs. However, the assumption that the management can *control* the behaviour of the workers in the public sector ignores the level of freedom that many workers have exercised in this sector, and the professional competencies *already* present in the services.

5.6 As part of the reforms, the power of the professions and the freedom of workers in this sector has to be controlled. A number of mechanisms can be used to achieve this: the appointment of general managers in the health service, and the provision of standards for service provision at given costs as accounting controls (performance measurement), are two such examples.

5.7 Research studies of public sector managers coping with financial constraints, and studies of field workers and their clients, suggest that successful public sector management is based on a high degree of *self managed modes of delivery* and *decentralisation*. This may well mean that there is little scope for *active* management, as services are locally organised.

(a) The nature of the services offered by parts of the public sector are client-led anyway. With limited resources, it is a rationing process which is juggled with at an individual level.

(b) Working in teams provides for a level of control over the delivery of the service and discipline.

(c) The group values (the ethics of public service provision) and group socialisation also provide a cultural control.

Management is then about maintaining a fair and reliable system of delivery and acting as a negotiator between the providers at ground level and the allocators of finance up the hierarchy.

5.8 Moreover, private sector activities are ultimately determined by the market. Services are provided by the private sector because there is a demand in the external market, or a demand can be created.

5.9   In many public sector services, on the other hand:

(a)   the size of the 'market' (or consumers of the service) is determined by the provider of the service (eg social security entitlement);

(b)   the consumers of the service do not have a choice of alternative providers;

(c)   their ability to complain is limited, especially as negligence, for example, is difficult to prove.

Therefore, in some instances, the public sector is less responsive to changes in its base of potential customers.

If standards are defined in advance, then this is a benchmark against which standards must be measured.

5.10   The limitations of market models is the thinking behind various quality initiatives introduced in a number of local authorities, taken up by the *Citizen's Charter*.

This proposes to give users of public services the right to redress for poor services. The hope is that this will encourage better service provision and not require the organisations to create complaints and refunding sections. European proposals on establishing a system of redress for poor service could give legal teeth to these initiatives. Other political parties are calling for a Quality Commission which could be added to the functions of the Audit Commission. The Quality Exchange established by the Audit Commission is providing a way of building up examples of good practice and disseminating them.

5.11   In addition, techniques such as Total Quality Management are being introduced to the Public Sector to enhance the quality of service delivery.

Leadership and cultural change

5.12   A new emphasis, in both the public and private sectors, is on *leadership* and the quality of the top management and the strategic core. This is emphasised by Tom Peters, in *A Passion for Excellence, The Leadership Difference. Organising for Local Government* (by Barratt and Downs) provides checklists on measuring the performance of *councillors* and the roles they have to play. The way in which local authorities are managed is the subject of a White paper from the Department of the Environment (July 1991) on *The internal management of local authorities*. Proposals being made on the internal management of local authorities suggest the creation of a strong mayor to run the authority or an executive board, or even an elected chief executive.

5.13   Tom Peters has also expressed his views on the roles of the public and private leaders. Both should be consensus builders, constantly willing to listen to their *customers* and constituents. Moreover 'the best managers consider their employees as customers, because the employee who cares about quality, who feels a sense of ownership or partnership in the enterprise, in turn communicates that to the customer'.

5.14   Many managers see people once every seven minutes. It might be argued that this is deleterious to performance and makes it hard to lead. However, the advantages of this approach are:

(a) managers can promote their vision, if they have one or their ideas, many times a day;

(b) they can keep in touch with what is going on;

(c) they can achieve minor, untraumatic changes which, in the long term add up incrementally to substantial changes;

(d) innovations can be tried, on an experimental basis without signalling a major change of policy;

(e) managers can involve others in the managerial process (if say, a manager is lacking in certain areas of expertise) without giving them formal authority;

(f) time spent in committees is minimised.

In short, a manager as 'teacher' or 'coach' needs to be in constant touch with his or her staff.

5.15 Therefore it appears that much of a leader's activity is involved in the organisation's day to day activities. Only rarely is a leader called upon to play a transforming role in organisational life.

5.16 In a local government context, it is argued by Barratt and Downs that councillors, as leaders although of a very special kind, have a similar role to play, eg:

(a) integrating strategy with operational effectiveness;
(b) establishing good relations with council officers;
(c) public relations.

5.17 To create consensus, Barratt and Downs propose that after an election the parties come together and agree matters of common interest, 'as leader of the council, work with the chairman of the council, the leader of the other parties/groups and the chief executive, to ensure that the maximum common ground is agreed upon. Where significant differing views are held enable these to be positively debated without detriment to the forward momentum of established policy or the public reputation of the council'.

5.18 In listening to the constituents and providing a political agenda for the local area, Barratt and Downs express the view that being out of touch damages the reputation of local government. 'Majority parties who hang on to power without clear, local, operationally meaningful policies or any rigorous assessment of their effects are neither governing nor furthering the cause of 'local government'. Similarly, opposition parties who are merely destructive and proffer no clear, local, operationally meaningful alternatives are equally useless'.

5.19 Barratt and Downs argue that to achieve change in local government *leadership* skills must be seen to be exercised.

(a) Conceive and communicate a vision, or even a sense of mission.
(b) Create a team to implement change.
(c) Communicate the change.

5.20 Barratt and Downs say these features of communication are relevant.

(a) Agreeing common values and objectives which bond people together
(b) Selling a vision
(c) Honouring the old ways but exchanging for the new
(d) Planning 'endings' positively – don't leave people or groups languishing
(e) Leading by example
(f) Creating local team spirit and will to win
(g) Making success possible and apparent
(h) Creating confidence
(i) Caring for people, including opponents
(j) Enjoying the challenge
(k) Proclaiming success
(l) Giving credit

This process should also encourage bottom up innovation. Change should not be imposed from the top.

Exercise

What would you say was the basic culture of the organisations or work groups described below?

(a) Camelot Ltd manufactures round tables. The company employs about twenty people. They work to strict deadlines, putting in overtime *if* necessary, and swapping tasks if the job needs it. There are usually two or three jobs at a time, and Arthur King, a project manager, sees his job as 'juggling the resources I have to ensure that both jobs are done on time. Of course, all my staff are specialists in this particular field, and I have to get them to work together. The chief technical officer looks after technical issues on each table.'

(b) Roland Bath is managing director of Bath Eurometrics which he set up with three partners, who are all board members. The only other employee is a receptionist. Although Roland has the title of managing director, this is largely for ceremonial purposes are most decisions are collective.

Solution

(a) A task culture, probably.
(b) An existential culture, possibly.

---

6. CONCLUSION

6.1 Trends in management thinking in the private sector are being adopted by the public sector.

6.2 These include:

(a) an emphasis on leadership;
(b) measurement of quality to empower the consumer of public services;
(c) a reassessment of necessary management competencies.

TEST YOUR KNOWLEDGE

The numbers in brackets refer to paragraphs of this chapter

1 List the ten roles for managers identified by Mintzberg. (1.7)

2 Why are executive agencies a new approach to public sector management? (2.6)

3 What are the 7 'S's? (3.2)

4 What does the Management Charter Initiative identify as being management competencies? (5.3)

Now try question 3 at the end of the text

PART B
ORGANISATION THEORY
AND STRUCTURE

Chapter 4

ANALYSING AND DEVELOPING ORGANISATIONS

This chapter covers the following topics.

1. Why organisations exist
2. The levels and dimensions of organisations

---

1. WHY ORGANISATIONS EXIST

1.1 The *Organisational Management* syllabus deals with the variety of organisation structures and the relationship between structure and objectives. Organisations pervade our lives; every individual is a member of many organisations and has to deal with a variety of public and private organisations for economic, social and political purposes.

An organisation can be defined as a 'social arrangement for the controlled performance of collective goals' (Buchanan and Huchzynski).

1.2 'Organising' in a management context means defining the tasks that must be completed to achieve the aims of the organisation, grouping the work into logical areas, and allocating authority, responsibility and resources to carry out the tasks.

1.3 As organisations grow in size and complexity, they require formal structures by which tasks are distributed and authority is defined. The allocation of resources to achieve the aims of the organisation has to be monitored to see that efficient performance levels are being achieved.

1.4 Organisations enable people to achieve more together than they could working individually. Specialisation means greater output from the same resource usage. This is sometimes referred to as synergy: 'the whole is greater than the sum of the parts'.

1.5 *Opportunities* and *risks* can be taken by organisations. From a private sector perspective, the emphasis needs to be on exploiting the opportunities and reducing risks to retain a competitive edge. In the private sector, there is a trade off between the risk of an enterprise and the reward of success.

So organisations are seen as:

(a) *risk managers* in the private sector;

(b) risk averse in the public sector (as they are required to maintain an equality of service).

1.6 Organisations depend on other organisations to supply a range of services and on facilitators or arrangers to reach the ultimate customer. Other organisations provide finance, trade company shares, set rules and regulations for the operation of the organisation.

1.7 Legal constraints operate over many of an organisation's activities, the functions it can perform, standards which it must observe, on health and safety, on pollution, the standards of its products, and its financial dealings.

1.8 As organisations grow in size and diversity then internal management and central services can become dominant issues. Communication problems emerge between the functional divisions, which can develop into conflict for resources.

1.9 It is possible to identify the following categories:

(a) private enterprises which are profit motivated;

(b) non profit making organisations (charities, professional bodies, interest and help groups);

(c) public sector organisations, national and local government, government agencies which are non profit making;

(d) public sector organisations which are given targets to achieve in making given returns on assets employed.

1.10 *Private enterprise* organisations are owned by individuals, partners, or shareholders and shares can be traded on the Stock Exchange. Large private enterprise organisations have shares owned by other financial institutions, through pension funds and banks and insurance companies.

1.11 Charities are owned by members and an elected board is responsible for the policy and structure of the organisation and appointed managers to run it. Finance may come from a wide range of sources from donations, from investments, from earnings and from providing a service. However, they are responsible to their donors.

1.12 *Public sector organisations* (non profit) are run by elected or government nominees, and financed from taxation. They are organised to provide a service, efficiently and effectively.

Links between private and public sector organisations

1.13 The public sector has always contracted out or bought services from the private sector. Examples include military procurement, road building, engineering works, trains, buses, planes, using national and local house building firms, purchasing drugs and medical equipment. Purchasing or contract relationships also cover the operational elements in the public sector (eg renting or purchase of buildings, buying or leasing office furniture and photocopiers, and a wide range of computing services).

1.14 Other links between the public and private sectors includes the use of:

(a) *agencies* to provide recruitment;

(b) temporary staff;

(c) consultants to advice on the management of the organisation, legal advice, auditing and payroll services.

1.15 *Partnership agreements* have also been used with Housing Associations, Training Agency and Enterprise Trusts which link the public to public organisations and also include voluntary and private sector organisations. The use of educational and training bodies to provide qualified staff again shows the integration across the public and private sector divides.

1.16 The financial resources of the public sector also have an impact on the private sector. Local authorities, for example will have funds on deposit at lending institutions. The scale of public sector *pension funds* means that the public sector has a powerful influence over some parts of the private sector (eg when some public sector pension funds have become involved with property or development companies).

1.17 The division between public and private sectors has become blurred in some instances. Examples are:

(a) central government economic regeneration schemes;
(b) 'economic development' activities;
(c) pension fund investment.

1.18 The public sector *supports* the private sector in many ways.

(a) It provides infrastructure (eg roads, railways).
(b) Government provides funding for various private sector interests (eg training schemes).
(c) Government tax policy can benefit or disadvantage some areas of the private sector.
(d) The public sector purchases goods and services from the private sector.

Regulation

1.19 Parliament and the Civil Service are responsible for the establishment and administration of the legislative framework which:

(a) defines and regulates the activity of the institution (eg company law); and

(b) *creates* public bodies such as the health trusts and local government which are funded from taxation, and requires these organisations to be accountable to Parliament for the money they spend and the implementation of government policy.

1.20 Various Acts of Parliament establish rules, regulations and standards which should be followed by both the public and private sectors. These include laws regarding employment, equal opportunities, health and safety, and pollution. The government may create and fund independent bodies to ensure that standards are being achieved, rules are obeyed and provide for grievances to be heard in tribunals where cases can be adjudicated.

1.21 *Regulatory organisations* have also been set up for privatised public utilities (eg OFTEL and OFGAS) to safeguard the interests of consumers and promote competition. A range of consultative committees work locally to review the activities of transport providers and the health service.

1.22 *Ombudsmen* are appointee by Parliament for Local Administration to take up citizens' complaints on maladministration. This approach has also been extended by the private sector (eg Bank ombudsman, advertising standards authority).

1.23 In the absence of a written constitution enshrining citizens' rights in law an elaborate system of checks and balances has developed. The process of *judicial review* and the development of the Queens Bench Division of the High Court into an Administrative Court of Justice by default, has been one way of enabling challenges to be made to administration or policy decisions made by Ministers of State and of public bodies.

1.24 Scrutiny may also be exercised by the institutions of the EC and other international bodies, as organisations and individuals can challenge government decisions in European Courts. These range from issues of water quality, prisoners' rights, and the interpretation of rights to benefits under social welfare legislation.

1.25 Independent reviews of the financial operation and good management practice in local government and health authorities is provided by the *Audit Commission*. With the reallocation of control of some functions of local government (polytechnics becoming independent of local government), then the Audit Commission itself will have to compete with the private sector in providing external auditing and providing management advice to these bodies.

Local authority contracting and regulation

1.26 The diagrams on the following pages show the division of local authorities into client and contractor roles. These show how the differences between purchaser and provider can be managed, and provide a framework for compulsory competitive tendering.

1.27 The transformation of the state from owner into regulator has a parallel, at local level, with the separation between the roles of:

(a) providing services to the public;
(b) managing and running those services.

1.28 Contracting out means, for example, that a local council, instead of setting up a direct service organisation staffed with council employees, purchases the services of a private contractor instead.

1.29 This means that local authorities now become regulators too, ensuring that the standards specified in the contract are upheld.

SEPARATING CLIENT AND CONTRACTOF ROLES
There are two main routes to achieving client and contractor separation

Clean separation at member and officer level

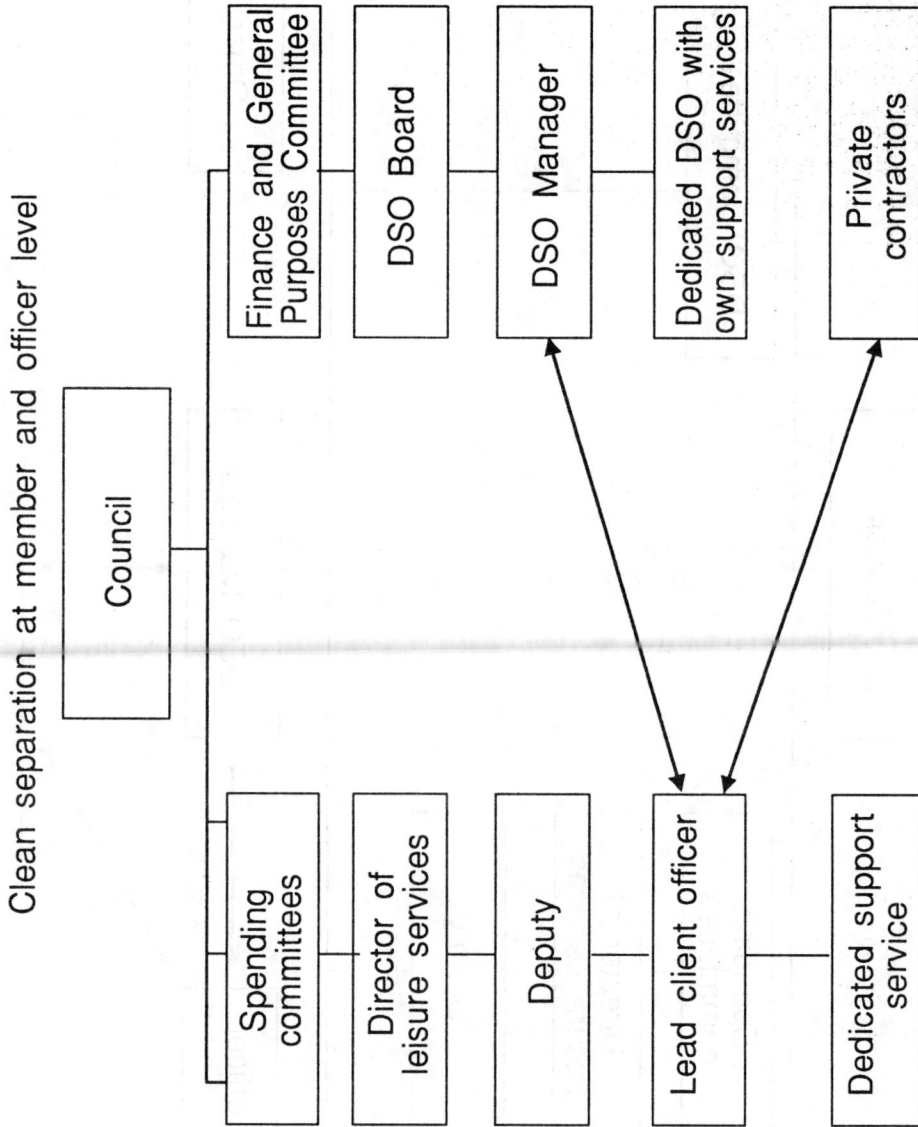

Clean separation at member level, separation below deputy at officer level

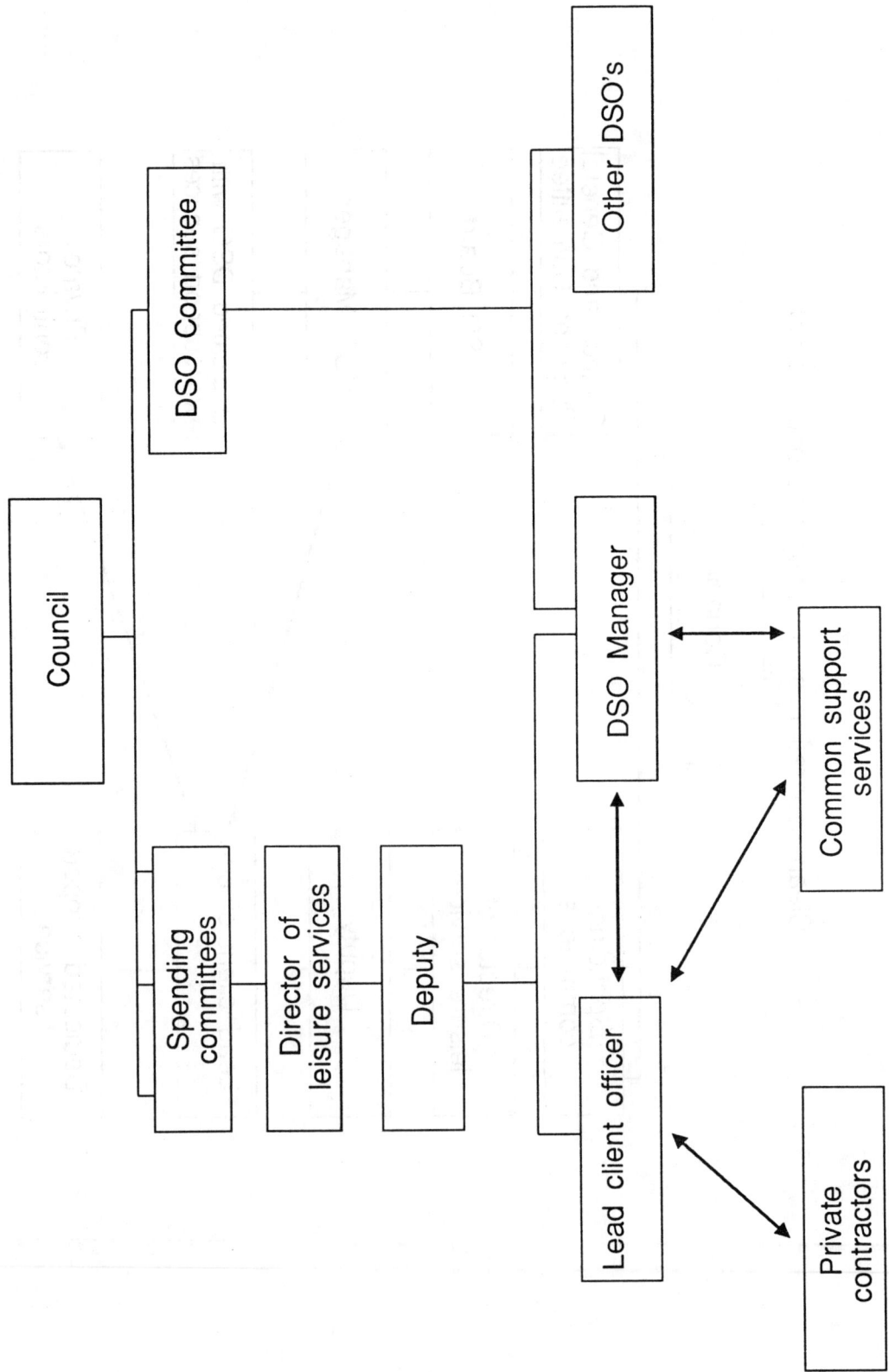

2. THE LEVELS AND DIMENSIONS OF ORGANISATIONS

2.1 The basic components of an organisation can be identified as follows.

(a) *Top management* who are concerned with setting the objectives and strategy for the operation of the organisation. They provide the link with the external environment. They may be representatives of the shareholders, or elected members of local government, or appointed chief executives.

(b) *Middle management* who are concerned with coordination and the implementation of the top management objectives with the operational levels of the organisation.

(c) *Operational core management* who are responsible for the direct performance of the technical or productive operation and implementing the tasks of the organisation, working on the production line, lecturing and serving the public.

(d) *Operational support managers* who are providing the back up services for the operational core and manage supplies and technical services.

(e) *Organisational support managers* who are responsible for providing services for the whole organisation but are not part of the daily operational work flow, these include personnel and management accounting.

(f) *The workers* in the organisation may have representation through trade unions or other negotiating machinery to cover health and safety and working conditions as well as pay and welfare services.

2.2 The *core* and the *service* functions can be subdivided in a number of ways. The structure which is adopted reflects the diversity of what the organisation does and how it chooses to do it. The creation of functional departments and the subdivisions of the tasks of the organisation creates diversity. The greater the diversity, the greater is the need for coordination, and the establishment of integrating procedures.

2.3 *Territory* is used to differentiate how people see their role in the organisation in physical and psychological terms. It is the space occupied by that person. People who do not have a clear territory in which to operate can feel aimless and having no control over their own work, and often are encroaching on other people's territory.

2.4 Many organisations in the public sector, which have a variety of unrelated activities, are sharply differentiated in terms of territory. Territories are drawn up on *professional* lines and in relation to particular discrete functions. The organisations are held together through rules and procedures and a hierarchical reporting system, up to committees of elected members or coordinating committees. *Accountability* becomes a factor in the setting of the organisational structures to perform particular tasks.

Strategic management

2.5 The introduction of *corporate management or strategic management* into the public sector has meant that the structure of the organisations has changed to bring in policy making bodies that are responsible for advising on policy options and evaluating the performance of policies and linking strategic and financial planning.

2.6 An example of corporate, or strategic management of public sector bodies is given in the recommendations of the Bains Report. Central coordinating bodies should exist to inject strategic management into an organisation.

(a) Central coordinating committees provide a network in which intelligence can be shared.

(b) Central coordinating committees often have access to funds (eg from contingency reserves) outside the main programmes, so as to encourage economic development.

2.7 With the introduction of compulsory competitive tendering, this strategic or even regulatory approach has taken greater prominence. The division between a local authority's role as a paymaster and a provider/manager of services has caused tensions.

2.8 Ultimately, this requires a new management style on the part of the provider/manager of services. An executive agency, for example, is now a separate cost and profit centre in its own right. At the same time, however, there can be competition, and so the purchaser of the service can expect higher standards.

The NHS

2.9 This new approach has permeated the National Health Service. From 1 April 1991 new funding and accounting relationships have been introduced into the Health Service at a number of levels.

The key changes are as follows.

(a) Districts will identify the health needs of its residents and will contract with hospitals to provide health care. A district's role becomes that of the *purchaser* of health care.

(b) Districts will be allocated funds on a weighted capitation basis. In other words, allocations will be based on the numbers of people in the district, with other factors taken into account. These funds will still be cash limited (ie there will be a maximum amount, in cash terms, available).

(c) Districts will draw up contracts with self-governing Trust Hospitals to provide health care. The district may set performance criteria to be met and require quality as well as cost measures to be included. The district may also contract with the private sector. Districts will still retain 'directly managed units' with which they will have more informal working, but may be required to achieve performance targets and demonstrate value for money through annual reports.

(d) Trust hospitals will be financed through public dividend capital and interest bearing loans. They will be set financial duties, financial targets and external financing limits. Business plans will be drawn up by each Trust and scrutinised by the government.

(e) Trust hospitals will have to produce an annual report with a statement that shows assets employed, results for the year, performance against financial duties and a range of performance indicators.

(f) A new Family Health Service Authority will replace the Family Practitioner Committee. This becomes responsible to the Regional Health Authority.

(g) Family Practitioners can now become budget holders. So far nearly 400 practices have taken up the opportunity. They can contract with a hospital to provide medical care for their patients.

2.10 The finance departments will have to take on new tasks of capital charging, contract setting, contract payment, contract monitoring and contract income collection.

Organisational arrangements will require the following.

(a) *District level*

   (i)   Purchaser contract setting
   (ii)   Purchaser contract monitoring
   (iii) Contract payment
   (iv)   Resource allocation
   (v)   Financial strategy
   (vi)   Financial services
   (vii) Internal audit

(b) *Unit level*

   (i)   Expenditure control
   (ii)   Financial planning
   (iii) Capital charging
   (iv)   DMU contract setting
   (v)   DMU contract monitoring

(c) *District or unit level*

   (i)   Contract income collection
   (ii)   Treasury management
   (iii) Financial accounting
   (iv)   Financial services

A typical structure at district level is as follows.

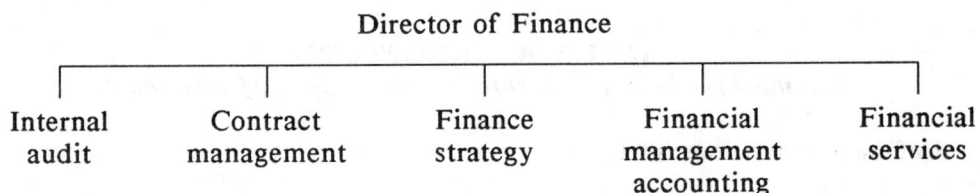

Director of Finance

Internal audit	Contract management	Finance strategy	Financial management accounting	Financial services

As more Trusts are established and further devolution of management to the directly managed units occurs, then more complex contracting and resource allocation procedures are likely to be put in place. Skill in contract management will become all important. The measurement of the performance of health units and control of costs to create value for money will be another important skill. Marketing and public relations will become important as the Trusts compete to maintain contracts with the General Practitioner Fund Holders who will be free to seek contracts to secure the best patient care.

Exercise

Find out the organisation structure of the local authority in which you live. How far does it exemplify the developments outlined in this chapter? Is it possible to detect an organisational split between the purchase and provision of services?

3. CONCLUSION

3.1 Organisations are social arrangements for the controlled performance of collective goals.

3.2 Public sector organisations are run by the State on behalf of the public.

3.3 There are many connections between public and private sectors.

(a) The public sector provides services to the private sector (eg infrastructure).

(b) The public sector regulates the activities of the private sector.

(c) The public sector purchases goods and services from the private sector for internal consumption.

(d) The public sector engages in contractual relationships with the private sector, for the provision of services to the public.

3.4 Contracting out is increasingly common. This means an enhancement in the strategic and regulatory, as opposed to organisational, goals of public sector bodies.

TEST YOUR KNOWLEDGE
The numbers in brackets refer to paragraphs of this chapter

1　Define organisations. (1.1)

2　Contrast the attitudes to risk in the public and private sector. (1.5)

3　What, and who, are the basic components of an organisation? (2.1)

4　What were the recommendations of the Bains Report? (2.6)

Questions 4 and 5 are best attempted after you have completed chapter 5

Chapter 5

TYPES OF ORGANISATIONAL STRUCTURE

This chapter covers the following topics.

1. Efficient organisation structure
2. Formal organisations
3. Scalar chain
4. Span of control
5. Line, staff and functional organisation
6. Departmentation
7. Centralisation and decentralisation
8. Divisionalisation
9. Matrix organisation

---

1. EFFICIENT ORGANISATION STRUCTURE

1.1 A formal organisation may be defined (Etzioni) as a social unit deliberately constructed to seek specific goals. It is characterised by:

(a) planned divisions of responsibility;
(b) power centres which control its efforts;
(c) substitution of personnel;
(d) the ability to combine its personnel in different ways.

1.2 Formal organisations have an explicit hierarchy in a well defined structure; job specifications and communication channels are also well defined.

1.3 An informal organisation, in contrast, is loosely structured, flexible and spontaneous. Membership is gained consciously or unconsciously and it is often difficult to determine the time when a person becomes a member. An example of an informal organisation is a group of managers who regularly go together for lunch to a local restaurant.

1.4 With every *formal* organisation there exists, to a greater or lesser extent, a complex *informal organisation*. The formal organisation is a structure of relationships and ideas; informal organisation, in practice, modifies this formal structure (Blau and Scott 1962).

The management task of organisation

1.5 Management has authority over the activities of an organisation. It can structure the work of the organisation and the jobs done within it to suit its requirements. The organisation structure it rules over will be inefficient or efficient. If it is inefficient it is management's duty to improve it.

1.6 The symptoms of a poor and inefficient organisation structure may be listed as follows.

    (a) The growth of many levels of management. An excessive number of management levels must inevitably involve the creation of much unnecessary work and reporting relationships. This can only result in inefficiency.

    (b) 'Frictional' or 'unprofitable' overheads - these are 'co-ordinators, expeditors or assistants' who have no clear job responsibility of their own, but are supposed to help their superior do his job.

    (c) The need for special co-ordinating measures, such as appointing liaison officers, or co-ordination committees, or holding numerous co-ordination meetings.

    (d) The tendency to 'go through channels' rather than go directly to the person with the needed information or ideas. 'It greatly aggravates the tendency of functional organisation to make people think more of their function than of the business'.

    (e) A lop-sided management age structure.

1.7 Efficient organisation structure does not necessarily ensure good and effective management, but with a bad or inefficient organisation structure, good performance is impossible, no matter how able management might be. 'The right organisation structure is a necessary foundation; without it the best performance in all other areas of management will be ineffectual and frustrated'.
(Drucker).

2. FORMAL ORGANISATIONS

2.1 The first responsibility of the manager as organiser is to divide the work and provide a means of co-ordination. There are two schools of thought on how this should be done.

    (a) Most companies adhere to the classical approach, which entails considering the work first, and the personalities second. The work is divided into jobs, and people are then appointed to do the work of each job.

    (b) There are, however, a few avant-garde organisations that follow the teachings of the behaviouralist school and consider that motivation of the people comes before division of the work in the apparently most logical way. Volvo's experiments with groups working in the automobile industry is probably the best known of the large organisations attempting to follow the behaviouralist theories. In this approach, employees are consulted about how a work process should be organised, and the organisation is then established in accordance with their preferences.

5: TYPES OF ORGANISATIONAL STRUCTURE

2.2 We have already briefly defined the concept of 'organisation'. This initial definition can now be developed by referring to the writings of Louis A Allen whose books *Management and Organisation* and *The Management Profession* discuss organisation principles. He tells us that 'organisation' is a mechanism or structure that enables living things to work effectively together. The basic elements of organisation are *division of labour*, a *source of authority* and *relationships*. This is true of all forms of organisation.

2.3 Management organisation, in these terms, means:

(a) identifying the work that must be accomplished to attain objectives, then grouping that work into logically related and balanced positions;

(b) next, responsibility and authority are defined and delegated.

(c) as a final step, relationships are established between positions and units to facilitate harmonious teamwork.

'One of the facts of life for organisations is that as they grow, they become more formalised... Just as growth sets up pressures for delegation, so it is also accompanied by formalisation' (John Child).

3. SCALAR CHAIN

3.1 The 'scalar chain' or 'chain of command' is the term used to describe the organisation's management hierarchy, that is the chain of superiors from lowest to highest rank. Formal communication runs up and down the lines of authority, eg E to D to C to B to A in the diagram below.

Note, however, that if communication between different branches of the chain is necessary (eg D to H) the use of a 'gang plank' of horizontal communication saves time and is likely to be more accurate, so long as superiors know that such communication is taking place.

Scalar chains: ———   A   Gang planks: - - - - - -

ABCDE

ABJL

ABJM   CG

AFGHI

AFKN   DH

AFKOP

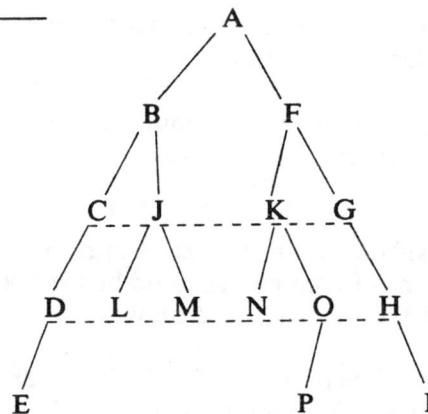

Scalar chains

3.2 Henri Fayol criticised government departments for making insufficient use of the *gang plank*. By this, he means that the subordinates refer too many problems up the scalar chain to their boss because the problem involves a person in another section or department. Instead, the subordinate could contact the other person directly and ask for a joint solution to the problem. In the diagram here, if C has a problem with affects G, instead of referring it up to B (who might then refer it to A) C could cross the 'gang plank' – communicate horizontally – with G. The problem might then be solved jointly by C and G, provided that B and F are aware that this is happening.

3.3 One important problem for efficient and effective management is establishing the most suitable *number of links* in the chains of command for the organisation concerned.

   (a) Townsend *(Up the Organisation)* estimated that the addition of each extra level of management into the hierarchy, adding one more link in the chain of command, reduces the effectiveness of communication within the organisation by about 25%.

   Peter Drucker cites the Roman Catholic Church as a classic example of an organisation with a short chain of command. From Pope down to parish priest there is only one intermediary layer of management, the Bishops, so that a papal edict comes down to parish priests in just one step.

   (b) Peters *(In Search of Excellence)* has expressed the view that, in future, organisations will have no corporate elite, no job descriptions, a destruction of bureaucracy and a totally flat organisational structure (see below), operating in a flexible network. The example may be the F1 Group. More than 1,000 highly qualified systems analysts, most of them women, work from home. They are networked to service clients' needs across the country.

3.4 There might be a tendency for chains of command within a single organisation to get longer as the organisation grows older. The length of the chains of command is a function of:

   (a) the size of the organisation;
   (b) the type and complexity of the products it makes or services it provides;
   (c) the diversity of its products and services;
   (d) its geographical spread;
   (e) the number and complexity of controls required; and
   (f) the type of people it employs.

3.5 No rules have been (or can be) laid down for how chains of command should be structured, but a general observation is that chains of command should be kept as short as possible, consistent with sound management, and the factors listed above.

   (a) Management structure should be organised for *business performance* - converting all the business activities into 'drive'. Managers should fulfil valuable operational needs in a simple environment, and organisations should avoid a red-tape bureaucracy working on a mountain of paper or in a maze of procedures.

   (b) Management structure should be organised so as *to direct the organisation's efforts away from bad performance*. Bad news should be communicated quickly so that problems can be rectified. Long chains of command create a tendency towards bad performance.

(c) *Short chains of command* help managers to develop. If future managers are in close and frequent contact with current managers, this is said to enable future managers to gain insight into being a manager. The use of mentors or management training and development programmes can be a formal way of encouraging this type of learning.

(d) The chain of command and management structure should enable the organisation to *train tomorrow's managers*. Drucker has cited cases of well known companies with as many as twelve links in the chain of command. Such a long chain makes promotion from the bottom to the top virtually impossible. To add to the problem, specialisation of skills in some management jobs (for example accountancy management) removes flexibility of appointments and restricts promotion prospects.

    (i) As a consequence, many large companies turn divisions into 'independent' subsidiary and sub-subsidiary companies, to ensure that its bright young managers with potential to rise to senior positions are given a more direct experience of running an organisation (albeit a subsidiary) from an early stage in their career. Within their subsidiary, the chain of command is short, and general management experience more easily gained.

    (ii) If large companies do not split their operations between subsidiary companies in this way, they will run the risk of losing their brightest management talents because managers will be frustrated by delays waiting from promotion, and will instead move to smaller companies to gain their experience and make their mark more quickly.

    (iii) The introduction in the public sector of devolved management to 'business units' or to contract management may be seen as creating opportunities for management development. Controlling budgets, producing business plans and having control over staff, working conditions and service delivery provides a good basis for management development.

3.6 In conclusion, chains of command should:

(a) reflect the business organisation, its environment, products, employees, diversity, spread and controls;

(b) be as short as possible consistent with efficiency and effectiveness;

(c) be short enough to provide a training ground for developing managers;

(d) in future everyone may be a manager as part of a network of providers, but being self employed.

4. SPAN OF CONTROL

4.1 The 'span of control' or 'span of management' refers to the number of subordinates working to the superior official. In other words, if a manager has five subordinates, the span of control is five.

Various writers of the classical school, such as Fayol, Graicunas and Urwick, argued that the managerial span of control should be limited to between three and six. Their arguments were based on the twin beliefs that:

(a) there should be tight managerial control from the top of the organisation; and

(b) there are physical and mental limitations to any single manager's ability to control people and activities.

4.2 To ensure effective control, the number of subordinates and tasks over which a manager has supervisory responsibilities should therefore be restricted to what is physically and mentally possible. A narrow span of control offers:

(a) tight control and close supervision; better co-ordination of subordinates' activities;

(b) time to think and plan; managers are not burdened with too many day to day problems;

(c) reduced delegation; a manager can do more of his work himself;

(d) better communication with subordinates, who are sufficiently small in number to allow this to occur.

4.3 The French writer V A Graicunas (1937) devised a formula to show how the number of possible relationships between members of an organisation increases geometrically in proportion to the number of members:

$$N = (2^{n-1} + (n-1))$$

Where N is the total number of possible relationships and n is the number of subordinates.

The greater the number of subordinates becomes, the supervisor finds himself managing a mushrooming number of organisational relationships (where $n = 1$, $N = 1$, and where $n = 7$, $N = 490$). This exploding complexity of larger and larger units must impose some limitations on the capabilities of management - the span of control is limited by the number of inter-relationships that one person can manage.

4.4 Urwick suggested a slightly different approach, in response to a report by James Worthy in 1950 that the policy of the American Sears Roebuck company was to have as wide a span of control as possible between stores managers and their subordinates, who were merchandising managers. A wide span of control forced stores managers to delegate authority, and the consequences, Worthy claimed, were improved morale and greater efficiency of merchandising management.

Urwick's counter-argument was that a wide span of control had been possible in this example of the Sears Roebuck company because the work of the merchandising managers did not interlock, therefore the need for co-ordination and integration was not present. This reduced the burdens of supervision and made a wider span of control feasible. Urwick concluded that the maximum management span of control should be six, when the work of subordinates interlocks.

4.5 A wide span of control offers:

(a) greater decision-making authority for subordinates;
(b) fewer supervisory costs; and
(c) less control, but perhaps greater motivation though job satisfaction.

Tall and flat organisations

4.6 The span of control concept has implications for the 'shape' of an organisation. A tall organisation is one which, in relation to its size, has a large number of management hierarchies, whereas a flat organisation is one which, in relation to its size, has a smaller number of hierarchical levels. A tall organisation implies a narrow span of control, and a flat organisation implies a wide span of control.

4.7 Some classical theorists accepted that a tall organisation structure is inefficient.

(a) It increases overhead costs.

(b) It creates extra communication problems, since top management is more remote from the 'actual work' done at the bottom end of the organisation, and information tends to get distorted or blocked on its way up or down through the organisation hierarchy.

(c) Management responsibilities tend to overlap and become confused as the size of the management structure gets larger. Different sections or departments may seek authority over the same 'territory' of operations, and superiors may find it difficult to delegate sufficient authority to satisfy subordinates.

(d) The same work passes through too many hands.

(e) Planning is more difficult because it must be organised at more levels in the organisation.

Behavioural theorists add that tall structures impose rigid supervision and control and therefore block initiative and ruin the motivation of subordinates.

4.8 Nevertheless, not all researchers favour flat organisation structures, and it can be argued that if work is organised on the basis of small groups or project teams (therefore narrow spans of control and a tall organisation structure) group members would be able to plan their work in an orderly manner, encourage participation by all group members in decision-making and monitor the consequences of their decisions better, so that their performance will be more efficient than the work of groups in a flat structure with a wide span of control. D Vander Weyer (*Management and People in Banking*, edited by Livy) suggested that in the case of large banking organisations 'it is virtually impossible for so complex an organisation as an international bank to work with less than five or six executive levels'. Specialisation and the importance of service delivery have seen local government develop with a number of small group or self managed teams as part of an organisation or three or four tiers.

4.9 There is a trade-off between the span of control and the tallness/flatness of an organisation. The span of control should not be too wide, but neither should an organisation be too tall.

Tall organisations

Reasons in favour	*Reasons against*
1 Keeps span of control narrow.	1 A wide span of control means that more authority will be delegated to subordinates. Greater discretion leads to job enrichment and motivation.
2 A large number of career/promotion steps are provided in the hierarchical ladder. More frequent promotions possible.	2 With many rungs in the hierarchical ladder, the *real* increases in authority between one rung and another might not seem obvious to managers.
	3 Tall organisations are more expensive in management overheads costs.
	4 Tall organisations tend to suffer from worse communications.

Span of control: conclusions

4.10 It is reasonable to accept the view that there is a limit to a supervisor's capabilities and that the span of control should be limited. However, the span of control is now thought to be dependent on several factors.

4.11 The nature of the manager's work load is likely to influence the span of control he or she can deal with efficiently.

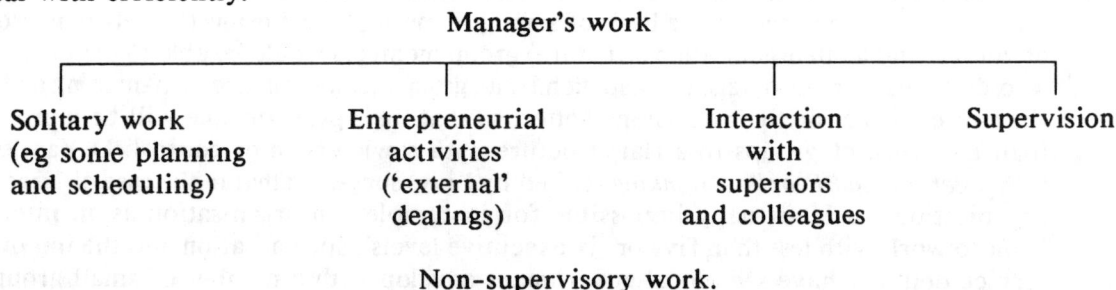

Manager's work

Solitary work (eg some planning and scheduling)	Entrepreneurial activities ('external' dealings)	Interaction with superiors and colleagues	Supervision

Non-supervisory work.

The greater the proportion of non-supervisory work in a manager's work load,

(a) the narrower the span of control should be; or
(b) the greater the delegation of authority to subordinates should be.

4.12 Other factors influencing the width of the span of control are:

(a) the geographical dispersion of the subordinates;

(b) whether subordinates' work is all of a similar nature (wide span possible) or diversified;

(c) the nature of problems that a supervisor might have to help subordinates with;

(d) the degree of interaction between subordinates (with close interaction, a wider span of control should be possible);

(e) the competence and abilities of both management and subordinates;

(f) whether close group cohesion is desirable. Small groups will be more cohesive, with a better sense of team work. This would call for narrow spans of control;

(g) the amount of help that supervisors receive from staff functions (such as the personnel department);

(h) the overlap of responsibilities and membership of groups (a link pin approach) to maintain communication and informed decision taking.

4.13 The is no universally 'correct' size for the span of management, and no current writer on organisations would suggest that a 'correct' span exists, without considering the particular circumstances of any particular individual organisation or department.

5. LINE, STAFF AND FUNCTIONAL ORGANISATION

5.1 There are two ways of looking at the distinction between line and staff management.

(a) Line and staff can be used to denote functions in the organisation. Line management consists of those managers directly involved in achieving the objectives of an organisation (that is all production and sales managers in a manufacturing company). Every other manager is staff (for example accounting, marketing, research and development managers).

> Rosemary Stewart wrote that 'Line functions are those which have direct responsibility for achieving the objectives of the company. Staff activities are those which primarily exist to provide advice and service.'

(b) As an alternative definition, line and staff can be used to denote *relationships of authority*. A line manager is one who has relatively unlimited authority over a subordinate to whom he gives orders. By this definition, any manager, no matter what department he works in (an operations department or an advisory department) will have line authority over his subordinates. Thus if the personnel department is a staff department, the manager in charge of recruitment and training will be subordinate in a line relationship to the personnel director. In other words, line authority can be a term used to describe the scalar chain of command in the management hierarchy.

5.2 Another popular distinction between line and staff is that:

(a) staff managers are thinkers and advisers; and
(b) line managers are doers.

5.3 Staff departments exist in many organisations where there is a need for specialisation. Accountants, personnel administrators, economists, data processing experts and statisticians are all experts in a specialised field of work. Where this expertise is 'syphoned off' into a separate department, the problem naturally arises as to whether:

(a) the experts exist to *advise* line managers, who may accept or reject the advice given; or

(b) the experts can step in to *direct* the line managers in what to do - to assume line authority themselves.

5.4 No organisation of substantial size can avoid operating problems unless there is a clear understanding as to the structure of the tasks and relationships of an organisation and as to where authority and responsibility rest. The creation of small teams or business units allocates 'staff' management as well as 'line' management duties. Decentralisation in organisations means 'staff' functions are operated closely with 'line' functions.

5.5 Unfortunately, this is an aspect of organisation which causes enormous friction. Line managers are thought of as 'first class citizens' and staff are relegated in status to the second rank as expensive 'overheads', who are not contributing anything of worth to the organisation. Staff managers may be seen to have an unfair level of access to top managers and influence policy more than line managers, as they report on the internal operation of the organisation.

The classical approach: planning and structure

5.6 An organisation is divided into functions, such as production, finance and sales. The functions required by each business will depend on the individual situation of the business. For example, some businesses may need a research and development department, or an advertising department, and others will not need them. Other functions, such as market research and public relations, may be provided by external services. In small companies and other such organisations, most staff functions may be provided by external agencies: for example, a businessman might hire the services of a professional accountant for a few hours each week and the services of a solicitor when required; a computer bureau may take on many data processing applications, including the weekly and monthly payroll work. Typing and secretarial services may be 'farmed out' to an agency. Some small manufacturing organisations may sell all their products through an agent; for example, a printing company may obtain business through a sales 'broker' who takes a commission on all work he finds for the company.

5.7 Owing to specialisation of work, there must be both line and staff management within an organisation:

(a) Line organisation establishes a direct relationship between the executive and his subordinates, and this order follows in the form of a *scalar chain* in a classical hierarchy.

(b) Line and staff organisations are based on both direct and functional relationships. In this system the line organisation is supplemented by staff organisation. The staff officers have no direct authority over the line organisation, but they provide assistance and service to the line personnel in an advisory capacity.

5.8 The conflict between line management, who may resent specialist advice, and staff management, who may be frustrated when their advice is ignored, has no organisational solution. The problem can be lessened, however, if:

(a) all vital activities of the business are line management functions; and

(b) staff management are kept in close proximity (either physically or by communications links) to the line management they advise.

5: TYPES OF ORGANISATIONAL STRUCTURE

Functional organisation

5.9 A development in more recent years has been the recognition that some 'staff' management has become highly specialised in areas of work which form a fundamental part of the line management positions. Examples are usually found in the fields of industrial relations and capital expenditure. In these areas the line manager would allow the staff manager to assume some of his or her responsibilities while still retaining final authority and responsibility. A typical example would be where the personnel manager specifies the rules for disciplining and dismissal of employees. The line manager recognises that the staff manager has greater knowledge and expertise on this subject and acquiesces in the carrying out of the prescribed steps of the procedure.

5.10 This role is clearly different from that of the traditional staff manager (eg work study, organisation and methods, 'personal assistant to' positions etc). Urwick and Dale have defined the distinction as being 'functional staff' as opposed to 'general staff'. General staff positions are seen as purely advisory positions.

Examples: line staff and functional staff

5.11 On the next page is a typical organisation chart of an international company, far from complex if compared with hundreds of large organisations but complicated enough to illustrate the positions of authority and responsibility and the distinctions between line and staff.

5.12 This organisation chart depicts a company with three businesses. It designs, makes and sells musical instruments, surgical instruments and sports equipment. It functions as a complete entity in three different countries to take account of the special needs of local markets.

(a) The *chief executive* very clearly has a line job. His responsibility is for all aspects of all functions of the organisation. He is truly a chief executive.

(b) The regional *managing directors* take their places one down from the chief executive in the scalar chain; they have line jobs with responsibility for the organisational structures in each region.

(c) It is equally clear that the *financial director* and the *personnel director* are staff functions. They report to the managing director, they are there to provide information and to recommend policies and procedures related to their professional skills and knowledge of the business. They have a functional authority over the equivalent staff at various levels of the company, but not a line authority.

(d) The *three group* directors are more difficult to classify. They are responsible to the managing director for all aspects of their part of the business and yet they do not appear from the chart to have a line relationship with their opposite numbers at national level.

This organisation structure may in fact be better classified as a 'matrix' structure, which is described later in this chapter.

MULTIMATICS LIMITED

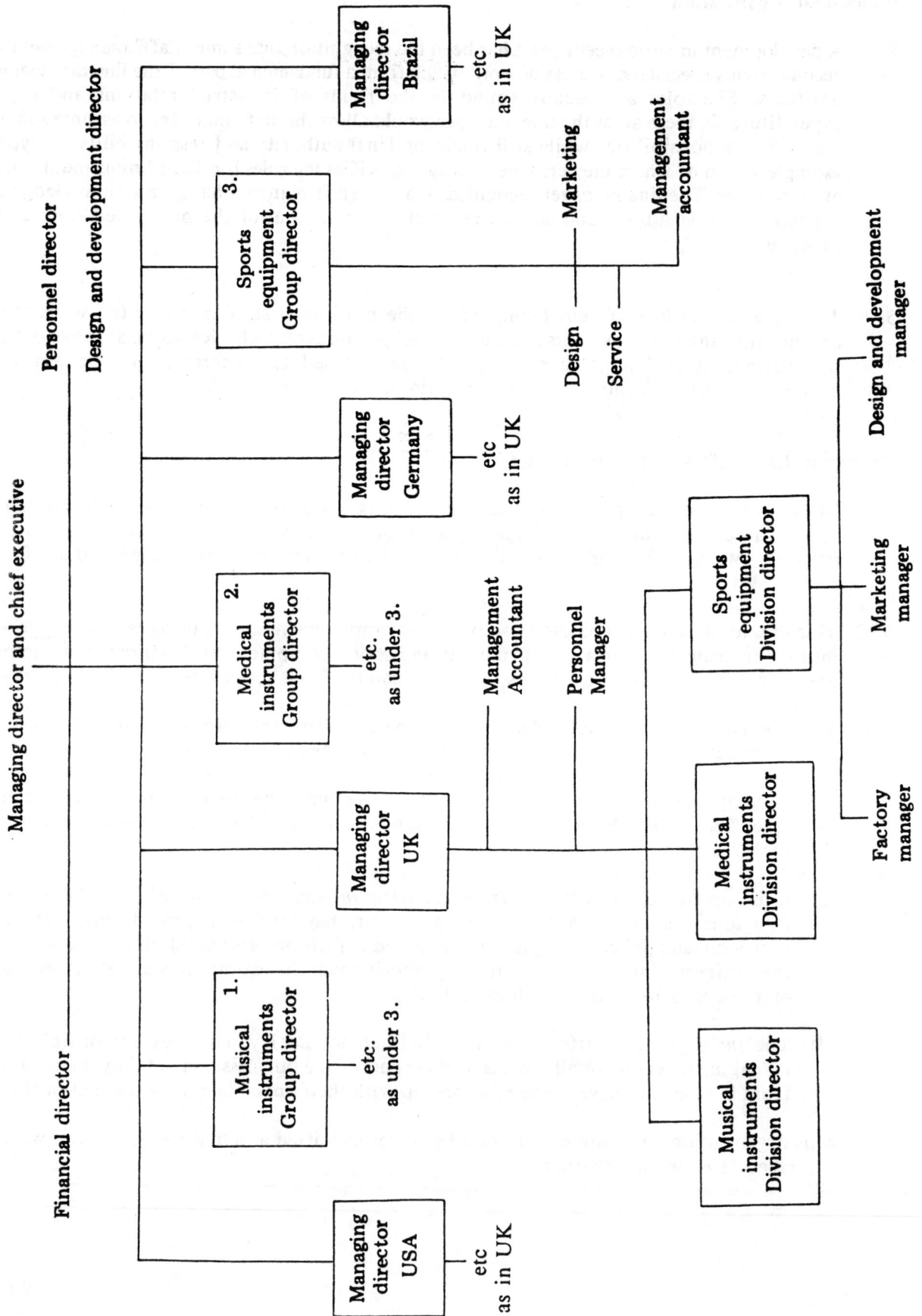

Managing director and chief executive

Financial director

Personnel director

Design and development director

Managing director USA
etc as in UK

1. Musical instruments Group director
etc. as under 3.

Managing director UK

2. Medical instruments Group director
etc. as under 3.

Managing director Germany
etc as in UK

3. Sports equipment Group director
Design
Service
Marketing
Management accountant

Managing director Brazil
etc as in UK

Management Accountant

Personnel Manager

Musical instruments Division director

Medical instruments Division director

Sports equipment Division director

Factory manager

Marketing manager

Design and development manager

74

5.13 An example of a similar structure in local government is present in the example 2 diagram on the next page. This demonstrates an integration of support services in both the management structure and as part of the operational line management.

Implications of line and staff for organisational design

5.14 There are drawbacks to using staff departments; a knowledge of the problems should enable management to deal with them, and thus use staff functions more effectively. These drawbacks are as follows.

(a) There is a danger that staff experts may, intentionally or not, undermine the authority of line managers. Subordinates might respect the 'expert power' of the staff man, and show a lesser willingness to accept the judgement of their line boss.

(b) Friction may also occur when staff managers report to a higher authority in the scalar chain of command. For example, a management accountant may submit reports about a line manager's performance to the production director or the managing director. The line manager might look on such reporting as 'telling tales' and resent the interference.

(c) Staff managers have no line authority and therefore no responsibility for what actually happens. If they give advice which is acted on, but fails to achieve desired results, staff men can blame the line managers for not acting on their advice properly.

(d) Because staff managers are 'thinkers' they may have their heads in the clouds. Their ideas may be unrealistic and impracticable; line managers, having received poor advice from one staff expert, might tar all staff managers with the same brush and resist all future expert help.

(e) Staff managers may attempt to usurp line authority. Any change in the boundaries of authority should be the result of conscious planning, and not surreptitious empire-building.

5.15 The solutions to these problems are easily stated, but not easy to implement in practice.

(a) Authority must be clearly defined, and distinctions between line authority and staff advice clearly set out (eg in job descriptions).

(b) Senior management must encourage line managers to make positive efforts to discuss work problems with staff advisers, and to be prepared to accept their advice. The use of experts should become an 'organisational way of life'.

(c) Staff managers must be fully informed about the operational aspects of the business on which they are experts. By providing them with detailed information they should be less likely to offer impractical advice.

(d) When staff advisers are used to plan and implement changes in the running of the business, they must be kept involved during the implementation, monitoring and review of the project. Staff managers must be prepared to accept responsibility for their failures and this is only really possible if they advise during the implementation and monitoring stages.

LOCAL GOVERNMENT DEPARTMENTAL MANAGEMENT STRUCTURE

CHIEF EXECUTIVE

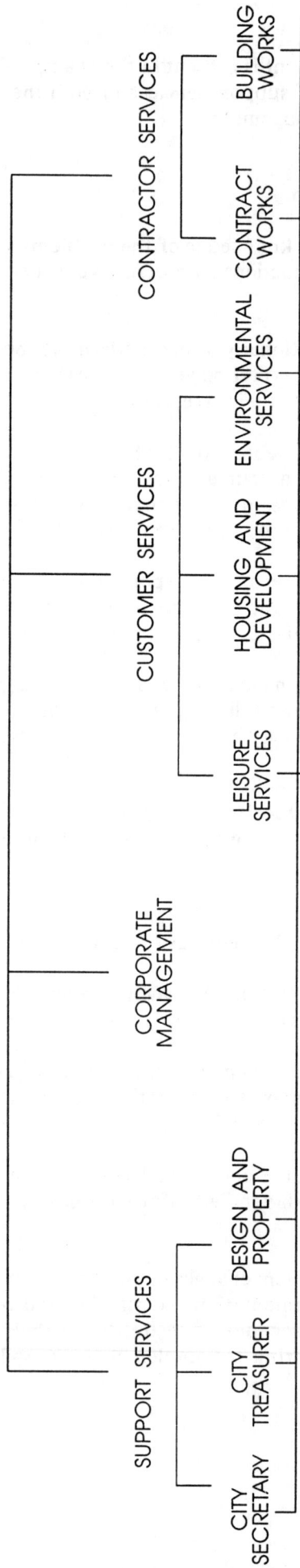

- SUPPORT SERVICES
  - CITY SECRETARY
  - CITY TREASURER
  - DESIGN AND PROPERTY
- CORPORATE MANAGEMENT
- CUSTOMER SERVICES
  - LEISURE SERVICES
  - HOUSING AND DEVELOPMENT
  - ENVIRONMENTAL SERVICES
- CONTRACTOR SERVICES
  - CONTRACT WORKS
  - BUILDING WORKS

MANAGEMENT TEAM

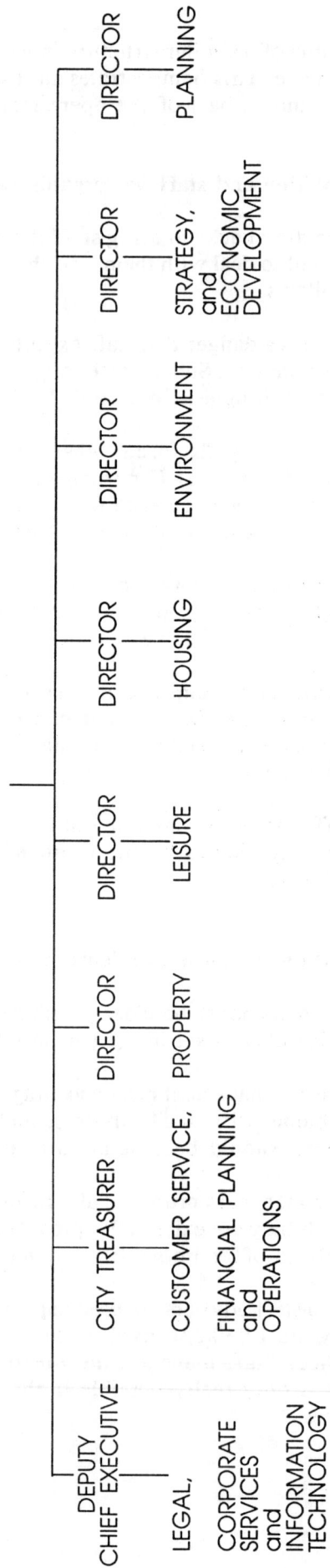

- DEPUTY CHIEF EXECUTIVE — LEGAL, CORPORATE SERVICES and INFORMATION TECHNOLOGY
- CITY TREASURER — CUSTOMER SERVICE, FINANCIAL PLANNING and OPERATIONS
- DIRECTOR — PROPERTY
- DIRECTOR — LEISURE
- DIRECTOR — HOUSING
- DIRECTOR — ENVIRONMENT
- DIRECTOR — STRATEGY, and ECONOMIC DEVELOPMENT
- DIRECTOR — PLANNING

Finding a 'balance' of influence between line and staff management

5.16 There has to be a balance between operations managers (line) and managers of support functions (staff). The problem for organisation is seen, typically, as follows.

(a) If operational managers had a superhuman ability to learn all the specialist skills necessary for management, there would be no need for support functions.

(b) It is only because specialist support is essential (eg accountants, computer specialists) or advisable (eg personnel specialists) - because operational managers would on their own be unable to make well-informed decisions - that the problem arises of finding a balance of authority or influence between line and staff.

5.17 Undue authority to line managers might result in rapid short-term business development, and high short term profits at high risk, with the danger that:

(a) legal restrictions (eg the rules of the Companies Act) will be inadvertently broken;
(b) personnel planning for the long term might be overlooked. Staff morale might be lowered;
(c) up to date technology and management techniques might be overlooked;
(d) important work not directly involved with day to day operations might be neglected.

The cumulative long-term effect will be damaging to the organisation.

5.18 On the other hand, it is unwise to give *too much* authority or influence to staff management.

(a) Staff management sometimes have divided loyalties between their organisation and their profession or speciality. Computer specialists might want to introduce up-to-date or 'perfect' computer systems when these might not be the most appropriate for the organisation. Accountants might show undue concern for the standards of their profession at the expense of the organisation's best interests.

(b) Many staff managers have skills which can be marketed to other organisations, so that their career is not necessarily tied to one company. Operational line managers, on the other hand, might be trained exclusively for service in one company, or one type of company or organisation (eg a bank or the Civil Service). When staff managers do not necessarily have a vested, long-term interest in their organisation, it might be argued that their authority should be kept under restraint.

(c) Staff managers tend to introduce rules and procedures - control systems, job evaluation and appraisal systems etc - and these tend to increase the bureaucratic nature of the formal organisation, with possible adverse repercussions on its efficiency due to excessive 'red tape'. This in turn might restrict an operational line manager's freedom of choice and flexibility. For example, a formal system of job descriptions might restrict the ability of management to make frequent reviews of their organisation's job structure.

(d) When an organisation has a multi-divisional structure, with international interests, each subsidiary or division (or sub-unit of a division) might have its own support functions. When there is staff management at group level, divisional level and below divisional level, a further organisational problem is created because of overlapping interests, boundaries of authority and influence, and conflicting advice and opinions between the different levels of functional staff.

(e) When staff departments build up an 'empire' of influence and authority, it may be difficult to measure the benefits to the organisation of various aspects of their work. Because the benefits of the work are 'indirect' they cannot always be measured in money terms. The only way to restrict the growth of costly, unjustifiable staff work might be to appoint outside consultants from time to time to carry out a cost-benefit analysis of a staff department on behalf of senior management.

5.19 In some cases, there might be a good argument for introducing elements of a matrix-management type of organisation (see later in this chapter) in which both operational (line) managers and support function (staff) managers have authority over the same managers below them in rank.

(a) The group head of marketing and public relations might have some authority over operational managers throughout the group, who will have responsibility for marketing performance and accountability to the head of marketing in this respect. Operational managers would also have their lines of responsibility to their senior operational management.

(b) Similarly, the group head of personnel might have some authority over operational managers, for example, with respect to job appraisal, manpower planning or recruiting and training.

5.20 The drawback to an excessive number of reporting lines (operational managers reporting to a number of different functional managers as well as their own operational superior) is that there will not be a clear source of authority in the organisation, and priorities might become uncertain and confused. Line managers may not get the personnel they want. They might be given inadequate training budgets to deal with change because staff managers have made the rules and control procedures governing resource allocation.

5.21 The argument of the classical school of management in favour of clear lines of authority is a valid one (although of course it is debatable whether a 'one boss for one subordinate' or 'unity of command' scalar chain of command is necessarily the only suitable way of establishing a clear authority structure).

5.22 Drucker argues that the traditional view of staff specialists as 'advisers with some authority' is a poor approach to organisation design. He suggested that 'as far as I have been able to grasp the concept, to be "staff" means to have authority without having responsibility. And that is destructive'. It is much better that (staff) functional departments, which are necessary in any large organisation:

(a) should have their own clear objectives;
(b) should have clearly stated areas of authority; and
(c) should be responsible and accountable for their exercise of that authority.

5.23 Traditionally in *central government* departments it has been the 'non expert' policy adviser or Treasury mandarin who has taken precedence over the 'line' managers (the experts in a particular field). The expert staff were a separate stream and did not move across to the policy or administrative side of the service. With the creation of 57 executive agencies to carry out government department work, a more decentralised structure has been created which works within a strategic framework.

5.24 The creation of 'business units', cost centres or internal contract arrangements in the public sector in health services and local government also reflect this approach.

Functional authority

5.25 *Functional authority* is a step further in the recognition that some 'staff' management has become highly specialised in areas of work which form a fundamental part of line management. This *expert power* becomes formally recognised in the organisation/management structure, merging line and staff authority. The expert is formally delegated the authority to influence specific areas (those in which he or she is a specialist) of the work of other departments and their managers. Functional specialists in, for example, financial control, industrial relations or public relations have the power to direct line managers within the well defined areas of their specialism.

5.26 This is a move towards *dual authority*, and carries elements of a *matrix structure* although the line manager retains ultimate authority for the functioning of the department. For this reason, and to avoid complex political problems, functional authority is usually exercised through the establishment of *systems, procedures and standards*, rather than by on-going direct intervention on the part of functional specialists. Management information systems and the availability of computer networks will be a vital part of this mixed line and staff management system.

Example: functional authority of the accounts department

5.27 Functional authority as described above is held by many different sorts of department but as an example let us examine how an understanding of functional authority underlies the organisation and management of an enterprise's accounting activity.

5.28 It is important for any function or department to understand the scope of its own authority, and to exercise that authority to an extent that is acceptable and effective in achieving organisational objectives.

5.29 If the accounts department of an organisation misunderstands the nature of functional authority, and assumes that it is in a 'staff' relationship with operational departments - or indeed if the accounts department *is* allocated a staff position in the organisation structure - the difficulties will be immense. If the department has no delegated authority to direct line managers in the areas of financial management and control, those activities will be at the mercy of line managers who may or may not choose to heed the advice, which is all the accounts department can give.

5.30 The complexity of the commercial environment and the requirements of financial management make it impossible in any but the smallest organisations for line managers to fulfil their operational duties and handle financial control at the same time. Devolved budget holders need to be trained and supported by the central finance management.

5.31 The application of functional authority, however, does have its problems, and an understanding of the nature of functional authority can again help in role definition and control with discretion: it is not 'staff' – but neither is it 'line' authority. Agreements have to be made across the 'functional' divide as to the purpose and procedures which will be followed as line and staff have different objectives.

5.32 Functional accounts managers must understand the boundaries of their authority: the purpose is not to undermine or curtail the authority of line managers who, after all, still retain ultimate responsibility. Given that corporate financial control is necessary in most organisations, especially in large, decentralised ones (where departments or divisions have a degree of autonomy), the problem is to reconcile the functional authority of the accounting department with the line authority of other managers. An understanding of the scope and nature of the two types of authority will at least point out areas of difficulty: rationalisation and role definition can therefore be carried out. For example, the ambiguous position of finance and accounting staff working in line departments should not be allowed to become a source of stress, and will require sensitivity: dual reporting (to the department – line – manager and to the accounts manager) must be handled with discretion, if role conflict and divided loyalties are not to arise.

5.33 Organisations generally delegate the management and control of financial affairs to an accounting and finance function/department which is responsible for the establishment and control of policies and procedures to which line and staff managers must adhere. The organisational difficulties arising from this common situation are mainly caused by lack of role definition: the solution then is to redefine clearly the nature and boundaries of functional authority. This may be difficult in value for money studies concerned with effectiveness. Resentment can occur when the accountant's measurement of performance extends to encompass a prescription for good line management (as has sometimes been done by the Audit Commission).

6. DEPARTMENTATION

6.1 As an organisation grows in size:

(a) it is able to take advantage of economies of scale, which in turn may call for the establishment of departments of specialists or experts (eg research and development, management scientists etc);

(b) the number of levels in the organisation hierarchy increases, so that problems of delegation of authority and control arise;

(c) specialist support teams (eg service and maintenance, quality control, corporate planning, organisation and methods, data processing etc) are created to ease the burdens and complexities of line management. Such support teams need to be slotted into the hierarchical structure;

(d) separate groups and departments continue to be formed as specialisation extends; new problems of communication and co-ordination (or integration) now arise;

(e) in public sector organisations, new functions may be added through legislation (eg Care in the Community; Children's Act);

(f)   as new intra organisational arrangements are established, additional departments may be required to deal with external and partnership arrangements.

Organisation by area, product, function, brand or customer

6.2   The creation of departments and divisions is known as *departmentation*. Different patterns of departmentation are possible, and the pattern selected will depend on the individual circumstances of the organisation. The organisational restructuring following the introduction of Compulsory Competitive Tendering (1988 Local Government Act) has meant new contract management functions have been located in additional departments or divisions.

6.3   Departments or divisions can be organised on the basis of the following.

(a)   *Function.* This accommodates the division of work into specialist areas. This can be seen in the Health Service with divisions between clinical, non clinical and support services, all with specialist tasks. In manufacturing, divisions may include production, sales, finance and general administration. Subdivisions of these areas may see sales divided into publicity, marketing and promotion, brand names and customer complaints. As new functions emerge they can be organised as subdivisions of existing departments or grow to become departments in their own right. This may be anything from energy saving to information systems to European dimensions for the organisation. Other functions may become dispersed or repackaged and operate as divisions of the organisation.

(b)   *Products.* Functional departments can be linked together to be concerned with a product so that individual managers can be held accountable for that product. This may be in the form of product teams. Japanese companies bring together engineers, designers, production managers and sales staff to develop a new product so that functional barriers are reduced at the outset. In the public sector the attempts to measure the unit costs are creating 'product' lines of management organisation. Business units are created to sell the 'product' to other parts of the organisation.

(c)   *Area.* This method of organisation is used when similar activities are carried out in widely different locations. Territorial departmentation means that services can be provided for local needs and that resource decisions can be more responsive to local conditions. The local management of schools demonstrates a level of devolved management. Central control is maintained by funding. The trouble with area departments is that overhead costs may increase and problems of coordination and integration become more acute.

Particular area-based problems arise when organisations that have to work together have different boundaries (eg local authorities and health authorities in 'care in the community', or coordinating gas, electricity and water services). Area-based solutions may be advocated for dealing with 'inner city' problems (eg task forces, 'city challenge').

(d)   *Markets.* Business organisations increasingly base organisational structure around market segments. A brand or market division may be most appropriate if customers' preferences are to be heeded (eg on design specifications). As competition is introduced into the public sector then marketing, brand or organisational identity is becoming more important. Public relations, marketing and promotion activities are used to attract purchasers or inward investors (eg to regions); and so the private sector's influence may see a shift towards market structured organisations.

Patient-focused organisation in a NHS hospital

6.4 These are situations where the organisational structure, and the physical disposal of those activities which reflects the structure, can have a direct impact on the actual service provided.

6.5 Hospitals are an example where both managerial and physical organisation around 'the customer' can lead to enhanced service efficiencies.

   (a) Many hospitals developed in a haphazard way, with equipment and service provision distributed over a wide physical area. One study revealed that junior hospital doctors walk up to seven miles a shift (using up three hours of possible productive time).

   (b) Furthermore, the physical location of equipment and services often reflect 'centralised' functional specialisms. In other words, a patient who needed complex treatment with a range of surgical and/or therapeutic procedures would be carted from department to department. Moreover, even those services delivered at the bedside would involve a large number of individuals.

      (i) One estimate supported that a patient who stayed five days in a hospital would encounter 47 different care providers.

      (ii) Work was specialised to the extent that there were 210 different job classifications.

   (c) Many procedures (eg quite simple blood tests) could be done at the bedside.

6.6 As an alternative, 'patient-focus' would require the following.

   (a) The establishment of a series of centres within separate parts of the hospital.

   (b) These centres would be staffed by *teams* with multiple skills. This would mean a reduction in the number of job descriptions. However, the multi-skilled team would have a complete responsibility for a group of patients.

   (c) It is hoped that the service would thus be designed around the needs of the patient, and would hence be more productive.

6.7 It has been estimated that, in some cases, patient-focused care could reduce operating costs by 10%. Moreover it would enhance productivity. It might enhance job satisfaction amongst medical personnel.

7. CENTRALISATION AND DECENTRALISATION

7.1 *Centralisation* and *decentralisation* refer to the degree to which authority is delegated in an organisation. The terms are thereby used to describe the level at which decisions are taken in the management hierarchy.

7.2   Complete centralisation would mean that *no* authority at all was exercised by subordinates; complete decentralisation would mean that *all* authority was exercised by subordinates (there would be no coordination of subordinates). It is doubtful whether any organisation approaches of either of these extremes.

7.3   Decentralisation has been seen as a way of being more responsive to customers' needs or providing a set of services in a local area. In local government, the successful decentralisation of functions to area or *neighbourhood offices* (eg housing neighbourhood offices) but has not been matched by the decentralisation of groups of functions (creating mini town halls). Decentralised provision of services means that political responses can also be made to local problems. As budgets and criteria for measuring performance criteria can be established for each decentralised area, it is possible to make comparisons between areas of relative expenditure and effectiveness. This is not possible with a centralised single function budgeting system. Resource allocation may be more responsive to area based budgeting than central budgets.

7.4   Delegation of decision making within established frameworks can save time, cut bureaucracy and, in the public sector, free senior managers and elected politicians to concentrate on strategic or policy issues. However, it may give more power to committee chairpersons and certain officers, which could result in arbitrary decisions in some cases.

The advantages of centralisation

7.5   The advantages of centralisation are as follows.

    (a)   Senior management can exercise greater control over the activities of the organisation and co-ordinate their subordinates or sub-units more easily.

    (b)   With central control, procedures can be standardised throughout the organisation.

    (c)   Senior managers can make decisions from the point of view of the organisation as a whole, whereas subordinates would tend to make decisions from the point of view of their own department or section. Sub-optimality occurs when one department makes a decision which appears to be a good one from the departmental point of view but which is actually damaging to the organisation as a whole. With centralisation, sub-optimality should not occur, but with decentralisation it would be a serious threat to the efficiency of the organisation.

    (d)   Centralised control enables an organisation to maintain a balance between different functions or departments. For example, if an organisation has only a limited amount of funds available to spend over the next few years, centralised management would be able to take a balanced view of how the funds should be shared out between production, marketing, research and development, provision of services and support to different departments.

    (e)   Senior managers ought to be more experienced and skillful in making decisions. In theory at least, centralised decisions by senior people should be better in 'quality' than decentralised decisions by less experienced subordinates.

(f)   Centralised management will often be cheaper in terms of managerial overheads. When authority is delegated, there is often a duplication of management effort (and a corresponding increase in staff numbers) at lower levels of hierarchy. To avoid such costs of duplication some specialised departments (eg data processing, the legal department) may remain centralised.

(g)   In times of crisis, the organisation may need strong leadership by a central group of senior managers. These managers may need to be in touch with the policy makers and the board or elected body to implement radical decisions.

The advantages of decentralisation

7.6   Some delegation is necessary in all organisations because of the limitations to the physical and mental capacity of senior managers. A greater degree of decentralisation - over and above the 'minimum' which is essential - has the following advantages.

(a)   It reduces the stress and burdens of senior management.

(b)   It provides subordinates with greater job satisfaction by giving them more say in decision-making which affects their work. Such participation in decisions, leading to job satisfaction, might motivate the subordinates to work harder and more efficiently and effectively to achieve the goals of the organisation.

(c)   Subordinates may have a better knowledge of 'local' conditions affecting their area of work. With the benefits of such knowledge, they should be capable of more informed, well-judged management. Unfortunately, local managers often think in the short term, whereas senior managers think in the longer term. A subordinate might therefore make a well-informed decision to win a short-term advantage when a different decision would have been preferable in the longer-term view.

(d)   Delegation should allow greater flexibility and a quicker response to changing conditions. If problems do not have to be referred up a scalar chain of command to senior managers for a decision, decision-making will be quicker. Since decisions are quicker, they are also more adaptable, and easier to change in the light of unforeseen circumstances which may arise.

(e)   By allowing delegated authority to subordinates, management at middle and junior levels are 'groomed' for eventual senior management positions, because they are given the necessary experience of decision-making. Delegation is therefore important for management development.

(f)   By establishing appropriate sub-units or profit centres to which authority is delegated, the system of control within the organisation might actually be improved. Targets for performance by each profit centre can be established, actual results monitored against targets and control action taken by appropriate subordinates with the necessary authority; the subordinates would then be held accountable and responsible for their results, and areas of efficiency or inefficiency within the organisation would be more easily identified and remedied.

SUMMARY

Arguments in favour of centralisation and decentralisation

Pro-centralisation

1 Decisions are made at one point, and so easier to co-ordinate.

2 Senior managers in an organisation can take a wider view of problems and consequences.

3 Senior management can keep a proper balance between different departments or functions - eg. by deciding on the resources to allocate to each.

4 Possibly cheaper, by reducing number of managers needed and so lower cost of overheads.

5 Crisis decisions are best taken at the centre.

Pro-decentralisation/delegation

1 Avoids overburdening top managers.

2 Improves motivation of more junior managers.

3 Greater awareness of local problems by decision makers. Geographically dispersed organisations should often be decentralised on a regional/area basis.

4 Greater speed of decision making, and response to changing events.

5 Helps junior managers to develop and helps the process of transition from functional to general management.

6 Separate spheres of responsibility can be identified, and control systems set up for junior management; controls, performance measurement and accountability are better.

7.7 Drucker argued in favour of more rather than less decentralisation, in order to provide a spur to management for better performance. An organisation should be structured so as to facilitate efficient and effective management. Drucker listed three major requirements for structuring.

(a) The organisation must be one which is directed towards *achieving business performance*. 'Organisation is the more efficient the more 'direct' and simple it is'.

(b) The organisation should contain the *least possible number of management levels*, so that the chain of command is as short as possible. 'Every link in the chain sets up additional stresses, and creates one more source of inertia, friction and slack'. There is a tendency (identified by C Northcote Parkinson) for levels of management to increase in number, but this is both unnecessary and inefficient.

(c) The organisation structure should provide jobs in which *young managers can be properly trained and tested* for more senior management positions in the future. 'It must give people actual management responsibility in an autonomous position while they are still young enough to acquire new experience'.

8.   DIVISIONALISATION

8.1   The two structural principles which meet these requirements in classical theories of organisational structures are:

(a)   *functional decentralisation*; and
(b)   federal decentralisation, or *divisionalisation*.

These are alternative organisation structures to greater centralisation of authority but with some functionally-organised or divisional-based decentralisation.

Of these, Drucker considered federal decentralisation much better where it could be applied but it can only operate at fairly senior management level and cannot go below a certain level in the management hierarchy. At lower management levels, functional decentralisation should be applied.

Federal decentralisation

8.2   Federal decentralisation, or divisionalisation, is the division of an organisation into autonomous regions or product businesses, each with its own revenues, expenditures and capital asset purchase programmes, and therefore each with its own profit and loss responsibility. Each division of the organisation might be:

(a)   subsidiary companies under the holding company;
(b)   profit centres or investment centres within a single organisation;
(c)   service functions operating as cost centres.

8.3   The rules for federal decentralisation should be as follows.

(a)   It must have properly delegated authority, but strong 'control' should be retained at centre by head office. In other words, management of federal units are free to use their authority to do what they think is right for their part of the organisation, but they must be held properly accountable to head office (eg for profits earned).

(b)   A decentralised unit must be large enough to support the quantity and quality of management it needs. It must not rely on head office for excessive management support.

(c)   Each decentralised unit must have a potential to be innovative and responsive in its own area of operations.

(d)   There should be scope and challenge in the job for the management of the decentralised unit.

(e)   Federal units should exist side-by-side with each other. If they deal with each other, it should be as an 'arm's length' transaction. Where they touch, it should be in competition with each other. There should be no insistence on preferential treatment to be given to a 'fellow-unit' by another unit of the overall organisation'.

8.4   The *advantages* of federal decentralisation are as follows.

(a)   It focuses the attention of management below 'top level' on business performance and results.

(b) It reduces the likelihood of unprofitable products and activities being continued.

(c) It therefore encourages a greater attention to efficiency, lower costs and higher profits.

(d) Management by objectives can be applied more easily. 'The manager of the unit knows better than anyone else how he is doing, and needs no one to tell him'.

(e) It gives more authority to junior managers, and therefore provides them with work which grooms them for more senior positions in the future.

(f) It tests junior managers in independent command early in their careers, and at a reasonably low level in the management hierarchy.

(g) It provides an organisation structure which reduces the number of levels of management. The top executives in each federal unit should be able to report direct to the chief executive of the holding company.

(h) It encourages experimentation in different management practices on a small scale.

8.5 The *limitations* to federal decentralisation are as follows.

(a) In some businesses, it is impossible to identify completely independent products or markets. In the telecommunications system, for example:

(i) federal decentralisation by region or area is not properly possible because customers in one region make inter-regional calls;

(ii) federal decentralisation by service (eg telephones, data transmission, or local calls and trunk calls) is not properly feasible because different services use common equipment.

(b) Federal decentralisation requires good quality local management, investment in management training, and the development of a strategy for the organisation. Investment is also required in information systems and monitoring procedures, so that good communications are maintained between the centre and the federal units. Resource allocation systems have to be created to help the weaker units in the federal structure.

(c) In federal structures, mechanisms are required to allow a federal voice in the decision making. The federal units are resource dependent on the centre and centre has to understand the 'street level' bureaucrat's problems in delivering the service on behalf of the centre. There should, however, be some mechanism whereby the collective issues are discussed.

(d) Federal decentralisation may lead to tension and conflicts result in a break up of the federal system. Independent units which can be externally resourced may be created through management buyouts or takeover by rival organisations. It may be difficult to disband federal structures when the centre has taken a policy decision to operate differently.

Functional decentralisation

8.6 Where federal decentralisation is not possible, Drucker argues in favour of functional decentralisation. Functional decentralisation exists when an organisation is structured on the basis of functional departments, and authority is decentralised as far as possible within each department.

8.7 Functional decentralisation has been the pattern of organisation in local government and health services. The introduction of general managers into the health service and an increasing concern with creating cost centres in local government. The integration of these functional divisions into a corporate entity has been a major problem. Making links across the organisation to bring together teams working on related issues or at the same level of responsibility has led to horizontal as well as vertical organisational structures being tried.

Decentralisation and NHS trusts

8.8 The recent organisational changes in the NHS (trust status for opted out hospitals, already touched on in an earlier chapter), indicate the potential pros and cons of decentralisation.

8.9 Ignoring the controversy surrounding the wider market led reforms, it is clear that many hospital managers have chosen this route as they feel it offers them advantages for their role as *managers*. 'Under the old system, hospital managers were constantly trying to fiddle with a few of the levers while changes outside our control were coming at us from district, government and regional level.'

8.10 An example has been The Central Middlesex Hospital (*Financial Times* 25 March 1991). The objective of moving to trust status was not so much financial but to support managerial freedom, in order to:

(a) 'make the hospital more patient focused';

(b) 'implement a wide ranging staff charter, designed to improve employees' attitudes, give them more rewarding careers and increase efficiency'.

8.11 Greater autonomy enables small, but beneficial, changes to be implemented. An example at the Central Middlesex Hospital was the replacement of inadequate signposting which, in a large 65-acre site, is an important operational issue. This had always been given a low priority in a centrally run service.

9. MATRIX ORGANISATION

9.1 Matrix organisation emerged in the USA during the 1950s and 1960s, and which is now widely practised in a variety of forms. Basically, a matrix organisation provides for the formalisation of management control between different functions, whilst at the same time maintaining functional departmentation.

9.2 A golden rule of classical management theory was unity of command – one person should have one boss. (Thus, staff management can only act in an advisory capacity, leaving authority in the province of line management alone.)

9.3 Matrix management is perhaps a reaction against the 'classical' form of bureaucracy by establishing a structure of dual command.

9.4 Matrix management first developed in the 1950s in the USA in the aerospace industry. Lockheed-California, the aircraft manufacturers, were organised in a functional hierarchy. Customers were unable to find a manager in Lockheed to whom they could take their problems and queries about their particular orders, and Lockheed found it necessary to employ 'project expediters' as customer liaison officials. From this developed 'project co-ordinators', responsible for co-ordinating line managers into solving a customer's problems. Up to this point, these new officials had no functional responsibilities.

Owing to increasingly heavy customer demands, Lockheed eventually created 'programme managers', with authority for project budgets and programme design and scheduling. These managers therefore had functional authority and responsibilities, thus a matrix management organisation was created. It may be shown diagrammatically as a management *grid*; for example:

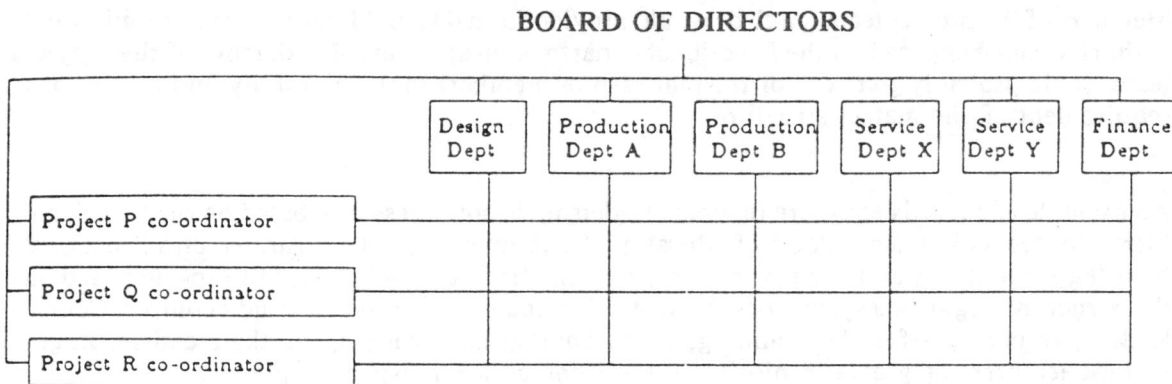

BOARD OF DIRECTORS

	Design Dept	Production Dept A	Production Dept B	Service Dept X	Service Dept Y	Finance Dept
Project P co-ordinator						
Project Q co-ordinator						
Project R co-ordinator						

9.5 Authority would be shared between the project co-ordinators and the heads of the functional departments. Functional department heads are responsible for the organisation of the department, but project co-ordinators are responsible for all aspects of the project itself. An employee in a functional department might expect to receive directions/commands from a project co-ordinator as well as from the departmental head - so there may be dual command.

9.6 Matrix organisations were also taken up by the public sector, particularly in local government, following the Bains' Report *(1972 Local Authorities: Management and Structure)*, which advocated a corporate approach to local government management. Bains introduced the idea of programme areas, and with the use of such techniques as 'planning programming and budgeting', the reformed local government system in 1974 adopted many of these ideas. This was achieved by the appointment of chief executives and the creation of directors for programme services establishing coordinating machinery in policy analysis units and corporate planning units, which went across departmental functional divisions.

9.7 The Policy and Resources Committee and the Chief Officers' Boards were established to coordinate an authority's activities rather than giving all the power to line functions. As cross departmental issues arose, working parties or project teams would be created to bring together a wide range of specialists to deal with the issues.

Project team matrices

9.8 Project teams are another example of a simple matrix structure. A project may be inter-disciplinary, and require the contributions of an engineer, a scientist, a statistician and a production expert, who would each be appointed to the team from their functional department, whilst still retaining membership and status within the department.

	Level in *departmental hierarchy*		*Department*			
		A	B	C	D	E
	1	x	⊗	x	x	⊗
	2	⊗	x	x	x	x
	3	x	x	⊗	x	x
	4	x	x	x	⊗	x

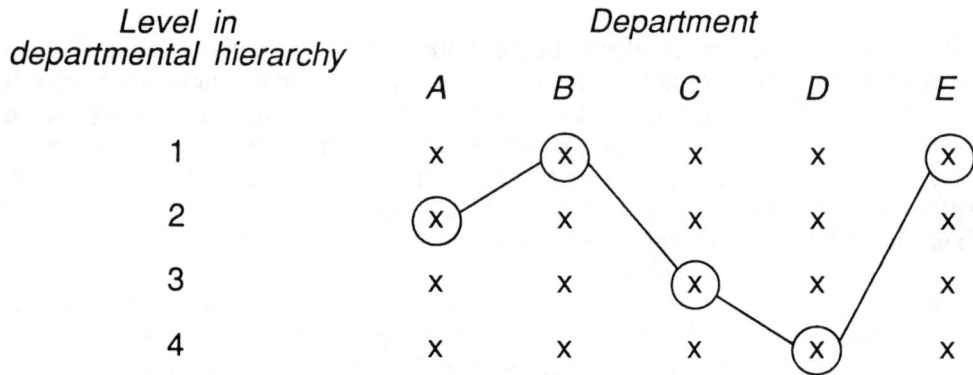

Members of the project team (circled) would provide formal lateral lines of communication and authority, superimposed on the functional departmental structure. Leadership of the project team would probably go to one of the more senior members in the hierarchy, but this is not a requirement of the matrix structure.

9.9   An example of a matrix structure in which leadership is not necessarily based on the functional hierarchy occurs in some colleges of education. Departments may be organised on a functional basis (eg accountancy and business studies, mathematics, economics etc) but superimposed on this structure might be a system of administration and organisation for study courses. Course leaders, responsible for the planning, co-ordinating and teaching of their course, might include lecturers of greater seniority in their course team. For example:

(a)   Course A might be led by a senior lecturer of the economics department, and include a junior lecturer from the same department and a principal lecturer from the mathematics department.

(b)   Course B might be led by a principal lecturer from the economics department and include a senior lecturer from each of the maths and accountancy departments.

(c)   Course C might be led by a principal lecturer from the accountancy department, and include junior lecturers from the accountancy and maths departments.

In a grid format this would appear as:

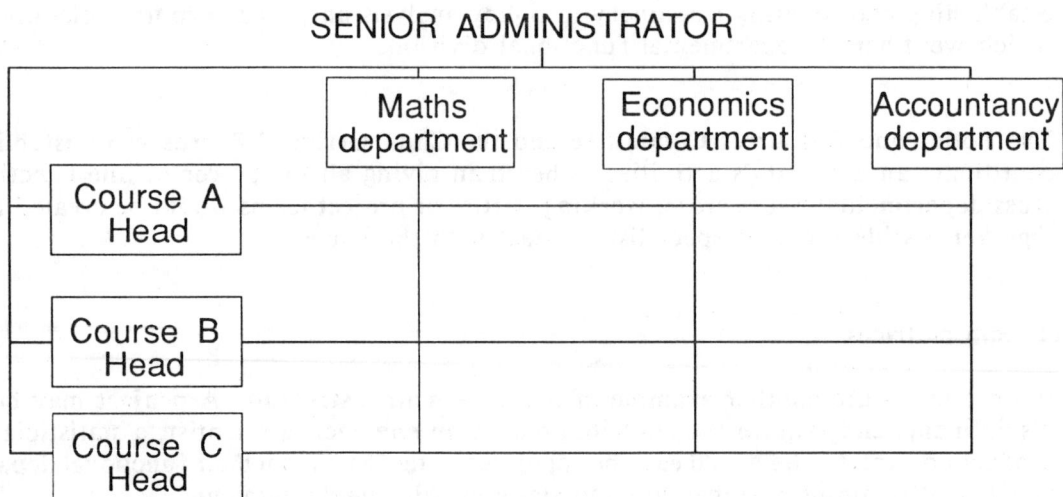

SENIOR ADMINISTRATOR

	Maths department	Economics department	Accountancy department
Course A Head			
Course B Head			
Course C Head			

9.10 A more detailed organisation chart might be drawn as follows:

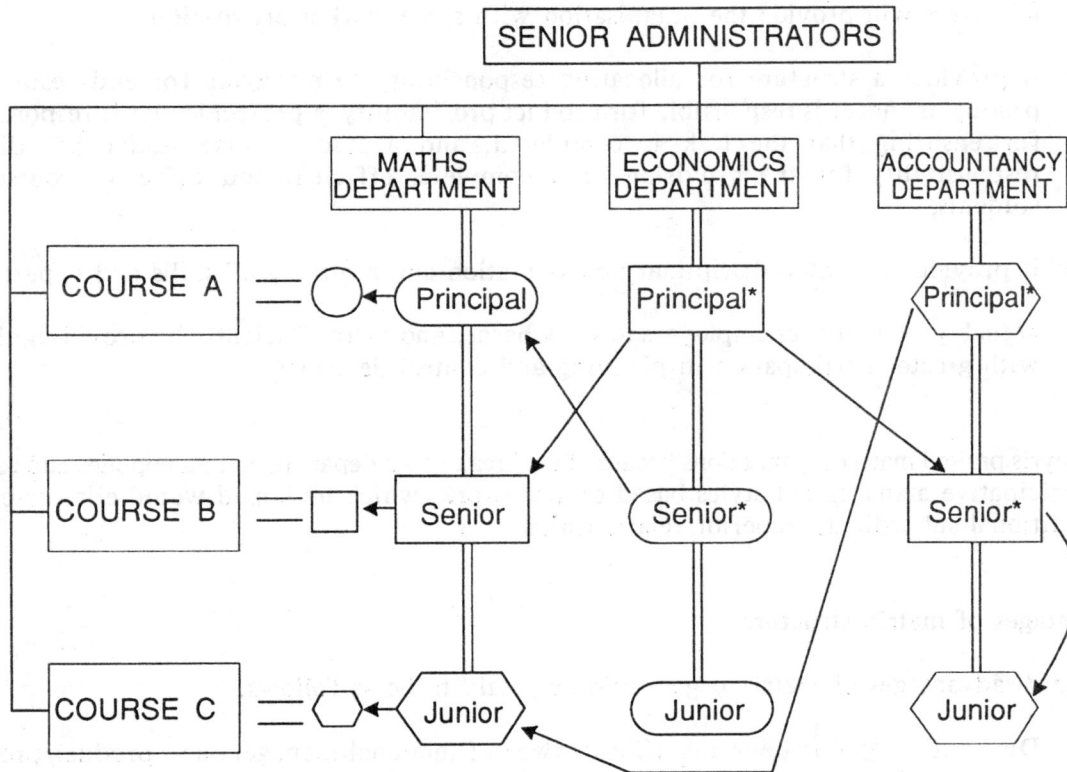

Key: *   Course leaders

_____ Lines of authority of course leaders

===== Departmental lines of authority

9.11 Matrix management thus challenges classical ideas about organisation in two ways:

(a) it rejects the idea of one man, one boss (unity of command); and
(b) its subverts the bureaucratic ethic of authority based on status in the formal hierarchy.

Advantages of a matrix structure

9.12 The advantages of a matrix structure are said to be:

(a) greater flexibility:

(i) of people. Employees adapt more quickly to a new challenge or new task, and develop an attitude which is geared to accepting change;

(ii) of tasks and structure. The matrix structure may be short-term (as with project teams) or readily amended (eg a new product manager can be introduced by superimposing his tasks on those of the existing functional managers).

Flexibility should facilitate efficient operations in the face of change;

(b) dual authority gives the organisation multiple orientation. For example, a functional departmentation will often be production-oriented, whereas the superimposition of brand managers will provide the organisation with some market orientation;

(c) it provides a structure for allocating responsibility to managers for end-results. A product manager is responsible for product profitability, a project leader is responsible for ensuring that the task is completed, and a study course leader has direct responsibility for the provision of a complete, efficient and effective course to students;

(d) it provides for inter-disciplinary co-operation and a mixing of skills and expertise;

(e) arguably, it motivates employees to work harder and more efficiently by providing them with greater participation in planning and control decisions.

9.13 Argyris praised matrix organisations because they break down departmental monopolies and foster participative management styles based on teamwork, which he hoped would eliminate the traditional subordinate-superior relationships.

Disadvantages of matrix structure

9.14 The disadvantages of matrix organisation are said to be as follows.

(a) Dual authority threatens a conflict between functional managers and product/project managers. Where matrix structure exists it is important that the authority of superiors should not overlap and areas of authority must be clearly defined. A subordinate must know to which superior he is responsible for a particular aspect of his duties.

(b) One individual with two or more bosses is more likely to suffer stress at work.

(c) They are sometimes more costly - eg product managers are additional jobs which would not be required in a simple structure of functional departmentation.

(d) It may be difficult for the management of an organisation to accept a matrix structure. It is possible that a manager may feel threatened that another manager will usurp his authority. (Where authority is not clearly defined, this is likely to happen. The decision-making process would also be expected to slow down.)

9.15 Many companies have recently moved away from matrix management as being far too complex to handle. An article in the *Financial Times* in June 1989 pointed out the danger of reacting too violently against what it describes as a management 'fad' such as matrices:

'[moving away from matrix-management] helped push multinationals such as Philips towards over-simplistic structures, in which most national power (and much sense of motivation) was given up in favour of strong global product divisions. Philips and others are now having to backtrack towards a hybrid structure which is more acceptable to the many nationalities who work within it.'

Exercise

Why do you think a large diversified conglomerate (like BTR) might have a relatively small head office function, despite the large number of businesses in this group?

Solution

Here are some possibilities.

(a) The various businesses are so different, that there are few scale economies to be had by integrating functions.

(b) Head office management might be committed to delegation: let the business managers get on with the job of managing providing they come up with the results at the end of the year.

---

10. CONCLUSION

10.1 An organisation can contain both a formal and an informal structure.

10.2 Formal organisations structure issues include scalar chains, spans of control, all of which deal with authority.

10.3 In addition, there is the distinction between line and staff managers. Line managers are directly involved in production or sales. Staff managers assist that function.

10.4 Centralised organisations encourage uniformity but can be overweighty.

TEST YOUR KNOWLEDGE
The numbers in brackets refer to paragraphs of this chapter

1 Describe some symptoms of pool organisation structure. (1.1)

2 What is a scalar chain (3.1) and span of control? (4.1)

3 Distinguish between tall and flat organisations. (4.6)

4 What is functional authority? (5.24)

5 Describe four methods of departmentation. (6.3)

6 What is a matrix organisation? (9.4)

Now try questions 4 and 5 at the end of the text

Chapter 6

ORGANISATIONAL CULTURE

This chapter covers the following topics.

1. Organisational change
2. Excellence and culture
3. Culture and organisation structure
4. Organisation style
5. The adaptive organisation

---

1. ORGANISATIONAL CHANGE

1.1 Handy sums up 'culture' as 'that's the way we do things round here'. A corporate culture 'defines appropriate behaviour, bonds and motivates individuals and asserts solutions where there is ambiguity. It governs the way a company processes information, its internal relations and its values' (*Corporate culture* Charles Hampden–Turner). The way things are done in the public sector has been changing in line with private sector management thinking described by Peters and Waterman *(In Search of Excellence)*. The Audit Commission *(Good Management Practice)* took up the idea of Peters and Waterman and found practical examples of management practice in local government.

1.2 It has sometimes been asserted that there is a conflict between:

(a) a professional culture;
(b) a public service culture;
(c) a managerial culture.

Each of these has been present to different degrees and at different times in the public and private sectors.

1.3 A 'professional culture' was one in which technical expertise (eg in surgery, or accountancy) is regarded as most important, and experts or committees of experts are responsible for decision making. The NHS was once run on a committee basis. Professional cultures have eschewed marketing (eg accountants were once forbidden to advertise their services) or overt competition.

1.4 It has been asserted that a public service culture has been present in many public sector organisations. A *popular stereotype* of the public service culture includes:

(a) devotion to wider values other than organisational advancement (ie fairly abstract notions of 'the public interest' 'the national interest');

(b) lack of interest in commercial disciplines (as not being relevant);

(c) a certain organisational rigidity, with relatively little attention paid to customer service at lower levels.

1.5 There are stereotypes, and each organisation has its own atmosphere or culture which to a degree structures the way in which individuals respond to each other within the organisation and to the users of the services provided.

1.6 A 'management' or 'commercial' culture on private sector lines is one which embraces 'marketing, and in which renewed emphasis is put on measures of cost.

1.7 An example of the introduction of a 'management' culture into the professional and service cultures of the NHS is provided by the Griffith report into NHS administration. Griffiths held that:

(a) general managers, rather than boards of professionals, should run the NHS;
(b) cost controls and financial awareness are also necessary amongst management.

So, for example, the relative values of preventative medicine (eg education campaigns) as opposed to treatments will be evaluated in financial as well as medical criteria.

1.8 An example of how a change in culture has taken place is given by British Airways. It has been discussed in detail by C Hampden-Turner in *Corporate culture*, but some of the salient points can be detailed here.

(a) Until the early 1980s BA's culture had the following characteristics.

(i) A military/technological tradition, rather than a tradition of service orientation.
(ii) A bureaucracy perceived as cold and inflexible by its customers.
(iii) A rigid hierarchy with achievement marked by rank.
(iv) The cabin staff – who delivered the service – were subordinated and disempowered.
(v) The cabin staff passed on these negative attitudes to the way they treated customers.

(b) *Before* privatisation, new management personnel were introduced, and the airline was reorganised (with some inspiration given by SAS). An example was the adoption of personal names instead of titles of rank on managers' doors.

(c) A new approach was implemented which:

(i) gave cabin crew greater discretion;
(ii) encouraged middle managers to be supportive and respectful of staff;
(iii) used measures to evaluate how middle managers treated their subordinates.

It was felt that if staff were more 'open' to customers, customers in return could provide more information about what they felt of the service. The strategy was 'putting people first'.

1.9   The result has been a business which is more customer orientated and which is making substantial profits. However challenges remain in that:

(a)   while it is desirable to breakdown barriers between functions, 'expertise' in a technical sphere is still necessary (eg obviously in engineering);

(b)   building networks that encourage the 'technical' jobs and the 'customer care' jobs (which Hampden describes as emotional labour) to cooperate together.

1.10   The example of British Airways occurred against a background of organisational change. Examples of public sector change include:

(a)   autonomous, or semi-autonomous, executive agencies set up to administer policy execution;

(b)   continuing privatisation of utilities and other state owned industries;

(c)   the purchaser-provider split in the health service (with budget-holders buying services);

(d)   changes in school funding and organisation (local management of schools, opting out);

(e)   the Citizen's Charter which might be a way in which service culture can be injected into the public sector.

1.11   These examples show the scale and pace of the changes going on at the boundary of the public and private sector. The transition into a competitive environment has required a challenge to existing cultures, and their replacement by new cultures.

1.12   These changes have been concerned with:

(a)   increasing the freedom of the organisation from political and bureaucratic controls;

(b)   providing clear goals and guidelines for these organisations;

(c)   opening up these organisations to competition or comparative performance measurement;

(d)   creating watchdog organisations to protect consumer interests;

(e)   introducing an enterprise culture;

(f)   changing management styles which are expected to be more aggressive;

(g)   creating financial management systems;

(h)   introducing new technology;

(i)   establishing personnel and staff management systems;

(j)   a commitment to quality;

(k)   establishing new decision making bodies and decision criteria which are market and business related.

1.13 Many of these organisational changes have also been accompanied by changes of image, the creation of new logos, painting of vehicles, new uniforms and slogans to identify the organisation (eg BT).

1.14 Culture can also embody the *mythology* of the organisation, what it did in the past, the characters that are remembered and the actions they are associated with them become the legends to retell at office parties and in committees.

1.15 A set of words of the new culture become established in the language of the people of the organisation and take on a new significance:

(a) 'shared values';
(b) 'the bottom line';
(c) 'economy, efficiency and effectiveness;
(d) 'the mission statement';
(e) 'quality'.

1.16 Culture is unique to an organisation. The prison service has a different culture to an advertising agency, which is different to a steel works or a car factory. Culture can also vary across the organisation.

The culture of a research and development department might be different from a marketing department, although they may both be concerned with innovation and taking risks. This has been described above in the case of BA.

1.17 In the public sector, culture can also be a reflection of *professional* training and practice. Professionals (eg doctors, accountants) are supposed to hold their *profession's* values, irrespective of the organisation they are in, and the profession's values are supposed to be more important than the organisation's priorities (eg particularly in ethical matters).

2. EXCELLENCE AND CULTURE

2.1 A criticism of the changes discussed above is that much of the cultural change is concerned with image rather than substance. Simply introducing a few new slogans backed up by advertising campaigns is not enough. If slogans do not reflect actual organisational practices they will be treated with derision by employees and cynicism by customers. The same staff are in the same posts by and large, they are doing the same job for the same level of reward. The consumers of the service or products are the same. The ownership or reporting systems may change but this may not be sufficient to change the *culture* of the organisation, especially if senior management is insufficiently energetic in promoting it.

2.2 The public sector has been characterised by a stable workforce with known positions and career prospects. This is now to be replaced with a performance related pay system, short-term contracts and an *exit culture*, replacing a *job for life* culture.

2.3 Uncertainty, even fear about the future, can be felt by many of the workers in the organisation undergoing changes in ownership and reporting systems, and the introduction of new values. What may be seen by some as an opportunity is seen as a threat by others.

2.4 Introducing a change in which customers are treated requires a change in the values of the employees who deliver the service.

2.5 Changing values can require a number of years, but ultimately, they must be communicated as part of the organisation's image to the consumer.

Some useful examples of cultural changes in the private sector can be relevant to the public sector, if the private sector is to be the model upon which the public sector is to be based.

The pursuit of excellence

2.6 In 1982 Tom Peters and Robert Waterman published what became a seminal book in management theory, *In Search of Excellence*. By an anecdotal technique they set about describing and analysing what it was that made successful companies successful.

2.7 By 'excellent' companies Peters and Waterman mean companies which have achieved a certain kind of innovative performance:

(a) they are usually good at producing commercially viable new products; *and*

(b) they are especially adroit at continually responding to changes of any sort in their environment.

An excellent company is a continuously innovative big company.

2.8 By observing and analysing in depth about thirty successful American companies (in terms of growth, market value, return on capital etc), Peters and Waterman noted that excellent companies share certain common characteristics:

(a) *thinking, wisdom* and *action* by managers were considered more important than tools, intellect and analysis;

(b) they worked hard to keep things *simple* in a complex world;

(c) they insisted on *top quality;*

(d) they paid huge attention to *customer care;*

(e) they listened to *employees* and treated them like adults;

(f) they gave rein to *innovators;* and

(g) they were prepared to put up with some *chaos* in return for quick action and experimentation.

2.9 These observed characteristics were analysed into eight key attributes of an excellent company and its culture.

> 1   A bias for action.
> 2   Closeness to the customer - quality, service and reliability.
> 3   Autonomy and entrepreneurship.
> 4   Productivity through people.
> 5   Hands-on management, driven by value.
> 6   'Stick to the knitting' - stick with what you know and can run.
> 7   Simple structures, small numbers of top-level staff.
> 8   Simultaneous loose-tight properties - they are at once centralised and decentralised. Autonomy is allowed on the shop-floor and in project teams but *all* parts of the organisation must adhere to core values.

Excellence and leadership

2.10 It is interesting to note that many of the 'excellent' companies showing these attributes were associated with very strong leaders who seemed to have a lot to do with making the company excellent in the first place. Provided this happened at an early stage in the company's life, the excellent value remained after the leader departed. The role of managers was to manage the *values* of the company.

2.11 A later work by Tom Peters with Nancy Austin, *A Passion for Excellence*, focuses on the importance of leadership and values. In particular, it advocates 'management by wandering about' (MBWA), by which it means that managers should keep in touch with what customers want, how products are produced and how employees are carrying out their work.

Excellence and the rational model of management

2.12 For many years the central theme of Western thinking on management was that managers make decisions in a rational way. Complex logical and mathematical methods were developed for the process: decision trees, critical path analysis etc.

2.13 However, behaviour in organisations is also about creativity, emotion, hunches, gut reactions, politics, enthusiasm and other unquantifiable human qualities that do not fit well into the rational model.

> '"Rational" has come to have a very narrow definition in business analysis. It is the "right" answer, but it's missing all of that messy human stuff, such as good strategies that do not allow for persistent old habits, implementation barriers and simple human inconsistencies.' *(Peters and Waterman)*

2.14 Peters and Waterman enumerate several shortcomings of the rational model of organisation, including the fact that:

(a) the numerative analytical component has in-built conservative bias and stifles innovation;

(b) it does not celebrate informality, internal competition and experimentation;

(c) it denigrates the importance of values; culture is essentially irrational;

(d) 'the rationalist approach takes the living element out of situations that should, above all, be alive'.

2.15 They suggest that the 'technology of reason' should be supplemented with a 'technology of foolishness': that sometimes, individuals should be free to act before they think. The right side of the brain - artistic and irrational - has its place in human behaviour. The decision making process should be like a 'garbage can': lots of ideas swirling around, mixing etc.

2.16 Above all, Peters and Waterman find that the central problem with the rationalist view of organising people is that people are not very rational.

Excellence and motivation

2.17 Peters and Waterman also discuss the central importance of positive reinforcement in any method of motivation. 'Researchers studying motivation find that the prime factor is simply the self-perception among motivated subjects that they are in fact doing well ... Mere association with past personal success apparently leads to more persistence, higher motivation, or something that makes us do better.'

2.18 At Mars Inc in America, Peters and Waterman observed that every employee - including the president - received a 10% pay bonus for each week in which he got to work on time every day. 'That's an ... example of creating a setting in which virtually everybody wins regularly ... When the number of awards is high, it makes the perceived possibility of winning something high as well. And then the average man will stretch to achieve. Many companies do believe in special awards, but use them exclusively to honour the top few (who already are so highly motivated that they would probably have done their thing anyway).'

2.19 The observations of Peters and Waterman on the 'culture' and motivational environment of 'excellent' companies in the USA may seem slightly eccentric to British managers, but part of the writers' profile of an excellent company is that 'excellent companies require and demand extraordinary performance from the average man'. They have gone to identify the same characteristics in business in the UK and Europe and have seen the same approach extended to the public sector in the UK.

2.20 Positive reinforcement - whether in the form of bonuses, prizes, 'reaffirming the heroic dimension' of the job itself, identifying workers with the company's success, or enhancing self-image in the workforce - is the method Peters and Waterman observed *succeeding*, although some research has shown that 'tough' managers, applying sanctions on undesirable behaviour, can also get improved performance out of their subordinates.

2.21 Peters and Waterman argue that employees can be 'switched on' to extraordinary loyalty and effort. How is this done?

(a) The cause is perceived to be in some sense great - 'reaffirming the heroic dimension' of the work. Commitment comes from believing that a task is inherently worthwhile. Devotion to the *customer*, and his needs and wants, is an important motivator in this way.

Shared values and 'good news swapping' - a kind of folklore of past success and 'heroic' endeavour - create a climate where intrinsic motivation is a real driving force. Arguably this might mean a new role for the idealism of public service.

(b) Employees are treated as winners. 'Label a man a loser and he'll start acting like one.' Repressive control systems and negative reinforcement break down the employee's self-image. Positive reinforcement, 'good news swapping', attention from management etc enhance the employee's self-image and create positive attitudes to work and to the organisation.

(c) They can satisfy their dual needs:

(i) to be a conforming, secure part of a successful team; and
(ii) to be a 'star' in their own right.

2.22 This means applying control (through firm central direction, and shared values and beliefs) but also allowing maximum individual autonomy (at least, the *illusion* of autonomy) and even competition between individual or groups within the organisation. Peters and Waterman call this 'loose-tight' management. Culture, peer pressure, a focus on action, customer-orientation etc are 'non-aversive' ways of exercising control over employees.

2.23 The implication of this for work behaviour affects the way in which individuals can be motivated and managed. As Peters and Waterman argue, a strong 'central faith', which binds the organisation together as a whole, should be combined with a strong emphasis on individual self-expression, contribution and success: individuals should be given at least the 'illusion of control' over their destinies, while still being given a sense of belonging and a secure, perceived meaningful framework in which to act.

Excellence and group behaviour

2.24 Peters and Waterman *(In Search of Excellence)* outline the cultural attributes of successful *task force* teams. They should:

(a) be small - requiring the trust of those who are not involved;

(b) be of limited duration and working under the 'busy member theorem' - ie 'get off the damned task force and back to work';

(c) be voluntary - which ensures that the business is 'real';

(d) have an informal structure and documentation - ie no bulky paperwork, and open communication;

(e) have swift follow-up - be *action* oriented.

Excellence and people

2.25 One of the prime attributes of 'excellent' companies identified by Peters and Waterman is what they call 'Productivity through People'.

2.26 The emphasis is on *enabling contribution*. They quote IBM: 'Our early emphasis on human relations was not motivated by altruism but by the simple belief that if we respected our people and helped them to respect themselves, the company would make the most profit.'

2.27 'Happy workers' are unlikely to be an end in themselves. A business organisation tries to get the best *out* of its people, not necessarily *for* them - unless the one cannot be achieved without the other.

2.28 We should also note that there are a great many other work and non-work variables in the equation. A 'happy' workforce will not *necessarily* make the organisation profitable (eg if the market is unfavourable): they will not necessarily be more productive (eg if the task itself is badly designed, or resources scarce) nor even more highly motivated. Nor is there a magic formula for making them happy by offering them opportunities suitable to their personality development (increased responsibility etc): their priorities may lie elsewhere, or they may be suffering frustration and failure in other areas of their lives that work cannot influence.

2.29 Economic conditions have changed since the Peters and Waterman studies and American companies like IBM and General Motors have cut their workforces and have had to adjust to competition which has produced financial losses. Some of the concepts about loyalty and effort have not been sustainable in the economic downturn.

2.30 The transfer of American cultural attitudes of having clear life goals and strategies, looking forward that than back, may not so easily be accepted in UK and European cultures. The public sector has also taken on board some of the recommendations made by Peters and Waterman. Again they may not be universally applicable and a more contingent approach may be required.

3. CULTURE AND ORGANISATION STRUCTURE

3.1 Analysis of an organisation's culture leads on to theories known as the cultures/structures approach. This states that the ideal organisation structure in any particular situation is dependent on the culture which exists within it.

3.2 Charles Handy is one of the theorists who developed this approach. He discusses four cultures but it is first of all important to note that an organisation might have a structure which reflects a single culture; on the other hand, different structures reflecting different cultures might also be found.

3.3 All organisations will generate their own cultures, whether spontaneously or under the guidance of positive managerial strategy. The culture will consist of the following.

(a) *Basic, underlying assumptions* which guide the behaviour of the individuals and groups in the organisation, e.g. customer orientation, or belief in quality, trust in the organisation to provide rewards, freedom to make decisions, freedom to make mistakes, the value of innovation and initiative at all levels etc.

(b) *Overt beliefs expressed by the organisation and its members*, which can be used to condition (a) above.

    (i)   These beliefs and values may emerge as sayings, slogans, mottos etc. such as 'we're getting there', 'the customer is always right', or 'the winning team'.

    (ii)   They may emerge in a richer mythology – in jokes and stories about past successes , heroic failures or breakthroughs, legends about the 'early days', or about 'the time the boss...'. Organisations with strong cultures often centre themselves around almost legendary figures in their history.

Management can encourage this by 'selling' a sense of the corporate 'mission', or by promoting the company's 'image'; it can reward the 'right' attitudes and punish (or simply not employ) those who aren't prepared to commit themselves to the culture.

(c)   *Visible artifacts* – the style of the offices or other premises, dress 'rules', display of 'trophies', the degree of informality between superiors and subordinates etc.

3.4   One way by which management can try to establish a culture is by drawing up a *mission statement*. A mission statement is a declaration of an organisation's aims, objectives and values. For example, J Sainsbury plc's mission statement states that the company's aim is:

'...to discharge the responsibility as leaders in our trade by acting with complete integrity, by carrying out our work to the highest standards and by contributing to the public good and quality of life.' (*Financial Times*, 11/1/1989)

3.5   Such statements generate high levels of cynicism if they are at variance with reality, and so for a mission statement to mean anything at all, it must be an expression of a sense of mission already existing. When defining what an organisation's mission is, management needs to consider four issues:

(a)   the organisation's *purpose* (eg maximise shareholder value);
(b)   the organisation's *strategy* (ie the business it is in, its intentions for the future);
(c)   the *values* that determine the treatment of employees, suppliers, customers etc;
(d)   whether the organisation does in fact *behave* in accordance with its stated mission.

3.6   It is not always clear to whom a mission statement is likely to be addressed, but mission statements are generally meant to encourage loyalty by giving employees motives for working other than pay and job security by providing a context of shared values. The mission statement can be used to attract sponsors and customers. The statement may well provide statements to measure the organisations performance.

3.7   A culture takes shape and colour in wide variety of ways, such as:

(a)   the extent of formalisation of the structure;

(b)   whether decisions are made by committees or individuals;

(c)   the degree of freedom allowed to subordinates to show initiative and innovation (and the degree of freedom which subordinates expect to be given);

(d)   communication - eg whether junior employees feel free to talk to senior managers;

(e)   the formalisation of clothing and office layout;

(f)   the kind of people employed (eg their education, age, ambition);

(g)   the symbols and 'legends' that matter to people in the organisation, the beliefs and attitudes that become shared in the organisation;

(h)   management style;

(i)   the organisation's goals and attitudes to risk;

(j)   attitudes to training, team-building and personal aspirations;

(k)   commitment to quality; and

(l)   attitude to technology.

Culture is unique to an organisation since it is made up of so many disparate elements and may be itself dynamic and adjusting as the organisation steers its way through the changing external environment.

Handy outlined four cultures, described below. We have briefly encountered them as 'gods of management' in Chapter 1.

3.8   *The power/club culture:* power and influence stem from a central source, perhaps the owner-directors. The degree of formalisation is limited, and there are not many rules and procedures. Important decisions are made by key people, and other employees tend to rely on precedent in the absence of other guidelines as to what to do. Other characteristics of the power culture are as follows.

(a)   The organisation, since it is not rigidly structured, is capable of adapting quickly to meet change. However, success in adapting will depend on the luck or judgement of the key individuals who make the rapid decisions.

(b)   Personal influence decreases as the size of an organisation gets bigger. The power culture is therefore best suited to smaller organisations, where the leaders have direct communication with all employees.

(c)   This may be expressed as a web organisational structure. The key to the organisation sits in the centre, surrounded by ever widening circles of intimates and influence. The organisation works like a club built around its head.

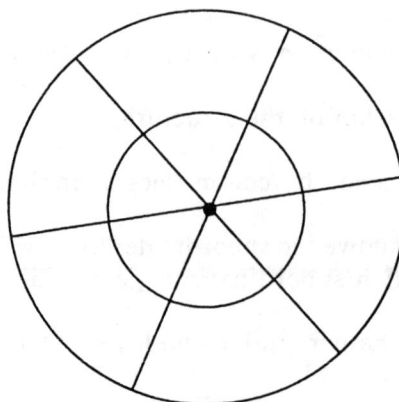

3.9   The *role culture* or *bureaucracy*

(a)   These organisations have a formal structure, and operate by well-established rules and procedures. Job descriptions establish definite tasks for each person's job, and procedures are established for many work routines, communication between individuals and departments, and the settlement of disputes and appeals. The organisation structure defines authority and responsibility to individual managers, who enact the role expected of their position. Individuals are required to perform their job to the full, but not to overstep the boundaries of their authority. Line management will accept advice from specialist staff experts only when such advice seems necessary or appropriate. Since a wide variety of people of different personalities are capable of doing the same job, the efficiency of this organisation depends on the structuring of jobs and the design of communications and formal relationships, rather than on individual personalities. Individuals who work for such organisations tend to learn an expertise without experiencing risk; many do their job adequately, but are not over-ambitious.

(b)   The bureaucratic style can be very efficient in a stable environment and when the organisation is of a large size. Thus the Civil Service, insurance companies and many large well-established companies with long-term products have been associated with bureaucratic organisations and the role culture. Unfortunately, bureaucracies are very slow to adapt to change and when severe change occurs (eg an economic depression) many run into financial difficulties or even bankruptcy (eg Rover and the British Steel Corporation in the late 70s).

(c)   This may be expressed as a Greek temple. A series of job boxes make up the departmental pillars which are then coordinated through the pediment at the top. The organisation works to the rule book and seeks predictability and certainty.

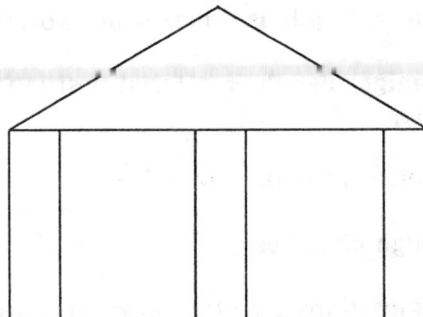

3.10 (a) *The task culture* is reflected in a matrix organisation or else in project teams and task forces. In such organisations, there is no dominant or clear leader. The principal concern in a task culture is to get the job done; therefore the individuals who are important are the *experts* with the ability to accomplish a particular aspect of the task. Each individual in the team considers he has more influence than he would have if the work were organised on a formal 'role culture' basis.

(b)   Such organisations are flexible and constantly changing; for example, project teams are disbanded as soon as their task has been completed. Project teams and task forces are useful in helping an organisation adapt to change. For example, if a large department were to change from an existing method of working to a new, real-time computerised system of operations, a task force of data processing experts and departmental managers would probably be created to implement the change.

(c)   Since job satisfaction tends to be high owing to the degree of individual participation and group identity, 'behavioural' management theorists might recommend this type of organisation structure as being the most efficient available. Handy would argue that this type of structure might only be successful if the nature of the work is suited to matrix organisation or project work, and the employees of the organisation belong to the task culture and therefore want the work organised in this way.

(d)   A net which can pull its cords this way and that and can regroup at will illustrates this culture. These cultures are suited to organisations who are concerned with problem solving and short term one off exercises. Young energetic people are attracted to this type of organisation.

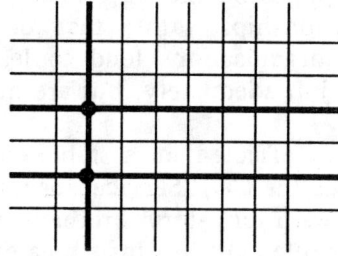

3.11   *The person culture*, formed in an organisation whose purpose is to serve the interests of a person or the individuals within it. These organisations are rare, although an example might be a partnership of a few individuals who do all the work of the organisation themselves (with perhaps a little secretarial or clerical assistance). It is quite common, however, for individuals to use an organisation to suit their own purposes - for example:

(a)   studio artists look on their job as a means of expressing themselves artistically;

(b)   university lecturers might use their official position as a springboard from which to launch a wider career;

(c)   doctors come together to provide a practice;

(d)   barristers work through chambers.

Management in these organisations are often lower in status than the professionals and are labelled secretaries, administrators, bursars, registrars and chief clerk.

The organisation depends on the talent of the individual - a set of stars that operate independently. They may be pulled into clusters more like the task culture or collegial model.

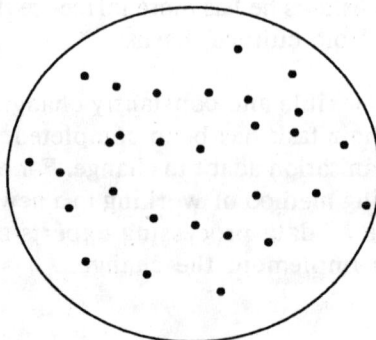

3.12 Cultures/structures theory clearly has implications for organisational design. In order to see how organisation design can 'mesh' culture with structure, we must begin by recognising the factors which help to determine, in any situation, what the predominant culture and therefore organisation structure will/should be.

   (a) *Size:* large organisations are more likely to favour a bureaucracy (role culture) as a means of organising the complexity of work.

   (b) *People:* some people like to be told what to do, and would favour an organisation structure based on power culture or role culture. Others enjoy the challenge of a complex job and 'ambiguity' and would therefore prefer (task-culture) project work. People with a strong need for security tend to prefer bureaucracies. Personal ambition is perhaps more associated with power culture and person culture, though it should be said that many bureaucracies are intensely 'political' with much energy spent on personal rivalry.

   (c) *The age of the organisation:* many businesses and other organisations begin to grow through the efforts of a few individuals (eg owner-directors, or the founder of a political pressure group) and tend to be highly centralised (power culture). As the organisations get older, and the former leaders are replaced by a new 'generation' of managers, systems tend to formalise and bureaucracy develops.

   (d) *The predominant goals or objectives of the organisation:* if the main purpose of an organisation is service to the community (eg hospitals, local government, railways, public utilities), a bureaucratic organisation will probably be most suitable for providing, monitoring and controlling the required level of service. If the predominant goal is growth or survival, an organisation based on power culture or task culture would be more efficient and successful.

   (e) *The technology of the organisation:* an important school of thought best known through the works of Eric Trist and Joan Woodward suggests that the most efficient structure of an organisation will be one which is suited to the technological conditions of the work (ie the equipment, methods of working, the nature of automation etc).

   (f) *The environment (economic, competitive, socio-cultural, legal, geographical etc):* examples of environmental influences are:

      (i) economic and market changes. Efficient organisations which adapt best are those structured according to a task culture or power culture;

      (ii) an organisation which is spread over a wide geographical area is likely to decentralise authority on a regional basis, so that different cultures might predominate in different regions;

      (iii) the appointment of worker-directors to the board of a company might betoken a change of attitudes towards decision-making within an organisation, from bureaucracy towards teamwork and group decisions (ie from a role culture to a task culture).

3.13 Most organisations do not have a *single* culture, but a mix of all four, and it may be difficult to change people and the structures in role cultures to task cultures. The cultural mix in any one organisation depends upon the relative importance of the factors covered above. You may find a role culture topped with a 'web' structure with task culture project groups round the edges and a few individuals of the person culture studded throughout the organisation. Some organisations operate in a federal structure with a number of separate club cultures, linked together by administrative departments with role cultures.

4. ORGANISATION STYLE

4.1 The term 'organisation style' refers to the characteristics which distinguish one organisation from another. It refers to the internal environment or 'atmosphere', including the attitudes, behaviour, values and relationships of all who work within the organisation. Style is less visible than culture, and may reflect the way things *actually* are, as opposed to the way they should be.

4.2 The style or 'climate' of any organisation determines the context in which work takes place and therefore affects the quality of the psychological and social life of its members. Organisational style will be influenced by the following.

(a) *Economic conditions*
The organisational climate will be influenced by the surrounding environment. In prosperous times organisations will either be complacent or be adventurous - full of new ideas and initiatives. In recession organisations will prefer to consolidate, retaining existing custom rather than attracting new clients, and concentrate on cutting costs rather than increasing revenues. To a large extent the opportunities for individuals to advance and develop their careers will depend on economic conditions.

(b) *Nature of the business and its tasks*
The different types of technology used in different forms of business create the pace and priorities associated with different forms of work, eg the hustle and frantic conditions for people dealing in the international money markets for a bank compared with the quiet studious life of a bank's economic research officers. Changing technology may require new structures and working conditions to be considered.

(c) *Leadership style*
The approach used in exercising authority will determine the extent to which subordinates feel alienated and uninterested or involved and important.

(d) *Policies and practices*
Attitudes to the level of trust and understanding which exists between members of an organisation can often be seen in the way policies and objectives are achieved, eg the extent to which they are imposed by tight written rules and procedures or implied through custom and understanding.

(e) *Structure and culture*
The values and beliefs of the management in relation to the way in which work should be organised, authority exercised and people rewarded may be highly formalised and centralised or informal and decentralised. New owners or new managers may be the catalysts that will introduce new cultures and structures.

(f) *Characteristics of the work force*
Organisation climate will be affected by the demographic nature of the workforce eg manual/clerical division, age, sex, length of service. Organisations which recruit a lot of school-leavers and graduates each year should have an atmosphere in which new ideas are welcomed and considered. The training and development of staff and preparing the next succession of senior staff is important.

(g) *The stage reached in the life cycle of the company*
Like products, organisations go through cycles of expansion, consolidation and decline. The climate will change as the company moves from one stage to another. For example, ideas for change will be welcomed in 'young' companies, carefully considered in mature ones and ignored in decaying ones.

(h) *Political changes*
As well as the other external environmental changes for the public sector the political climate may be a crucial factor in allocating resources to particular activities and introducing structural changes, for example in the Health Service.

(i) *Ideas in fashion*
Certain management theories became popular. An example is the imitation of Japanese quality control techniques, an end to hierarchy and so forth.

4.3 Developing an organisational style has been important for organisations such as Polytechnics which are directly resourced by the Government but which are self-managing corporations. The composition of governing bodies, half of whose members represent the private sector has led to a shift from local authority control. The appointment of directors or chief executives whose job is to create a high profile for the institution, to attract financial sponsors from the private sector, to improve public relations and to attract students, also has also an effect.

4.4 The outward and visible signs of the inward changes may well include a 'new logo' for the organisation, a new set of letter headings, signs on buildings and new advertising copy. The corporate image is extended throughout the organisation even to the wrapping on the sandwiches. The use of the logo on pens, sweaters, ties or mugs are all part of the new image or style.

4.5 In producing annual reports, image is important in demonstrating to stakeholders as the quality of brochures and literature has to be of the same high standard as the product or service.

4.6 The creation of new structures, mainly at the top, to provide a club culture and a way of coordinating the federal structure of the organisation can add a managerial style to previously administrative jobs. New functions, like marketing, public relations and estate management, personnel have to be introduced into the new self-managed organisation. The organisational style becomes important in negotiating with outside bodies (eg government, colleges in Europe, research foundations or private sponsors).

4.7 Most organisations exist in a changing environment and must adapt in order to survive. Although formalisation and bureaucratic organisation help a small organisation to develop into a large one, they may be insufficient to enable the organisation to survive continuing environmental changes.

5. THE ADAPTIVE ORGANISATION

5.1 Handy states that, depending on its culture and structure, an organisation adapts to change in one of three ways.

(a) *By deliberation:* the organisation 'seeks to reinforce the formal structure by more formal structures'. Companies or governments might establish committees with powers to investigate the state of affairs and recommend or even make decisions. Special project teams might be created, or new departments established (eg corporate planning department or economic advisory section).

(b) *By reproduction:* large national organisations might delegate authority ('decentralise') to regional headquarters. Unfortunately, decentralisation of this nature usually results in regional organisation structures which duplicate the former national structure. Bureaucracy remains in the same form, but on a smaller scale. Unless the environment is fairly stable, such organisational adaptation is likely to be inefficient.

(c) *By differentiation:* the organisation employs different structures with different cultures, in separate parts of the organisation, using a contingency approach - choosing the most suitable structure for each particular situation:

   (i) stable, routine work will be performed in a formalised bureaucratic manner (role culture);

   (ii) adaptation to change (development of new products and new markets, or meeting environmental 'threats') should be organised on a task basis;

   (iii) any sudden crisis might have to be dealt with by key individuals with emergency powers (power culture);

   (iv) overall policy decisions of the organisation should be set by a ruling body of key individuals (board of directors, the Cabinet of government ministers, or the supreme policy-making councils of other organisations) (power culture).

5.2 These can be seen in the example of Polytechnics.

(a) Formal structures (eg Faculties, School Boards, Deans) have been delegated powers and control over resources. Special groups or committees have been established on communications, Europe, franchising, credit transfers, and new units on public relations and a commercial centre.

(b) In a federal structure the smaller territorial divisions have to take on more bureaucratic responsibilities (eg payroll).

(c) In a self-managed organisation a strong central policy making body might be introduced. Units to oversee change may also be developed. Jobs relating to staff development, enterprise and so forth might also be created.

5.3 To be an adaptive organisation successfully, Handy found that 'One culture should not be allowed to swamp the organisation'.

5.4 However where differentiation, on a contingency basis, is applied in an organisation structure, there is a potential for conflict. Project teams might resent policy decisions of senior managers because they believe them to be inappropriate to the problems of the organisation; line managers might resent 'free-wheeling' 'undisciplined' members of project teams. The management of an organisation must be capable of reconciling differences and integrating the work of all employees towards a common aim.

5.5 In his book *The Age of Unreason*, Handy set down his views of future organisational cultures. Made possible by technological advances, these new structures might have the following features.

(a) A core of full-time staff supported by a greater number of part-time, temporary or subcontracted workers.

(b) Loose organisational structures in which subgroups have a high degree of autonomy.

(c) Personal, as opposed to standard, employment contracts.

(d) A reduction in the levels of middle management.

Organic and mechanistic organisations

5.6 Burns and Stalker contributed significant ideas about managing organisation growth and change. They identified the need for a different organisation structure when the technology of the market is changing. They also found that innovation is crucial to the continuing success of any organisation operating in the market.

5.7 They recommended an *organic structure* (also called an 'organismic structure') which has the following characteristics.

(a) There is a 'contributive nature' of specialised knowledge and experience to the common task of the organisation.

(b) Each individual has a realistic task which can be understood in terms of the common task of the organisation.

(c) There is a continual re-definition of an individual's task, through interaction between the individual and others.

(d) There is a spread of commitment to the concern and its tasks.

(e) There is a *network* structure of authority and communication.

(f) Communication tends to be *lateral* rather than vertical.

(g) Communication takes the form of information and advice rather than instructions and decisions.

5.8 Burns and Stalker contrasted the organic structure of management, which is more suitable to conditions of change, with a *mechanistic* system of management, which is more suited to stable conditions. A mechanistic structure has the following characteristics.

(a) Authority is a hierarchical formal scalar chain.

(b) Communication is *vertical* rather than lateral.

(c) Individual tasks are not clearly related to the goals of the organisation, owing to specialisation of work.

(d) Individuals regard their own tasks as something distinct and divorced from the organisation as a whole.

(e) There is a precise definition of duties in each individual job (eg rules, procedures, job definitions).

5.9 Mechanistic systems are unsuitable in conditions of change for three reasons:

(a) the *ambiguous figure system:* in dealing with unfamiliar problems authority lines are not clear, matters are referred 'higher-up' and the top of the organisation becomes over-burdened by decisions;

(b) *mechanistic jungle:* jobs and departments are created to deal with the new problems creating greater problems;

(c) *committee system:* committees are set up to cope with the problems. The committees can only be a temporary problem-solving device, but the situations which create the problems are not temporary.

Can a culture be changed?

5.10 Edwin Baker, in 1981, observed twelve corporations which developed unhealthy corporate cultures. He found a common pattern.

(a) The organisation flourished initially under its founder who created, usually without conscious effort, a cohesive group of employees who shared his beliefs and values.

(b) On the founder's retirement the organisation continued to flourish but many employees become rigid and insular in their thinking and behaviour.

(c) Concern for survival faded and, as a result, so did values regarding speed, flexibility, innovation and concern for the customer.

(d) Increased growth led to formalisation and the development of rules and procedures. Divisions occurred between employees and management because of specialisation. Communication and willingness to accept responsibility decreased.

(e) Employees identified with their departments, not with the organisation as a whole.

(f) Corrective action needed to challenge problems of mature products and markets met inertia. It was thwarted by the rigid culture.

5.11 In one case the rigidified culture led directly to bankruptcy. Baker warned that: 'changing the distinctive culture of a large, old organisation is enormously difficult and may take years'.

5.12 Ralph H Kilmann suggests the following steps for closing 'culture gaps':

(a) find out about what norms of behaviour are currently present (ie behaviour which is expected by a group of its members);

(b) decide the ways in which norms need to be changed;

(c) establish new norms;

(d) identify culture gaps; and

(e) close culture gaps.

5.13 The sorts of norm which Kilmann is talking about relate to attitudes toward performance/ excellence, teamwork, communication, leadership, profitability, staff relations, customer relations, honesty and security, training and innovation. Positive norms of behaviour are those where individuals identify their own goals with those of the organisation. Negative norms are represented by insularity, slowness, complacence and hostility.

5.14 The difficult task, obviously, is to establish new and positive norms of behaviour. A consistent approach is needed, requiring:

(a) top management commitment;

(b) modelling behaviour – management should be seen to be acting on the new norms themselves, not merely mouthing empty words about change;

(c) support for positive behaviour and confrontation of negative behaviour;

(d) consistency between the evaluation and reward system and positive behaviour (linking pay to acting on positive norms);

(e) communication of desired norms;

(f) recruitment and selection of the 'right' people;

(g) induction programmes for new employees on the desired norms of behaviour; and

(h) training and skills development.

5.15 Most research has shown that, in a large organisation, shifting the value system or culture can take between three and eight years to bring about.

5.16 Changes in the NHS over the last ten years demonstrate the extent to which the public sector has adapted. The National Health Service Management Inquiry (The Griffiths Report) proposed radical changes in the management of the health service (eg establishing a ministerial management board to introducing general managers in all levels of the service).

5.17 The NHS was defined as a system of administration which doctors treated patients in the light of professional judgement and they required technical and administrative support. In other words the 'NHS' is just a system that pays the bills and provides the hospitals. However, power was dispersed among a variety of clinical and professional groups with no clear focus or coordination to provide health care. The organisational style was reactive. There was a commitment to the status quo, and it was held that staff interests, rather than patient interests, were most influential in setting the organisation's direction. Changes were patchy and inconsistent and depended on individual or small team decisions. This provides an example of the *role/power culture* with the clinicians and especially consultants setting the agenda.

5.18 The report proposed a culture based on an increased prominence on proactive management rather than reactive administration. This would be economy and efficiency led and be based on value for money. A concern to use the estate asset base of hospitals to raise finance was an area of management highlighted by Griffiths. More attention would need to be given to the needs of the patient. Objectives and targets would be set for the functional divisions of the health service and new structures would be developed to change organisational thinking.

5.19 Further changes have taken place to maintain the momentum of change in the NHS and give more power to the managers and in particular the financial managers in the NHS. The creation of Hospital Trusts, contract provision and clear divisions between purchasers and providers in the system, have continued the structural reforms. The culture has been changed, emphasising *performance measurement*, costing of activities, use of information technology to monitor what is happening, rewards by performance related pay. The system has not had time to establish a new position as continuous change has been the norm for ten years and will continue for a while.

If anything, a 'management of change' culture has become the norm.

Exercise

Why do you think British Rail now refers to passengers as 'customers'? What do you think might be the importance of this development to BR's (i) passengers and (ii) staff?

Solution

Arguably this is more important to staff than to passengers, whose main concerns will be punctuality, reliability, safety, seating room and cleanliness. These require capital investment, which is largely determined by central government. While being called 'customers' might be greeted with cynicism by some passengers, it is a public statement on behalf of the management that:

(a) BR realises its passengers have a choice of transport modes; and

(b) it is more than just a service but a business. As such it should communicate, on the surface at lease, a customer orientation to staff.

A basic problem with these imposed 'cultural changes' is that other areas of morale must be right too. In another context, BT's new customer-orientated reorganisation, supposed to empower staff, got a surprising response when far more than anticipated applied for voluntary redundancy.

---

6. CONCLUSION

6.1 An organisation's culture is the values and assumptions held by the people who work for it.

6.2 Culture has an important effect on how organisations respond to their customers and cope with change.

6.3   Culture can result from structure. Changing one, without changing the other, is difficult.

TEST YOUR KNOWLEDGE
The numbers in brackets refer to paragraphs of this chapter

1   What is culture? (1.1)

2   What do Peters and Waterman define as the shortcomings of rationality in organisational life? (2.14)

3   What are the constituent parts of a culture? (3.3)

4   Distinguish between power cultures and role cultures (3.8, 3.9). What sort of organisation structure will these exhibit? (3.8, 3.9)

5   What are the structural factors affecting culture? (3.12)

6   How can an organisation adapt? (5.1)

Now try question 6 at the end of the text

Chapter 7

RELATIONSHIPS WITHIN AND BETWEEN ORGANISATIONS

This chapter covers the following topics.

1. Conflict
2. Networks
3. Bureaucratic and adaptive structures
4. 'Adhocracy'
5. Enablers, facilitators and arrangers
6. Partnerships
7. Organisation development

---

1. CONFLICT

1.1 Relationships between different groups in an organisation can lead to disagreement, hostility and open conflict, as a result of which the organisation will be operating well below their optimum level of performance. *Conflicts* may produce strikes or disruption to the work programme and require lengthy and costly periods of resolution. Organisations may become fragmented: elements split off as separate organisations when their aims are only capable of being fulfilled outside the existing structures. When organisations or, for that matter, functions or departments are taken over the new set of businesses may not all fit well together, merging of departments or functions can take place, and again some units sold or hived off. The cultures of the combined entities may differ. The merging of the Audit Commission and Health Auditors from the Civil Service demonstrates some of the problems.

1.2 The symptoms of organisation conflict are listed by Handy as follows.

   (a) Poor communications
   (b) Intergroup hostility and jealousy
   (c) Interpersonal friction
   (d) Escalation of arbitration
   (e) Proliferation of rules and regulations, norms and myths
   (f) Low morale and frustration at inefficiency
   (g) Anger directed at higher levels of the organisation.

1.3 The size of many organisations in the public sector creates problems of *communication* both because of:

    (a)   the links in the chain of the hierarchy;
    (b)   the diversity of the organisations' activities;
    (c)   secrecy in the decision making process is still seen as important.

Information may only be communicated to those that 'need to know'. The requirements of the Freedom of Information Act and Finance Acts to make material available to the public, has improved internal communications too.

1.4   Communication is still seen as 'top down' activity putting policy or higher order decisions into effect and providing some reasoning for the action being taken. Little communication is upwards except in appraisals or performance reviews. Internal memoranda and meetings are the most common form of communication for giving direction. Bulletins, or news sheets with annual reports can be used to show how the organisation is working and developing.

Inter group friction

1.5   Horizontal communication *between* divisions or sections may be poor because of jealousy over resource allocation, power positions, or fear of the auditor, or the interference of other professions or administrators in another's territory. The culture of the organisation and the myths and group norms of behaviour between the divisions can create barriers to working together. Creating horizontal links and matrix structures may break down some of these barriers. Joint training programmes, for example, can be used to improve contacts and cooperation.

Interpersonal friction

1.6   It may be more difficult to deal with *interpersonal* friction and 'opponent - centred episodes' and 'incompatibility' between individuals working in different divisions or the same office. So to avoid conflict, differences need to be recognised and interactive skills developed both within and between groups. This aims to encourage the expression of emotions and feelings and to reduce the possibility of such feelings being the seeds of conflict. *Integrators* are seen from group studies to be important and the creating of situations for open argument and debate can help in conflict management. When the differences are not about substantive issues but really about values and goals, then conflict resolution may not be so easy.

Arbitration

1.7   Mechanisms for negotiation may include third parties. The staff or personnel department who may sort out differences or provide training and staff development or be able to transfer staff or help individuals to leave. Trade unions may be willing to take cases to arbitration and use the Arbitration Service, or Equal Opportunities tribunals to deal with cases of alleged violations of the legislation or issues of sexual harassment.

1.8   Implementation of the 'Social Charter' concerning workers' rights, and the European models of worker participation in organisations, may become accepted ways of dealing with many of these problems. The Health and Safety at Work Act has been used as a way of negotiating over working conditions. The use of institutional mechanisms for dealing with differences is thus a search for rules for *every* occasion, establishing norms of behaviour and devising ways of dealing with those exceptions which have got through the system.

1.9 Conflict can be seen as endemic in any organisation.

'Organisational conflict is something we all experience more or less on a day to day basis as we attempt to perform our role and manage our careers in complex organisations.'

'The hard design choice involving structures, technologies and tasks needed to accomplish the mission of the organisation often create and reinforce differences in the operations, goals, and orientations between organisational members and sub units. Moreover, the external environments of organisations sometimes change in ways that necessitate a reshuffling of priorities and resource allocations among internal sub units and stimulate shifts in the balance of power and patterns of influence between them.'

(R H Miles *Organisational Conflict 1980*)

The diagram shows the sources of organisational conflict.

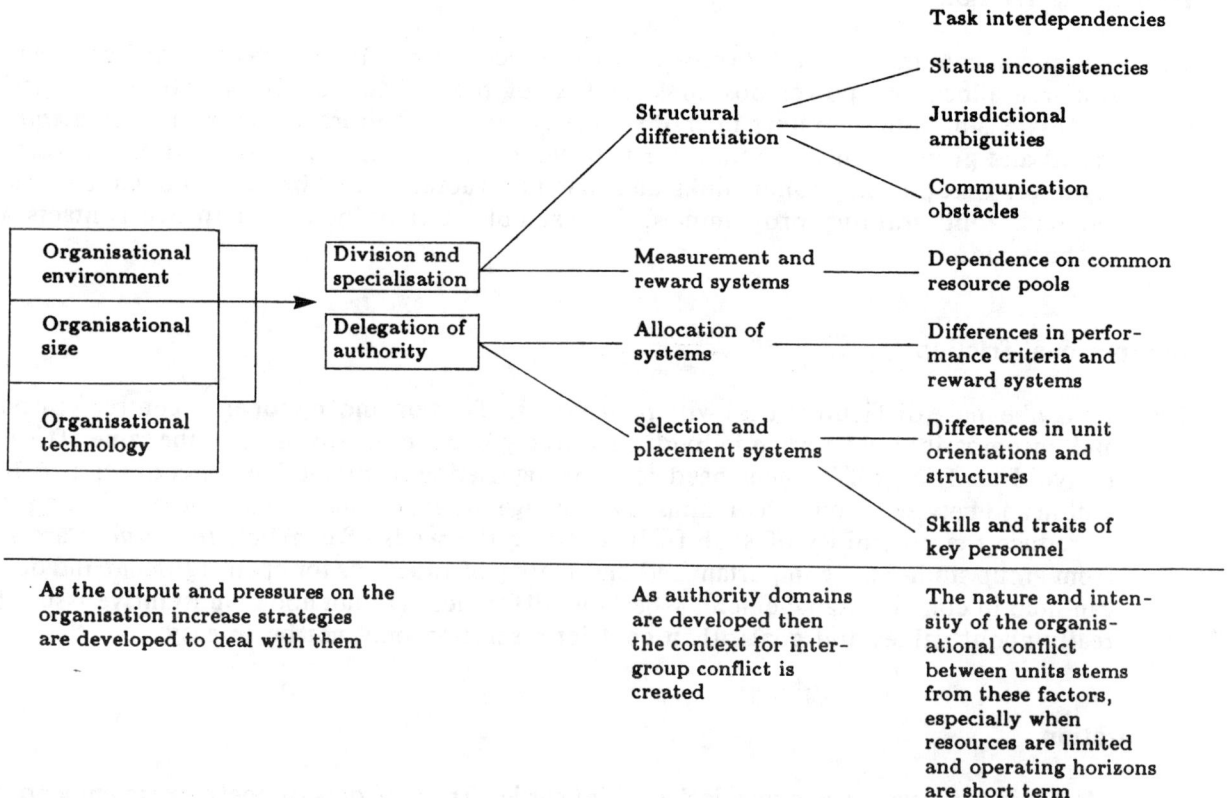

Sources of organisational conflict

		Task interdependencies
		Status inconsistencies
	Structural differentiation	Jurisdictional ambiguities
		Communication obstacles
Organisational environment	Division and specialisation	
	Measurement and reward systems	Dependence on common resource pools
Organisational size	Delegation of authority	
	Allocation of systems	Differences in performance criteria and reward systems
Organisational technology	Selection and placement systems	Differences in unit orientations and structures
		Skills and traits of key personnel

As the output and pressures on the organisation increase strategies are developed to deal with them	As authority domains are developed then the context for inter-group conflict is created	The nature and intensity of the organisational conflict between units stems from these factors, especially when resources are limited and operating horizons are short term

1.10 On the other hand, S Robbins in *Conflict Resolution and Control*, asserts that 'more organisations are dying from complacency and apathy than are dying from an over abundance of conflict'. This may be due to the feelings of individuals that they are not important enough to be consulted, that they are short-term assets which can be dispensed with, especially in times of recession and high unemployment. It may be felt that it is the external environment that is producing the changes in the organisation and that individuals are powerless to do anything about it.

1.11 In the public sector there are many sources of potential conflict.

(a) Anger and frustration may be expressed at the controlling political interests of elected members or at Ministers who are seen as being 'politically motivated' in their actions.

(b) Professional interest and current practice may be threatened by new legislation or changes to working practices (eg compulsory competitive tendering). The frustration may be with outside bodies or interests who set the political agenda (eg think tanks) or ministers who push or pull in particular directions.

(c) It may be felt that the organisation gets an unfairly bad press. The few examples of things going wrong might be far outweighed by the majority of things that go right, but errors make good headlines.

(d) The conflict with the external environment also arises when the organisation in the public sector is being asked to do things for which it has not got the resources or technical skills in the short term.

1.12 Interpersonal communications are essential in organisational relationships. Communication is a two-way exchange.

(a) The sender of the message formulates the message, and transmits the message through speaking or writing.

(b) The receiver gets the message, through listening or reading, interprets the message and its meaning, seeks clarification and responds or takes action.

The process may be disturbed by 'noise' which interferes at various places along the line of communication and distorts the message. Noise can be caused by:

(i) the interpersonal relation between sender and recipient;
(ii) lack of clarity;
(iii) differences in language and use of concepts;
(iv) an inappropriate interpretation of the message caused by other messages in the organisation (eg contrasting information offered by the grapevine).

2. NETWORKS

2.1 Networks are semi-formal communications systems within organisations, whose existence can be facilitated by technology. They exist outside the formal organisation hierarchy, and develop, perhaps from personal contact:

(a) on the job;
(b) at working parties;
(c) at conferences;
(d) at joint training sessions;
(e) outside organisational life (eg the 'old school tie' network).

2.2 A network of this sort can be used to trade information, or to set up informal alliances (eg before meetings). Alternatively it can be a channel for mutual advancement.

2.3 Networks can also involve necessary commercial contacts from outside the organisation.

2.4   A typical network might be a group of middle managers, whose day to day jobs are important in the implementation of corporate plans and strategies. These middle managers are key tactical and operational decision-makers. They will not be functional heads, as these people are too far removed from the decisions under review.

2.5   A network is more than just a 'task force' or project team set up to review a particular issue or problem.

        (a)   Networks are often supposed to identify problems. To a degree, they are set their own agendas, reflecting tactical and operational issues, rather than responding simply to issues raised by senior management. In many cases, senior management may not be aware of the problems in any case, or may not have the particular knowledge or expertise to deal with them.

        (b)   Networks can also be institutionalised in regular meetings to obviate the need for tactical and operational decisions to pass up and down the management hierarchy.

2.6   Finally, a network does not deal with issues of 'team spirit', 'culture' or 'morale', but is a means by which information and experience can be shared across functional and geographical lines, so that other individuals in the organisation can learn from them.

Network technology

2.7   Information technology can be a facilitator of this type of information communication, although at the outset, this might appear rather strange: it is traditionally supposed to be concerned with 'hard' facts.

        (a)   Electronic mail, on computer networking systems (see your BPP *Information: Systems and Control* text for technical details) enables individuals, who do not meet each other, or who may not even communicate on the phone, to establish a communicative relationship.

        (b)   Electronic bulletin boards are a use of *computer conferencing techniques* which allow each member connected to the system to communicate with all other members. it can mean the display of and discussion of controversial ideas.

        (c)   Another technique is viedo-conferencing, by which managers from different regions can 'meet' without the trouble of travelling to a single destination.

        These innovations mean that relatively informal networks are no longer limited by geography. Communication on a horizontal level between diverse areas is now cheaper than it might have been previously.

2.8   Networking between organisations is seen as a way forward for business. Examples of medium size companies in Italy cooperating in product development and responding to customer demand are seen as demonstrating this approach. The development of the 'European company' may be created through networking rather than takeovers or mergers between companies, to be able to be flexible but also compete with international companies with large market shares. Linking the management and operational aspects of businesses, in response to customer needs, can mean added value can be achieved with limited investment and training.

2.9 In short, it is possible that fixed hierarchies in organisations will break down, as networks become more common, linking individuals within organisations, and linking companies. This is discussed further in the next section.

3. BUREAUCRATIC AND ADAPTIVE STRUCTURES

3.1 'Networks' can be a model for future organisations. R B Kanter in her book *When Giants Learn to Dance*, compares *bureaucratic* organisations to *post entrepreneurial* organisations.

Bureaucracy is ..	The Post-entrepreneurial organisation is ..
Position centered (status)	People centered (relationships)
Repetition orientated (codifying)	Creation orientated (innovative)
Rules oriented (procedures must always be followed)	Results oriented (end justifies the means)
Pay is position based	Pay is related to performance
Formal structure Limits on access to information	Communication links inside and outside the organisation are maximised
Mandates are restricted to territory and function	New relationships should be established across territory and function
Ownership and control	Leverage and experimentation

The concept of the post-entrepreneurial organisation has various implications, both for organisation structure, and for employees.

Post-entrepreneurial organisations and organisation structure

3.2 Post-entrepreneurial organisations have a relationship with the environment which is more open than bureaucracies.

(a) They seek commercial/competitive opportunities through the expansion of information flow.
(b) Links with outsiders are maximised, and outsiders are brought in more often.
(c) The organisation's 'boundaries' become less easy to determine.
(d) The organisation will have to do 'more with less' (certainly true of the public sector).

3.3 Moreover, the deployment of individuals within the organisation will change.

(a) A 'leaner' organisation will require individuals to assume a variety of roles at different times.

(b) Individuals will regularly be redeployed in a number of different creative combinations.

3.4   The belief underlying this theory is that human creativity can be channelled for organisational benefit if bureaucracy is abandoned. Moreover, Charles Handy in *The Age of Unreason* questions the concepts of 'unemployment' and 'employment' as being rigid categories. As with Rosabeth Moss Kanter he sees that we could have a portfolio of jobs and do different jobs and different times of our lives. So organisational structures would be more flexible with short term contracts and more temporary work.

3.5   This new theory can be summarised in four Fs: being focused, fast, friendly and flexible.

3.6   The 'free flowing organisations' and the 'employee as chameleon' required by these post entrepreneurial organisations may be some way in the future. However the sorts of changes implied in these models are beginning to happen:

(a)   individual work contracts;
(b)   performance related pay;
(c)   decentralised budget holders;
(d)   contracting of work;
(e)   maternity and paternity leave schemes;
(f)   job swaps and sabbaticals;
(g)   job sharing.

Contingency theory of relationships

3.7   Organisations operating in a period of rapid change need to be flexible and have what Burns and Stalker call an *organic system*. An organic system is one in which the boundaries of jobs are fluid and there is more consultation and exchange of information than in mechanical systems. Interaction takes place laterally as well as vertically in organic organisations. *Contingency theory* is the theory that the nature of the organisation is contingent upon its situation. Its situation reflects its position in its environment, as well as the age structure and functions of the organisation. The more dynamic the external environment the greater is the differentiation required in the tasks of the organisation and so in the integration necessary to hold the organisation together.

3.8   To cope with rapid change the organisation might use outside consultants to advise it on how:

(a)   to adjust the organisation to meet the challenge of change;

(b)   to fight change (eg to provide arguments and data on why the county council tier of local government should not be abolished).

3.9   Many inter-organisational relationships are contingent on a range of factors and can vary over time and are not always going to be stable and mechanistic.

3.10   The table below describes the type of relationships which can exist between central and local government. As can be seen the characteristics of the relationship are based on its functions.

Model of central/local relationships

Type	Basis of relationship	Characteristics
Conflict	Defining boundaries. Regulation.	Antagonistic. Adversary. Use of the courts.
Cooperative	Economic problems. Distress.	Collaboration. Supportive. National planning.
Concentrated	Shared expertise.	Professional. Objective service standards.
Creative	Bid/grant schemes. Innovation.	Participation. Project grants. Developmental.
Competitive	Coordination. Delivery systems.	Tension. Rivalry. Centre imposing schemes.
Calculative	Accountability. Overtly political.	Information exchange. Gamesmanship. Creative accounting.

4. 'ADHOCRACY'

4.1 The contingent approach has been developed into a positive means of establishing and running organisations in new and fluid environments. In local government, the setting up of local *economic development units* demonstrated a responsive and creative approach to managing organisational relationships.

    (a) The limited legal foundation on which economic development was based until 1989 (Housing and Local Government Act) meant that powers and financial commitment from many local authority functions (land and buildings, town planning, traffic, environment, marketing and promotion) had to be brought together.

    (b) Bridges had to be built with the central government departments, of the Environment, of Trade and Industry, of Transport and the Manpower Services Commission and the Training Agency.

    (c) Links to local business representatives (eg Chambers of Trade and Commerce), and with bodies like Business in the Community, were also important.

4.2 Innovative ways of directing main programme finance and winning special urban programme funds and private sector funding to regenerate run down areas of our cities has required the development of 'networking' skills. The latest schemes, associated with *City Challenge*, have required area regeneration programmes to bring together public, private and voluntary sectors to both draw up the strategies and to have a board to oversee their implementation.

4.3 Organisations, at arms length from the local authority, have been set up to work with venture capital organisations. The secondment of staff from the private sector into these organisations has been important in breaking down the barriers between the sectors. Government 'task forces' have also tried to bring central and local government departments together. The creation of Urban Development Corporations has also been a way of bringing together the public and private sectors.

4.4 Many of the activities connected with local economic development may be new or 'one off' and require negotiating both with funding bodies and with a number of interest groups concerned with a particular development scheme. For these schemes to be a success, the participants have to communicate well and trust each other because there are few ground rules to work with. A pilot project funded from European Social Fund may have implications for the development of future funding far beyond the scale of this single scheme. These types of initiatives often attract publicity and political interest, and so have to be open to public discussion.

4.5 The operation of local government economic development units then provides an interesting example of setting up organisational relationships.

4.6 Toffler in *The Adaptive Corporation* refers to this trend as adhocracy.

'In the Super-Industrial society, however, bureaucracy will increasingly be replaced by *adhocracy*, a frame-like holding company that coordinates the work of numerous temporary work units, each phasing in and out of existence in accordance with the rate of change surrounding the organisation.

This development is already foreshadowed in many industries by rapid proliferation of temporary organisations - task forces, problem solving groups, project teams, and the like. The adhocracies of tomorrow will require a totally different set of human characteristics. They will require men and women capable of rapid learning (in order to comprehend novel circumstances and problems) and imagination (in order to invent new solutions). In short to cope with first time or one time problems, the corporate man of tomorrow will not function 'by the book'. Instead, he must be capable of exercising judgement and complex value decisions rather than mechanically executing orders sent down from above.

He must be willing to navigate through a diversity of assignments and organisational settings, and learn to work with an ever changing group of colleagues.'

4.7 For a responsive organisation that covers a wide range of professional disciplines and nascent economic development functions then 'adhocracy' provides an appropriate model to apply.

(a) Sophisticated innovation requires a configuration that is able to fuse experts drawn from different disciplines into operational ad hoc project teams.

(b) As the range of tasks undertaken and the large number of contracts required in the operational network increases then an *adaptable* team becomes essential. The team must be willing to treat existing knowledge and skills merely as bases on which to build new ones. Training schemes for members of economic development teams are having to provide both new knowledge and a new way of working.

(c) The environment in which the economic development teams operate is both very volatile and uncertain.

(d) A set of functions established initially for other purposes have to be drawn together to achieve some stated goal of economic regeneration.

Some organisations have been established outside the machinery of local government to achieve economic development: Development Commission, Development Agencies, Highland and Islands Development Board, Enterprise Boards. It is to be expected that they will tend towards the use of adhocracy.

Economic development units

4.8   The main function of *economic development units* has been as much to change attitudes as to provide catalysts for looking at the way a local economy can be managed. The units themselves are small but because of the political importance attached to them and the necessity to build up credibility outside the local authorities, they have come to exercise an important role in local government.

4.9   The range of activities covered by local economic development show the diversity of skills required and the suitability of using a frame like holding company to coordinate efforts and to use temporary work teams to deal with particular issues. The preparation of a *strategic plan* with clear measurable objectives and identification of projects and expenditure is now required. In producing such a plan many local influential bodies need to be consulted and involved in setting the objectives.

The activities of economic development units may include the following.

(a)   Research into the local economy.
(b)   Marketing and promotion.
(c)   Inward investment.
(d)   Identify infrastructure investment needs.
(e)   Providing infrastructure, premises, land.
(f)   Assisting business development financial assistance.
(g)   Specialist business advice. European issues.
(h)   Bidding for funding Urban Programme European Funds.
(i)   Project development schemes, derelict land.
(j)   Training schemes.
(k)   Cooperatives, community schemes.
(l)   Monitoring and evaluating performance of the unit.

Most of these activities will mean working in teams or partnerships with other members of the authority or a range of outside bodies or interests, which may include central government departments, the European Commission, business groups, developers, individual companies, voluntary groups, political groups and so forth. The ebb and flow of the work and the need to work with others may make the 'adhocrative' approach most suitable.

5.   ENABLERS, FACILITATORS AND ARRANGERS

5.1   As the public sector and, in particular, local government is seen to act as an *enabler* rather than a *provider*, the problems of inter organisational relationships, between purchaser and provider and between partners on the operation of contract managers becomes important. The setting up of *direct service organisations* for highway services under the 1980 Local Government Act and compulsory competitive tendering have required local authorities to review their role and operational structures.

5.2 An enabling authority would have powers of general competence as with 'local economic development', to intervene in any area if feels is relevant to its residents' interests. This is more like the European local government system with a *general* competence given to authorities and then limitations set on what can be done. Even before legislation clarified the functions to be included in local economic development, most authorities used enabling powers to involve themselves in local economic regeneration. In the interests of residents (using s 137 monies to help the local communities under the 1972 Local Government Act) local authorities were able to allocate up to 2p rate for local economic development and other community interests. Local authorities would also work with tourist boards, Countryside Commission and the Arts Council to promote that area. Local authorities would mount campaigns to seek investment in improved road and rail communications or to keep a hospital or factory open.

5.3 The enabling authority is also seen as a way of dealing with inefficiency in local government and health authorities. A way of achieving this is to release the local authority from providing and managing services itself. Arms length companies could be set up to run a service (eg local economic development, waste disposal, transport, airports). Other services like libraries and social services community care provision are being considered for 'arms length' provision.

5.4 Local authorities have also used *voluntary organisations* and *community initiatives* to provide help and support for local areas. The management of these organisations may cause problems as they have different objectives and operational ethics than the local authority. As a *facilitator* of community initiatives, the authority may have little say on how the agency operates and the lack of managerial and financial expertise may result in problems of reporting to the district auditor on how money has been spent. The ability of the authority to control these organisations may be very limited and result in some conflicts over measuring performance.

5.5 As authorities have a *regulatory function* to perform as well as a facilitator role, these two functions may conflict at times. This leads to the argument that all services should be run by the private sector and the public sector should have a regulatory role only. However, having a clear separation of functions can be a problem when the powers of regulatory bodies, the support they provide, or the sanctions they impose are limited.

5.6 Some local authorities have restructured their service provision to put functions at 'arms length' to make them managerially accountable, in response to compulsory competitive tendering and the competitive market philosophy behind these changes. The views of the Audit Commission on good management practice, the results of value for money studies and comparative performance studies have added to the pressures for change.

5.7 The creation of management posts and decentralised controls over budgets and the organisation of work can create conflict within the organisation.

(a) The costs allocated for central services, the way in which the legal, financial and personnel services operate may provide points of conflict.

(b) This is a general trend which includes a new definition of service standards, creation of cost centres, budgeting, creation of trading accounts, new management information systems, more meetings and communication problems.

5.8 An emerging pattern of management in the enabling authority is creating three different management functions which have to be interrelated for the authority to meet and respond to local needs.

(a) At the centre will be found a core of strategic planners and regulators who will work closely with the politicians. A consultative paper on the Internal Management of Local Government discusses the options of elected chief executives or mayors and having a cabinet to run the authority.

(b) The middle line, or operating core is made up of entrepreneurial officers who will run services either as independent agencies, private sector companies, voluntary bodies or direct services organisations, at arms length from the authority, and having made a total discretion over how the service will be provided in accordance with agreed specifications.

(c) The third element will be the support services (accountants, valuers, lawyers, architects, information systems and purchasing professionals). These functions are being considered for competitive tendering. If they are to survive they will have to operate as *Direct Service Organisations*, having to compete for custom from independent or quasi-independent service providers. As many of these functions (valuers, architects and lawyers) operate in the private sector, competition (and management buy outs) might be feasible in the short term. If the functions remain *inside* the local authority they will tend to operate through service level agreements or direct time charging systems.

5.9 The ability to bargain, to negotiate, to set up and run contracts and to manage staff within set costs will all be important skills required in this management structure. The dangers of failure have been demonstrated with contracting operations which have not reached the required standards within costs, the problems of contract compliance and enforcement of agreements. Working together to achieve agreed specifications and meeting the 'purchaser' and 'consumers' requirements will need new partnership agreements.

6. PARTNERSHIPS

6.1 As organisations become reliant on each other and require some agreement to work together, the establishment of *partnerships* between organisations become common. As organisations expand across Europe, formal legal working partnerships are being drawn up. Working together for common, mutually beneficial, purposes can be achieved by contract or service agreements or can be a set of wider agreements which share work responsibility and inputs from the partners. Partnership is a formal way of bringing together fragmented activities under an umbrella control agreement and its success will depend on drafting contracts and ensuring adherence.

6.2 Partnerships require that the organisations can agree on:

(a) shared goals, objectives and business plans;
(b) the way resources are to be allocated and any mutual financial dealings.

All these will be embodied in legal agreements.

6.3 In the public sector, partnerships between *local* and *central* government have been created to deal with 'inner city' problems. These partnerships have allocated resources to a particular locality over a given time period to achieve agreed sets of goals. The partners in this case negotiate over additional resources.

6.4   In any partnership, information and powersharing are important for success. The objectives of providing *added value* through the partnership arrangements need to be identified clearly before the partners commit themselves. Partners have to respect each other and be prepared to work reciprocally. However, the partners may have different basic interests and see the partnership's purpose differently. Mechanisms for resolving conflict and for arbitration, may be required when partners no longer agree.

6.5   Partnerships in the public sector have also been seen as ways of shifting the public/private sector boundary. The latest efforts in inner city regeneration *(City challenge)* have tried to bring public/private community interests together in certain localities to achieve urban redevelopment over a short five year period. Partnerships have also been created between local authorities and housing and property companies for building projects. Partnerships between local authorities and housing associations also exist.

6.6   Partnerships like the *Glasgow Eastern Area Renewal Project* linked together Glasgow District Council (Housing), Strathclyde Regional Council (Education), Health boards, Manpower services, Scottish Housing, the Housing Corporation and the Scottish Development Agency in a ten year redevelopment project in Glasgow. Each of the organisations made financial and staffing commitments to the renewal scheme. Other examples of the Scottish Development Agency (now a partnership *Scottish Enterprise*) developing are projects in Dundee, Leith and Edinburgh showing that specific project partnerships can work successfully and can bridge the gap between public and private sectors and voluntary groups.

7.   ORGANISATION DEVELOPMENT

7.1   *Organisation development* can be seen as a process by which an organisation can create a collaborative management culture. It is a process which can be used to break down organisational conflict and relate the overall strategy of the organisation to the behaviour of the individuals within the organisation.

7.2   Bennis (1969) says that organisation development 'is a complex educational strategy intended to change the beliefs, attitudes, values and structure of organisations so that they can better adapt to new technologies, market and challenges and to the dizzying rate of change itself'.

From the definition of Bennis, two important points must be emphasised:

(a)   organisation development is an *educative* process; and

(b)   it is based on the prescription that there is no ideal form of organisation design, but that organisations must be *adaptive* in order to survive.

7.3   Organisation development is a long range effort to improve an organisation's problem solving and renewal processes.

(a)   This is done by establishing a collaborative management culture through work teams.

(b)   To bring about this cultural change, a *change agent* or catalyst is used to identify the problems of the organisation and develop appropriate solutions. The approach used follows human resource management and applied behavioural science, including action research. This means that the consultants may be used with internal staff to look at the effectiveness of the whole organisation. At the individual level, schemes may be drawn up to provide training for individuals in relationship skills, process skills and transactional analysis.

7.4 Organisation development might also be concerned with marshalling the capabilities of people meeting their own as well as organisational objectives. It is seen as a process of planning and implementing change in such a manner that enterprises have an increased capacity for survival and growth. Breaking down the resistance to change and being able to deal with change at all levels, a number of companies have embarked on organisation development schemes from corporate strategy to management training.

7.5 Organisation development is a means of improving the relationships within the organisation through the use of *team building exercises*, getting groups to come together in *diagnostic review sessions*, and working together on managing the group process. These team building activities:

(a) are built around task accomplishment exercises;

(b) are also concerned with building and maintaining effective interpersonal relationships, boss and peer group relationships. Issues concerned with interpersonal or inter unit conflict and under utilisation of each other as resources are faced head on. Communication problems and role analysis and role negotiation are dealt with in group exercises.

7.6 Team building can also be used to establish goals and improve the decision making in the group. In 'cascading' ideas down the organisation, the work teams can enable goals and the managerial decision making process to be clarified. In using organisation development interventions over a number of months, and with a wide set of staff, changes in working practice and motivation have been implemented. When changes in management objectives change or innovations are being introduced, improving and building up communications is seen as vital in the process of change.

7.7 *Consultants*, working with members of the organisation, are often employed as both organisation development experts and as change agents. Consultants are invited in when a need for change has been identified. The consultant having diagnosed the problems selects a technique to bring about the needed change. The change agent supervises and facilitates the change process.

7.8 The organisation development approach may take some time and be very demanding of staff time and cooperation. Taking staff out of the work situation may be an important part of the programme. During an extended organisation development process an organisation may undergo fundamental changes in structure and in culture. Organisation development can be seen as a way of putting strategic change into effect.

Exercise

(a) Do you agree with the proposition that conflict in the work place is inevitable?

(b) How far do you think conflict is caused simply because of institutional pressures within the organisation, as opposed to outside forces?

Solution

Hints

(a) There is no right answer to this question, but here are some ideas. Perhaps conflict is inevitable because organisations with *multiple goals* will frequently find those goals in conflict. Moreover, there is always an element of personal politics involved in the organisation between different individuals in the battle for resources.

(b) The answer to this question will, in part, depend on your wider assumptions about conflict in society as a whole. Some feel that organisations are simply the arena in which wider social conflicts are reproduced or fought, the main cause being wider social factors. For example, industrial conflict was held to be inevitable, and necessary, in the 'Marxist' view, on the grounds that the class interests of workers and owners were dialectically opposed.

---

8. CONCLUSION

8.1 In the public sector, there are trends towards changes in roles and relationships between public, private and voluntary sectors are likely to become a great deal more fluid.

8.2 Relationships might be determined by adhocracy. This is a breakdown of bureaucratic structures into looser sets of relationships between individuals brought together, on temporary bases, for specific sets of tasks.

8.3 These will be established by 'networking' both within and outside organisations. Boundaries between organisations and departments are likely to be characterised by greater fluidity.

8.4 Managing these new relationships requires a new set of skills.

TEST YOUR KNOWLEDGE
The numbers in brackets refer to paragraphs of this chapter

1 List some symptoms of conflict. (1.2)

2 What is networking? (2.1)

3 Differentiate bureaucracies from post entrepreneurial organisations. (3.1)

4 What is adhocracy? (4.6)

5 Describe an 'enabling authority'. (6.2)

Now try question 7 at the end of the text

PART C
THE ORGANISATION
IN ITS ENVIRONMENT

Chapter 8

THE GOALS AND OBJECTIVES OF ORGANISATIONS

This chapter covers the following topics.

1. The goals of the organisation as a reason for its existence
2. The conversion of goals into strategy
3. The internal and external environment
4. Compatible and incompatible goals

---

1. THE GOALS OF THE ORGANISATION AS A REASON FOR ITS EXISTENCE

1.1 An organisation should have a reason to exist and a reason for its activities. Many organisations have several reasons for its existence (eg the survival of management careers!) but an organisation's activities usually have some rationale.

1.2 Goals can be simple. They might be expressed in a *mission* statement and include objectives such as:

    (a) the maximisation of shareholder value;
    (b) devotion to customers' needs;
    (c) to produce a car that is best value for money.

1.3 Goals can thus be outlined covering the organisation's treatment of a number of stakeholder groups (eg customers, employees, shareholders). If the mission statement is published, it is evidence of an organisation's commitment.

1.4 There are a number of advantages to having stated goals.

    (a) They provide a touchstone in case of conflicting decision choices.
    (b) They can inspire employees.
    (c) They can be used in marketing.
    (d) They are the start of planning.

1.5 On the other hand, too rigid adherence to goals can conceal a lack of imagination with regard to:

    (a) new technology or working practices;
    (b) environmental changes.

In short, goals can inhibit future reflection on the organisation's direction.

8: THE GOALS AND OBJECTIVES OF ORGANISATIONS

The importance of goal setting

1.6 It is possible to analyse two types of organisational goals, primary objectives and secondary objectives.

(a) In the private sector, the primary objective is ultimately to make money and realise a return on the investment. The secondary objective will be the means that carries this out (eg make a car).

(b) In the public sector, the situation is not clear cut. This is because the benefits to society are harder to measure, even in cost-benefit analysis. Arguably then, the public sector's objective is to provide services within current resources.

1.7 Moreover, the goals of the *organisation* or an entity may differ from the goals of the *individuals* within it. In order for success, the individual's goals have to be allied to the organisational goals. Management by objectives (MBO): a way in which organisational goals are allied to individual performance. This has been implemented by British Rail.

Types of goals

1.8 Goals can be directly related to concepts of *compliance* (Etzioni). These can be described as follows.

(a) *Order goals* operate through constraints on people and require compliance (as in military organisations).

(b) *Economic goals* are concerned with the production process or services to the customer and are based on utilitarian compliance (ie the greatest happiness for the greatest number.)

(c) *Culture goals* are concerned with value systems, as in educational institutions.

1.9 A *systems view* of goals is used by Perrow in this classification.

(a) *Societal goals* which are concerned with meeting the needs of society and may be incorporated in most organisations.

(b) *Output goals* are ways of measuring the performance of the organisation in meeting customer needs.

(c) *Systems goals* are concerned with the running of the organisation to provide the services to customers in an efficient way.

(d) *Product goals* are about the quality of the product or service provided and its attractiveness to consumers.

(e) *Derived goals* outlined the influence the organisation is expected to have on its environment, the members of the organisation and the development of the organisation and its members.

1.10 Note that a goal is an 'end'. It may be that the pursuit of goals has unintended and undesirable consequences if the 'means' are inappropriate.

2. THE CONVERSION OF GOALS INTO STRATEGY

2.1 Goals express a desirable situation. Goals need to be given detail before they can be used to manage the operational system. Objectives set out the way in which goals can be achieved and the expected end results. Policy is developed within the framework of the objectives and identifies a course of action to achieve the objectives.

2.2 The terminology is not always exact, but you might care to keep in mind the following.

(a) Objectives are the 'what' is to be achieved.

(b) Policies are the 'how', 'where' and 'when' they are to be achieved.

(c) Goals and missions are about 'why' it is being done at all.

2.3 The setting of *objectives* and the laying down of *policies* are the essential elements in creating a strategy to achieve the goals for the organisation. The organisation needs to know what is being achieved, relating the outputs to the inputs and the use and adequacy of resources being allocated to secure the desired outcomes.

2.4 Organisations have multiple objectives and subscribe in general to social goals as expressed by Sir John Harvey-Jones, that business 'is not just about the creation of wealth, its about the creation of a better world for tomorrow and the building and growing of people'. However, when social goals and profit are not compatible, real choices are determined by ownership.

2.5 The components of the strategy are a reflection of its goals. It deals with:

(a) the continuation of the organisation;

(b) its survival in providing goods or services at least cost and added value, produced with regard to the social responsibility of the organisation and the use of resources;

(c) the development of the managers and workers in the organisation.

2.6 This means interpreting the external environment and adjusting the internal environment of the organisation to meet the changing conditions in which the organisation operates.

Strategies in the public sector

2.7 Public sector organisations have developed a series of strategic documents. Examples are in central government and the new Executive Agencies.

In achieving the goals or vision for the organisations core operating values have been identified, which cover:

(a) customer service;
(b) caring for staff;
(c) a bias for action;
(d) value for money.

2.8 Strategies for *local government* and the introduction of corporate planning go back to the *Maud Report on the Management of Local Government (1967)*. The *Maud Report* advocated the co-ordination of committees and the work of officers through a chief executive and a management team. The American experience of 'planning programme budgeting systems' was copied:

(a) to provide for clear statements of the authority's objectives;
(b) 'programme areas' which grouped the authority's activities together;
(c) an authority's budget was presented under the programme headings, and monitoring was introduced to measure results.

The Bains Report, *The New Local Authorities - Management and Structure (1972)* further encouraged the adoption of more streamlined structures and corporate working. The management of the authority would be a shared responsibility between councillors and officers, who would be organised into a 'policy and resources committee' for members and a 'chief officers board' coordinated by a chief executive. The policy and resources committee had a set of sub committees which would cover, land, performance review, staffing, and finance and policy issues.

2.9 Both public and private sector organisations deal with strategic thinking or *corporate planning*. The view of Bains was that the *corporate system* should be a *network* across the whole organisation, not just an additional unit or department. A matrix organisation was seen as a way of integrating the corporate thinking into the existing patterns of the service function based sections.

2.10 The management approaches of corporate planning were seen to be a failure in local government in the 1980s. Commitment from Councillors was weak and front line staff were not made part of the change in *culture* required by the corporate approach. The 'planning programme budgeting system' jargon was hard to understand (the Greater London Council employed American corporate planners to introduce the system).

2.11 There were other difficulties in corporate planning for local government.

(a) Different planning areas had different decision timescales (eg road building, refuse collection).

(b) People had entrenched empires to defend.

(c) Some plans (eg relating to land use) were very complex.

2.12 Attempts, say, to forecast the next twenty years of economic and social change and the resulting changes in land use patterns resulting from them were mainly concerned with *ends* rather than the processes involved in achieving them. Thus strategic planning tended to be seen as waste of time and energy, especially as the economic and financial basis for the forecasts were soon undermined by events (eg little capital investment was made in the London Underground network in the 1970s on the assumption that usage would decline, whereas the 1980s however, have seen a large increase in usage).

2.13 A beginning of the strategic planning process, once the organisation knows more or less where it is, can be seen in SWOT analysis.

   (a)   Strengths
   (b)   Weaknesses
   (c)   Opportunities
   (d)   Threats

The idea is to convert weaknesses to strengths, and threats to opportunities. SWOT indicates the organisation's position in relation to other organisations.

2.14 In converting strengths into weaknesses and threats into opportunities, a number of different strategies may be identified. There may be several ways of achieving the desired result. How do you evaluate between them?

   (a)   In simple economic terms (eg discounted cash flow).

   (b)   By using *risk analysis*. Each alternative strategy is assessed according to the potential cost of failure, and how critical they are for the organisation's continued existence.

   (c)   By identifying the goals and assessing the impact of one set of strategies on the others.

   (d)   Finally, the degree to which each alternative is in line with the various goals outlined in the mission statement must be assessed (eg if the mission statement promises that the organisation's activities will not cause environmental degradation, then a strategy which would cause pollution, in pursuit of one of the organisation's other goals, would not be recommended).

2.15 *Practical plans* or annual *business plans* link the strategy to the budget. The business plan will cover the resources to be used, the processes required to achieve the goals, the task to be performed. The business plan may cover deadlines and identify the way progress can be measured along the way, and pinpoint critical strategic factors which have to be dealt with to achieve the established goals.

2.16 The design of suitable monitoring and *performance measurements* forms an integral part of the corporate planning. Monitoring and the budgetary framework form part of the control mechanisms of keeping the strategy on target and measuring performance and seeing that given 'milestones' have been achieved.

2.17 Strategic planning is seen as a major event in an organisation's life and is undertaken at high cost, due to the disturbance it can create in the organisation and time involved in carrying it out.

One view of strategic planning is that an *ad hoc* exercise which is only undertaken at moments of crisis or major external change. Another view is that it should be a continuous process and be part of the formal management of the organisation.

Formal planning

2.18 Most writers favour a disciplined approach, for many reasons.

(a) Many organisations are large, have a complex structure and operate in many different markets. Conglomerates and multinationals are among the most complex. Without discipline, planning would be unmanageable and in the case of multinationals or conglomerates, a failure to impose the discipline of strategic planning would result in the fragmentation of the organisation into separate uncoordinated parts.

(b) The rate of change in production, technologies and markets is very fast. A manager must be able not only to deal with change when it occurs, but to be able to foresee changes before they happen in order to be better prepared to meet them. Unless planning is disciplined, managers will think in the short term, and not far enough ahead.

(c) Because of the complexity of many business decisions, there is need for an information system which provides information of a sufficient quality to enable better decisions to be made. A formal information system, drawing from external sources as well as internal feedback, should be linked to a formal system for corporate planning and control.

(d) There is still a growing tendency for managers to be less authoritarian in style and to allow subordinates a greater scope of authority. The objectives set by management to subordinates have therefore, in many instances, become more generalised and longer term.

(e) If there is discipline in budgeting, we should expect to find discipline at the higher level of strategic planning. Planning itself is a discipline which focuses attention on significant issues which might otherwise be ignored.

(f) A disciplined approach to strategic planning should ensure that:

(i) all the stages in the planning process are carried out;
(ii) it is a continuous system, not an occasional 'one-off' exercise, so that there is a monitoring and review process;
(iii) the entire organisation is coordinated, from the decisions of top managers to those of factory foremen and other front line supervisors.

Informal planning

2.19 The second approach to strategic planning is to operate a system whereby opportunities are exploited as they arise. They are judged on their individual merits and not within the rigid structure of an overall corporate strategy. This approach contrasts with the generally accepted principles of disciplined strategic planning, and is called *freewheeling opportunism*.

2.20 The advantages of this approach are as follows.

(a) Opportunities can be seized when they arise, whereas a rigid planning framework might impose restrictions so that the opportunities are lost.

(b) It is flexible and adaptable. A formal corporate plan might take a long time to prepare and is fully documented. Any sudden, unexpected change (eg a very steep rise in the price of a key commodity) might cause serious disruption, so that the process of preparing a new components plan would be slow. A freewheeling opportunistic approach would adapt to the change more quickly.

(c) It might encourage a more flexible, innovative attitude among lower-level managers, whereas the procedures of formal planning might not.

2.21 Professor Bernard Taylor in his paper *New Dimensions in Corporate Planning* reiterates the fact that the way strategic planning is practised will vary with circumstances. Fitting the planning 'mode' to the situation will require a good deal of skill and experience.

(a) In a large bureaucratic organisation, this will probably require the introduction of a formal planning system.

(b) In circumstances where growth or innovation are required, it will be important to organise for new projects.

(c) In an uncertain situation with many interest groups involved, it may be advisable to use an organisational 'learning' process - to improve mutual understanding, to explore the problem, and possibly to evolve a consensus.

(d) If it is necessary to influence decisions in other organisations there may be a need for special arrangements to improve formal and informal contacts, eg through joint committees, liaison officers etc.

(e) Where there is a 'crisis of identity' in the organisation (eg if it is not thought to be socially valuable or if the future of the enterprise is tied up with the creation of a new technology with important social implications) it may be particularly important to re-examine the future role of the enterprise in society.

2.22 A shift in the role of management has been taking place from operational management to strategic management. Once an organisation was launched upon a course of action, operational management made nearly all the decisions, often including the major non-recurring decisions. The view that managers are now more able to manage and control staff and trade unions reflects the changing emphasis. In the public sector the creation of 'Agency status' for large parts of the Civil Service introduces a stronger strategic management element.

2.23 Strategic management continuously evaluates:

(a) change;
(b) its opportunities in new markets;
(c) the use of new technologies.

A corporate rationale replaces operational/product issues. This can result in uncertainty as maintaining the operational base has a lower priority than new projects.

2.24 The strategy needs to be prepared with a concern for the *operational* aspects of the organisation, to link *bottom up* and *top down* planning approaches. Bridging the gap between strategy and implementation is the job of middle managers who are the main channel of communication up and down the organisation. For the strategies to work they have to get the backing of the operational side of the organisation and not be diverted from them. The strategy choices have to be explained and evaluated in operational terms. Any major change creates a threat to existing positions and fear among the workforce. If the change involved restructuring, new technologies, new product development or ways of delivering a service, then dealing with threats to existing working positions has to be part of the strategy.

2.25 In public sector organisations that have multiple goals, and limited power of control over the service provider, it may be difficult to link the *regulatory* to the *provider* strategies. This may be so with regulatory bodies set up for the privatised utilities of water, electricity, gas and telecommunications.

(a) The regulatory bodies are concerned with pricing policy, the social service element of the service, the opening up of competition and a concern with the consumer and public interests.

(b) It may be difficult to reconcile these objectives and to bargain with the *provider*, whose goals are set by shareholders and they have to operate in a commercial rather than public service environment.

2.26 In setting up appropriate organisation structures to deliver a strategic approach it is advocated that you need to start with political or member commitment in the public sector and especially in local government. In the private sector this may be the board of directors.

The elements of a successful strategy are then as follows.

(a) Commitment from members (political or board).

(b) Adequate data for making the decisions.

(c) A procedure for the strategy formation, proper timetables for implementation, outline of communication expected.

(d) Involvement of the implementers and operational levels of the organisation.

(e) Leadership of the team of sufficient status acceptable to the members and operational managers.

(f) A strategy team that has power to bargain and negotiate change.

(g) A mechanism for resolving disputes - an ultimate decision maker.

(h) An implementation strategy to carry the proposals through to a conclusion.

3. THE INTERNAL AND EXTERNAL ENVIRONMENT

3.1 Strategies for achieving long term goals and objectives the need to consider the external environment in which the organisation operates and how internal resources can be acquired and directed to achieve overall goals.

(a) *Planning the level of product or service levels to be provided.* This requires market-research and knowledge of customers and forecasts of future demand and consumer interests. Knowledge about the market the consumers about competitors, about new approaches to providing a service has been continually revised as new data appears.

(b) *Using the resources effectively* to achieve the expected levels of product or service required. These resources will include finance, personnel and equipment.

3.2 Plans, structures and techniques to keep in touch with the market are tools used to understand the environment. Using internal technique, say, to show value for money in the use of public finance are all factors in the of manipulation of the external environment. The calculation of the Revenue Support Grant, the factors used for deciding on financial bids for capital investment, for housing or urban programme monies need to be understood if the local authority is going to secure the required resources for its communities' needs. This level of understanding of resource allocation and policy making now has to extend to Europe and to world organisations.

3.3 If the public and private sector are to work together each has to understand the way in which the other relates to its external environment. Some contrasts can be outlined.

3.4 In the *private sector* the manager has control over the resources and the results within the organisation. This can be represented as a closed system. (Note, however, that *no organisation* is a closed system, simply because all organisations staffed by human beings are open systems. However, from the manager's *point of view*, the system might appear relatively closed, if resources are provided by other departments, and results are measured by sales, say).

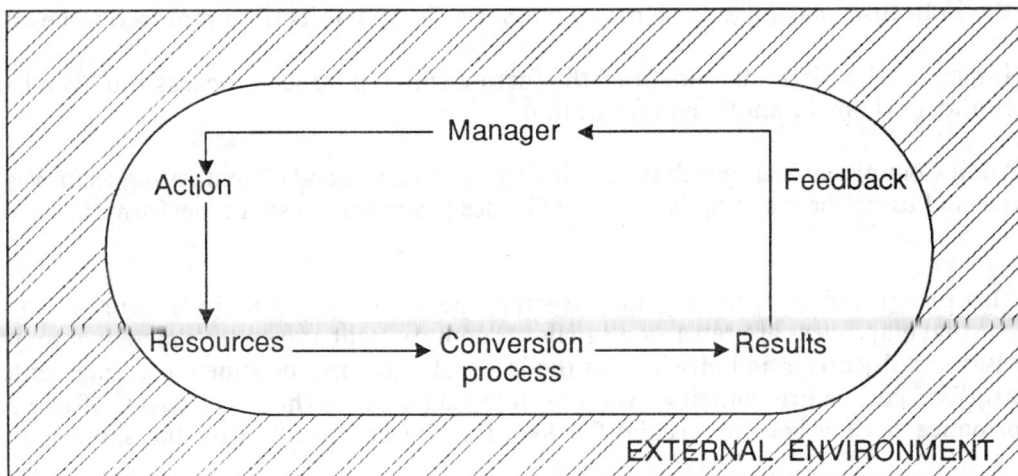

3.5 In the public sector, the system appears more open and both the resources and the results can be seen as part of the external environment because the manager has less control over them.

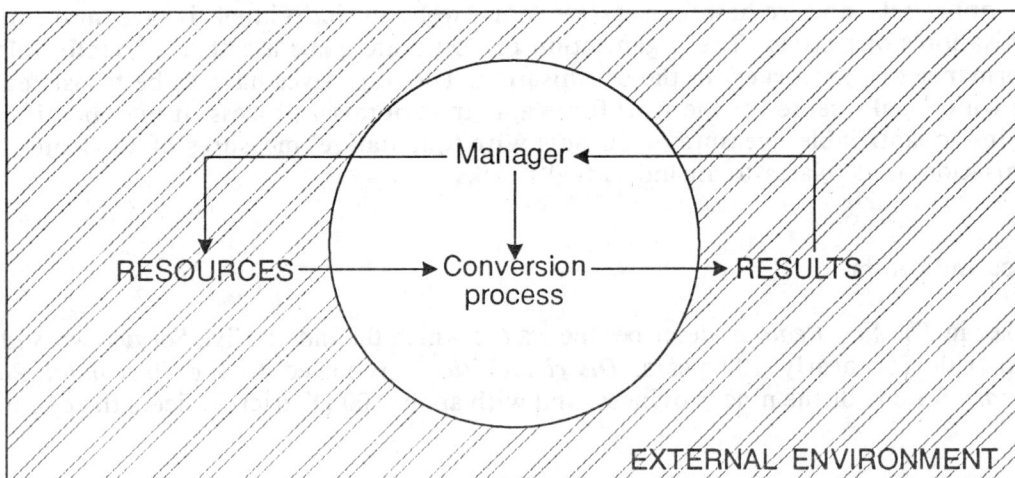

141

3.6 The open system makes planning harder because the organisation has continually to adjust its position in regard to the information and resource flows from the external environment. The moves to give public sector organisation greater control over resources and to encourage improved efficiency in staffing, and use of assets are an attempt to internalise resource management. The linking of resource allocation to performance standards or to a 'purchaser' role through contracts to provide a service (health or education) relates the resource, conversion process and results together. The measurement of the outcomes as well as the inputs becomes important to seeing what has been achieved with the available resources.

3.7 Performance review can be seen as a means of securing better value for money, by covering the achievements of *targets* and the resources used, and identifying areas for improved performance. Performance review can concentrate then on the role of management and the 'conversion' process as shown in the diagrams above. Comparative performances over time, between organisations and different organisational structures and 'conversion processes' are necessary to relate the organisation to its wider environment. The problems associated with using performance indicators are:

(a) that they can generate a lot of data which is difficult to interpret;

(b) the indicators may have to be proxy measures for the objectives required to be obtained;

(c) it may also be difficult to identify the factors which produced success and even harder to replicate them in another organisation.

The Audit Commission's approach to identifying best practice and disseminating examples of best practice and using them as a basis of Audit Guides is one way to set up performance standards.

3.8 It is also recognised that, in the public sector, the staff are the main 'resource', so it must be clear that employees are rewarded fairly for commitment and compliance in achieving the organisations objectives and mission. As the internal structures become more fragmented with decentralised cost centres and devolved resource management the mechanisms of *comparative* performance review become crucial for keeping the organisation on the same path.

3.9 The overall performance target of the organisation may be translated into section and individual performance targets. The use of performance related pay can bring clear performance measures down to the individual level (eg in health authorities and parts of British Rail).

3.10 Staff appraisals and review can assess how well an individual is accomplishing the organisation's objectives. The organisation or corporate goals are then formally related to performance of the workers in the organisation. The objectives have to be translated into a form which make sense for the workforce and any appraisal process. It may be difficult to combine 'quantifiable' measure of outputs with 'qualitative' measures of outcomes for the organisation as it relates to an individual's tasks.

Performance indicators

3.11 Drucker in *The New Realities* describes the way in which the Indian Civil Service worked under British rule for nearly 200 years. *District Officers* reported to the *Provincial Political Secretary* for one of the nine provinces, and with about 100 District Officers the country was administered by under 1,000 civil servants. Each month the District Officer prepared a report for the Provincial Political Secretary which covered his principal tasks:

(a) to prevent outbreaks of disorder (eg racial and religious conflicts);
(b) keep down banditry;
(c) dispense justice impartially and honestly;
(d) assess and collect taxes.

In the report the District Officer indicated what he had expected at the beginning of the month, the actual outturn, and an explanation of any discrepancy. Then he forecast the next month's activities, asked questions about policy and commented on long term opportunities, threats and needs. The Provincial Political Secretary in return commented on each of the tasks and other issues raised in the report. This seems to represent the ideal way of setting up a system of monitoring performance indicators.

3.12 Performance indicators exist to provide a way of measuring progress over time.

(a) They are used to improve performance by advice being given on how to deal with poor or below standard performance.

(b) They provide a way of seeing that the tasks are done and aims and objectives are being met.

(c) They act as a control mechanism to establish tasks and standard performance levels.

(d) They can be used to modify behaviour and change policy if it is not working.

(e) They allow comparative performance between organisations or individuals carrying out the same tasks.

The model developed in the Indian Civil Service seems to meet most of these objectives for performance indicators. They have been adopted, in the wake of the Citizen's Charter, as a means by which the performance of local authorities will be measured.

3.13 Over reliance performance indicators can cause management problems.

(a) The mechanical reporting of set tasks and standards can harm initiative and innovation especially as the centre wants to maintain control.

(b) The limitations of the pursuit of indicators at the expense of objectives may be seen in the failure of the economies of the former USSR and COMECON block. In achieving the performance level required, organisations may concentrate on short term measures rather than long term. They may distort what is actually happening to comply with the performance measure. For example, *volume of output* was measured, which meant that no attention was paid to output quality.

(c) The effects of producing the performance indicators may mean rigid structures are created to report on work done.

(d) The indicators chosen may be irrational or produced bias results in the way they are translated by the centre.

4. COMPATIBLE AND INCOMPATIBLE GOALS

4.1 The strategic management of the organisation and the operational management of the organisation may have incompatible goals. The time and resources to achieve the changes set out in the strategy may be insufficient. The problem faced at the operational level to achieve higher productivity to take on new working practices or technologies may have been underestimated by the strategists.

4.2 The *political* and *professional* stakeholders in the public sector with professional ethics and standards conflicting with political objectives. Incompatibility at the level of introducing 'business' goals into the public sector which has traditionally followed 'social' goals may produce conflicts over working practices.

4.3 Furthermore, many of the management concepts adopted by both public and private sectors originate in America or Japan. The values of these cultures, which are reflected in management philosophy, may be different from that of the UK. The systems of public/private sector relationships in these countries' organisations may mean that the delivery of services is seen in a different way.

4.4 Private sector goals may not always be appropriate to public sector organisations. In an industrial organisation, activities can be divided into sales, production and research. Japanese management approaches have developed a culture based on shared commitments to the same corporate goal. In some Japanese companies, the rigid demarcations between the three functions have been reduced and teams have been created to overcome the barriers between sales/production and research.

4.5 For industrial organisations it is assumed that they are able to identify concrete goals, formal authority, task interdependence and clear performance measures. In the public sector on the other hand, goals tend to be abstract, authority is diffuse, there is a low interdependence between tasks and they have had few measures of performance. To overcome these problems in the public sector work has to be related to strategic goals, but this may not always be easy, when so many different demands are placed on it.

4.6 The regulatory bodies for the privatised utilities demonstrate some of the problems of having a multiple set of goals to achieve. Regulatory bodies (eg OFGAS, OFWAT, OFTEL) are supposed:

(a) to control price increases;
(b) to maintain competition;
(c) to oversee the social implications of the operator's actions in the public interest.

The operators have a duty to shareholders to make a return on their investment and to develop business opportunities, while having a commercial duty of care to the customer. The regulatory bodies are adding a third factor being responsible to the public interest.

Exercise

Brittania Hospital has just received a new Chief Executive, Mr Jerry Flashman, who had previously been a senior executive in a medium-sized company, which made a variety of high tech products for the youth market. Mr Flashman has said 'Britannia Hospital needs a culture of continuous innovation in *all* our products. Brittania Hospital must thrive on the chaos of dynamic rapidly changing environments. We must reach our customers, and create new markets'. He does not believe in formal planning, as 'when you're eyeball to eyeball with change you don't want to look at ten-year old policy documents'.

What do you think of Mr Flashman's approach to Brittania Hospital?

Solution

Again, no right answer, but here are some hints.

Mr Flashman has not adjusted to the different planning and operating timescales in the fashion industry and in the public sector. While private sector disciplines may be appropriate, a hospital is providing services not consumer goods. Continuous innovation has often been a feature of medical practice (eg with new drugs and treatments), but it is important to remember that *patients* do not change very much. Their broken legs, and the remedies for them, will be broadly similar year on year. Any changes in the patient population will be *long-term*, with the increasing proportion of the elderly in the population, given the considerable resources that must be devoted to meet *future* needs. He also has a naive view of the nature of formal planning – it is about taking necessary decisions *now* to cope with developments *in future*, not blind subservience to the past.

5.   CONCLUSION

5.1   An organisation's goals are the rationale for its existence.

5.2   Public sector organisations have multiple goals:

(a)   service delivery;
(b)   cost containment,

with less control over inputs which are externally determined. Local authorities provide a number of different services, with sometimes conflicting timescales.

5.3   Goals must be translated into strategies and strategies into performance measures.

TEST YOUR KNOWLEDGE

The numbers in brackets refer to paragraphs of this chapter

1   What are the advantages of having organisational goals? (1.4)

2   Describe some difficulties in corporate planning for local authorities. (2.12)

3   What is SWOT analysis? (2.14)

4   What differences in the control spans of management exist in private and public sectors? (3.4, 3.5)

Now try question 8 at the end of the text

Chapter 9

THE NATURE OF THE ORGANISATION'S ENVIRONMENT

> **This chapter covers the following topics.**
>
> 1. The changing environment
> 2. Comparative performance
> 3. Marketing and organisational style
> 4. Management principles and the global context

1. THE CHANGING ENVIRONMENT

1.1   The external environment in which any organisation operates contains four sets of factors.

(a) Politico-legal
(b) Economic
(c) Social
(d) Technological

A useful acronym is PEST.

1.2   Each of these can be addressed in different ways. The public sector is more vulnerable to political pressures than the private sector, but perhaps less influenced, in the short term, by the fluctuations of the business cycle.

1.3   As described in the previous chapter, a task of the management process is to assess the factors in the external environment which have implications for the organisation, and to try and tie it in with its internal resources and abilities.

1.4   Some factors in the environment in which organisations develop are touched on below.

Green issues

1.5   Concerns about the natural environment have been taken up by pressure groups and have become part of the political agenda. As legislation on pollution and control of waste products becomes more restrictive, the internal practices of organisations must respond.

1.6   The *Pearce Report* on *Greening Accountancy* would extend the accountant's remit to the environment and consumption of energy and non renewable resources, and introduces ideas of *environmental audits*. These are studies of the impact that all of an organisation's activities have on the environment. Pressures from the European Community have pushed for the use of Environmental Impact Studies to accompany major development proposals like new roads, or major industrial development. These have already caused controversy in the UK, with the European Commission overriding government policy.

Investing in technology

1.7   The purpose of capital investment in advanced manufacturing technologies (eg with computer aided design computer robotics used in manufacturing), is to achieve a competitive advantage. Quantifiable benefits can be identified (enhanced quality, guaranteed delivery times, increased production flexibility). Many of the advantages will be long term and will require the use of appraisal techniques such as sensitivity analysis over different scenarios encompassing view of how the external environment may develop.

1.8   Information technology is likely to be an increased investment for the public sector, as it is possible that better information may lead to the better allocation of resources, and also, savings in clerical time. The cost of failures of IT projects can be significant. The NHS is introducing national guidelines for IT to avoid failures, and to standardise systems (eg there will be a common directory of clinical terms).

Personnel

1.9   The power of organised labour has been much reduced, through recession and government policy. The setting up of single union deals and plant based negotiation has reduced inter-union disputes. Legislation on the powers of unions and establishing procedures for taking industrial or strike action has set a new basis for dealing with the workforce.

1.10   Legislation which is concerned with health and safety at work can also be used to alter working practices and provide a forum for worker participation.

1.11   Workers have certain rights to information on the operation of the business. The encouragement of worker participation is found in the Employment Act 1982. With European Legislation on the Social Charter and the acceptance of workers' rights and workers' involvement in running business in Europe, it is possible that this trend might emerge in the UK.

EC and international agreements

1.12   As companies operate on a European scale with plants in different member states, moves to harmonise working practices would seem to offer some advantages in strategic planning for European Businesses. From 1993 the European regulatory controls over businesses will become more important, especially if European institutions become interventionist in industrial policy.

1.13 Companies operating on the world stage have to adapt to many different rules and regimes. International agreements through the *General Agreements on Tariffs and Trade* can provided breakthroughs in removing barriers for businesses.

The role of the *International Monetary Fund* and credit agencies become important for helping set up new trading opportunities.

1.14 The EC provides funds for economic and social development. Many local authorities have appointed *European Development Officers*. Lobby organisations have grown up in Europe to promote or safeguard the interests of particular groups. *Euro Cities* has been created by six cities across Europe to argue for city aid rather than regional aid.

1.15 The development of closer economic and political union in Europe, the need to comply with European legislation on company law, on standards and quality of products, and requirements for procurement in the public sector, must all be taken into account by organisations over the next few years.

Consumerism

1.16 Consumer rather than producer interests are gaining more attention. Carrying out *market research*, and conducting follow up studies of consumer satisfaction, are ways of keeping in touch with the external environment. This is even being applied to the public sector. The Department for Education has decided to use market researchers to assess the opinions of students, potential students, parents and employers before issuing a Charter for higher education.

1.17 Consumer interests have also been safeguarded by the setting up of regulatory bodies and the introduction of the Citizens Charter. It is possible that this approach will be extended in other European countries.

1.18 The European Courts will exercise a greater say over citizens rights, and over the implementation of European Regulations and Directives. The European Charter on Human Rights, the Social Charter, and the Charter on Local Self Government, are all concerned with maintaining the rights of individuals and providing for support to be provided for individuals to achieve a basic quality of life.

1.19 Watchdogs to look after consumer interests have been developed in response to the monopoly position of some privatised public utilities (eg OFTEL, OFGAS). The role of the Audit Commission has been extended to be concerned with the quality of services. The achievement of 'Quality Standards' at the European level, for both products and the operation of organisations, is becoming an issue for the public as well as the private sector.

1.20 Commissioners for Administration for Parliament, and for Local Administration (Ombudsmen) investigate complaints about maladministration and the treatment of users of central and local services. This approach has spread to the private sector (eg the Banking Ombudsman).

1.21 The use of local regulatory control systems through Inspectorates, Trading Standards and Environmental Health are becoming more important, as society becomes concerned with improved quality of services.

1.22 The internal structure of the organisation reflects these outside influences (for example by creating European centres in the organisation, or quality control centres, or public relations units).

2. COMPARATIVE PERFORMANCE

2.1 The way an organisation can judge how it is doing is to make comparisons of its performance against other organisations, in relation to standards of performance or targets, or comparison over time. This is sometimes referred to as *benchmarking*. However it is interesting to compare what has occurred with the UK with some other countries.

Australia

2.2 In Australia, a business approach has been introduced into state government with public administrators becoming managers. The public administrators work according to managerialist models, with an emphasis on cost cutting, performance measures, management by objectives, computerisation, strategic management, efficiency and scrutiny. The reforms have been more thorough and better managed than in the UK.

2.3 These Australian reforms have seen a typical state cabinet becoming the 'corporate board'. This determines the strategy, uses the budget as a planning instrument and produces a corporate plan for the whole government. Outside advisers and business experts are used to advise the cabinet and its committees. The cabinet hires and fires the chief executives of government bodies and agencies.

2.4 Ministers have become 'executive directors' running streamlined organisations with annual performance contracts. They set fiscal limits and targets for their own organisation. The emphasis is an economy, productivity, efficiency and effectiveness, using performance indicators and efficiency audits. A comparison with the UK can be found in the structure of the ministerial responsibility for the health service and the creation of trust hospitals.

2.5 The Australian Civil Service has become output orientated. Performance related pay is widely used but managers are allowed to manage with flexibility, be 'entrepreneurial' and are concerned to redeploy public resources where they can be best used. Organisational structures have become flatter, red tape has been reduced with improved service to customers. Operations are simpler with shared use of integrated common services.

2.6 Public enterprises are expected to pay their way, make adequate returns on capital and reduce the social *cost* element of service delivery. These enterprises are expected to act commercially and are *taxed* in the same way as private companies. The public service principles of probity, accountability and fair dealing are retained but are being added to by taking a business like approach to running public enterprises and the government service.

2.7 The Financial Management Initiative, the Rayner scrutiny, Executive Agencies and the introduction of business planning and performance measurement for chief executives, are applications of the same philosophy in the UK. The approach in the UK may be more piecemeal and less radical than in Australia and New Zealand in the reform of the government machinery.

New Zealand

2.8 In the 1980s the New Zealand government, facing unsustainable levels of government borrowing, and a sluggish over-protected economy, instituted major reforms in public institutions and economic management. Government support for businesses would be reduced and there would be a clear separation of the private sector and the public sector. In a policy of 'corporatisation' state corporations were established which were autonomous financial entities separate from the state, run as commercial business lines. The bodies created as 'state owned enterprises' are Electricorp, Telecom, Forestcorp, Landcorp, Post Office Bank, NZ Post, Airways Corporation of NZ and Coal Corp and they are required to fund their activities from commercial returns and private sector loans.

2.9 The State Reform Act of 1988 in New Zealand introduced managerialism into the rest of the public services. Managers were given greater freedoms, but were subject to value for money auditing. Contract theory and public choice theory underly the market approach used to change bureaucratic behaviour and dependency on state handouts. The same theories apply in the UK.

2.10 The measurement of the performance of these semi-autonomous organisations means distinguishing between *specific* outcomes on the one hand and the achievement of *overall* social goals on the other.

The UK

2.11 In the UK, the development of audit controls and value for money audits by the Audit Commission have provided measures of performance between groups of local authorities. Studies by the Audit Commission have looked at good management practice across authorities and in relation to managing particular activities. Management of new services like *Care in the Community* are being studied as the policy is put into operation.

2.12 Since 1982 the typical local authority has produced reports which compare its performance, according to a number of measures, with similar and adjacent authorities. This enables councillors, officers and the public to see how an authority is performing. Detailed analysis can then be used to look at performance, staffing, costs, use of assets and methods of carrying out tasks. These reviews can be a means of learning as well as control.

2.13 Comparative performance can be used to stimulate competition. The managerial implications are that improvements are best achieved by adopting business like approaches and financing.

2.14 Comparative performance measures are always going to be open to challenge but the models used are becoming more accurate. Standard levels of performance are becoming the accepted norms. Reporting mechanisms have to be harmonised and the danger is that all organisations adopt practices like the average. This may limit desirable innovation. Organisations are now seeking 'quality' management standards in the public sector which provide a further base for comparing performance and the way the management itself is organised. Savings have been achieved, productivity increased, new working practices introduced.

3.   MARKETING AND ORGANISATIONAL STYLE

3.1   Performance of demonstrably high quality can then be used as a *marketing* tool for attracting customers and investors. Marketing as a concept, as understood in business, is the identification and satisfaction of customer needs at a profit. Marketing activities are the deployment of the *marketing mix* of:

   (a)   the product;
   (b)   its price;
   (c)   place (where it is sold, how it is distributed);
   (d)   promotion (eg advertising, direct selling).

3.2   Parts of the public sector have had little need of *marketing* many of their services as they have been free at the point of consumption and are available on demand. Some marketing has been in evidence in some quasi-commercial activities (eg the tourism officer, inward investment, HMSO). The information aspect of marketing can be used to publicise and advertise changes in services (eg encouraging more people to take up disability benefit). Advertising has also been used to encourage changes in public attitudes and behaviour (eg AIDS, tobacco use, solvent abuse and drunk driving). These have an educational purpose.

3.3   The role of marketing and advertising will inevitably increase, as hospitals, and even schools, compete for 'clients' (ie patients and pupils) for the services being provided. Competition within the public sector is exemplified, with private hospitals and trust hospitals and directly controlled hospitals now competing for patients and general practitioner contracts.

3.4   In the private sector it is the customer who sees a benefit in purchasing a product or in using a service. If the customers do not like the product they will not buy it. To obtain sales, firms do a lot of persuading and reading of public tastes to maintain or increase their 'market share'. They need to see that they are not upstaged by competitors in the market and it is this competitive motivation which keeps the organisation active.

3.5   Public sector reforms in a number of countries have attempted to introduce a similar mentality. As the public services have captive customers (children *have* to attend school):

   (a)   the first set of responses were to improve efficiency to obtain value for money, through reducing costs;

   (b)   the second stage of reform has been about establishing targets or standards of performance, again related to costs and use of resources;

   (c)   the third stage is now competition.

3.6   Public services tailored for individual needs, similar to market segmentation strategies might be employed by the public sector. This can be seen in *Care in the Community* with proposals to develop *individual care packages* for those being helped, and the use of public, private, voluntary agencies to provide the care. The development of 'modular courses', 'credit transfer and access', negotiated learning, distance learning and open education to enable individuals to create their own tailor-made courses is a similar example.

3.7   Individuals have exercised 'choice' over housing, medical insurance, private transport, private recreation. The demands of the users of the services are improved quality and conditions in social benefit offices, in hospitals and in schools. The public sector has to respond to the clients it serves.

3.8   Management decisions have been devolved to the provider unit (eg the school), and by involving the customers in the management process (as school governors). The organisations have become more open: they might have to report to the customers, carrying out customer surveys, evaluating customer needs. Schools have to earn money through the school meals service, can raise funds through sale of school uniforms, book fairs, and so have to take on a marketing role, however reluctantly teachers might assume it.

3.9   As marketing and presentation have been well established in the private sector the quality of 'marketing' presentations in the public sector are expected to be of the same standard. The availability of desk top publishing computer packages, laser printers and colour printing have meant that the quality of presentational material can be achieved relatively cheaply.

3.10 The points of contact with the public as the customer have also been subject to reassessment from attractive entrance foyers, well sign posted buildings, friendly and helpful staff, to customer satisfaction surveys. In reporting on the performance of the organisation on an annual basis to the local taxpayers and other stakeholders, authorities are now including the results of customer reactions to service provision. Local authorities also produce lots of literature on the services they provide and have free newspapers, leisure newspapers and information materials.

3.11 All these changes have meant that public sector organisations have become image conscious. Marketing and public relations experts have been employed by universities, in hospitals and in local authorities. Concern with design and with presentation in a commercial sense has meant organisations in the public sector have new *logos*. Pens, bags, ties, even wine are used to promote the organisation. An example is the fact that many former polytechnics have decided to call themselves universities once this option was open to them, with a consequent redesign of logos, letterheads and so forth. The workers and the students in these organisations are all seen as ambassadors of the organisation. Partnerships with the private sector are set up, to add to the marketing package.

3.12 The organisational style changes to being concerned with the customer and the maintenance of a position in the market place. Style is indeed the mission and strategy for the organisation. External marketing can also be translated into internal communication (eg demonstrating the shared values, and success of the organisation). The operational aspects of the organisation have to be related to the image of the organisation being presented in the marketing material. The Civil Service college for example, now an agency, has to demonstrate that it can 'earn a living' and find a niche in a wider market place.

3.13 The product must also be designed to satisfy customer needs. The product itself may be subject to debate: in education is it the finished student who is being sold with added value? or is it the education provided? or the learning environment?

3.14 New organisational style can be adopted to meet the new product requirements to cater for new customers. In Higher Education lecturers become 'resource centres' rather than teachers or researchers. Teaching patterns change to semesters covering fifteen weeks. Short courses, distance learning, cumulative credit systems are introduced.

3.15 Conflicts may arise over the purpose and the nature of the products being offered. Indeed, are consumers of the service *customers* or *citizens*, from the point of view of the organisation?

3.16 The main problem for the public sector, even those parts of it given freedom to be 'entrepreneurial', is that it is still restrained by *resource limitations* For example, public bodies are still subject to overall discipline of public expenditure. Being successful in the market may mean having to make better use of existing facilities and capacities, improving productivity, but resource and space constraints may mean students are unable to find a seat in the lecture theatre or the library.

4. MANAGEMENT PRINCIPLES AND THE GLOBAL CONTEXT

4.1 *Comparative management* is concerned with analysing the job of *managing* in different environments (eg different countries), and the reasons why enterprises show different results in different environments.

4.2 *International management* is concerned with the way in which local conditions affect the operation of management in multinational and international organisations.

4.3 So far in this text we have tried to illustrate general principles of management, and our assumption has been that such principles have universal validity. This chapter examines some of the limitations in that assumption. The need to question the assumption arises primarily from the fact that nearly all research into management and organisation has taken place in societies which are economically and culturally advanced, and which have a strong basis of private enterprise. This inherent bias may lead to distortion if research is used as the basis of general conclusions. Furthermore, for UK managers the Single European Market of 1992 means that they must increasingly think globally - but continue to manage locally as well. Public sector managers will have to relate to rules and regulations drawn up at the European level and relate to external objectives.

Comparative management

4.4 Two American writers, Gonzalez and McMillan, suggested that 'American management experience abroad provides evidence that the uniquely American philosophy of management is not universally applicable but is a rather special case . . . That aspect of management which lacks universality has to do with interpersonal relationships, including those between management and workers, management and suppliers, management and the customer, the community, competition and government'. This conclusion was based on a two-year study of management in Brazil.

4.5 This suggests that *no* general conclusions on management principles can be arrived at, and that different principles will apply in different cultures. It even opens up the possibility that a single general set of management principles may not be applicable even within a large country such as the United States, because of the variety of subcultures that may exist.

4.6 Despite this, Gonzalez and McMillan believe that the export of managerial know-how from the United Stages has benefited other countries. American ideas (such as innovation etc) may at first be greeted with scepticism, but eventually the objective and systematic approach is welcomed.

4.7 Koontz, O'Donnell and Weihrich (KOW) have argued that apparent differences between management *principles* in different countries are actually differences of *application,* and that this distinction has been blurred by careless use of terminology. Their idea is that certain universal *fundamentals* of management exist, which may be applied in different ways depending on the local culture.

4.8 The variations may also arise by scale of organisation, in that large (international) businesses may demonstrate courage in how they are managed having to operate in the international cultural setting. At the other end of the scale small companies may be more charismatic in style and are more responsive to local conditions.

The Farmer-Richman and KOW models

4.9 R N Farmer and B M Richman emphasise the importance of the external environment in which an organisation operates. They developed a model to illustrate the distinction between the management process and the environment of managing

The Farmer-Richman model

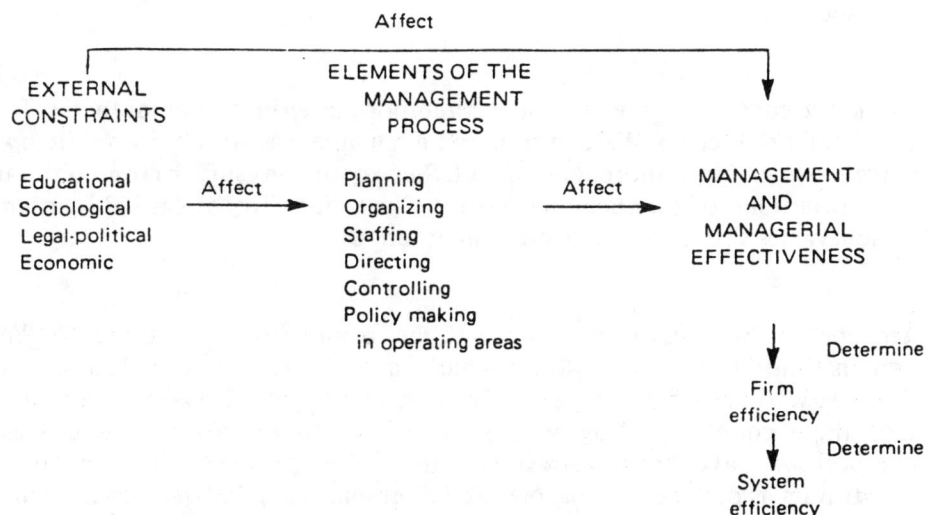

```
                                    Affect
          ┌──────────────────────────────────────────────────┐
          │          ELEMENTS OF THE                          │
  EXTERNAL             MANAGEMENT                              ▼
  CONSTRAINTS            PROCESS

  Educational    Affect   Planning      Affect    MANAGEMENT
  Sociological    ───▶    Organizing     ───▶     AND
  Legal-political         Staffing                MANAGERIAL
  Economic                Directing               EFFECTIVENESS
                          Controlling
                          Policy making
                            in operating areas
                                                       │
                                                       ▼    Determine
                                                     Firm
                                                   efficiency
                                                       │
                                                       ▼    Determine
                                                    System
                                                   efficiency
```

4.10 Farmer and Richman elaborate on the four categories of external constraints identified in the model.

4.11 *Educational* constraints include the level of literacy in the environment (country) and the availability of secondary education, vocational training and higher education. Poor educational facilities will inevitably result in poor management.

4.12 *Sociological* constraints are the most numerous category. For example, one country may have a tradition of antagonism between trade unions and management whereas another might have a history of mutual trust and co-operation. In some societies there may be an inflexible class structure which prevents some members of society from entering management. One country might have a conservative outlook and incline to resist change, whereas the society of another country might favour radical change. In some countries there might exist a prejudice against careers in commerce, so that educated people would prefer professional careers. Different societies might take different views on the desirability of wealth and material gain.

4.13 *Legal and political* constraints are analysed by Farmer and Richman under six headings:

(a)   the 'rules of the game', including legislation on prices and competitions, health and safety, contracts, taxation, hours and conditions of work;

(b)   defence policy and national security. This often has a considerable effect on the allocation of labour and resources;

(c)   foreign policy, including tariffs and quotas, protection of local trade, exchange controls and restrictions on foreign ownership and investment;

(d)   political stability. Political uncertainty in a country may affect management's ability to carry out its planning functions;

(e)   political organisation, including the degree to which a country's government is federal or centralised;

(f)   the flexibility of law, ie the ease with which legal charges are brought about in a society.

4.14 *Economic* constraints are obviously an important environmental factor. In some countries the means of production, distribution and exchange are largely in public ownership; in others, private ownership is more widespread. Some countries suffer from high rates of inflation and other symptoms of economic instability. The availability of capital is another important factor which varies from one environment to another.

4.15 The opening up of Eastern Europe and the former Soviet Republics to 'Western' management demonstrates the clash of cultures which have operated over the last seventy years. The use of 'know how' funds from Europe has meant that managers have taken European and American ideas into these countries. Programmes of reform to privatise state bodies and to introduce competition have been restrained after initial problems in some of the countries. The constraints as outlined by Farmer and Richman vary between each country, and within the countries (between regions) because of the scale and ethnic and religious differences) and between urban and rural areas.

4.16 The ideas and practices being introduced into these Eastern European countries not only refer to the future private sector but also extend to the public sector and include organising central and local government bodies (some countries having no local government), health services or higher education. One export has been in setting up 'management schools' to train managers through links with UK management education centres.

4.17 The political, legal and economic instability in these countries emerging from central state control may make it difficult to separate the management process from the external environment as clearly as is implied in the Farmer-Richman model. Managing under resource constraints and having central objectives set, may mean an emphasis on the operational aspects of management rather than the strategic. As firms and companies move in from the 'West' and market conditions are established perhaps more convergence of the management process may be seen.

KOW model

4.18 Although they accept the broad outline of Farmer and Richman's model, KOW continue to maintain their belief in universal management fundamentals. They believe that the Farmer-Richman model only illustrates the different applications of these fundamentals in different environments.

4.19 The KOW model is an attempt to go beyond the Farmer-Richman model. While accepting the Farmer-Richman environmental constraints as valid, it tries to show that a belief in universal management fundamentals is still tenable. The model is based on the idea that management knowledge is only a part of the total knowledge utilised in an enterprise. Enterprise activities fall into the two categories of managerial and non-managerial.

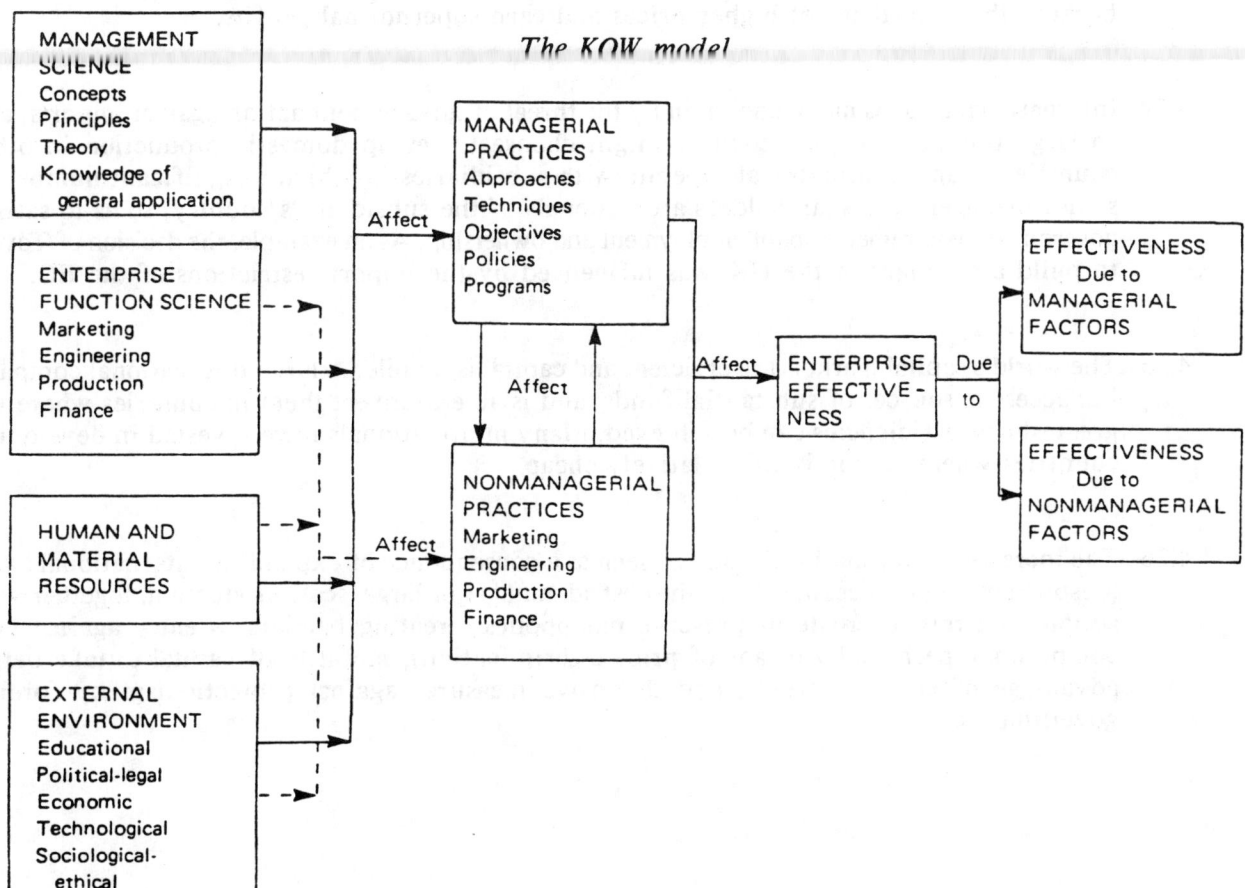

The KOW model

4.20 The KOW model refers to environmental factors not as constraints, but as *variables* which may constitute constraints or opportunities. It may be that in Eastern Europe the dominant variables have been the non managerial aspects.

4.21 One example of comparative management might help to illustrate the effect of environmental factors on managerial practices. In Japan, social and cultural conditions have led to a situation in which some large companies attempt to look after their employees and provide lifelong employment. Authority is based on seniority and respect for age, although employees at lower levels are positively encouraged to contribute to the process of making planning decisions. In return companies expect complete loyalty to the firm from all employees. This socio-cultural background therefore affects the management tasks of planning (consultation), organising (seniority), staffing (lifelong employment) and leadership (loyalty to the firm, respect for age). However there is evidence that these practices are changing in response to adjusted economic conditions.

International management

4.22 *Multinational companies* are groups of companies with a head office and parent company in one country, and subsidiaries in other countries. (An *international company* might be based in one country, but sell goods to other countries. It would not then be a multinational.)

4.23 There is a continuing growth in the development of multinationals, for a variety of reasons. There are economies of scale to be obtained, even when a company operates with foreign subsidiaries. Distribution of production saves transport costs. In addition, there is the advantage to suppliers in achieving a monopolist or oligopolist status within world markets, because they can then set higher prices and earn supernormal profits.

4.24 International trade is made uncertain by the threat of government action against imports, and so large producers in one country might choose to set up domestic production in other countries. Many multinationals operate with subsidiaries in which a significant number of senior managers and shareholders are nationals of the subsidiary's country, so as to satisfy government requirements about employment and ownership. As an example, the decision of Toyota to build a car plant in the UK was influenced by the import restrictions of the EC.

4.25 The world's capital markets are efficient and capital is mobile. A large international company has access to sources of substantial funds, and is able to invest them in countries where the greatest cost efficiencies can be achieved. Many multinationals have invested in developing countries where labour is still relatively cheap.

4.26 The increase in multinationals may be seen as a consequence of expanding international trade (despite temporary recessions) and the cost advantages of large-scale production, together with action by firms to create or preserve monopolies (creating barriers to entry against new competitors, perhaps by means of price discrimination), mobility of capital to take better advantage of labour markets, and defensive measures against protectionism by foreign governments.

Disadvantages of multinationals

4.27 Although multinationals can exploit a number of advantages over smaller firms (eg economies of scale, access to capital markets worldwide, ability to manufacture and produce in countries where material and labour resources are cheap), they also suffer from a number of specific managerial disadvantages. These will be examined by looking in turn at the management function of planning, organising, staffing, leading and controlling.

4.28 *Planning*. The environmental variables within which an organisation operates make planning difficult even in local terms. But a multinational faces problems of forecasting environmental variables over many countries, possibly throughout the world. Plans which look promising in the local environment may founder abroad.

4.29 *Organising*. The possible structures of an organisation have been discussed in earlier chapters. Multinationals face the problem that no one structure can meet the needs of the many different environments in which they operate.

4.30 *Staffing*. The basic problem here is whether managers should be chosen from the home country or selected locally. Home-grown managers may be familiar with headquarters philosophy, but may find it difficult to get on with local staff from a different background. Differences in language are an obvious problem. On the other hand, use of locally-selected managers may lead to a lack of homogeneity in the multinational's trading efforts.

4.31 *Leading*. In Western countries a participative style of management is generally practised, or at least aimed at. But this may be difficult to transfer to other countries where there is a tradition of autocratic rule. Again, the problem of different languages is relevant: effective leadership is hardly possible without good communication.

4.32 *Controlling*. Effective control depends on accurate measurement of performance. When many aspects of performance are measured in monetary terms this means that currency differences are a serious obstacle to control. In addition, accounting practices, financial reporting and taxation may all vary from country to country. Inflation rates may be different, and exchange rates will exacerbate the problem. The sheer size and geographical dispersion of multinationals mean that delays elapse between the measurement of performance and the taking of corrective action.

Europeanisation

4.33 With the coming together of a 'federal' Europe, harmonisation of products, working practices and a Social Charter will mean a new 'environmental' culture emerging in the 1990s.

4.34 Many companies will be European and have a European-wide market area with no customs or trade barriers. Working practices, social provision and access to health and education are expected to converge in Europe.

4.35 European political and economic union, exemplified by a central European Bank are all part of the changes which are *possible* in the 1990s. The political, economic, and financial climate which set the external non management variables will become subject to a European view of issues. The European Community could grow to include some of those from the Eastern bloc. There is a possibility that conflicts between European goals and local goals will increase.

4.36 An alternative scenario is to see more transnational or subfederal, city or regional units joining together to deal with common problems across Europe. The setting up of a representative body of the local governments of Europe is one step along the way of establishing a machinery for working together.

4.37 European integration could develop a particular model of management principles, based on partnership, and concerned with collective views, and with a strong cultural base, to rival the Americans and Japanese. However, given the disparities in management culture (with the UK sharing many American management practices) it might be unlikely that a European management culture will emerge.

Cultural differences and management

4.38 The social or environmental 'climate' or 'culture' of a country may be defined as 'all the social factors that affect the way people behave' (Rosemary Stewart) or the sum of all its environmental influences; ie the class structure, economy, political structure, legal framework, employee representation structure, education, culture, lifestyle, level of technology etc created by the socio-political and economic trends in the country's history.

4.39 Four features of this climate that may affect the attitudes and practices of managers in different countries include the following.

(a) *Class structure*. The class structure of a nation is likely to influence the way in which management and workforce perceive each other, and the way in which both regard their work. It is an accepted fact that in Britain there is a greater perceived social distance between manager and worker, leading to greater formality in interpersonal relations and a greater stress in management attitudes on the traditional hierarchical aspects of organisation than is evident in Japan or America, where informality and worker participation in management are far more developed. According to Rosemary Stewart, 'the gap, or social distance, that exists between different levels in the organisation reflects both the class structure in the society as a whole and management's place in it'.

(b) *The labour relations climate* - including governmental influences (ie employment law), regulation and the structure of worker representation/trade unionism. The attitudes of management to labour is reflected in how authority is exercised and how conditions of work and employee services are regarded. Governmental intervention may shape management policy in these areas: in Latin America, the government is a vital intermediary in industrial relations, and in the early days of industrialisation in Britain, many factory owners had to be forced by the Factory Acts to provide minimum conditions, pay and welfare for their employees, to stop child labour etc. There are other influences: a paternalistic approach to the employment relationship might grow out of a feudal social structure (as in Japan) or out of a strong traditional class/family structure (as in Italy). A history of industrial disputes in a country may reinforce managerial stereotypes of the militant worker etc.

(c) *The dominant values of the society.* Whether they arise from history, religion, politics or any other source, there will be certain mainstream cultural characteristics which will affect the manager himself and the conditions within which he operates. Where materialistic values are uppermost, eg in countries like America, the manager will have high status, which will be reflected in his attitudes to his work and to his subordinates. Japanese cultural values, such as concern for the individual, respect for seniority and the concept of 'wa' or 'harmony', are closely bound up with the managerial practices of consensus decision-making, paternalism, 'nenko' or lifetime employment etc.

(d) *Technological advancement.* The extent to which technology is an accepted part of the social structure will influence managers' attitudes to its implementation and advancement in the workplace, and possibly to change in general. Managerial attitudes to work patterns, eg pace of work, and place of work - with networking eroding the supremacy of the office as the administrative heart of the organisation - have to take into account the level of technology available, employed by the competition etc. Workers with new technology are considered to be 'knowledge' workers with necessary skills and experience: administrative staff in countries where information technology is less advanced are likely to be less highly regarded, and the few who may have gathered technology-based skills elevated.

(e) *The occupational / professional structure.* This will depend on how organised and how highly-regarded the occupations and professions are in a country. The medical and teaching professions may be very highly prized in some cultures, whereas in more materialistic cultures, financial professions have the highest status. This will affect managers' attitudes to their own position in their society, and to their importance in the organisation. Accountants may run companies in Britain, where engineers or production designers are in senior positions in Germany etc.

Exercise

Your company which is based in the UK has recently developed a new drug to combat Alzheimer's disease. As this is a major breakthrough technologically, your company wishes to sell it throughout the world. Given the wide disparity in economic sophistication and development between countries, what questions would you consider when introducing the drug to:

(a) a poorer country in the Third World;
(b) an affluent country in the West?

Solution

You could write reams here, and the suggestions below do not attempt to encompass every issue that could be raised.

(a) Effective demand. In poorer countries, people die younger. A drug such as this may be too expensive anyhow, and the country might have much more pressing claims on the limited resources at its disposal (eg basic health care, infant mortality etc).

(b)   In an affluent country on the other hand, Alzheimer's disease is seen as problem.

    (i)   Culture. What are the cultural attitudes to the elderly?
    (ii)   Geriatric health care. Who looks after the elderly?
    (iii) Would the drug be prescribed by a doctor, or could it be available over the counter?
    (iv) How would you publicise the drug to potential buyers?
    (v)   Does the country regard Alzheimer's disease as a serious problem anyway?

---

5.   CONCLUSION

5.1   The organisation's environment is comprised of those political, economic, social and technological factors which affect an organisation's performance.

5.2   It is possible that the external environment can provide examples and models for the public sector.

5.3   The public sector is likely to make more use of marketing.

TEST YOUR KNOWLEDGE
The numbers in brackets refer to paragraphs of this chapter

1   What, briefly, are factors in the EC which must be taken into account in organisational life? (1.15)

2   What is a likely result of marketing in service provision? (3.6, 3.8)

3   What is the public sector's main problem in being 'entrepreneurial'? (3.16)

4   Distinguish between the Farmer-Richman and KOW models. (4.9, 4.10)

5   Describe some factors affecting managerial practice in different countries. (4.40)

Now try question 9 at the end of the text

Chapter 10

MANAGING IN TURBULENCE

This chapter covers the following topics.

1.   The nature of turbulence
2.   Strategy in turbulent times
3.   The information based organisation
4.   The competitive local authority

---

1.   THE NATURE OF TURBULENCE

1.1   The external environment of organisations is in a state of change.

(a)   This might require a major change in the way the organisation works rather than minor adjustments to existing practices.

(b)   However, a series of minor changes themselves can add up to a strategic change of direction for an organisation that is continually adjusting its internal operations to meet external pressures. These adjustments may be occurring at the same time as the introduction of new information systems, decentralisation, financial restrictions, cuts in staff, all of which can result in crisis management.

1.2   The danger is that an organisation's response to changes in the external environment, especially if these are rapid, may be *disorganised* and ad hoc, especially if managerial attention is concentrated elsewhere. Management may not see the wider significance of environmental changes, and so the organisation may eventually fail.

1.3   To move from crisis management to strategic management is seen as requiring a certain level of stability. Contingency planning can be a move towards taking a strategic approach.

1.4   The opportunities for change may be seen as threats, and expose the weaknesses of the organisation or require a high risk cost response in the short term. It may be difficult to see what will come after the period of turbulence. Will things return to normal? Will a more stable situation return again?

'Turbulence' and local authorities

1.5   Perhaps the best case of turbulence in the public sector is in local authority finance.

(a) The Community Charge (Poll tax) was introduced in a short time period.

(b) This required new computer systems.

(c) Public opposition was intense, with non-payment campaigns making the task of collection and drawing up the register even harder.

(d) On top of the expense and difficulty of introducing the poll tax it has been abolished, and a new tax, the Council Tax, is to replace it.

1.6 At the same time as the community charge was being introduced other changes were taking place.

(a) Compulsory competitive tendering of services.

(b) A new political goal was outlined for local government as an enabler not a provider.

(c) Restraints on spending. Capping of authorities' expenditure.

(d) The abolition of metropolitan county councils.

(e) Changes to the housing benefits system and housing finance.

(f) Use of the housing revenue account and use of capital receipts were limited.

(g) Changes proposed for social services, with legislation such as the Children's Act and Care in the Community.

(h) Changes in education service with local school management, opting out of schools, transfer of Polytechnics and Colleges from local governments to central governments control.

1.7 The level of turbulence is expected to increase in local government with proposals for establishing a new structure for local government moving towards unitary authorities after a set of local studies by a Local Government commission. A consultation paper on the internal management of local government proposes that elected mayors or chief executives be *considered* to run local government in the middle 1990s. The extension of Compulsory Competitive Tendering to white collar jobs in local government is also being introduced.

1.8 The *Health Service* has been under a similar level of turmoil, with Hospitals Trusts, General Practitioner Fund Holding, changes in Community Health Care, and the introduction of management systems at all levels in the service, and opening up the service to competition.

1.9 As well as coping with the *administrative and operating* changes that have been introduced from the political agenda, local governments and health authorities have to deal with other factors in the *external environment* which have an impact on their services. These include the following.

(a) *Economic changes*, which have an impact on inflation, unemployment, and ability of other organisations to provide services, the level of benefits paid, the levels of homelessness and so forth.

(b) *Demographic changes*, with fewer young people and more old people in the population, which affects the services to be provided and on staffing in health authorities.

(c) *Technological changes*, with changes in information systems, and a plethora of new treatments in medicine.

(d) *Social changes*, the increasing expectations of customers for a high quality of service, the attitudes to the payment (or non payment) of local taxes, the demands for more post school education, returning long stay mental patients to the community.

(e) *Political changes* include the reduction in the size and cost of the public sector, the opening up of the public sector to competition, closer links with Europe and the requirements to follow European Laws.

(f) *Administrative changes* in the organisation of public services, include the introduction of market systems in creating purchaser and provider relationships, the establishment of regulatory bodies, the setting of performance measures and value for money studies.

All these changes adding to the management problems of the public sector and the difficulties of managing change itself.

1.10 Managers' resistance to change may be due to lack of perception of the need for change, and a lack of information of why change is required. This may reflect the uncertainty about the consequences of changes in one part of the organisation in relation to the rest of the organisation.

1.11 Uncertainty, ambiguity and frequent adjustments to what is being required and the way in which the changes are introduced (the national curriculum and testing for pupils) increases frustration and can undermine cooperation of supporters of the idea. With high levels of uncertainty, it is difficult to plan ahead, and disruptive adjustments have to be made frequently in respect to the changes in the external environment.

2. STRATEGY IN TURBULENT TIMES

2.1 In turbulent times it is necessary to take a dynamic view of strategic management. No longer can organisations simply extrapolate the future from historical experience. A future scenario is required to reassess the operation of the organisation to maintain its survival and operational efficiency. *Strategic management* is the process of trying to understand where the organisation will be in tomorrow's world, and then managing the changes (eg management style, the structure of the organisation, in the mix of products or services and the way they are delivered). Managing in turbulence is the ability to deal with unforeseen changes in a thoughtful strategic way and relate the capabilities of the organisation to deliver at different levels of turbulence.

2.2 In a paper by R Sykes *Strategy in Turbulent Times* (in Management 1992) a typology of responses to different *levels of turbulence* is mapped out. Sykes has a five point scale to measure levels of turbulence.

Level of turbulence	Driving factor
1 Repetitive	Precedent
2 Expanding	Efficiency
3 Changing	Market
4 Discontinuous	Environment
5 Surpriseful	Research and development creating its own environment

An organisation has to identify the level of turbulence to which the organisation is exposed. Not all parts of the organisation will have the same level of turbulence.

2.3 The organisation then has to review the nature of the capabilities that would be appropriate for the level of turbulence which has been identified. The organisation may call in consultants to assist in managing the change when they are dealing with high levels of turbulence.

2.4 In the public sector since 1980, the *discontinuous* level of turbulence has been the norm. The transfer of public corporations to the private sector has required new structures to serve future needs. The creation of Hospital Trusts has meant new structures and faster organisational responses to change. The proposals for unitary local authorities to replace the existing two tier structure will be a major discontinuity in the operation of local government.

2.5 The *changing* level of turbulence, has been seen in the market driven approach to opening up the public sector to competition and differentiation in services giving wider choice to consumers. Competitive tendering in health, local authorities and the civil service has required developing new capabilities in contract specification, contract negotiation and contract management. The decentralisation of management and the creation of profit or cost centres in health and in education has meant adopting management cultures, seeking operating efficiency and meeting performance targets.

2.6 Sykes holds that matrix organisations and decentralised profit centres are the best structures for managing turbulence. In the *surpriseful* level of turbulence, the organisation requires creative charismatic leadership and is capable of establishing its own environment. This is when the organisation is driven by the research and development function and new venture departments. The organisation develops pioneering technologies and identifies latent needs. This means being proactive rather than reactive or relying on process efficiency. Change may be fast and erratic.

2.7 To operate at the surpriseful level of turbulence it is necessary for managers to appreciate new ways of working. *Leadership* is important in closing the gap between the capability of the organisation and the strategy for managing in the level of turbulence.

2.8 Leadership is the process of influencing others to work willingly towards an organisation's goals, and to the best of their capabilities. 'The essence of leadership is followership. In order words it is the willingness of people to follow that makes a person a leader.' (Koontz, O'Donnell, Weihrich). Leaders in times of high turbulence need *personal charisma* as well as *expert powers* and be able to act as change agents in the organisation. Leaders have to be able to motivate others to accept the challenge of change and seek opportunities for developing the organisation and enhancing its position in the external environment. It is discussed later in this Text.

3. THE INFORMATION BASED ORGANISATION

3.1 In his book, *The New Realities* Drucker discusses the impact of information technology on the structure and operation of large organisations. Drucker identified a number of changes which could result from the use of information in organisations.

(a) A much flatter organisation with a number of tiers of management being lost.

(b) The organisation will be staffed by specialists who direct and discipline their own performance through organised feedback from colleagues and customers. Drucker cites hospitals, universities and the symphony orchestra as examples of *information based organisations*.

3.2 Faster and more accessible computer technology also provides access to information, and with computer networks, easy exchange of information. *Decentralised management* and immediate links to the 'centre' or to specialists can now be obtained, using computer mail and conference links and such technologies as telephone voice messaging to keep in contact.

3.3 As an example of a decision process which is changed through the use of computer technology, Drucker used *capital investment decisions*. Capital investment decisions are seen as being transformed from opinion into diagnosis, from being opportunistic, financial decisions governed by numbers, into a business decision based on alternative strategy assumptions.

3.4 The information required for investment decisions includes:

(a) the life of the project;

(b) costs of deferring;

(c) timescales;

(d) cost compared to alternatives (eg in the case of a speculative property development, the market rent);

(e) support and infrastructure required for the project.

A lot of this information must be obtained from the external environment of the organisation.

3.5 The information-based organisation, as described by Drucker, might be based around teams of an interdisciplinary or specialist nature. Information systems become the vital challenge through which their activities can be reviewed and coordinated.

3.6 In an organisation which is based around a core and a number of satellites, a number of management problems arise.

(a) Senior managers with no specialist knowledge may lack credibility in getting things done.

(b) Two separate structures - specialist or administrative - might recruit from different catchment pools, and so cultural differences and hostility might develop between specialist and administrative tasks. This might be a particular problem in the NHS, although the combination of clinical and managerial roles might reduce this problem.

3.7 Information technology will help provide the necessary coordinating channel between the centre and the teams on the periphery. To this end:

(a) the information system must be coherent;

(b) it must enable shared access;

(c) all hardware and software must be compatible;

(d) different departments must be prepared to share this information (although this must be fiercely resisted).

3.8 While computers were originally brought in as a cost-saving exercise, computers are now used as tools in the management decision making process. For example:

(a) spreadsheets allow investigation of different variables;
(b) input/output analyses can model the economy;
(c) expert systems provide technical backup.

3.9 In 'data hungry' organisations like the NHS, an information base is vital. There is now to be a coherent strategy for information systems.

3.10 With the introduction of competitive tendering into local authorities and health authorities, the need for *information* and performance measurement has increased. The information needs can be seen from the client and contractor positions.

Client	*Contractor*
Service needs	Quantity of work done
Service objectives	Quality of work done
Contract price	Costs incurred
Quantity of work	Profit and cash flow
Quality of work	

3.11 The information gathering process can be expensive in person-days of work, setting up hardware and developing the appropriate software. The range of uses for the data collected also means that the end users have to be considered in setting up the system. The work required for setting up an information base for an Education Authority can cover the following.

      (a)   Staff payrolls
      (b)   Property valuation, property inventory
      (c)   Equipment inventories
      (d)   Valuation of Equipment
      (e)   Food material inventories
      (f)   Technical food specification
      (g)   Location schedules for contracts
      (h)   Monitoring changes

3.12   The changes in the information requirements in *local authorities*, and the use by a wide range of people of computers, has resulted from legislative changes, a move to contract agreements and the reduction in costs and increase in capacity of computers. The legislation has covered the community charge and its replacement, education reform, housing policy, financial reporting and competitive tendering. The latest proposals are that computing services themselves be open to competition and possible privatisation.

3.13   The *centralised computer service* is under threat as the shift to decentralised data inputs and interrogation facilities though the use of microcomputers and networks are set up. The requirements of decentralised accounting and management means that central departments can not manage the wide range of activities being established. With contracting out a need for commercially orientated information and analysis has been created with the need for information more frequently than traditionally available in local government. The development of computing expertise in the decentralised or contract units is becoming more common.

3.14   Technology is becoming a tool of management and goes along with decentralisation of management control. The emphasis on performance measurement, efficiency and value for money depend on information systems. The access to computer networks changes the availability of information and the potential development of local analysis suited to local need. The changing structures in the public sector in creating contract units and splitting contractor/client services are going to require extensive and accurate information systems.

4.   THE COMPETITIVE LOCAL AUTHORITY

4.1   As part of its general aim to change the way that the public sector is managed, the government has been attempting to introduce competition and market processes into local government. The competitive approach was first introduced in the Local Government Planning and Land Act 1980, which required competition for building and highways construction and maintenance. Local authorities had often contracted out some activities, used consultants, provided services through agency agreements but those required particular procedures to be followed to open up services to the private sector. The Audit Commission added to the notion of competition through the use of comparative authority performance measures and identifying best management practices.

4.2   The competitive approach was extended by the Local Government Act 1988 which *requires* local authorities to subject to a number of services to competitive tendering.

     (a)   Refuse collection
     (b)   Street cleaning
     (c)   Building cleaning
     (d)   Schools and welfare catering, other catering
     (e)   Vehicle maintenance
     (f)   Grounds maintenance and the management of sports and leisure facilities

Local authorities will only be allowed to provide these services by using their own staff if they have won the right to do so in open competition. Competition has led to major changes in the way that local authorities manage themselves.

4.3   Proposals have been made to extend competitive tendering to 'white collar' areas of local authority services. There are defined as the provision of *professional advice* or other professional services, involving the application of any financial or technical expertise.

4.4   It is possible to identify four classes of service.

     (a)   *Direct to the public services:* the management of theatres and arts facilities, library support services and parking services are to be defined activities under the 1988 Act.

     (b)   *Construction related services:* architecture, engineering and property management. These would be subject to an evaluation of quality of services.

     (c)   *Corporate services:* corporate and administrative, legal, financial personnel, computing will have to introduce trading accounts to facilitate easier privatisation in the future.

     (d)   *Manual services:* cleaning of police buildings and the maintenance of police vehicles; maintenance of fire service vehicles; and provision of home to school transport are to be defined under the 1988 Act.

The government has also said it will issue a consultation paper on competitive tendering in housing management.

4.5   The main organisation impacts of competitive tendering have been changes in:

     (a)   committee structure;
     (b)   departmental structure;
     (c)   operational structures;
     (d)   management roles;
     (e)   relationships between central, support and contract units;
     (f)   role of councillors and the operation committees.

4.6   The changes which have taken place vary between authorities and are different for county, metropolitan district, large city district and rural district.

```
                            COUNCIL
                               |
                       POLICY COMMITTEE
          _____|_____
         |                     |                     |
                          CLIENT                 CONTRACT
                         COMMITTEES              COMMITTEE
         |                     |                     |
     SUPPORT               CLIENT                CONTRACT
     SERVICES            DEPARTMENTS            DEPARTMENTS
         |                     |                     |
         |                     |____\   DIRECT  ___\  SERVICE
         |                          /  SERVICE      /  PROVISION
         |                                  |
         |_____\  ORGANISATION
                                       /   MANAGERS
```

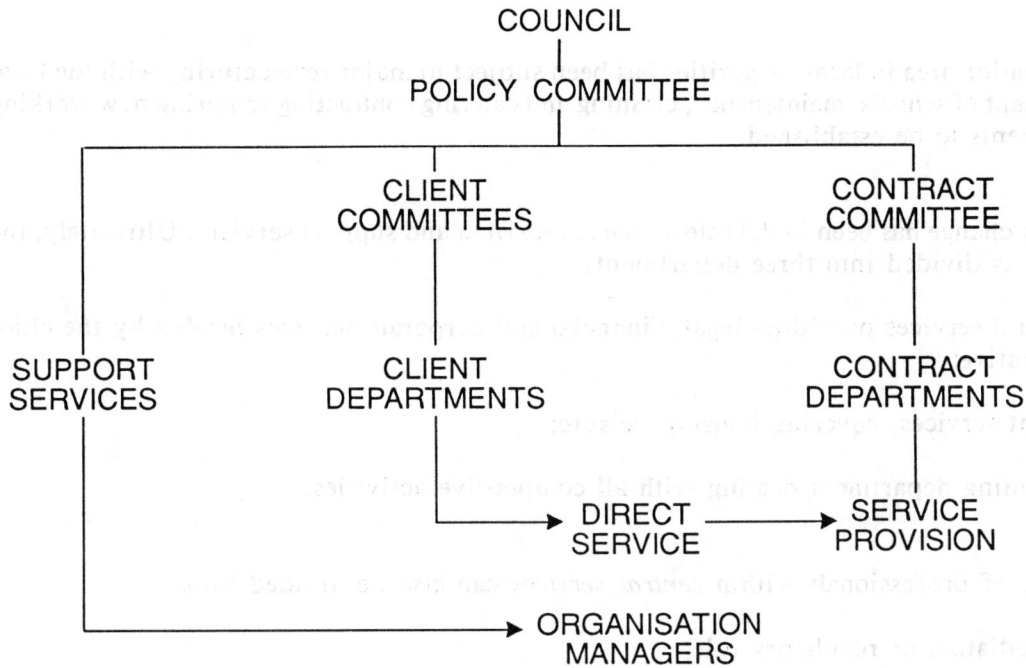

4.7 Operational structures are even more varied. Direct service managers or contract managers are located in a specialist department. Coordination across some areas has created a contract service organisation for cleaning or catering services. An example provided by K Walsh (1991 Competitive Tendering for Local Authority Services) shows a county authority with detailed contract management being conducted through the education department.

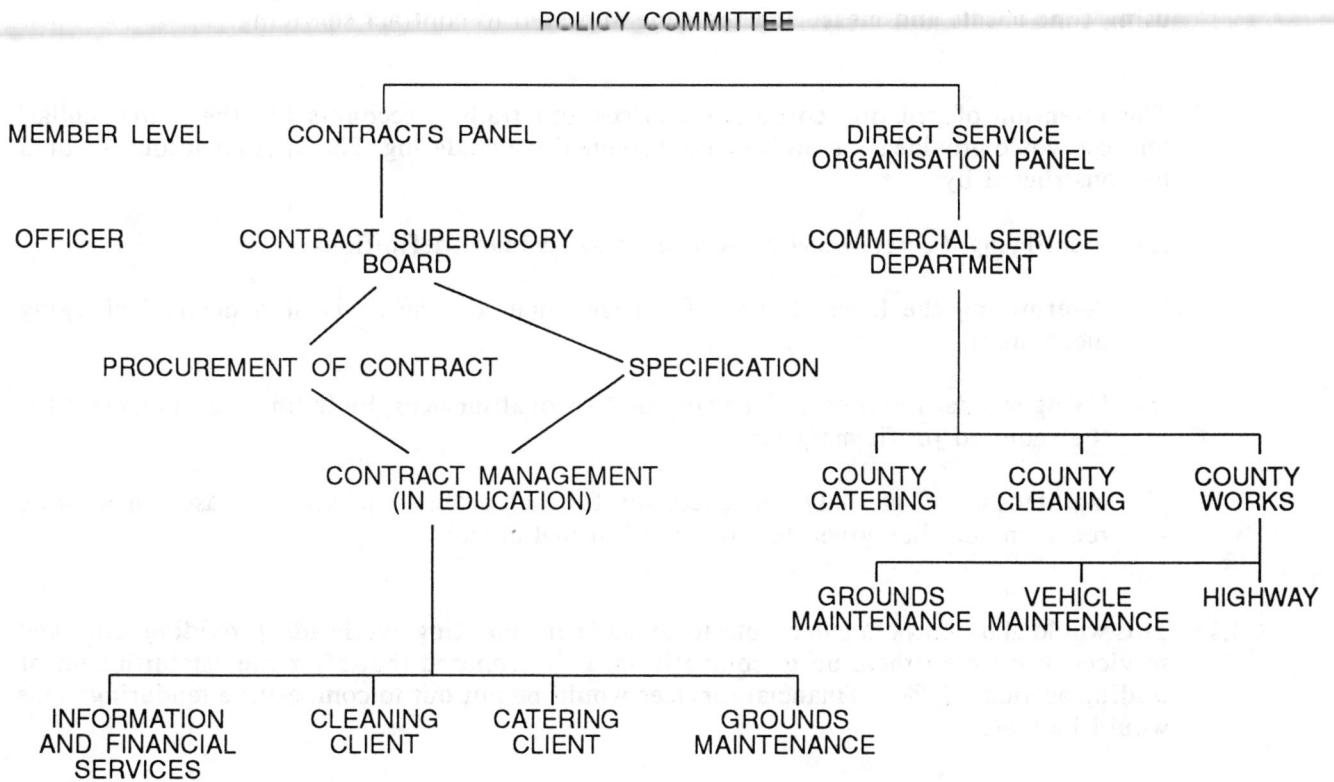

```
                            POLICY COMMITTEE
               _____|_____
              |                                           |
MEMBER LEVEL  CONTRACTS PANEL                   DIRECT SERVICE
              |                                 ORGANISATION PANEL
              |                                           |
OFFICER   CONTRACT SUPERVISORY                  COMMERCIAL SERVICE
              BOARD                                 DEPARTMENT
            /        \                                   |
 PROCUREMENT OF CONTRACT      SPECIFICATION              |
            \        /                          _____|_____
      CONTRACT MANAGEMENT                       |       |        |
        (IN EDUCATION)                       COUNTY   COUNTY   COUNTY
              |                              CATERING CLEANING WORKS
              |                                      _____|_____
              |                                     |      |      |
              |                                  GROUNDS VEHICLE HIGHWAY
              |                                  MAINTENANCE MAINTENANCE
   _____|_____
  |           |           |               |
INFORMATION  CLEANING   CATERING       GROUNDS
AND FINANCIAL CLIENT    CLIENT         MAINTENANCE
SERVICES
```

4.8 The education area in local authorities has been subject to major restructuring with the local management of schools, maintenance, cleaning and catering contracting requiring new working arrangements to be established.

4.9 The other change has been in the role of *central services* and support services. Ultimately, the authority is divided into three departments:

(a) central services providing legal, financial and corporate services headed by the chief executive;

(b) client services, covering housing, leisure;

(c) a trading department dealing with all competitive activities.

4.10 The roles of professionals within *central services* can also be divided into:

(a) a mediating or regulatory role;
(b) a client support role;
(c) a contractor role.

Internal trading accounts

4.11 The central service function is less of that concerned with control than about advice. The charging of central services is based upon time of the service used, calculated at the start of the year. A time charging system requires the central department to know its total costs, the total hours available and the proportion of total hours that are chargeable. This requires using time sheets and measuring the time allocated to contract servicing.

4.12 The intention of creating corporate services and trading accounts for the 'white collar' services would provide the basis for future competitive tendering. The internal accounts would be constructed by:

(a) identifying discrete services according to standard definitions;

(b) determining the level of work for each client on the basis of a defined charging mechanism;

(c) fixing standard unit costs for using professional services, including a cost element for the required profit margin;

(d) maintenance of internal trading accounts for each professional service, based on accurate recording of time given to work for internal clients.

4.13 This would allow corporate decisions to be made on allocating overheads, providing improved services or opening them up to competition. It is proposed that after the establishment of trading accounts 25% of financial services would be put out to competitive tendering. This would include:

    (a) financial planning;
    (b) internal audit;
    (c) exchequer services;
    (d) cash collection;
    (e) payroll administration;
    (f) accounting services;
    (g) investment management.

4.14 Corporate administration would be expected to put 15% of its services out to competition, legal services 33%, personnel services 25% and computing services 90%. The implications for financial services of having the associated services, and especially computing, open to competition would be to establish *service level agreements* with these other services.

4.15 Service level agreements provide a way of managing the client/contractor relationship through defining the service to be provided in terms of quantity, quality and price and agreeing contract terms. The service level agreement would be expected to cover:

    (a) a description of the service;
    (b) a definition of what is provided for measuring performance;
    (c) a basis for charging for the defined activities;
    (d) a basis for marginal changes;
    (e) procedures for dealing with disputes;
    (f) a timescale and renewal dates for the agreement.

The agreement helps in establishing responsibility for services at the centre and at a cost centre and provides a way for measuring and charging the use of central services.

4.16 It is important to identify corporate costs as well as the support service costs, however apportioned and charged. Corporate costs apply to *all* the council's activities. The costs of 'democracy', members' allowances, elections and civic duties are excluded from competitive tendering for corporate services. Other corporate and statutory functions exist, including committee support, press and public relations, overall financial control and budgetary procedures, setting the local charges on rates, policy formulation and monitoring.

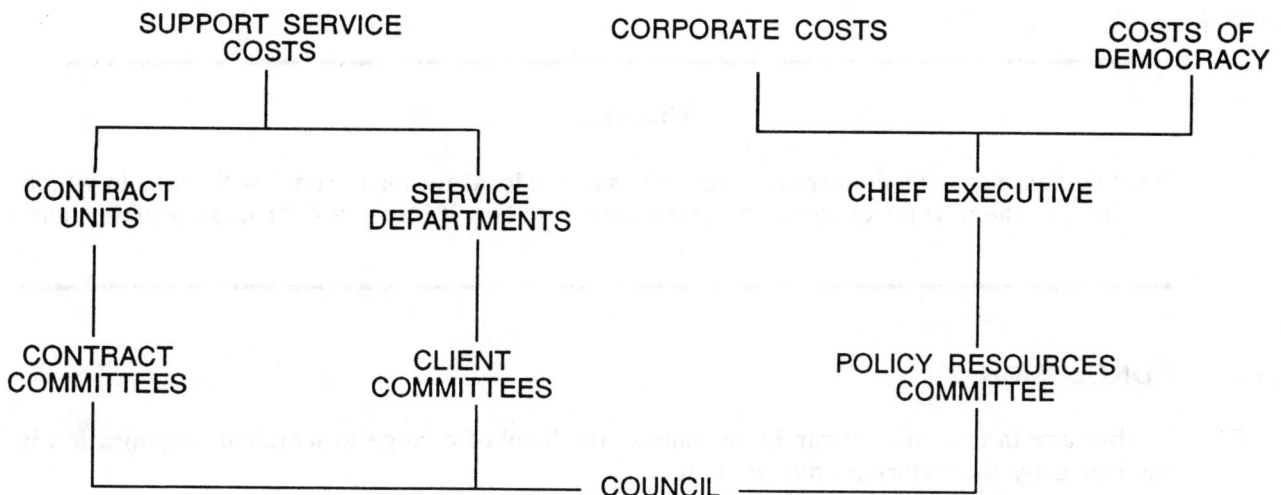

4.17 Problems arise as to how functions are charged and allocated, especially when the 'costs' may be seen to be imposed by the policy decisions of the council or Policy and Resources Committee. Personnel costs may increase because of an *active* recruitment policy targeting particular groups which adds to the recruitment cost for the service and contract units.

4.18 Councillors and client committees are concerned with:

(a) assessing the needs and wants of the electorate;
(b) policy formulation and strategic planning;
(c) identifying service priorities; and
(d) evaluating the performance of the contract and service activities of the authority.

Members will be removed from the day to day decision making and so may meet less frequently. Consultation papers on *The Internal Management of Local Authorities* suggest having directly elected *mayors* or chief executives, and a cabinet like structure for running the authority.

4.19 At the officer levels these changes mean more delegation of responsibility, clearer lines of accountability and more freedom to manage on a day to day basis. The *professional* heads of sections and service departments may be replaced by generalist or trained managers, whose skill is in *management*. The direct service organisation/contract unit manager becomes more concerned with income, having invoices paid quickly, being concerned with marketing and customer relations. The need is for good financial information for both the client and contractor roles within local government. The majority of contracts have been won by the in house organisation. They have now to demonstrate that they can achieve the quality, costs and returns established in the contract agreements.

4.20 Competition has highlighted the problems of management and organisation in local government, and it has meant a different way of looking at service provision. The lack of adequate information systems on the work to be done, together with the lack of inventories and the problems of preparing specifications, have been a problem for contract management. At the next stage, the monitoring and performance review work also requires good information systems and clear positions established for client and contractor responsibilities. Quality assurance and quality management has been a major shift in local government management attitudes. A new management role has been established for officers: the council members take on a more strategic role.

Exercise

What evidence can you find from the activities of the local authority running the area in which you live, of the new purchaser and contractor roles? Has it improved the quality of service?

---

5. CONCLUSION

5.1 Turbulence in this context can be defined as the level of change to which an organisation is subjected by the external environment.

5.2   The public sector has experienced a great deal of turbulence relating to:

   (a)   ownership (privatisation);
   (b)   government policy (the hectic farce of local authority finance);
   (c)   organisational purpose (as a purchaser of services rather than a provider of them).

5.3   Competitive tendering has meant:

   (a)   new organisational structures, separating core management from service departments or contractors;

   (b)   a greater need for accurate performance information to assist decision making.

TEST YOUR KNOWLEDGE
The numbers in brackets refer to paragraphs of this chapter

1   Can an organisation's survival be threatened by turbulence? (1.2)

2   What are the factors which create turbulence? (1.9)

3   What strategies are available for managing turbulence? (2.3 - 2.8)

4   What is the basis for information organisations? (3.1)

5   How useful are information systems for management decision-making? (3.7)

6   What have been the organisational impacts of competitive tendering? (4.5)

Now try question 10 at the end of the text

PART D
MANAGEMENT PROCESSES

Chapter 11

POLICY, POLITICS AND THE DECISION MAKING PROCESS

This chapter covers the following topics.

1. Policy and politics
2. The decision making process
3. Power
4. The role of the Chief Executive
5. Leadership and decision making

---

1. POLICY AND POLITICS

1.1 Public sector policies have some element of overt political choice attached to them. Responsibility for the actions taken by the public sector ultimately rests at the highest political level (eg the Cabinet, Cabinet committees). Ministerial decisions are made within an agreed policy framework. At this level the Treasury is also involved to assess the financial implications of policy.

What is policy?

1.2 Policy is a way of expressing the broad purposes of government activity in a particular field, with some desired outcome in mind.

(a) A policy may be a *specific* proposal (eg to replace the community charge as a way of raising local taxation revenues).

(b) Policy may also be about establishing procedures to achieve objectives such as improving education (eg through schools opting out of local authority control and reducing the political and bureaucratic controls of local government).

(c) Policy can also be a vague direction for change with no *specific* outcome intended. The disillusionment with government's ability to deliver services and provide value for money has meant a move towards a market orientated response. Consequently, separating the purchaser of services, the provider of services and the regulation of services has become an underlying policy principle.

1.3 Policy results from the interaction of a range of interest groups which come together to inform the decision making arena. Ideas may come from politically motivated sources and think tanks, or from special interests who lobby the government, from pressure groups, and from the civil service.

1.4 *Policy making* is a process of problem-identification, consultation and decision-making.

1.5 The government can solicit a number of sources for advice, or in turn, may be lobbied by them.

   (a) The Civil Service exists to advise the government, although views expressed in different areas are likely to differ (eg differences in the Foreign Office view and that expressed by the Prime Minister's policy advisers are sometimes reputed to have characterised much of Margaret Thatcher's administration).

   (b) There may be a number of experts on particular areas, who are outside the government. Academics, 'think tanks', for example, may be asked for their views. Recently, the Treasury has established a semi formal arrangement with various academic bodies to improve its economic forecasting.

   (c) *Royal Commissions* might be set up. An example related to local government was The Widdicombe Committee on the conduct of local authority business.

   (d) *Special interest groups* might also pitch in. Charities are often asked for advice. Representatives of the food industry advise on nutrition.

1.6 Implementing policy, however, is perhaps a more tortuous process than making it. After all:

   (a) the division of responsibilities between separate civil service departments has to be sorted out;

   (b) the department responsible for implementing it must negotiate the necessary funds from the Treasury, which might take a more sceptical view of the expenditure;

   (c) if legislation is required, a slot must be negotiated in the parliamentary timetable, where it will be competing with other parliamentary work;

   (d) furthermore, if the policy requires legislation, it is quite possible that this will be amended by the House of Commons, or indeed the House of Lords.

1.7 If the policy is poorly drafted in legislation its actual effect might be confusion. Problems arise in the way legislation is drafted, or in unforeseen anomalies.

1.8 Few policies are 'new' in that they are built upon an existing set of policies which are not working or are no longer relevant. The policy making process is a pattern of continuous readjustment of policy actions. Few policies then run their course and so the link between cause and effect and the use of the appropriate actions is difficult to demonstrate.

1.9 Policies which have elements of political and resource choice in them may be strong on rhetoric but weak on funding, as the power system for allocating funds is not the same as that for getting the issue on to the political agenda.

1.10 Policy formulation is rarely the responsibility of one single ministry. In launching *Action for Cities* (1986) the Prime Minister was flanked by six ministers who were associated with the bundle of policies aimed at dealing with inner city problems. The problem of the inner cities covers a number of interrelated issues (eg housing, education, the environment, social issues, crime, unemployment, the development process and local economic development). Similarly, environmental issues affect, say, transport, trade and industry, and energy policy.

1.11 Policy implementation is not always the responsibility of a single organisation either. The release of long term patients from psychiatric hospitals into the community means the coordination of a number of policy areas (eg the organisations responsible for health, social welfare, housing and employment). The funding for these organisations may not be well related or coordinated with the policy objectives.

1.12 The policy can be communicated through legislation, circulars at conferences, or meetings, and then use of professional bodies to promote the policy. The policies for changes in the health service were presented to health authority staff through meetings and use of video and presentation packs. Advertising has become more widely used in recent years.

1.13 With the intermingling of policies, and of the agents which implement them, it may be difficult to identify clearly the impact of a particular policy. Unintended consequences may also result from the implementation of the policy.

1.14 In the policy making process, objective setting for the public sector is based upon political values. The public sector objectives are often diffuse, unclear, unspecific or internally inconsistent and are subject to political legitimation. The implementation process may well involve another tier of political decision makers (eg local government, appointed boards who have their own set of priorities). The local or organisational interests have again to legitimate the decisions being made. The field officers, street level bureaucrats and teachers have then to put the policy into practice in the work situation. A simple example is the sale of council houses, implemented far more swiftly by some local authorities than others.

1.15 The organisation implementing the policies has to make decisions about priorities from among several objectives, which may all be equally desirable but which cannot be achieved due to limited resources. The controls on both capital and revenue expenditure are such that the art of public management at an organisational level is the manipulation of limited funding within the political decision making process.

1.16 The intent to satisfy policy objectives may be qualified by the statement 'within the resources available'. Public sector management becomes a rationing process, a resource allocation problem. 'Need' may also be a matter of professional judgement or an interpretation of the administrative rules, which can be questioned in the courts. Need may be demonstrated through statistical measures or consumer surveys but the interpretation of these findings will requires ethical and social judgements.

1.17 Priorities in the health service have always been subject to resource limitations and professional judgements on need and resource allocation. Lind and Wiseman (1978) identify six dimensions which can be used for ranking health service resource allocations in order of priority.

1   Between geographical areas: Area equalisation expenditure
                                    Access to services

2   Between population groups: Deprived groups
                                    At risk groups

3   Between disease and dependency groups: Cancer sufferers or old people
                                    How treatable is the group?
                                    Research into treatment: cause

4   Between different services or In patient – out patient
    care activities: Hospital service or use of general practitioners

5   Between different forms of
    intervention: Health promotion

6   Between different agencies: Community care
                                    Private residential homes

These need to be linked together to establish comparative indicators of priority.

1.18 Lind and Wiseman feel that dependence on statistical information can mean a concentration on what is *measurable* (throughputs) rather than what is important, the quality of medical care. In areas of ill health a wide range of action may be required and may relate to wider social and economic issues (eg to do with unemployment, poverty and poor housing and education) which it may be ideologically acceptable.

2.   THE DECISION MAKING PROCESS

The rational model of decision making

2.1 The *rational model of decision making* is a systematic approach, which takes in all relevant factors, and weighs them carefully before the final choice is made.

Five steps can be identified.

1   Identify and define the problem.
2   Decide how to deal with the problem.
3   Generate and evaluate possible solutions.
4   Decide on the solution, and implement.
5   Check that the decision has worked.

2.2   The rational model makes assumptions that the process takes place in discrete steps.

    (a)   These assumptions may not be valid, thanks to the limited time people have in which to make decisions, and the information they have available.

    (b)   Moreover, the way the problem is identified and defined may depend on *value judgements* about what the problem is, and so what the solutions are. By defining the problem in a particular way, the possible solution is also often being defined (ie the range of available solutions is limited).

2.3   In the public sector it may be difficult to isolate a problem and deal with it in a simple manner. The problem manifested may only be a symptom of other problems which should be dealt with.

2.4   In the public sector, the information and theoretical base for evaluating possible solutions may be rather limited. The need for research and testing possible solutions can mean a delay in taking action.

2.5   Policy makers might tend to confine themselves to considering variables and issues that will have immediate consequences to themselves and which vary only a little from the existing position. The uncertainty of knowledge and the ambiguity that exists about how to evaluate possible solutions means that the process is again often limited in its scope.

The 'partisan mutual adjustment' model of decision making

2.6   The view that policy making is a process of political and social interaction – negotiation, bargaining, making agreements among groups promoting and protecting differing and competing interests and values - is from a 'partisan mutual adjustment' perspective. This model of the policy making political process contrasts with a view that policy is driven by *centralised* information-based decision making.

2.7   Choosing an action implicitly includes a view about possible or likely outcomes of the decision and has considered the 'trade offs' or 'opportunity costs' of making the particular choice of actions. So when it comes to check on the decision taken, it is being evaluated against a speculative outcome.

2.8   Decision making in practice depends on the judgement, intuition and experience of the decision maker. This might mean the decision makers will play safe and in a political context provide the citizens with what they want in the short term.

2.9   On the other hand, decision-makers develop a new set of values, and so the response to a problem may be more than a pragmatic tinkering with known instruments, but wholesale changes of direction. The Lange Government of New Zealand started a thorough root and branch reform of New Zealand's institutions.

2.10 The rational model of decision making assumes that in the implementation process, all managers carry out the duties allocated to them, and only make decisions which fall within the scope of their individual authority. This view of implementation may not be relevant to the public sector. The range of the public sector is so wide that a *variety* of agents and bodies will be responsible for implementing the policy decisions, and the links between them may not be all that tight.

2.11 The content of public sector decision making can be wide.

(a) Decisions can be about long term as less specific issues, about ill defined issues of policy direction.

(b) Decisions can be about control mechanisms to see that action is taken and performance is monitored.

(c) Decisions can be about short term issues related to staff problems or reacting to complaints.

(d) Decisions can be routine about organising work, recording work being done.

(e) Decisions can be made by individuals on a face to face basis, or by committees or groups as the organisation on a formal or informal basis or can be imposed from outside the organisation.

2.12 Decisions are needed to resolve problems, when there is a choice about what to do, or how to do it. Problems vary, not just in subject matter, but also according to other factors.

(a) How easy or complex are they to resolve?
(b) How frequently do they arise?
(c) Can the problem be quantified, or are there qualitative matters of judgement involved?
(d) How much information is available?
(e) What are the costs/time implications of obtaining more information?
(f) How serious are the consequences of making a bad decision?
(g) Can the decision be changed quickly?
(h) Whose job is it to make the decision about how to deal with the problem?

2.13 As opposed to what is suggested by the rational model, decisions are made to achieve not an optimal outcome but a *satisfactory* outcome - something that will do for *now*.

(a) Passing the decision upwards or downwards, to get someone else to make it for you. Delegation offers a quick and simple solution to *your* problem.

(b) Putting off the decision in the hope that people will forget or the problem goes away, or someone else solves it anyway.

(c) Use the solution adopted in a similar situation. Copy what was done previously.

(d) Find out what sort of decision the boss requires, or the people or groups who identified the problem. A solution might be suggested by them.

(e) Making a quick decision which you can revise if it does not work.

2.14 The decision making process may be initiated by a strong leader who is able to provide a strong direction for the followers to make decisions. Decisions are then made as the leader would like them. This can provide a way of maintaining positions of power in an organisation and limiting discussion on alternative approaches. The use of external agencies may be used for the same purpose (ie you cannot do that, because the government/trade unions/regulatory body would not agree).

2.15 The other important aspect of decision making as well as the 'power' to make decisions is the need to *communicate* the decisions. In times of change it is necessary to be able to explain why the decision was made and what the ends are which the decision is hoping to achieve. Decisions at the top of the hierarchy may never be put into action because they are not communicated to those responsible for carrying out the action.

2.16 In public sector organisations, there are many professional staff and a number of interlocking work groups with a high degree of loyalty among members. In these situations, the manager will be expected to adopt a *consultative* and *participatory* style of leadership and decision making. Group members will expect to be consulted on deciding the group's objectives and in problem solving.

2.17 The involvement of those implementing the decision and the interest groups being affected by the policy decisions has become a vital part of the decision making process in the public sector. It is felt that a better decision will be reached and implementation will be easier, if there has been wide-ranging consultation amongst interested parties.

2.18 In the public sector, decision making has often been based around committees and committee procedures. The ability to influence the committee to make a decision becomes an important skill of managers in local government. There is some evidence that managerial autonomy will reduce the need for decision making by committees who will take a more strategic role.

2.19 Corporate decision making in local government can be represented as follows.

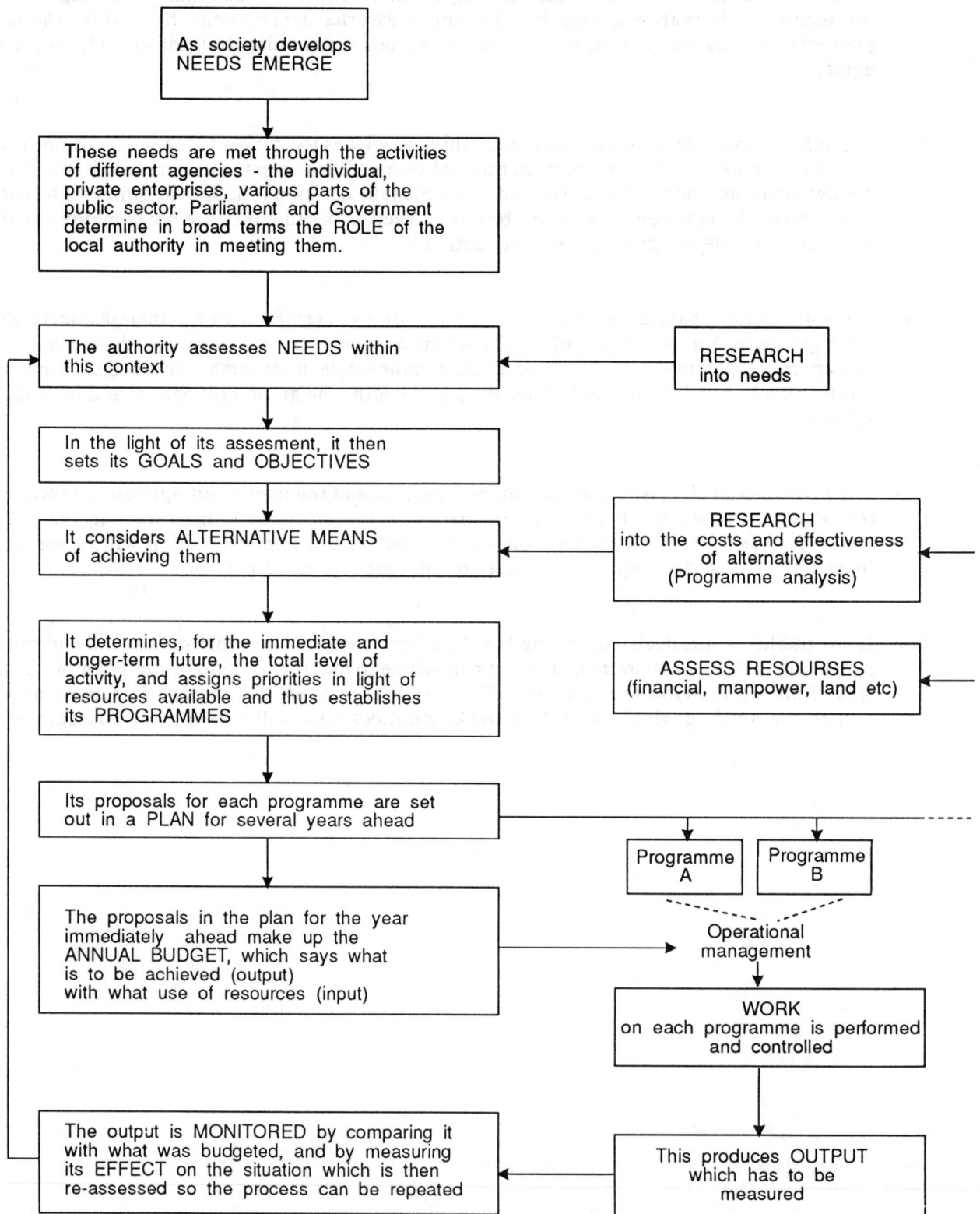

```
                    ┌──────────────────────────┐
                    │   As society develops    │
                    │     NEEDS EMERGE         │
                    └──────────────────────────┘
                                 │
                                 ▼
          ┌───────────────────────────────────────────┐
          │ These needs are met through the activities │
          │ of different agencies - the individual,    │
          │ private enterprises, various parts of the  │
          │ public sector. Parliament and Government   │
          │ determine in broad terms the ROLE of the   │
          │ local authority in meeting them.           │
          └───────────────────────────────────────────┘
                                 │
                                 ▼
  ┌──────────────────────────────────────┐        ┌─────────────────┐
  │ The authority assesses NEEDS within   │◄───────│   RESEARCH      │
  │ this context                          │        │   into needs    │
  └──────────────────────────────────────┘        └─────────────────┘
                     │
                     ▼
  ┌──────────────────────────────────────┐
  │ In the light of its assesment, it then│
  │ sets its GOALS and OBJECTIVES         │
  └──────────────────────────────────────┘
                     │
                     ▼
  ┌──────────────────────────────────────┐      ┌──────────────────────────────┐
  │ It considers ALTERNATIVE MEANS        │◄─────│        RESEARCH              │
  │ of achieving them                     │      │ into the costs and           │
  │                                       │      │ effectiveness of alternatives│
  │                                       │      │ (Programme analysis)         │
  └──────────────────────────────────────┘      └──────────────────────────────┘
                     │
                     ▼
  ┌──────────────────────────────────────┐      ┌──────────────────────────────┐
  │ It determines, for the immediate and  │      │ ASSESS RESOURSES             │
  │ longer-term future, the total level of│      │ (financial, manpower, land   │
  │ activity, and assigns priorities in   │      │ etc)                         │
  │ light of resources available and thus │      └──────────────────────────────┘
  │ establishes its PROGRAMMES            │
  └──────────────────────────────────────┘
                     │
                     ▼
  ┌──────────────────────────────────────┐      ┌───────────┐ ┌───────────┐
  │ Its proposals for each programme are  │      │ Programme │ │ Programme │
  │ set out in a PLAN for several years   │      │     A     │ │     B     │
  │ ahead                                 │      └───────────┘ └───────────┘
  └──────────────────────────────────────┘              │
                     │                            Operational
                     ▼                            management
  ┌──────────────────────────────────────┐
  │ The proposals in the plan for the year│
  │ immediately  ahead make up the        │      ┌──────────────────────────────┐
  │ ANNUAL BUDGET, which says what        │      │          WORK                │
  │ is to be achieved (output)            │      │ on each programme is         │
  │ with what use of resources (input)    │      │ performed and controlled     │
  └──────────────────────────────────────┘      └──────────────────────────────┘
                     │                                        │
                     ▼                                        ▼
  ┌──────────────────────────────────────┐      ┌──────────────────────────────┐
  │ The output is MONITORED by comparing  │◄─────│ This produces OUTPUT         │
  │ it with what was budgeted, and by     │      │ which has to be              │
  │ measuring its EFFECT on the situation │      │ measured                     │
  │ which is then re-assessed so the      │      └──────────────────────────────┘
  │ process can be repeated               │
  └──────────────────────────────────────┘
```

This represents a rational view of the decision making process.

3. POWER

3.1   To make the decision effective, the decision makers need power. *Power* does not mean the ability to exercise *control*, but has a more general meaning to do with the ability to affect a situation. When power is legitimate, recognised and acknowledged, it is called *authority*.

3.2   Authority may be exercised by someone occupying a position or formal role in an organisation. This is *position power* according to Handy because the authority is the post or function. The position power in local government is possessed by the 'council' and its leader and the 'legal' decisions are made in the name of the council. Most local authorities have appointed chief executives to manage the operation of the authority.

3.3   *Resource power* includes control of money and information. As chief executives in local authorities are the main link between the officer and councillors and so have a uniquely widespan of information in the decision making process, they are in a position to influence many decisions.

3.4   In the public sector, a level of knowledge or expertise has been expected of chief officers, as lawyers, accountants or planning backgrounds. This expertise provides *expert power*. The person is seen as being 'an authority on' a particular topic.

  (a)   In local government, traditionally the way to senior posts has traditionally been through *professional posts* in local government hence expert power must be required first.

  (b)   In the civil service however the technical expert has been less important than the generalist administrator, with 'position power'.

3.5   An individual may have *personal power* due to their charisma or personality. Association with charismatic leaders may provide *referent power* as someone can operate in the name of the leader, or is known to have easy access to them.

3.6   Sources of power are various.

  (a)   Resource power and position power are usually given from above, or from outside the organisation.

  (b)   Expert power and personal power are given from underneath from the people over whom the power will be exercised. Expert power may be gained through education and training or professional qualification. It may provide a knowledge base to carry out an activity but not competence. In management training the move has been away from an academic base to personal competence or vocational base. The development of competence also reinforces the personal qualities required for exercising power.

3.7   Resource power and position power allow a manager to lay down rules and regulations, issue orders and instructions, take decisions about other people and act as the boss. If this position power is not backed up with some *personal power*, then a lot of time has to be spent on seeing that rules are being complied with. To get people in the organisation to work with the leader, it is important they identify with the approach of the leader and even internalise the leader's wishes. Just because you have authority you cannot expect everyone to agree with you even if they have to obey you. People have *negative power* if their non-cooperation would be a serious worry.

4. THE ROLE OF THE CHIEF EXECUTIVE

4.1 The enhanced role of the chief executive in local government can be traced back to reports of the 1970s about the management of local authorities. Rather than being a clerk often taking a legal and procedural view in administrating the operations of the authority, the chief executive was seen to be a manager or coordinator of the authority's activities.

4.2 The role of the chief executive was studied by the *Widdicombe Committee* on the conduct of local authority business. The views expressed in the report reemphasised the propriety roles of the management, coordination and personnel, and finance.

4.3 Legislation has since clarified the finance role and there is requirement to have an officer concerned with propriety issues. The level of 'power' that would have been given to the chief executive, under Widdicombe's recommendations would have diminished the power of the councillors. The ability to determine what information councillors have on a particular subject and being able to exclude a councillor from a decision because of their interests.

4.4 The *Audit Commission* also reviewed the role of chief executives in *First Among Equals*, and identified the key tasks and the key success factors for better management.

Key success factors

Key tasks	Understand customers	Respond to electorate	Consistent achievable objectives	Clear respons- ibilities	Train and motivate people	Communicate effectively	Monitor results	Adapt to change
Manage internal relation- ships				X		X		X
Convert policy into action	X	X	X	X		X	X	X
Develop processes, people and skills			X	X	X		X	
Review performance		X	X	X	X	X		X
Think and plan ahead		X	X			X		X

4.5   The Audit Commission identified several roles for the chief executive.

    (a)   *Strategic:* as a corporate manager and as a political manager.

    (b)   *Coordinating:* as the focus of communication between the council and its employees; as a trouble shooter coping with crises; as an honest broker, or umpire between chairpersons of committees and departmental heads.

    (c)   *Operational:* running the policy and chief executives section; being responsible for the legal and financial administration of the authority; taking on specialist roles like economic development; being a project manager for dealing with particular schemes, such as bids for urban programmes, town twinning.

    (d)   *Representative:* acting as a representative of the council at civic functions and with members; as a salesperson to external bodies, government department, the business community; as a figurehead providing a model for staff.

These roles also overlap with councillors' roles and require coordination with councillors' activities in policy making and decision-making.

4.6   A consultation paper on the *Internal Management of Local Authorities* (April 1991) sets out the following options for change.

    (a)   An executive would be elected separately from the council, to run the council on a day to day basis, including decisions on policy.

    (b)   Alternatively, the council could elect a small executive committee to carry out day to day executive tasks, although some of this authority would be *delegated* to an appointed council.

4.7   The future role of councillors is to oversee contractual arrangements:

    (a)   setting standards where appropriate;
    (b)   specifying service requirements;
    (c)   awarding contracts fairly;
    (d)   monitoring performance;
    (e)   taking action if performance falls short of the required level.

4.8   This creates a *managerial function* for councillors, as opposed to the view of their role as:

    (a)   representing their constituents;
    (b)   getting involved in policy decisions.

The party and political aspects of local government decision making will be replaced with managerial ones.

4.9   As the roles of a local authority changes from being a provider to an enabling or facilitating body, then the need to work through other organisations becomes even more important. The local authority will have to act in a range of modes, as clients and contractors and as regulators and inspectors of other bodies, and as advocates and enablers on a wide range of policy issues.

4.10 Management then varies with technology used, and with the conditions and tasks it has to deal with. Local government is concerned with the collective interests of the community, and the range of diverse interests it services, from big business to small companies to individuals.

4.11 The private sector also has to serve a number of interests (eg shareholders' desire for short term profits, the consumer's wish for good quality and cheap products, the state, suppliers, sale outlets, workers).

4.12 Different parts of the business may call for different management styles and processes. Common to all the management processes should be an element of planning, but with a range of varying time horizons, today's delivery of goods, next year's budget, future investment plans.

4.13 The *general manager* concept identifies someone who can organise the work of others, has control of resources, is a point of communication up and down and is part of the review process of activities as well as operational tasks.

R Steward (1979) *The reality of management* provides a definition of the manager's job as 'deciding what should be done and then getting other people to do it'.

A longer definition would be concerned with how these tasks are to be accomplished.

(a) The first task comprises setting objectives, planning (including decision making), and setting up formal organisation.

(b) The second consists of motivation, communication, and control (including measurement), and the staff development.

4.14 When it comes to research studies of how managers *actually* do their jobs (Carlson Broussine) it seems that much of a manager's time is taken up with short conversations, telephone calls, which are unscheduled, and organised meetings. Only a minority of their time is spent on 'planning' and 'organising'.

4.15 Communication and cooperation are the main activities of the manager who may be required to make a lot of decisions 'on the hoof'. The manager does have lots of information and a wide range of sources of information. Most of the information will either be oral form or short memos rather than lengthy well formulated and analytical reports. At times it may be necessary to take a stock check of decisions and draw a group of people together in a meeting and produce some more formal and recorded decisions.

4.16 While the interest and participation of staff is advocated as best management practice, the pace and speed of time required to react to problems that occur is such that full participation is impossible. Others have to be told about decisions and their agreement sought after the event.

4.17 People may become demotivated if they feel that they are not included in the decision making process, or what they say or believe they have agreed is ignored. Judging levels of motivation and understanding the energy and capacity people have to do the job, and providing the right mix of encouragement, criticism, and teaching is an integral part of management.

4.18　The organisational hierarchy and spans of control limit the area over which the officers can make decisions. Referral up and down the hierarchy creates its own bureaucratic decision making procedure. In the public sector, the image of posts with specific levels of responsibility and authority, in the context of a strict grading system, still applies. Efforts to create more dynamic and open structures makes it harder to identify accountability for a decision. The need to demonstrate that the process of decision making was fair, and that rules and procedures were followed, is both part of the *culture* and a *requirement* (eg in any case of alleged maladministration). Thus it helps to know that procedures and due care and attention were given to the matter concerned. This may be important in financial transactions and recording expenditure undertaken in relation to particular budget headings.

4.19　Competences which are being promoted by Management Charter Initiative require managers to be good listeners and analysts, as well as being able to give orders. The training of staff in management techniques is *not* yet a major part of the staff development in the public sector. However the Health Service has identified 250,000 posts as having managerial responsibility. In local government, perhaps 20% of staff require some management training (500,000 posts).

5.　LEADERSHIP AND DECISION MAKING

5.1　Leadership is the process of influencing others to work willingly towards an organisation's goals, and to the best of their capabilities. 'The essence of leadership is followership. In other words it is the willingness of people to follow that makes a person a leader' (Koontz, O'Donnell, Weihrich).

5.2　Leadership comes about in a number of different ways.

(a)　A manager is appointed to a position of authority within the organisation, and relies mainly on the (legitimate) authority of that position. Leadership of subordinates is a function of the position.

(b)　Some leaders (eg in politics or in trade unions) might be elected.

(c)　Other leaders might emerge by popular choice and through their personal drive and qualities. Unofficial spokesmen for groups of people are leaders of this style.

Our main concern, of course, is with managers who are appointed as leaders by virtue of their position in the organisation. Leaders are *given* their roles by their putative followers; their 'authority' may technically be removed if their followers cease to acknowledge them. The *personal, physical* or *expert* power of leaders is therefore more important than position power alone.

5.3　The subordinates of a manager with indifferent or poor leadership 'qualities' and skills would still do their job, but they would do it ineffectually or perhaps in a confused manner. By providing leadership, a manager should be able to use the capabilities of subordinates to better effect; leadership is the 'influential increment over and above mechanical compliance with the routine directives of the organisation' (Katz and Kahn *The Social Psychology of Organisations*).

'Since people tend to follow those whom they see as a means of satisfying their own personal goals, the more managers understand what motivates their subordinates and how these motivations operate, and the more they reflect this understanding in carrying out their managerial actions, the more effective leaders they are likely to be. '   *Koontz, O'Donnell and Weihrich*

Trait theories of leadership

5.4   Early theories suggested that there are certain qualities, personality characteristics or 'traits' which make a good leader. These might be aggressiveness, self-assurance, intelligence, initiative, energy, a drive for achievement or power, appearance, interpersonal skills, administrative ability, imagination, a certain upbringing and education, the 'helicopter factor' (the ability to rise above a situation and analyse it objectively) etc. Taylor believed the capacity to 'make others do what you want them to do' was an inherent characteristic.

5.5   This list is not exhaustive, and various writers attempted to show that their selected list of traits were the ones that provided the key to leadership. The full list of traits is so long that it appears to call for a man or woman of extraordinary, even superhuman, gifts to be a leader.

5.6   Ghiselli did show a significant correlation between leadership effectiveness and personal traits of intelligence, initiative, self-assurance and individuality. Hunt found a similar correlation between effectiveness and the 'helicopter factor'.

5.7   Jennings (1961) wrote that 'Research has produced such a variegated list of traits presumably to describe leadership, that for all practical purposes it describes nothing. Fifty years of study have failed to produce one personality trait or set of qualities that can be used to distinguish between leaders and non-leaders.'

Trait theory, although superficially attractive, is now largely discredited. Although it may be possible to show that, without certain characteristics, it is difficult to be a good leader, it has proved impossible to show that all people with certain characteristics are good leaders.

5.8   Alternative approaches to leadership theory have been developed over the years, and some of these will be described under the headings of:

(a)   style theories, mainly of the 'behaviouralist' school of thought;
(b)   systems theory and leadership;
(c)   contingency theories of leadership.

Style theories

Huneryager and Heckman

5.9   Four different types or styles of leadership were identified by Huneryager and Heckman (1967).

(a) *Dictatorial style*: the manager forces subordinates to work by threatening punishment and penalties. The psychological contract between the subordinates and their organisation would be coercive. Dictatorial leadership might be rare in commerce and industry, but it is not uncommon in the style of government in some countries of the world, nor in the style of parenthood in many families.

(b) *Autocratic style*: decision-making is centralised in the hands of the leader himself, who does not encourage participation by subordinates; indeed, subordinates' ideas might be actively discouraged and obedience to orders would be expected from them. The autocratic style is common in many organisations, and you will perhaps be able to identify examples from your own experience. Doctors, matrons and sisters in hospitals tend to practise an autocratic style; managers/directors who own their company also tend to expect things to be done their way.

(c) *Democratic style*: decision-making is decentralised, and shared by subordinates in participative group action. To be truly democratic, the subordinate must be willing to participate. The democratic style is described more fully later.

(d) *Laissez-faire style*: subordinates are given little or no direction at all, and are allowed to establish their own objectives and make all their own decisions. The leader of a research establishment might adopt a laissez-faire style, giving individual research workers freedom of choice to organise and conduct their research as they themselves want (within certain limits, such as budget spending limits).

5.10 These four divisions or 'compartments' of management style are really a simplification of a 'continuum' or range of styles, from the most dictatorial to the most laissez-faire.

Dicta-torial	Autocratic		Democratic				Laissez-faire
Manager makes decisions enforces them	Manager makes decisions and announces them	Manager 'sells' his decisions to subordinates	Manager suggests own ideas and asks for comments	Manager suggests his sketched ideas, asks for comments and amends his ideas as a result	Manager presents a problem, asks for ideas, makes a decision from the ideas	Manager presents a problem to his group of subordinates and asks them to solve it	Manager allows his subordinates to act as they wish within specified limits

This 'continuum' of leadership styles was first suggested by Tannenbaum and Schmidt (1958).

5.11 There are differing views as to which of these leadership styles (especially (a), (b) or (c)) is likely to be most effective. The probable truth is that the degree of effectiveness of a particular leadership style will depend on the work environment, the leader himself and his subordinates.

The Ashridge studies

5.12 A slightly different analysis of leadership styles, based on this continuum, was made by the Research Unit at Ashridge Management College, based on research in several industries in the UK (reported 1966). This research distinguished four different management styles.

(a) The autocratic or *tells* style. This is characterised by one-way communication between the manager and the subordinate, with the manager telling the subordinate what to do. The leader makes all the decisions and issues instructions, expecting them to be obeyed without question.

(b) The persuasive or *sells* style. The manager still makes all the decisions, but believes that subordinates need to be motivated to accept them before they will do what he wants them to. He therefore tries to explain his decisions in order to persuade them round to his point of view.

(c) The *consultative* style. This involves discussion between the manager and the subordinates involved in carrying out a decision, but the manager retains the right to make the decision himself. By conferring with his subordinates before making any decision, the manager will take account of their advice and feelings. Consultation is a form of limited participation in decision-making for subordinates, but there might be a tendency for a manager to appear to consult his subordinates when really he has made up his mind beforehand. Consultation will then be false and a facade for a 'sells' style of leadership whereby the manager hopes to win the acceptance of his decisions by subordinates by pretending to listen to their advice.

(d) The democratic or *joins* style. This is an approach whereby the leader joins his group of subordinates to make a decision on the basis of consensus or agreement. It is the most democratic style of leadership identified by the research study. Subordinates with the greatest knowledge of a problem will have greater influence over the decision. The 'joins' style is therefore most effective where all subordinates in the group have equal knowledge and can therefore contribute in equal measure to decisions.

5.13 The findings of the Ashridge studies included the following.

(a) There was a clear preference amongst the subordinates for the *consultative* style of leadership but managers were most commonly thought to be exercising the 'tells' or 'sells' style.

(b) The attitudes of subordinates towards their work varied according to the style of leadership they thought their boss exercised. The most favourable attitudes were found amongst those subordinates who perceived their boss to be exercising the *consultative style*.

(c) The least favourable attitudes were found amongst subordinates who were unable to perceive a consistent style of leadership in their boss. In other words, subordinates are unsettled by a boss who chops and changes between autocracy, persuasion, consultation and democracy. The conclusion from this finding of the study is that *consistency* in leadership style is important.

		Strengths		*Weaknesses*
• *Tells style*	(1)	Quick decisions can be made when speed is required	(1)	It does not encourage the subordinate to give his opinions when these might be useful.
	(2)	It is the most efficient type of leadership for highly-programmed routine work.	(2)	Communications between the manager and subordinate will be one-way and the manager will not know until afterwards whether his orders have been properly understood.
			(3)	It does not encourage initiaive and commitment from subordinates.
• *Sells style*	(1)	Employees are made aware of the reasons for decisions.	(1)	Communications are still largely one-way. Subordinates might not buy his decisions.
	(2)	Selling decisions to staff might make them more willing to co-operate.	(2)	It does not encourage initiative and commitment from subordinates
	(3)	Staff will have a better idea of what to do when unforeseen events arise in their work because the manager will have explained his intentions.		
• *Consultative style*	(1)	Employees are involved in decisions before they are made. This encourages motivation through greater interest and involvement.	(1)	It might take much longer to reach decisions.
	(2)	An agreed consensus of opinion can be reached and for some decisions consensus can be an advantage rather than a weak compromise.	(2)	Subordinates might be too inexperienced to formulate mature opinions and give practical advice.
	(3)	Employees can contribute their knowledge and experience to help in solving more complex problems.		
• *Joins style*	(1)	It can provide high motivation and commitment from employees.	(1)	The authority of the manager might be undermined.
	(2)	It shares the other advantages of the consultative style.	(2)	Decision-making might become a very long process, and clear decisions might be difficult to reach.
			(3)	Subordinates might lack enough experience.

Theory X and Theory Y

5.14 The theory X and theory Y of Douglas McGregor can be applied to leadership style. We saw that leadership style may be affected by which theory of human nature the particular manager subscribes to:

(a) *Theory X* - the average human being has an inherent dislike of work and will avoid it if he can; or

(b) *Theory Y* - the expenditure of physical and mental effort in work is as natural as play or rest.

5.15 Managers who consciously or unconsciously hold the view that most people belong, to different degrees, in the Theory X group will tend to adopt styles which are 'harder line' - the tells, dictatorial or autocratic end of the spectrum. Conversely, a manager who believes in Theory Y will be more participative and adopt a style closer to 'joins'.

5.16 Although Theories X and Y are extreme views, they do serve to define the two ends of a spectrum into which human attitudes towards work fall. Similarly, the strength of a manager's convictions about his subordinates' attitudes will define where his leadership style falls in the Ashridge or Tannenbaum and Schmidt continuum. Through the theories therefore we can see how a manager's leadership style links in with his attitudes to motivation - a Theory X autocrat will probably believe that only attractive pay and coercion will get a job done, whilst a Theory Y democrat will acknowledge participation as a motivator.

Rensis Likert

5.17 As we have seen early on in this Study Text, Rensis Likert distinguished four styles of management:

(a) exploitive authoritative;
(b) benevolent authoritative;
(c) consultative authoritative;
(d) participative group management.

Managers, to be effective and to communicate, must adjust to the people they are managing.

5.18 Likert attempted to show that the effective manager is one who uses the participative style of management, although the ideal manager must be able to use the right leadership style for the right situation. Everyone in an organisation is interdependent with other people (as a manager is dependent upon his subordinates). Authority alone is insufficient to obtain good performance. It can only be effective in certain situations and with certain people. The complete manager is one who uses (normally) a supportive, participative approach but who can use any style effectively in the right situation.

5.19 In his books *New Patterns of Management* and *The Human Organisation* Likert attempted through research to answer the question 'what do effective managers have in common?' His research showed that four main elements are normally present in effective managers.

(a) *They expect high levels of performance*. Their standards and targets are high and apply overall, not only to their subordinates' performance, but also to other departments and their own personal performance.

(b) *They are employee-centred*. They spend time getting to know their workers and develop a situation of trust whereby their employees feel able to bring their problems to them. When necessary, their actions can be hard but fair, akin to the actions of a fond and responsible parent. Such managers are typified by their ability to face unpleasant facts in a constructive manner and help their staff to grow and develop a similar constructive attitude.

(c) *They do not practise close supervision*. The truly effective manager is aware of the performance levels that can be expected from each individual, and has helped them to define their own targets. Once this has been achieved, the manager judges results and does not closely supervise the actions of his or her staff. Thus the manager not only develops his or her people, but is also free to spend more time on other aspects of the job (for example, planning decisions, communications with other areas and personnel problems).

(d) *They operate the participative style of management as a natural style*. This means that if a job problem arises they do not impose a favoured solution. Instead, they pose the problem and ask the staff member involved to find the best solution. Having then agreed their solution the participative manager would assist his staff in implementing it.

5.20 Likert emphasises that all four features must be present for a manager to be truly effective. For example, if a manager is employee-centred, if he delegates and is participative, then he will have a happy working environment but he will not produce a high performance unless he also establishes high standards of performance. A manager's concern for people must be matched by his concern for achieving results. This linking of the human relations approach with scientific management targets will provide the recipe for real effective performance.

It is important to remember that management techniques such as time and motion study, financial controls etc are used by high producing managers 'at least as completely as by the low producing managers, but in quite different ways.' The different application is caused by a better understanding of the motivations of human behaviour.

5.21 Likert's research showed that, on the whole:

(a) supervisors with the best performance were those who concentrated their main efforts on the human aspects of their staff's problems and attempted to build work groups with high performance standards;

(b) supervisors with poor performance spent more time in ensuring that their staff were busily employed in fulfilling specified stages of work;

(c) the participative, supportive supervisor who was transferred to a low-production unit was able to raise the performance at a fast rate.

Likert's conclusion was that the style of supervision is more important in achieving better results than any more general factors such as job interest, loyalty towards the company etc.

Blake's grid

5.22 The writings of the human relations school (McGregor etc) tended to obscure the 'task' element of a manager's responsibilities. By emphasising style of direction and the importance of human relations, it is all too easy to forget that a manager is primarily responsible for ensuring that tasks are done efficiently and effectively.

5.23 Robert R Blake and Jane S Mouton designed the management grid (1964). It is based on two fundamental ingredients of managerial behaviour, namely:

(a) concern for production or the 'task'; and
(b) concern for people.

5.24 The results of their work were published under the heading of 'Ohio State Leadership Studies', but are now commonly referred to as Blake's grid.

Blake's grid

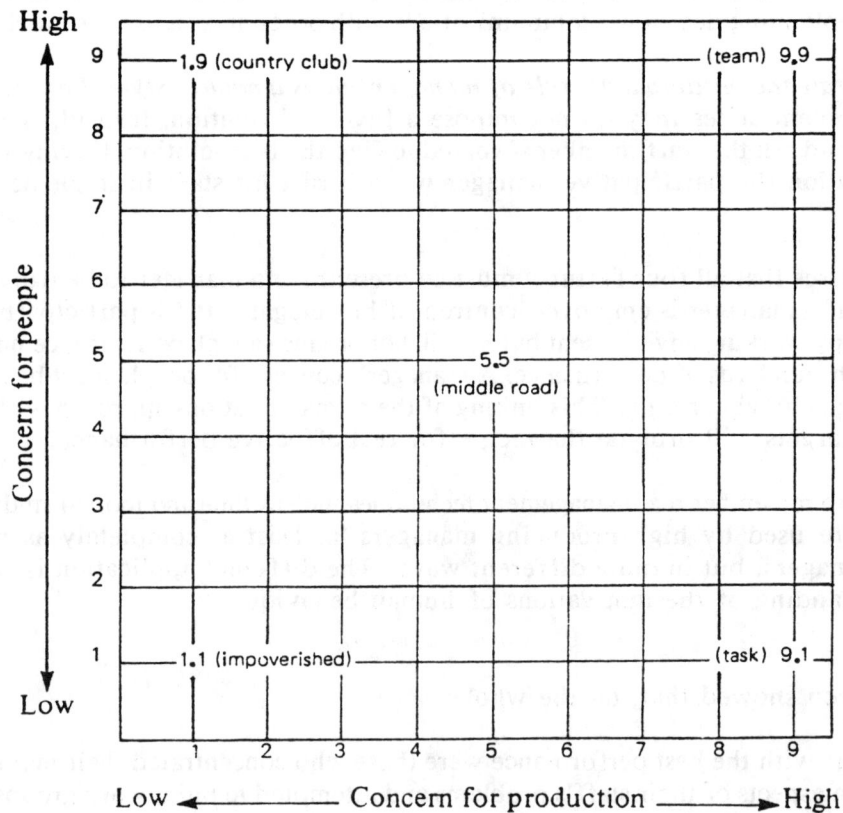

5.25 The extreme cases shown on the grid are defined by Blake as being the following.

    (a) 1.1 *impoverished*: manager is lazy, showing little effort or concern either for staff or work targets.

    (b) 1.9 *country club*: manager is attentive to staff needs and has developed satisfying relationships. However, there is little attention paid to achieving results.

    (c) 9.1 *task management*: almost total concentration on achieving results. People's needs are virtually ignored and conditions of work are so arranged that people cannot interfere to any significant extent.

    (d) 5.5 *middle of the road or the dampened pendulum*: adequate performance through balancing the necessity to get out work while maintaining morale of people at a satisfactory level.

    (e) 9.9 *team*: high performance manager who achieves high work accomplishment through 'leading' committed people who identify themselves with the organisational aims.

5.26 It is worth being clear in your own mind about the possible usefulness of Blake's grid. Its primary value is obtained from the appraisal of a manager's performance, either by the manager himself or by his superiors. The ideal manager is a 9.9 man or woman with high concern for both production and people. An individual manager can be placed on the grid, and his position on the grid should help him to see how his performance as a leader and a manager can be improved. For example, a manager rated 3.8 has further to go in showing concern for the task itself than for developing the work of his subordinates.

5.27 You should also be aware that Blake's grid is based on the assumption that concern for production and concern for people are not incompatible with each other. In this respect, Blake and Mouton accept the Theory Y view of leadership style.

A systems approach to leadership

5.28 Systems theory is concerned with the complex inter-relationships between the many different parts of a system (organisation), and the effect of the environment on the system (and vice versa). Katz and Kahn have developed ideas on how leadership can contribute to the better functioning of a system.

5.29 Early research by Katz and Kahn (reported in 1951) into the effect of leadership style on productivity suggested that there were three aspects of leader behaviour which affected productivity:

    (a) assumption of the leadership role;
    (b) closeness of supervision; and
    (c) degree of employee-orientation.

5.30 Comparisons were made between high-productivity and low-productivity groups.

    (a) In the most efficient groups the supervisor assumed the leadership role and used his supervisory talents to get the best out of the group. He realised that the leader has special functions and cannot therefore behave as an ordinary group member (be 'one of the boys'). In large organisations the assumption of the supervisory role is often made easier by transferring staff on promotion so that they can make a fresh start among strangers.

(b) Supervision was closer in low-production than in high-production groups. Workers expect to have some control over the means by which they perform a set task, and they resent having means specified in too much detail. Supervisory behaviour was found to reflect management leadership styles, so the organisational context affects leadership.

(c) Studies of the attitudes held by supervisors towards their subordinates revealed that the men in charge of high-production groups were more employee-oriented (intent on promoting their welfare). In the research experiment, the attitudes of a manager were gauged by asking subordinates to rate bosses; results showed that the efficient bosses were seen by their subordinates to be more *considerate*.

5.31 Katz and Kahn have since developed their ideas and have suggested that the reason why the most effective managers show consideration and understanding towards their subordinates is because they supplement their formal position in the organisation and appreciate that their employees:

(a) have interests and roles outside their job;

(b) are subject to pressures and influences from their external environment;

(c) need information to do their job with greater understanding; and

(d) need to be guided in the dynamic, changing organisation, and to understand the significance of change.

5.32 Good leaders show a true awareness that organisations are 'open' systems, reacting to and changing with their environment, of which their subordinates are also a part. Leaders influence those aspects of their subordinates' interests, energies and drive which cannot be harnessed by simple organisation structure, job definitions, or more formal management techniques.

A contingency approach to leadership

5.33 A contingency approach to leadership is one which argues that the ability of a manager to be a leader, and to influence his subordinate work group, depends on the particular situation, and will vary from case to case. Factors which vary in different situations are:

(a) the personality of the leader
(b) his leadership style
(c) the nature of the group's tasks
(d) the nature and personality of the work group and its individual members
(e) conditions of work, and
(f) 'external environmental' factors.

Handy's 'best fit' approach

5.34 Charles Handy has suggested a contingency approach to leadership. The factors in any situation which contribute to a leader's effectiveness are:

(a) the leader's personality, character and preferred style of operating;

(b) the subordinates' individual and collective personalities, and their preference for a style of leadership;

(c) the task: the objectives of the job, the technology of the job, methods of working etc; and

(d) the environment.

Essentially, Handy argues that the most effective style of leadership in any particular situation is one which brings the first three factors - a leader, subordinates and task - into a 'best fit'. For each of the three factors, a spectrum can be drawn ranging from 'tight' to 'flexible'.

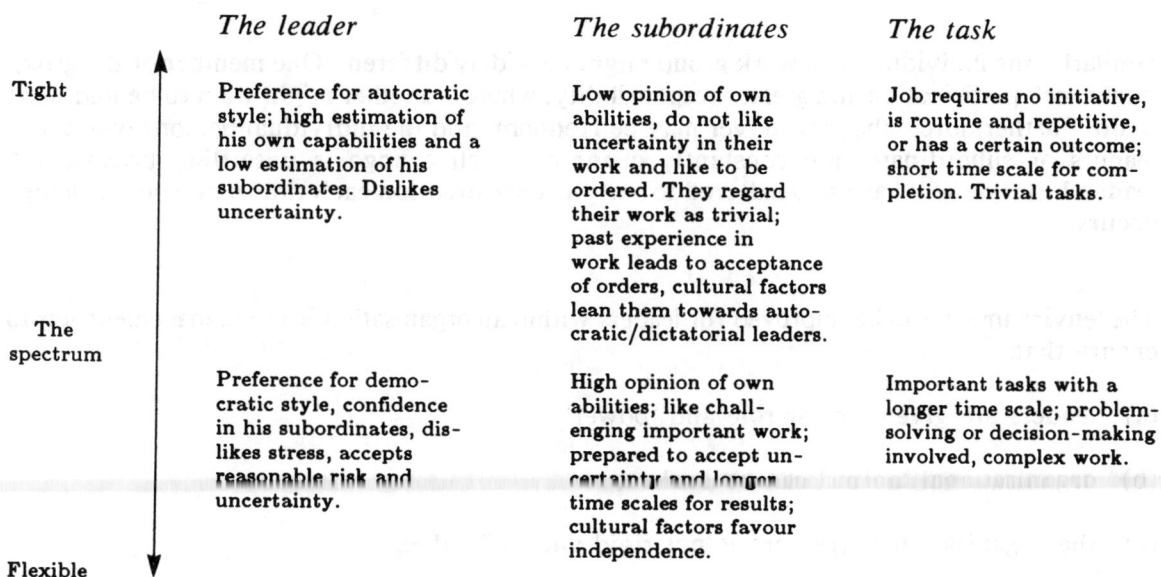

	The leader	The subordinates	The task
Tight	Preference for autocratic style; high estimation of his own capabilities and a low estimation of his subordinates. Dislikes uncertainty.	Low opinion of own abilities, do not like uncertainty in their work and like to be ordered. They regard their work as trivial; past experience in work leads to acceptance of orders, cultural factors lean them towards auto-cratic/dictatorial leaders.	Job requires no initiative, is routine and repetitive, or has a certain outcome; short time scale for com-pletion. Trivial tasks.
The spectrum			
	Preference for demo-cratic style, confidence in his subordinates, dis-likes stress, accepts reasonable risk and uncertainty.	High opinion of own abilities; like chall-enging important work; prepared to accept un-certainty and longer time scales for results; cultural factors favour independence.	Important tasks with a longer time scale; problem-solving or decision-making involved, complex work.
Flexible			

5.35 A best fit occurs when all three factors are on the same level in the spectrum. In practice, there is likely to be a misfit. Confronted with a lack of fit, the leader must decide which factor(s) should be changed to bring all three into line. The factor over which a leader has most influence is himself and his style; hence, Handy argues, the great emphasis on 'leadership style' in management literature. However, although the leader's style is theoretically the easiest to alter in the short term, there are often long-term benefits to be achieved from re-defining the task (eg job enlargement) or from developing the work group.

5.36 The fourth factor identified by Handy in the situational jig-saw is the *environment*.

(a) *The position of 'power' held by the leader in the organisation and the relationship of the leader and his group*. Power might be a position of authority but it might also be the expertise or the charisma of the leader. A person with great power has a bigger capacity to set his own style of leadership, select his own subordinates and re-define the task of his work group.

(b) *Organisational 'norms' and the structure and technology of the organisation.* No manager can flout convention and act in a manner which is contrary to the customs and standards of the organisation. If the organisation has a history of autocratic leadership, it will be difficult to introduce a new style. If the formal organisation is highly centralised, there will be limits to how far a task can be re-structured by an individual manager. In mass-production industries where routine, repetitive work is in-built into the production technology, challenging tasks will be difficult to create, and leadership will tend, perforce, to be autocratic.

(c) *The variety of tasks and the variety of subordinates.* If the tasks of a work group are simple, few in number and repetitive, the best style of leadership will be different from a situation in which tasks are varied and difficult. In many groups, however, tasks vary from routine and simple, to complex 'one-off' problem-solving. Managing such work is complicated by this variety.

5.37 Similarly, the individuals in a work group might be widely different. One member of the group might seek participation and greater responsibility, whereas another might want to be told what to do. Furthermore, labour turnover may be frequent, and the individual persons who act as leaders or subordinates are constantly changing; such change is unsettling because the leadership style will have to be altered to suit the new situation each time a personnel change occurs.

5.38 The 'environment' can be improved for leaders within an organisation if top management acts to ensure that:

(a) leaders are given a clear role and 'power';

(b) organisational 'norms' can be broken;

(c) the organisational structure is not rigid and inflexible;

(d) subordinates in a work group are all of the same quality or type;

(e) labour turnover is reduced, especially by keeping managers in their job for a reasonably lengthy period of time.

Exercise

From your experience at work, or in some other structured area of your life, how would you assess whether people in charge of your activities were leaders as opposed to managers. Where would you place your superiors on Blake's grid, for example, and why?

---

6. CONCLUSION

6.1 'Policy' arises both from conscious direction and from ad hoc decisions made 'on the hoof'.

6.2   As a lot of management time is spent in short 'ad hoc' situations, so much policy development often reflects this fact.

6.3   Policy is often made by negotiation with, and the satisfaction of, a wide range of interests. The rational model of decision making is flawed as it ignores the social, political and cultural context of decision making.

6.4   There are a number of sources of power in the organisation. To exercise leadership skills requires the tapping of many of these sources.

TEST YOUR KNOWLEDGE
The numbers in brackets refer to paragraphs of this chapter

1   How are priorities of NHS resources worked out? (1.21)

2   What are problems in taking decisions? (2.12)

3   What are the roles of the chief executive of a local authority? (4.4)

4   Distinguish trait theories from style theories of leadership. (5.4, 5.6)

Now try question 11 at the end of the text

Chapter 12

STRATEGIC MANAGEMENT

This chapter covers the following topics.

1. The elements of strategic management
2. Strategic planning
3. Implementation
4. Marketing and the public sector
5. Monitoring and performance review

---

1. THE ELEMENTS OF STRATEGIC MANAGEMENT

1.1 Strategic management involves:

(a) taking a long term view on current activities;
(b) acting in the light of the strategic plan.

1.2 One model of strategic management, provided by Johnson and Scholes gives three main elements.

(a) Strategic analysis (covering the external environment, the resources available, and the objectives of those leading the organisation).

(b) Strategic choice (including generating alternative strategies and selecting the Eight ones).

(c) Strategy implementation (involves planning the resources available).

Environmental monitoring

1.3 Environmental *attitudes* can be monitored by surveys of opinion. As an example, surveys conducted during the Widdicombe report revealed that 90% of those surveyed believed that local authorities had a role in providing housing, in contrast to government policies which reduced that role. There are three possible responses.

(a) You can simply 'follow' public opinion.
(b) You can implement the policy anyway in the hope that people will come round to it.
(c) You can make strenuous efforts to convince people of the merits of the new policy.

1.4 Environmental monitoring, as has been mentioned already includes paying attention to:

(a) relevant economic factors directly affecting current performance;
(b) future economic factors (eg trends);
(c) long term and short term political strategies.

1.5 Strategic management also involves marrying the resources currently available, or those anticipated to be available, with the demands of the external environment, or trends within it. For example:

(a) there is a change in the age structure of the population, so the work of a strategic management is to develop the appropriate personnel practices to deal with it;

(b) resources, too, can change. New forms of treatment or new attitudes may encourage a shift to preventative medicine.

1.6 The other problem for many organisations is knowing 'where they are' at the moment and in which direction they are going. The organisation cannot stop functioning while the strategic analysis is undertaken. The fundamental questions may be the most difficult to answer.

(a) What are we currently doing?
(b) What is it costing?
(c) What effect is it having?

1.7 Having established the present position of the organisation and identified the key variables for the operation of the organisation, then another set of questions become appropriate.

(a) Where do we want to go?
(b) What is the vision for the future?
(c) How are we going to get there? (Strategy)
(d) What is the plan of action? (Resources)
(e) How do we know we are on the right course? (Monitoring and Evaluation)
(f) How can we keep on the right course? (Decision processes)

2. STRATEGIC PLANNING

Position audit

2.1 The first step in preparing a strategic plan is to carry out a *position audit* or situation audit. The results have to be related to the objectives and any mission statement for the organisation. As well as an audit of markets or activities, and the profits and costs associated with existing operations, it may be appropriate to introduce databases and information systems that cover financial management. The use and development of information technology and the application of computer use has now to be part of the situation audit. A review of resources will be expected to cover both *physical assets* and *staff skills* and motivation.

2.2 An analysis of how the organisation arrived at its current position is also necessary. The *critical strategic factors* in the management process, which produced one type of outcome rather than another, need to be identified. The organisational structure and communications are a vital part of the analysis of the management arrangements. This can be an extension of value for money studies. Audits of management arrangement and the use of organisation fitness tests, (the type you tried in Chapter 1) can assist in this type of critical review.

2.3 *Intangible resources* may also be relevant (the level of goodwill, how the organisation is seen by rival organisations, how customers feel about how it goes about its business, how staff feel about working for such an organisation). This 'feel' for the organisation can include issues which may be difficult to quantify, such as the state of the buildings used by the organisation, the reception one gets on first arrival, the literature it produces. All these provide clues on the culture of the organisation.

SWOT analysis

2.4 Secondly, forecasts have to be made of changes in the key variables which have been identified as significant for the operation of the organisation. These may be quantifiable or intangible (attitudes to change, and keeping in touch with changing consumer demand). In identifying how the key variables relate to each other, an analysis can be carried out.

    (a)   The organisation's Strengths
    (b)   The organisation's Weaknesses
    (c)   The prospective Opportunities
    (d)   The prospective Threats.

2.5 SWOT appraisal covering internal and external issues can be brought together.

A model for a Polytechnic 'university' might include at the present time.

Strengths	*Weaknesses*
Physical assets	Need to maintain and provide new buildings
Number and quality of courses	Ability to adapt to consumer demands
Expertise and staff quality	Ageing staff profile, attract new specialist staff
High application levels	Marketing and public relations
Low costs per student	

Threats	*Opportunities*
Overcrowding: growing too fast for capacity of facilities	Franchising courses Distance learning Fast track two year courses
Other competitive institutions	Attracting more mature students
Government funding limitations	Raising finance from private sources, from Europe
Government policy	Education is an important political issue

2.6   A number of different strategies can be developed from this SWOT analysis for a Polytechnic, although it needs to be supported by more detailed audits and a review of the management processes in the particular institution.

(a)   A range of individual strategies might be developed to deal with opportunities (eg to raise additional finance, to make better use of existing resources through fast track two year and short courses).

(b)   Weaknesses which can be dealt with in the short term for little cost may also be tackled, such as marketing and public relations, staff recruitment and staff development.

(c)   The threats may be more difficult to deal with as they are more uncertain and long term in relation to external policy changes, but internal studies of the use of buildings, library arrangements, timetabling, term dates student placements, programming of short courses are all ways of dealing with the threat of overcrowding.

2.7   Forecasts of *student demand*, and the levels of demand in the post-qualification job market for graduates from different disciplines, are affected by professions and companies recruiting graduates, schools and educational advisory bodies, training organisations, the government and other funding agencies. Because of the complex levels of interaction between the interests concerned, the use of *scenario building* in developing ways of creative thinking may held in judging future patterns of demand.

2.8   A *scenario* is a 'model' of the future. Several scenarios are devised, incorporating varying assumptions (eg demand, interest rates). These can be compared to find the most appropriate policy. Scenarios can be developed by a review of currently held opinion through literature reviews and questionnaires of leading people in the area of forecasting. The experts may be brought together to test out their ideas. Forecasting models developed by one of the interested parties may be used as a starting point and current for short term funding allocations. Such analysis might reveal areas to which more attention must be given in terms of resources, lobbying for policy changes and so forth.

3.   IMPLEMENTATION

3.1   Strategic planning is sometimes a one off and expensive exercise which provides a framework for future actions, or it can be a more integral part of management and performance review. An overall set of strategic objectives can provide guidance for subdivisions of the organisation to produce their strategic plans. Strategy can be reviewed on a three to five year basis, with business plans and budget, or financial plans being prepared on an annual basis. Strategic planning then becomes part of the every day management process, in measuring performance against milestones of the strategy, and in the use of indicators to steer the immediate decisions back on the strategic course.

3.2   The purpose of the strategic plan can be seen to be as follows.

(a)   To interpret future research and scenarios, to identify key areas for strategic choice (eg introducing new technology like the electric car, to meet environmental controls which are expected to be introduced over the next decade for city traffic).

(b) To introduce a process of innovation and organisational change to achieve agreed goals (eg to research and develop materials for production of electric cars at a price and level of reliability which will meet demand in ten years time).

(c) To assess the interests of stakeholders in the future plans and be aware of the competitors' progress in the same field (developing an electric car, or cleaning up existing cars to meet the environmental controls must be done with an eye to competition).

(d) To be part of the central control system which establishes specific objectives and draws up action plans (eg produces timetables and budgets for producing the electric car and develops joint ventures with other companies and component producers so that the car is assembled on time and within budget).

3.3 The obstacles to strategic planning and strategic management are the unwillingness of people to move from entrenched positions.

(a) Senior management and operational management perhaps have the most to lose.

(b) Middle management is too busy trying to do the job, dealing with the next crisis that they have not got the time, energy or information to work strategically.

3.4 A number of features must be present for successful implementation.

(a) The plan should have something which can be done quickly and show results, but which also puts the organisation on a course for change.

(b) It needs agreement or understanding from all those involved about the direction in which the organisation is going and 'why' and, if possible, 'how' it will manage the process.

(c) The strategic process should be integrated with the budgetary process. The development of detailed business plans and schedules for implementing policy follow on from the strategic management plan.

3.5 Strategic management must be more than generating expensive plans concerned with historical rather than future trends. The 1970s saw a strategic planning vogue in local government town planning with the *Greater London Development Plan* and *Third London Airport plan* which had little impact on the 'real world'.

3.6 In fact, strategic thinking about the future for local government has come from such external bodies as the Institute of Economic Affairs and the Adam Smith Institute 'Omega Report' on local government although internal think tanks have declined in influence recently. The proposals set out by these think tanks have been put into practice over the last seven or eight years. The strategy being established for local government and the public sector in general, is being set by those *outside* the organisations concerned. This is quite unlike the private sector.

3.7 The new public management is concerned with performance review which can be used to identify needs for change and secure the better implementation of change rather than just measuring success against targets. The monitoring process is the element of the strategic management which is the most difficult to maintain but is the key to success.

3.8 In the private sector, the importance of strategic management is that it helps the organisation to survive, to maintain its position in the market and to grow and adapt to change. The financial backers, shareholders and particular institutional shareholders also take a view of the company's performance in its sector and they see how well the company is making plans for change. If they feel that environmental changes are meeting an inappropriate response, then support may be withdrawn from existing managers.

3.9 A private sector analogy for the public sector could describe central government as a holding company wanting to see returns on its investment and the companies in the group adapting to change and providing an effective set of services that customers want at least cost.

3.10 The use of assets and improved *asset management* has been a new strategic objective for the public sector. *Cost control* has been another factor which has been highlighted as part of strategic management. Pricing and full cost recovery has become an element of strategic management. The measurements of performance may not be comparable, such as profit as a percentage of sales, sales capital employed ratio, profit as a percentage of capital employed. Alternative measures, concerned with providing *added value*, might be appropriate and developing such measures in higher education is as important as performance indicators at the operational level (eg staff student ratios, research grants obtained).

3.11 In the private sector, the function of strategic management is to ensure the continuing health of the company's mix of products and business activities by 'positioning' the company, in other words by entering new areas of opportunity and by establishing corporate policy.

The growth in earnings per share that is required is the ultimate responsibility of top management and will be contributed to by both operating and strategic management, with the latter probably playing the preponderant role. This it will achieve by the continuous positioning of the company in the best product mix.

Strategic management is therefore seen as having three specific tasks.

(a) To see that the mix of products provides the optimum return on investment and stability commensurate with the company's strengths and weaknesses. New products can be identified for development, unsuccessful ones for withdrawal.

(b) To maximise the value of the shareholder's investment.

(c) To ensure that management skills are not excessively diluted by trying to do too much at once. It is better to do a few things well than many badly. The range of activities chosen for the future should be within the capacity of management, either existing or potential, and will of course be selected on a basis of mutual compatibility.

3.12   The strategic management process continuously evaluates change and the opportunities it brings in terms of established criteria. Rather than *specific* definitions of products or services, these will comprise a statement of corporate purpose and product rationale, the growth forces upon which to build, the emerging markets to serve and the growth technologies from which to benefit.

3.13   Successful corporate development is the result of separating the functions and responsibilities of *operating* and *strategic* management. The functions of the chief executive are to organise and staff the subordinate positions, to ensure that individual actions conform to long-term objectives and policies, and to act as a link with investors and external agencies. Subordinate levels of management would be allocated to the function that accords the closest with their talents and interests.

3.14   The strategic management process needs to establish a clear position as part of managing the efficiency and effectiveness of the operation of the organisation. This can be done through establishing action plans for departments to achieve the strategic objectives. This will require information systems and analytical skills in judging how well the organisation is doing in achieving the strategic objectives. The test may be the market place or institutional and government support.

4.   MARKETING AND THE PUBLIC SECTOR

4.1   Central government, in the promotion of policy, uses the media to market particular programmes (eg on the inner city when six ministers and the Prime Minister appeared on a platform to present the latest policies). Advertisements on job schemes, health warnings, privatisation issues are an example.

4.2   Marketing, the art (or science as some would have it) of anticipating customer needs and promoting products to satisfy them, exists in the public sector in several areas.

   (a)   Agencies marketing their services to central government.
   (b)   The NHS internal market.
   (c)   British Rail markets quite aggressively.
   (d)   Schools might market themselves on examination performance.

4.3   The *marketing of services* is inherently more difficult than the *marketing of products*. Services are consumed as they are created. Perhaps the purchaser/provider split, and the establishment of executive agencies not only allows the purchaser to set detailed performance targets, but might also encourage the growth of marketing culture in service providers.

4.4 There still remains inevitable differences between them. The table below draws upon distinctions make by Ransom (1988).

Factor	Private sector	Public sector
Decision-making agents	Individual choice (in market)	Collective choice (though representative institutions)
Decisions influenced by:	Demand, price	Resources, needs
Rights of access to decision making	Closed (ie private) interests	Open (ie public) interests
Rights of access to goods/services	Equity of the market	Equity of need
Criterion of success	Market satisfaction	Justice
Legitimation	Customer sovereignty	Citizenship
Getting things done	Competition as market instrument	Collective action as policy instrument
Motivator	Exist as the stimulus (a company might go out of business, so it is prodded to action)	Voice as the condition (ie public's expressions of concern, to bring a matter to policy maker's attention)

4.5 The public sector is criticised because consumers are trapped and have no choice. It is held that bureaucratic structure and the monopoly position of the state organisations prevents competition.

Quasi-markets have been introduced:

(a) to provide an element of choice for the consumers, who now need information on which to base their choice;

(b) to separate the purchaser from the provider;

(c) to establish performance standards to enable good performers to be rewarded (eg courses of a certain quality are given a subsidy of up to 20%);

(d) to enable management to search for low cost inputs and to manage resources more efficiently;

(e) to create exchange relationships between the purchaser and provider, so that the purchaser, still the central or local state, can exercise some choice about where the money is spent and can shift the monies to achieve value for money. A contractual relationship is thus created and a requirement for contract compliance mechanisms.

4.6 In some circumstances the availability of funding may mean rationing or even demarketing to reduce demand. If services are marketed the possibility that there will be endless demand which cannot be satisfied.

5. MONITORING AND PERFORMANCE REVIEW

5.1 The success of strategic management can be monitored through the business plan and the annual budget and performance review cycle, and in the internal and external auditing processes. Comparisons of actual outcomes against standard levels of performance and against similar organisations can also be useful.

5.2 Butt and Palmer provide a series of checklists for value for money audits which relate well to the strategic management approach. They identify a set of processes which flow from:

(a) an agreement of strategic objectives;
(b) to establishing priorities and agreeing budgets for set service levels;
(c) setting the targets and operational objectives in the annual plan;
(d) to agreeing performance measures and standards;
(e) setting up a rolling view programme.

The value for money audit is used to check this process.

An example of strategic management: the Benefits Agency

5.3 The Strategic Plan produced for the Social Security Benefits Agency identifies a strategic vision based upon the delivery of social security benefits, in a manner which meets customers' needs and achieves the best possible value for money. Details of how this will be measured include:

(a) a helpful public interface;
(b) faster query turnaround;
(c) fewer errors;
(d) a telephone information service;
(e) pleasant offices;
(f) improvements in technological back up for staff;
(g) more discretion for local managers;
(h) an efficient service to ministers;
(i) living within the budget.

All these are to be achieved from 1992 to 1997. This agency has nearly 70,000 staff and budgeted running costs of £1,575 million.

5.4 To realise this vision, four core operating values have been identified:

(a) customer service;
(b) caring for staff;
(c) bias for action;
(d) value for money.

5.5 Proposed changes in:

(a) technology;
(b) staffing;
(c) policy

are assessed for the impact they will have on the consumer of the service.

5.6 A set of targets or performance measures were determined for 1991/92 (eg times taken to deal with particular types of cases) and a customer satisfaction rate of 85% established. Other milestone targets have been set such as the introduction of an interim accruals accounting system and an asset register by 1 March 1992).

5.7 The strategic planning process should now 'cascade' down to the divisions. Strategic planning should be taken into account when resources are bid for. Strategic plans could be built up again into a rolling programme, which would feed into the Public Expenditure Survey rounds and become part of the overall review process of the government's social benefits policy.

5.8 The use and development of performance review in central government departments goes back to 1970 and the introduction of the Central Policy Review Staff and a system of scrutiny and action, *Programme Analysis and Review*. In 1979, Programme Analysis Review was replaced with another scheme from Lord Rayner (of Marks and Spencer), known as the *Rayner Scrutinies*. Their aim was to investigate specific policy areas and to identify those areas where money could be saved and effectiveness improved, with agreed solutions and timetables for achieving agreed levels of savings. Over a period of eight years, some 300 scrutiny exercises had generated savings of £1 billion.

5.9 Alongside this development of value for money studies and scrutinies grew up a whole range of output and performance measurement. This approach of performance review was initiated in the 1982 White Paper on Efficiency and Effectiveness in the Civil Service. The aims of the Financial Management Initiatives announced in the White paper were to:

'Promote in each department and organisation a system in which managers at all level have

(a) a clear view of their objectives, and means to assess and, wherever possible, measure outputs or performance in relation to those objectives;

(b) well defined responsibility for making the best use of their resources, including a critical scrutiny of output and value for money;

(c) the information (particularly about cost), the training and access to expert advice which they need to exercise their responsibilities effectively.'

5.10 In the private sector, the overriding objective is to make acceptable profits, and so the units in the company and individuals can be judged by their contribution to achieving profits. The contribution of personnel function, the research department and the finance department may be difficult to quantify other than as a cost. The same difficulties apply to much of the public sector.

5.11 The final piece of the process in central government has been to establish trading organisations or Executive Agencies in government departments: *Improving Management in Government: The Next Steps*. Each Executive Agency will be required to produce a strategic plan for the Agency within a framework document guidelines which sets out the business of the agency. The departments or subsections of the agency will also have to prepare strategic management schemes.

5.12 Strategic management plans are also being drawn up in other parts of the public sector, especially in health and education. This will be a way of negotiating contracts, raising investment finance and planning the operation of the organisation and demonstrating the use of resources to obtain the corporate and unit objectives.

Exercise

Draw up a SWOT analysis for the Arts and Libraries service of your local authority. (You may need to do a little research on this.)

---

6. CONCLUSION

6.1 Strategic management includes the development and implementation of strategic plans.

6.2 These plans have a distant time horizon, but the long term perspective must be kept in mind while operating decisions are being made.

6.3 Strategic plans are developed by public sector bodies the better to plan ahead. Strategic planning is likely to increase as more public sector organisations will exist in a quasi-market.

TEST YOUR KNOWLEDGE

The numbers in brackets refer to paragraphs of this chapter

1   What are the elements of strategic management? (1.2)

2   Describe SWOT analysis. (2.4, 2.5)

3   What are the purposes of a strategic plan? (3.2)

4   What factors differentiate the public and private sectors? (4.4)

Now try question 12 at the end of the text

Chapter 13

MANAGING FINANCIAL AND HUMAN RESOURCES

This chapter covers the following topics.

1. The role of finance specialists
2. Financial management
3. Managerial roles and effectiveness
4. Human resource management

---

1. THE ROLE OF FINANCE SPECIALISTS

1.1 Both the public and the private sectors depend on people, materials, the use of equipment, buildings and machinery. All this involves money. Monitoring the way the money is used in the organisation, its cash flow, how the money is raised used, the repayment of debts and investment decisions, are all part of the process.

1.2 In the private sector, the finance function is responsible for:

(a) maintaining accounts and records;
(b) internal financial control over budgets;
(c) payment systems;
(d) inventory control.

1.3 The economic position of the organisation may be studied by the finance section, with reports on:

(a) the economy of the market areas in which the organisation operates;
(b) international finance, and changing exchange rates;
(c) the political economy of different countries;
(d) taxation and controls over financial dealings in stocks and shares; and
(e) the presentation of accounts and accounting standards.

1.4 The finance section has always been involved in *information technology* with the use of computers to record the use of resources, payments, inventory control and analysis of business performance. Consequently, the control of computer communication, and audits of computer usage may come under finance management. The setting up and maintenance of accounting and other data systems, the purchase and development of computer hardware and software may also be part of the finance and the resource management function.

1.5   In the *private sector*, financial management is an integral part of the working of the organisation and actively assists in achieving profits, generating cash, chasing up payments, demonstrating earnings ratios and return on capital investment. Financial management is part of the central management function of the private organisation and part of the strategic and business planning activities. Finance directors are on the board of companies and are often appointed as chief executives.

1.6   In the *public sector* the finance management function has been mainly concerned with:

      (a)   setting budgets;
      (b)   creating accounting systems to record the expenditure of the organisation;
      (c)   internal audit (and seeing the procedures are followed for external audit checks).

Financial management is again concerned with information systems and control of the money flow within the organisation. Capital borrowing and debt repayments are established by the Treasury and supporting Ministries, and in negotiation on individual projects. However, money is still invested in the money markets and on short term deposit, the management of the organisation's debt repayments and borrowing, are important in controlling the flow of money.

1.7   The public sector provides some services free at the point of consumption. For others, fees are set by the government. Many public sector organisations rely on revenue payments from the Treasury, rather than the consumer. Public sector organisations then have to operate under externally imposed resource controls, and cannot set own prices for their services.

1.8   In service organisations, and especially in the public sector, the costs and benefits are the factors to be considered in providing the service. The effects of charging or setting a price for the service may reduce demand so it may be difficult in determining the service's worth.

The questions which have to be considered in financial management control are as follows.

      (a)   *What is the social benefit arising from the activity?*
           As services are intangible, it may be difficult to determine what the users get out of the service. The social benefit may be politically determined. Alternatively, economic methods can be used to *estimate* the value of the service (eg building new roads).

      (b)   *Which outcome indicators are best for demonstrating the social relevance of the organisation's activity?*
           In services production and consumption are inseparable. Services are expected to meet agreed targets which have been defined in advance.

      (c)   *Which output indicators are best for specifying the volume of activity within the organisation? (ie how much service is to be provided, and how can this be measured)?*
           Services may have to be rationed, using waiting lists or means testing. The capacity constraints on the service may be a way of rationing. (*Marginal* improvements in capacity may be limited. The addition of new capacity may require large blocks of capital investment (a new school or hospital) and a commensurate increase in revenue expenditure.) An example could specify the number of eye operations done per day.

(d) *Which input indicators are best for monitoring the utilisation of resources?*
The service may depend on an individual officer, their competence, courtesy, work load, the particular work situation, previous investment, staff recruitment and training and human resource management. Any simple indicator might miss some of the main issues.

(e) *How do these resources use indicators get translated into costs?*
The problem is of finding standards of performance for comparative study, manday costs of the service are one way to set a time and a cost for providing a service.

1.9 Finance specialists are generally employees of organisations. They prepare the budgets and provide the financial analysis and advice for the corporate planning process, record and monitor the flow and use of money in the organisation. Finance specialists will also work for accountancy and management consultants, for tax consultants, for merchant banks, commercial banks and building societies. In government, finance specialists will be found in the Treasury, Inland Revenue, national Audit Office, HM Customs & Excise, the Department of Trade and Industry, the Department of the Environment, Offices of Fair Trading and in every Ministry. Finance specialists can also be found in regulatory bodies such as the Audit Commission and Small Claims Court.

1.10 The government schemes of privatisation and the creation of Next Steps Agencies and the setting up of trust hospitals have all required a chance in public approaches to accountancy. Greater freedom for internal management has often meant more devolved financial management. The *management* of assets, the split between capital and revenue and the use of capital receipts and depreciation have all become more important as the organisations have had to prepare 'stand alone' accounts.

1.11 Strategic and business plans have been drawn up for these new trading organisations. Some of these plans must be developed for the privatised utilities. Financial advice on diversification on acquisitions have been important for the new privatised businesses. Taxation strategies now has to be considered.

1.12 In the Health Service and local government work on compulsory competitive tendering and the separation of client and customer and contractor has meant that input costs and outputs requirements must be known in drawing up the contract specifications. Financial assessments of assets, working capital and labour force costs have had to be considered in relation to specific areas of work. If the services are won in-house then it is necessary to prove the services offered are provided at a good price in manday costs and that the required quality, reliability, and return on capital assets is achievable. Contract management and decentralised service provision will require reporting mechanisms to maintain central control, and control process audits.

2. FINANCIAL MANAGEMENT

2.1 The objectives of financial management are:

(a) to find ways of allocating the resources available;

(b) to provide the financial information and advice on the organisation's overall strategic goals;

(c) to provide information and critical analysis of current performance and advising on how the operations could be improved;

(d) to ensure the effective use and control of the available resources;

(e) to provide information for the Board or the Council, shareholders, external auditors, the Inland Revenue and HM Customs & Excise;

(f) to provide information to employees;

(g) to see that the organisation is run with probity and that accounting standards are followed. In the public sector this may imply compliance with some statutory reporting or accounting obligations.

2.2 Financial managers have a number of duties.

(a) *Management duties*

(i) Produce the section or department's own strategy, business plan and work schedules. Maintain by the staff and working resources of the section or department.

(ii) Control the work activity so that the services can be provided as required and within acceptable costs. If financial services are to be opened up to competition and contracting out, then the costs and quality of service have to be defined.

(iii) Participate in the wider management team, or chief officer's board, advising on economic and financial issues.

(iv) Maintain external relations and public relations in relation to finance issues, such as explaining the council tax.

(v) Control flows of information for monthly, quarterly reviews within set times for having the work completed.

(vi) Ensure information is available at the required time, for annual reports, external audit, tax returns, the budget cycle.

(b) *Accountancy duties*

(i) Being responsible for accounting systems and accounting records and related computer systems and paper records.

(ii) Carrying out value for money audits.

(iii) Providing an advice function on processes and methods in accounting to service department heads, devolved managers and contract supervisors.

(iv) Preparing the budget and negotiating the budget presentation.

(v) Preparing the annual statement and comparative statistics.

(vi)   Preparing other company reports.

(vii) Carrying out the internal audit function.

(viii) Providing reliable information to users which can be used for basing decisions.

(c) *Investment duties*

    (i)   Advising on investment decisions and risks involved, timing, pay back periods, alternative means of funding.

    (ii)   Advising on acquisitions and mergers and disposal of assets.

    (iii) Advising on the investment outside the organisation.

    (iv) Advising on the use of pension funds.

    (v)   Securing long term capital investment or permanent shareholding capital.

    (vi) Securing short term loans.

    (vii) Negotiating with banks, insurance and pension investors, with quasi-government bodies like 3i (Investors in Industry), development agencies, the European Commission, European loans.

    (viii) Negotiating and bidding for funding, capital credits, supplementary grants for transport, urban programme, city grants, with government departments for development projects in local government.

    (ix) Advice on property portfolios and economic development

    (x)   The use of monies to invest before final payments or transfer.

(d) *Security duties*

    (i)   Security of cash and receipts.

    (ii)   Inventories and control of equipment.

    (iii) Stock records and control and procedures for keeping records.

    (iv) Computer control to limit fraud, control of access to certain data.

    (v)   Overseeing centres for covering costs, revenues, profits and other centres of financial responsibility.

(e) *Payroll and payment duties*

    (i)   Cash flow.

    (ii)   Paying invoices.

(iii) Staff payments, tax and superannuation deductions.

(iv) Community charge collection or local taxes.

(v) Maintaining a collection account.

(vi) Payment of contractors for capital works.

(f) *Other duties*

(i) Reporting to the Finance Committee, finance directors or the board.

(ii) Producing annual reports.

(iii) Legal duties on probity.

(iv) Training for new legislation on community charge and council tax, general training of staff in being familiar with procedures.

(v) Training for accountancy professions, updating of professionally qualified staff.

2.3 The financial specialist in that capacity might have relevant professional interests outside the organisation. Such interests and the activities related to them can include the following.

(a) The development of professional practice standards.

(b) In institutions representing the profession, learned bodies and associations of local authorities, or trade associations, or Chambers of Commerce.

(c) Taking part in setting cash limits and rules of procedure in consultative committees on local government finance with the Department of the Environment.

(d) Continuing professional development and updating practice knowledge.

(e) Working with partners on financial support of schemes.

(f) Representing the authority on other bodies (eg in economic development funds).

(g) As member of European lobby groups to promote the organisation's interests.

(h) Being aware of City and money markets and investment of surplus funds.

(i) Keeping up to date with insurance and the insurance fund market.

(j) Seeing what the competitors are doing.

(k) Keeping up with computer packages which could be used by the organisation, and the development of computer and communications technology.

2.4 In local government, the director of finance acts as the legal head of the service. He or she provides financial information and analyses of the financial consequences of the organisation's major decisions.

2.5 A director of finance is responsible for the availability of resources for medium and long term projects, and the capital and revenue implications of any proposed changes in the function and operation of the organisation (eg privatisation, management buy out, the setting up of partnerships, new legislation, European funding for economic development, physical development projects). Other roles include:

(a) setting the costs of existing services, and looking for reductions;

(b) identifying the savings which could be made from rationalisation of services, creating service cost centres, decentralising, advising on financial management organisational structures;

(c) managing the timing of resource availability and the impact on borrowing and capital debt charges;

(d) as a member of the management team advising on financial aspects of management decisions;

(e) advising elected members (eg of the authority) on the budget and on the financial implications of any particular action they may propose.

The role of the Treasury in financial management

2.6 Treasury organisation covers the economic service, public expenditure, finance, economic responsibility for forecast and analysis and medium term policy and with public expenditure on public enterprises.

2.7 The Treasury provides advice on how to carry out some tasks. Sources of advice include the following.

(a) The Treasury Green Book (on economic appraisal, raising rates of return in public sector from 5% to 8% in real terms, details expected earnings from nationalised industries).

(b) Economic appraisals in central government: a technical guide (April 1991).

(c) Discount rates of return in the public sector: economic issues (Treasury Working paper 58).

(d) Expenditure appraisal in central government: Treasury Bulletin (Winter 1990/91).

2.8 The *National Audit Commission* oversees government expenditure and reports on the way the government funds have been spent. Special audits have reviewed particular policy areas (inner cities, regional policy, privatisation) and have been critical of the government's financial management in some of these areas.

3. MANAGERIAL ROLES AND EFFECTIVENESS

Managerial roles

3.1 Mintzberg defines ten roles for the manager, which are grouped under three headings: interpersonal roles, information roles and decision roles. We have briefly discussed these already, but just to recap, they are as follows.

(a) *Interpersonal*

  (i) *Figurehead role:* as a symbol of the organisation representing the organisation on formal occasions, signing documents, being available to those who want the boss.

  (ii) *Leader role:* the authority of the post to make certain levels of decision to provide guidance for others and to take critical decisions.

  (iii) *Liaison role:* linking with others at the same level, making and maintaining contacts with the external environment.

(b) *Informational*

  (i) *Monitor role:* seeking and obtaining information which enables the manager to understand the operation of the organisation in its environment.

  (ii) *Disseminator role:* this entails the transmitting of information from the external environment into the internal environment.

  (iii) *Spokesperson role:* this involves transmitting information more formally to the media, to the public, to the board, to inspector or investigatory bodies.

(c) *Decisional*

  (i) *Entrepreneurial role:* to initiate and plan controlled change and taking action to improve the existing situation and solve problems.

  (ii) *Disturbance handler:* this means dealing with unpredictable events and requires the manager to calm the situation down.

  (iii) *Resource allocator:* making choices on the allocation of resources such as money, materials and manpower, deciding on a programme of work and deadlines to be met.

  (iv) *Negotiator role:* to negotiate with individuals or organisations and make agreements on actions to be taken.

In practice these roles are seen to overlap and are part of the reasons why organisations need managers, to negotiate, to sort out disturbance problems and allocate resources in relation to the information being received.

Managerial effectiveness

3.2 A clear distinction has grown up between 'efficiency' and 'effectiveness'. Efficiency is concerned with how the work is done and how the resources are managed to achieve the objectives of the organisation. Efficiency is about measuring the inputs and used to achieve the given outputs. Effectiveness is concerned with the outcomes, with what has been achieved. Managerial effectiveness is seen by Drucker as 'doing the right things'. Drucker is concerned with how managers do the job, the management of their time, making a contribution to the development of the organisation, being able to prioritise work activities, exercise judgement and work well with other people.

3.3 Measuring effectiveness can cover the following.

   (a) Time taken to carry out tasks.
   (b) Errors or mistakes in the work.
   (c) Complaints from customers or suppliers or other departments.
   (d) Organising work and maintaining productivity.
   (e) Keeping within budget.
   (f) Response time to changes in objectives.
   (g) Morale of staff.
   (h) Development of staff.
   (i) Work record of staff, timekeeping, absences, sickness.
   (j) Staff recruitment and retention.
   (k) Making critical decisions.
   (l) Innovation in working practices.
   (m) Contribution to strategic management.
   (n) Own development.

3.4 In the public sector the cost of the workforce can be 60% of the costs of the organisation. The most important resource of the organisation is the people it employs. This means that the *financial resource management* has to be linked with *personnel management*.

3.5 Without competent and well motivated people at all levels, the organisation will either pursue inappropriate or unreachable goals or find it difficult to operate effectively. Together with financial management, the effective management of people come before the details of operation management in achieving the goals of the organisation.

3.6 A measure of effectiveness is how well the manager can balance the achievement of objectives, with dealing with the people they have to manage. These relationships have been mapped by *Blake and Mouton* in *the Managerial Grid* which we discussed in an earlier chapter.

3.7 Organisations are training managers to develop the attitudes and working practices identified with the *team manager* (ie position g.g on Blake's grid). The training programmes have used a case study group working approach to develop these team and sharing skills. The identification and training in competencies can also be seen to have grown out of this behaviouristic approach to the role of the manager and managerial effectiveness.

3.8   To recap, management competencies can be stated to include the following.

(a) *Dealing with people:*

(i)   those for whom one has responsibility;
(ii)   peers;
(iii) those to whom one reports;
(iv)   clients, customers and citizens.

(b) *Managing activities:*

(i)   financial activities;
(ii)   system control;
(iii) techniques;
(iv)   functional activities.

(c) *Sensitivity to the environment:*

(i)   the political world;
(ii)   customer expectations/needs;
(iii) legal considerations;
(iv)   organisational, social, economic and technological change.

(d) *Personal effectiveness:*

(i)   communication;
(ii)   numeracy and the use of numerical techniques;
(iii) people orientation;
(iv)   results orientation;
(v)   self awareness/development orientation.

Motivation

3.9   To be able to develop these competencies the people in the organisation have to be motivated to use them to for the goals of the organisation, which may differ from the goals of the individual. It is argued that if individuals can be motivated, they will work more efficiently (productivity will rise) and will produce a better quality product.

3.10   Motivation theories have been based on certain assumptions about human behaviour.

(a) *Satisfaction theories.* These theories are based on the assumption that a 'satisfied' worker will work harder, although there is little evidence to support the assumption. Satisfaction may reduce labour turnover and absenteeism, but will not necessarily increase individual productivity. Some theories hold that people work best within a compatible work group, or under a well-liked leader.

(b) *Incentive theories.* These theories are based on the assumption that individuals will work harder in order to obtain a desired reward - this is positive reinforcement, although most studies are concentrated on money as a motivator. Incentive theories *can* work, if:

    (i)   the individual perceives the increased reward to be worth the extra effort;

    (ii)   the performance can be measured and clearly attributed to that individual;

    (iii) the individual wants that particular kind of reward; and

    (iv) the increased performance will not become the new minimum standard.

    (c) *Intrinsic theories*. People will work hard in response to factors in the work itself - participation, responsibility etc: effective performance is its own reward.

3.11   Frederick Herzberg in his book *Work and the Nature of Man* (1966) identified the elements which cause job dissatisfaction (hygiene factors), and those which can cause job satisfaction (motivator factors). We have already touched on these.

Factors which cause dissatisfaction at work are:

(a)   company policy and administration;
(b)   salary;
(c)   the quality of supervision;
(d)   interpersonal relations;
(e)   working conditions;
(f)   job security.

He calls such factors *hygiene* or *maintenance* factors (because they are essentially preventative). They prevent or minimise dissatisfaction but do not give satisfaction, in the same way that sanitation minimises threats to health, but does not give 'good' health. They also have to be continually reviewed. Satisfaction with environmental factors is not lasting. In time dissatisfactions will occur.

3.12   The important point is that *motivation* through the above-mentioned factors is a necessary but thankless task. It is never-ending. Even if effective it will still not motivate the employee to work well (at a higher than usual level of performance) except for a short period of time.

On the other hand, if the environment is deficient in some way then the subordinates are likely to become annoyed and show their displeasure by industrial conflict, decreased productivity, grumbling etc. Yet if the deficiency is corrected the best that can be expected is that output/effort will return to 'normal'.

3.13   *Motivator factors* actively create job satisfaction and *are* effective in motivating an individual to superior performance and effort. These factors consist of:

(a)   status (although this may be a hygiene factor as well as a motivator factor);
(b)   advancement;
(c)   gaining recognition;
(d)   being given responsibility;
(e)   challenging work;
(f)   achievement;
(g)   growth in the job.

3.14 Herzberg saw two separate 'need systems' of individuals.

(a) There is a need to *avoid unpleasantness*. This need is satisfied at work by hygiene factors. Hygiene satisfactions are short-lived; individuals come back for more, in the nature of drug addicts.

(b) There is a need for personal growth, which is satisfied by motivator factors, and not by hygiene factors.

A lack of motivators at work will encourage employees to concentrate on bad hygiene (real or imagined) such as to demand more pay. Some individuals are not mature enough to want personal growth; these are 'hygiene seekers' because they can only ever be satisfied by hygiene factors.

The job as motivator

3.15 The job itself can be interesting and 'exciting'. It can satisfy the desire for a feeling of 'accomplishing something', for responsibility, for professional recognition, for advancement and so on, and the need for self-esteem.

3.16 'Dissatisfaction arises from environment factors - satisfaction can only arise from the job.' (Herzberg).

If there is sufficient challenge, scope and interest in the job, there will be a lasting increase in satisfaction and the employee will work well; productivity will be above 'normal' levels.

The extent to which a job must be challenging or creative to a motivator seeker will, in relation to each individual, depend on:

(a) ability; and
(b) tolerance for delayed success.

3.17 Herzberg suggested means by which motivator satisfactions could be supplied. Stemming from his fundamental division of motivator and hygiene factors, he encourages managers to study the job itself (the type of work done, the nature of tasks, levels of responsibility) rather than conditions of work. Only this way will motivation improve. (Concentrating on environmental factors will merely stave off job dissatisfaction.)

3.18 He specified three typical means whereby work can be revised to improve motivation. These are as follows.

(a) *Job enrichment:* this is the main method of improving job satisfaction and can be defined as 'the planned process of up-grading the responsibility, challenge and content of the work'. Typically, this would involve increasing delegation to provide more interesting work and problem-solving at lower levels within an organisation.

(b) *Job enlargement:* although often linked with job enrichment, it is a separate technique and is rather limited in its ability to improve staff motivation. Job enlargement is the process of increasing the number of operations in which a worker is engaged and so moving away from narrow specialisation of work. Herzberg tells us that this is more limited in value, since a man who is required to complete several tedious tasks is unlikely to be much more highly motivated than a man performing one continuous tedious task.

(c) *Job rotation:* this is the planned operation of a system whereby staff members exchange positions with the intention of breaking monotony in the work and providing fresh job challenge.

Expectancy theory

3.19 Expectancy theory states that the strength of an individual's motivation to do something will depend on the extent to which he *expects* the results of his efforts to contribute towards his personal needs or goals, to reward him or to punish him.

3.20 Put another way, expectancy theory states that people will decide how much they are going to put into their work, according:

(a) to what they perceive they are going to get out of it (expectancy);

(b) to the value that they place on this outcome (whether the positive value of a reward, or the negative value of a punishment) which Vroom called 'Valence'; and

(c) to the strength of their expectation that behaving in a certain way will in fact bring out the desired outcome (force of motivation).

$$\text{Expectancy} \times \text{Valence} = \text{Force of motivation.}$$

3.21 For the public sector, rewards have often been related to the post or position in the hierarchy and have not reflected effort. The hierarchical structure and national agreements on wage levels have meant rigid pay and organisational structures. The changes going on in the structure and operation of the public sector are hoping to improve flexibility of payment and performance rewards and so are aimed at changing workers' expectancy.

3.22 Charles Handy (*Understanding Organisations*) puts forward an 'admittedly theoretical' form of expectancy model.

Handy suggests that for any individual decision, there is a conscious or unconscious 'motivation calculus' which is an assessment of three factors:

(a) the individual's own set of needs;

(b) the desired results - what the individual is expected to do in his job;

(c) 'E' factors. Handy suggests that motivational theories have been too preoccupied with 'effort'. He notes that there seems to be a set of words, coincidentally beginning with 'e', that might be more helpful. As well as effort, there is energy, excitement in achieving desired results, enthusiasm, emotion, and expenditure (of time, money etc).

Handy's motivation calculus

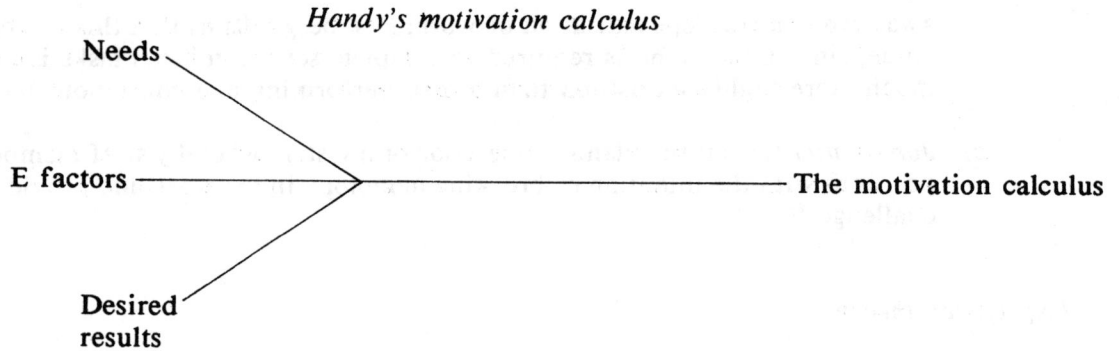

3.23 The 'motivation decision' – how strong the motivation to achieve the desired results will be – will depend on the individual person's judgement about:

(a) the strength of his needs;

(b) the *expectancy* that expending 'E' will lead to a desired result; and

(c) how far the result will be 'instrumental' in satisfying his needs.

> A man may have a high need for power. To the degree that he believes that a particular result, such as a completed task, will gain him promotion (expectancy) *and* that promotion will in fact satisfy his need for power ('instrumentality') he will expend 'E' on the task.

3.24 In terms of organisation practice, Handy suggests that several factors are necessary for the individual to complete the calculus, and to be motivated.

(a) *Intended results* should be made clear, so that the individual can complete his 'calculation', and know what is expected of him, what will be rewarded and how much 'E' it will take.

(b) Without knowledge of *actual results*, there is no check that the 'E' expenditure was justified (and will be justified in future). *Feedback* on performance – good or bad – is essential, not only for performance but for confidence, prevention of hostility etc.

3.25 Handy's calculus helps to explain various phenomena of individual behaviour at work.

(a) Individuals are more committed to specific goals – particularly those which they have helped to set themselves.

(b) If an individual is *rewarded* according to performance tied to standards ('management by objectives'), however, he may well set *lower* standards: the 'instrumentality' part of the calculus (likelihood of success and reward) is greater if the standard is lower, so less expense of 'E' is indicated.

Systems and contingency approaches to motivation

3.26 Stemming from the early research work of Elton Mayo, a systems and contingency approach to motivation has been developed by a number of writers, notably Kurt Lewin. A systems and contingency approach means that:

(a) the motivation of an individual cannot be seen in isolation. It depends on the system within which he operates, his work group and his environment;

(b) the motivation of the individual will also depend on circumstances. Different people react to the same environment in different ways, and a person's motivation is likely to vary from day to day, according to his mood, events at work and his fatigue as well as 'hygiene' and 'motivator' factors in his work.

3.27 Writing in 1938, Lewin developed his 'field theory' in which he compared an individual's environment to a magnetic field, with various forces in that field pulling him in different directions and affecting his attitudes from day to day. His formula for human behaviour was:

$B = (P,E)$ where

B is a person's behaviour, which depends on
P (the person himself/herself) and
E (his or her environment).

3.28 This means that an individual's motivation, varying over time, could be illustrated on a graph as follows:

Amount or degree of motivation of individual

Individual's motivation graph

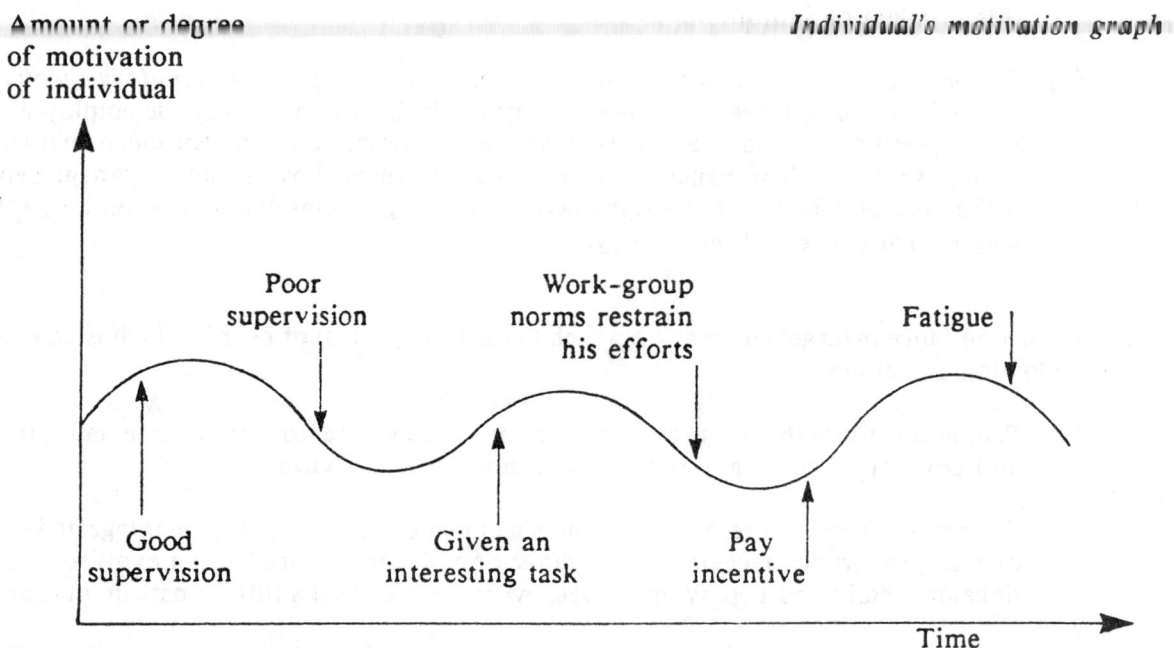

3.29 The systems and contingency school of thought is that if a manager wishes to improve the motivation of subordinates, he or she must take all the circumstances of the particular situation into account, being differences between individuals, the external environment, individuals' expectations, work groups, variations in circumstances from day to day or month to month etc.

3.30 Motivation is something which is complex and requires constant attention and be easily damaged. The balance of motivational factors inside and outside the workplace can be subject to many changes and shifts in emphasis.

4. HUMAN RESOURCE MANAGEMENT

4.1 Drucker (writing before Herzberg) suggested that motivation through 'employee satisfaction' is not a useful concept because employee satisfaction is such a wishy-washy idea. It doesn't mean anything in particular, and if it is to have some meaning, it must be defined more constructively. His suggestion was that employee satisfaction comes about through encouraging - if need be, by 'pushing' - employees to accept *responsibility*. There are four ingredients to this.

(a) *Careful placement of people in jobs.* The selection or recruitment process is an important one, because the person selected should see the job as one which provides a challenge to his abilities. There will be no motivation for a university graduate in the job of shop assistant, whereas the same job can provide a worthwhile challenge to someone of lesser academic training and intelligence.

(b) *High standards of performance in the job.* Targets for achievement should be challenging. However, they should not be imposed in an authoritarian way by the employee's bosses. Employees should be encouraged to expect high standards of performance from themselves.

(c) *Providing workers with the information they need to control their own performance.* The employee should receive routine information about his or her performance on the job, without having to be told by the boss. (The design of a reporting system is important in this respect.) Being told by a boss comes as a praise or reprimand, and the fear of reprimand will inhibit performance. Access to information as a routine matter overcomes this problem of inhibition.

(d) *Opportunities for participation in decisions that will give the employee managerial vision.* Participation means having some say and influence in the way the employee's work is organised and the targets for work are set. Participation does not mean that the boss relinquishes the job of managing the business! However, bosses should manage people to make them efficient; and managing people to manage themselves is a potentially valuable way of achieving such efficiency.

4.2 Human resource management is an approach to the management of people which is based on the following principles.

(a) People constitute the resource by which the inanimate factors of finance, land, property and equipment are converted into the delivery of services.

(b) Policies and practices regarding the management of people need to be integrated with the overall process of managing the organisation. Strategies need to be evolved to obtain, develop, retain and deploy employees with the required skills across the organisation.

(c) Leadership and motivation is a task for all managers. No jobs are self-contained. They all interact.

Personnel planning

4.3 Compared to machines, materials and money, labour is a relatively unpredictable and uncontrollable resource for a number of reasons.

(a) Environmental factors such a government decisions or the state of the markets create uncertainties in the *demand* for labour, whereas other factors (such as education or the demands of competitors for labour) create uncertainties in the *supply* of labour.

(b) Employees as individuals may have their own personal goals, and make their own decisions about, for example, whether to leave the organisation, whether to co-operate with management strategies and whether to undertake further training. When large numbers of individuals are involved, the pattern of behaviour which emerges in response to any change in strategy may be hard to predict for reasons such as local culture and attitudes and industrial relations in the local area or plant.

Management and employees may be capable of adapting to change by accepting changes in job content, work organisation or retraining. However, it may be necessary to negotiate rather than impose changes and to accept the consequences of changes for labour turnover and employee motivation.

(c) Legislation as well as social and ethical values constrain the ways in which labour may be used, the controls which may be placed over labour, the ease with which labour may be replaced, the criteria which may be used in recruitment or promotion and, in some cases, the rate of pay.

4.4 The purpose of manpower planning in both the short and the long term is therefore:

(a) to estimate the (uncertain) demand for each grade and skill of employee;

(b) to estimate the (uncertain) supply of labour for the appropriate grades and skills;

(c) where there is a discrepancy between demand and supply, to take measures which will reduce demand or improve supply. Attention must be given to pay, productivity, labour turnover, training, career structure, job enrichment etc.

This purpose can perhaps be stated more simply as being the objective of having the right people in the right jobs at the right time.

4.5 The process of manpower planning may be described in general terms as follows.

(a) Obtaining information on current manpower analysed by grades, skills, ages and retention rates, on which to base estimates of future manpower.

(b) Forecasting manpower requirements, by grades and skills, to meet the long term and short term needs of the organisation.

(c) Devising a strategy to meet the projected manpower requirements by grades and skills.

(d) Acquiring manpower and controlling its 'flow' through the organisation; these are the personnel issues of conditions of employment, pay, training, welfare, recruitment, promotion etc.

(e) Developing the skills of individuals so that with experience, they will become more productive and effective (eg management development).

(f) Attempting to persuade employees to adapt to changes in technology, organisation structure, the social habits of co-workers etc.

(g) Attending to the human relations factor so that corporate goals are achieved in a manner acceptable to and approved by the workforce.

Manpower planning as supply and demand forecasting

4.6 'The general aim of corporate manpower planning is to reduce the risk of either surplus or shortage of particular kinds of manpower, because any imbalance between personnel and other resources or corporate needs is likely to involve waste.' (Smith 1971)

4.7 The demand for labour must be forecast by considering the following.

(a) The objectives of the organisation, and the long and short term plans in operation to achieve those objectives. Where plans are changed, the effect of the change must be estimated.

(b) Manpower utilisation – how much labour will be required, given the expected *productivity* or work load of different types of employee. Improvements in productivity might be estimated on the assumption that concessions will be made on pay to the employees concerned.

The manpower plan

The manpower plan is prepared on the basis of the analysis of manpower requirements, and the implications for productivity and costs. The plan may consist of the following.

● *The recruitment plan:* numbers, types of people, when required; recruitment programme.

● *The training plan:* numbers of trainees required and/or existing staff needing training; training programme.

● *The redevelopment plan:* programmes for transferring, retraining employees.

● *The productivity plan:* programmes for improving productivity, or reducing manpower costs; setting productivity targets.

● *The redundancy plan:* where and when redundancies are to occur; policies for selection and declaration of redundancies; re-development, re-training or re-location of redundant employees; policy on redundancy payments, union consultation etc.

● *The retention plan:* actions to reduce avoidable wastage.

The plan should include budgets, targets and standards. It should allocate responsibilities for implementation and control (reporting, monitoring achievement against plan).

Recruitment and selection

4.8 Note that there is an important distinction between recruitment and selection.

(a) *Recruitment* is the part of the process concerned with finding the applicants: it is a 'positive' action by management, going out into the labour market, communicating opportunities and information, generating interest.

(b) *Selection* is the part of the employee recruiting process which involves choosing between applicants for jobs: it is largely a 'negative' process, eliminating unsuitable applicants.

Job description

4.9 A *job description* is a broad statement of the purpose, scope, duties and responsibilities of a particular 'job'. It is used to determine and specify:

(a) the content of a job; and

(b) its relative importance in comparison with other jobs. (This does not mean necessarily that the job is evaluated quantitatively, although job evaluation can be carried out when a job description is prepared).

4.10 The first step is to prepare a *job analysis*. This is 'the determination of the essential characteristics of a job' (British Standards Institution) - that is, the process of examining a job to identify its component parts and the circumstances in which it is performed. The product of the analysis is usually a *job specification* - a detailed statement of the activities (mental and physical) involved in the job, and other relevant factors in the social and physical environment.

4.11 Information which should be elicited from a job analysis is both task-oriented information and worker-oriented information, including the following.

(a) *Initial requirements* of the employee: aptitudes, qualifications, experience, training required etc.

(b) *Duties and responsibilities:* physical aspects; mental effort; routine or requiring initiative; difficult and/or disagreeable features; consequences of failure; responsibilities for staff, materials, equipment or cash etc.

(c) *Environment and conditions:* physical surroundings, with particular features - eg temperature or noise; hazards; remuneration; other conditions such as hours, shifts, benefits, holidays; career prospects; provision of employee services - canteens, protective clothing etc.

(d) *Social factors:* size of the department; teamwork or isolation; sort of people dealt with - senior management, the public etc; amount of supervision; job status.

4.12 The fact that a job analysis is being carried out may cause some concern among employees: fear of standards being raised, rates cut, redundancy etc. The job analyst will need to gain their confidence by:

(a) communicating: explaining the process, methods and purpose of the appraisal;

(b) being thorough and competent in carrying out the analysis;

(c) respecting the work flow of the department, which should not be disrupted; and

(d) giving feedback on the results of the appraisal, and the achievement of its objectives. If staff are asked to co-operate in developing a framework for office training - and then 'never hear anything' - they are unlikely to be responsive on a later occasion.

4.13 The job description is prepared from the job analysis and will list:

(a) job title;

(b) location of the job (department, place);

(c) the relationship of the job to other positions (especially to a senior manager and to subordinate employees, ie to whom is the job holder responsible and who are the job-holder's subordinates)?

(d) the main duties of the job;

(e) the responsibilities of the job holder;

(f) the limits to the job holder's authority;

(g) major tasks to be accomplished by the job holder;

(h) any equipment for which the job holder is responsible.

Some job descriptions include objectives and expected results, whilst others might also describe terms and conditions of employment.

4.14 A job description can then be used:

(a) to decide what skills (technical, human, conceptual, design etc) and qualifications are required of the job holder (ie when interviewing an applicant for the job, the interviewer can use the job description to match the candidate against the job);

(b) to ensure that the job:

(i) will be a full time job for the job holder and will not under-utilise him by not giving him enough to do;

(ii) provides a sufficient challenge to the job holder - job content is a factor in the motivation of individuals;

(c) to determine a rate of pay which is fair for the job, if this has not already been decided by some other means eg a separate job evaluation exercise;

(d) to provide information from which particular job vacancies can be advertised.

Induction and training

4.15 Both selection and training are concerned with:

(a) fitting people to the requirements of the job;

(b) securing better occupational adjustment; and

(c) in methodological terms, setting and achieving targets, defining performance criteria against which the success of the process can be monitored.

> 'Training is to some extent a management reaction to change, eg changes in equipment and design, methods of work, new tools and machines, control systems, or in response to changes dictated by new products, services, or markets. On the other hand, training also induces change. A capable workforce will bring about new initiatives, developments and improvements - in an organic way, and of its own accord. Training is both a cause and an effect of change.'
>
> Brian Livy: *Corporate Personnel Management*

On the job training or coaching

4.16 On the job training is very common, especially when the work involved is not complex. Trainee managers require more coaching, and may be given assignments or projects as part of a planned programme to develop their experience. Unfortunately, this type of training will be unsuccessful if:

(a) the assignments do not have a specific purpose from which the trainee can learn and gain experience; or

(b) the organisation is intolerant of any mistakes which the trainee makes. Mistakes are an inevitable part of on-the-job learning.

4.17 Experienced supervisors and managers, either promoted from within the organisation or recruited from outside, will need a period of orientation in their new job. It takes time to settle down, and learn the way the 'system' operates. There must be tolerance of mistakes during this orientation period, because it is a form of on-the-job training.

4.18 Different methods of on the job training include the following.

(a) *Coaching:* the trainee is put under the guidance of an experienced employee who shows the trainee how to do the job. The length of the coaching period will depend on the complexity of the job and the previous experience of the trainee.

(b) *Job rotation:* the trainee is given several jobs in succession, to gain experience of a wide range of activities. (Even experienced managers may rotate their jobs, to gain wider experience; this philosophy of job education is commonly applied in the Civil Service, where an employee may expect to move on to another job after a few years).

(c) *Temporary promotion:* an individual is promoted into his/her superior's position whilst the superior is absent due to illness. This gives the individual a chance to experience the demands of a more senior position.

(d) *'Assistant to' positions:* a junior manager with good potential may be appointed as assistant to the managing director or another executive director. In this way, the individual gains experience of how the organisation is managed 'at the top'.

(e) *Committees:* trainees might be included in the membership of committees, in order to obtain an understanding of inter-departmental relationships.

4.19 Essential steps in the training/coaching process are as follows.

(a) *Establish learning targets.* The areas to be learnt should be identified, and specific, realistic goals stated. These will refer not only to the 'timetable' for acquiring necessary skills and knowledge, but to standards of performance to be attained, which should if possible be formulated by agreement with the trainee.

(b) *Plan a systematic learning and development programme.* This will ensure regular progress, appropriate stages for consolidation and practice. It will ensure that all stages of learning are relevant to the trainee and the task he will be asked to perform.

(c) *Identify opportunities for broadening the trainee's knowledge and experience* - eg by involving him in new projects, encouraging him to serve on interdepartmental committees, giving him new contacts, or simply extending his job, giving him more tasks, greater responsibility etc.

(d) *Take into account the strengths and limitations of the trainee*, and take advantage of learning opportunities that suit his ability, preferred style and goals. A trainee from an academic background may learn best through research-based learning - eg. fact-finding for a committee, off-the-job study etc; those who learn best by 'doing' may profit from project work, hands-on training etc.

(e) *Exchange feedback.* The supervisor will want to know how the trainee sees his progress and his future. He will also need performance information in order to monitor the trainee's progress, adjust the learning programme if necessary, identify further needs which may emerge and plan future development for the trainee.

All the above will require the commitment of the organisation, and the department manager in particular, to the learning programme. They must 'believe' in training and developing employees, so that they are prepared to devote money, opportunity and the time of all people concerned. The manager will largely dictate the department's attitude to these things. His own time and support will be required to give praise and constructive criticism, to show an interest etc.

Technical training

4.20 Technical training is concerned with teaching a person how to do a particular job, or how to do it better.

4.21 A systematic approach to technical training involves identification of technical work which will lend itself to training, the design of a training scheme, implementation of the scheme and subsequent review to decide whether or not it has succeeded in achieving its purpose at a reasonable cost. The stages in a systematic approach of this kind may be listed as follows.

(a) Identify areas where training will be beneficial.

(b) Set training objectives.

(c) Decide on the training method.

(d) Compare the costs and benefits of the proposed course.

(e) Introduce a pilot or test scheme.

(f) Implement the scheme in full.

(g) Monitor the results to check that:

(i) training works; and
(ii) benefits exceed costs.

Group learning: 'T' groups

4.22 Group learning is not common in industry but is common in organisations such as social services departments of local government authorities. The purpose of group learning is:

(a) to give each individual in a training group (or T group) a greater insight into his own behaviour;

(b) to teach an individual how he 'appears' to other people, as a result of responses from other members of the group;

(c) to teach an understanding of intra-group processes, or how people inter-relate;

(d) to develop an individual's skills in taking action to control such intra-group processes.

'Encounter groups' for therapy are a development of the T-group principle.

4.23 Group learning may be of educational value to individuals whose job is dealing with other people. This process must have the full co-operation of all participants in the group if the training is to provide positive educational results.

4.24 The underlying concept of T-groups is that groups will study their own behaviour with the help of an experienced trainer. They will meet in sessions of about 1½ -2 hours each, and will be left to decide for themselves how to organise their time and what to talk about. The purpose of T-groups training in management would be:

(a) to give individuals more awareness of being part of a group of people;

(b) to help individuals to understand their attitudes to other people, and to improve these attitudes when they are harmful;

(c) to make individuals more sensitive to the opinions of other people;

(d) to learn how to help others;

(e) to learn how to let other people become the leader in a situation where that other person emerges as the most natural leader for the situation. (This in turn might help a manager to delegate work more freely).

4.25 T-groups can therefore be used to develop human relations skills. 'Participation in any group activity probably enhances a person's sensitivity to how others see him and his skill in assessing the behaviour of others and the reasons for it.' However, it can be argued that membership of committees can also be a useful aid to development without the intense pressures that may arise in T-groups.

Staff appraisal

4.26 Staff appraisal is the process of:

(a) looking at the past performance of an employee, and assessing his strengths and weaknesses;

(b) considering the suitability of the employee for promotion (ideally, by considering his potential to do a more senior job well);

(c) considering how the performance of the employee can be improved (or developed) by training, moving to another job to obtain more experience or counselling about his faults and how to overcome them.

In many organisations, a formal appraisal is carried out once each year, and an annual report on the employee prepared for personnel records.

Appraisal schemes

4.27 The purpose of formal appraisal schemes is:

(a) to gather information about the skills and potential of existing employees;

(b) to assess the performance of employees, so as to reward them (eg with the promise of promotion);

(c) to let the employee know how well he or she has performed, and give an assessment of his/her strengths and weaknesses;

(d) to allow the person being appraised and his/her superior to discuss how they should plan to achieve the objectives of both the person and his/her job.

4.28 Appraisal schemes are therefore means of rewarding, criticising, encouraging and counselling. The superior of the person appraised is meant to be both critic and counsellor, but in practice these twin roles tend to be incompatible.

Appraisal techniques

4.29 As well as completing appraisal forms appraisal can include the following.

(a) *Overall assessment*. This is the most simple method, requiring the manager to write in narrative form his judgement about the appraisee, possibly with a checklist of personality characteristics and performance targets to work from. There will be no guaranteed consistency of the criteria and areas of assessment, however, and managers may not be able to convey clear, effective judgements in writing.

(b) *Guided assessment*. Assessors are required to comment on a number of specified characteristics and performance elements, with guidelines as to how the terms (eg 'application', 'integrity', 'adaptability') are to be interpreted in the work context. This is a more precise, but still rather vague method.

(c) *Grading*. Grading adds a comparative frame of reference to the general guidelines, whereby managers are asked to select one of a number of levels or degrees to which the individual in question displays the given characteristic. These are also known as *rating scales*, and are much used in standard appraisal forms. Their effectiveness depends to a large extent on:

 (i) the relevance of the factors chosen for assessment. These may be nebulous personality traits, for example, or clearly defined job factors, eg job knowledge, performance against targets, decision-making etc;

 (ii) the definition of the agreed standards of assessment. Grades A–D might simply be labelled 'Outstanding – Satisfactory – Fair – Poor', in which case assessments are subject to much variation and subjectivity. They may, on the other hand, be more closely related to work priorities and standards, using definitions such as 'Performance is broadly acceptable, but employee needs training in several major areas and/or motivation is lacking.'

Numerical values may be added to ratings to give rating 'scores'. Alternatively a less precise *graphic scale* may be used to indicate general position on a plus/minus scale, eg:

Factor: job knowledge

High ————————————— Average —————————— Low

(d) *Behavioural incident methods*. These concentrate on employee behaviour, measured against definitions of 'typical' behaviour in each job, which are based on common 'critical incidents' of successful and unsuccessful job behaviour reported by managers. Time and effort are required to collect and analyse reports and to develop the scheme, and it only really applies to large groups of people in broadly similar jobs. However, it is firmly rooted in observation of 'real-life' job behaviour, and the important aspects of the job.

(e) *Results-orientated schemes.* The above techniques may be used with more or less results-orientated criteria for assessment - but are commonly based on trait or behavioural appraisal. A wholly results-orientated approach (eg Management by Objectives) sets out to review performance against specific targets and standards of performance agreed in advance by manager and subordinate together. The advantages of this are that:

(i) the subordinate is more involved in appraisal of his own performance, because he is able to evaluate his success or progress in achieving specific, jointly-agreed targets;

(ii) the manager is therefore relieved, to an extent, of his role as critic, and becomes a 'counsellor';

(iii) learning and motivation theories suggest that clear and known targets are instrumental in modifying and determining behaviour.

> The effectiveness of the scheme will still, however, depend on the targets set (are they clearly defined? realistic?) and the commitment of both parties to make it work. The measurement of success or failure is only part of the picture: reasons for failure and opportunities arising from success must be evaluated.

Promotion

4.30 Promotion is not only useful from the firm's point of view - in establishing a management succession, filling more senior position with proven, experienced and loyal employees. It is also one of the main forms of reward the organisation can offer to its employees, especially where, in the pursuit of 'equity', employees are paid a rate for the job rather than for performance: pay ceases to be a prime incentive. In order to be a motivator, promotion must be seen to be available, and fair. It can also cause political and structural problems in the organisation if it is not carefully planned.

4.31 A coherent policy for promotion is needed. This may vary to include provisions such as:

(a) all promotions, as far as possible, are to be made from within the firm; this is particularly important with reference to senior positions if junior ranks are not to be discouraged and de-motivated;

(b) merit and ability (systematically appraised) should be the principal basis of promotion, rather than seniority (years of service). Loyalty and experience will obviously be considered but should not be the sole criterion. Management will have to demonstrate to staff and unions, however, that their system of appraisal and merit rating is fair and fairly applied if the bases for promotion are to be trusted and accepted;

(c) vacancies should be advertised and open to all employees;

(d) there should be full opportunities for all employees to be promoted to highest grades;

(e) personnel and appraisal records should be kept and up-dated regularly;

(f) training should be offered to encourage and develop employees of ability and ambition in advance of promotion;

(g) scales of pay, areas of responsibility, duties and privileges of each post etc should be clearly communicated so that employees know what promotion means – what they are being promoted *to*.

The prevention of high labour turnover

4.32 A systematic investigation into the causes of labour turnover will have to be made, using the following information.

(a) Information given in *exit interviews* with leaving staff, which should be the first step after an employee announces his intention to leave. It must be recognised, however, that the reasons given for leaving may not be complete, true, or those that would be most useful to the organisation. The interviewer should be trained in interview techniques, and should be perceived to be 'safe' to talk to and objective in his appraisal of the situation (rather than being the supervisor against whom the resigning employee has a complaint, the manager who is going to write a reference etc).

(b) Information gleaned from interviews with leavers, in their homes, shortly after they have gone. This is an occasionally-used practice, intended to encourage greater objectivity and frankness, but one which requires tact and diplomacy if it is not to be resented by the subject.

(c) Attitude surveys, to gauge the general climate of the organisation, and the response of the workforce as a whole to working conditions, management style etc.

4.33 Some reasons for leaving will be genuine and largely unavoidable, or unforeseeable, eg:

(a) illness or accident, although transfer to lighter duties, excusing the employee from shiftwork etc might be possible;

(b) a move from the locality for domestic reasons, transport or housing difficulties;

(c) marriage or pregnancy (many women still give up working when their family situation changes);

(d) retirement;

(e) career change.

4.34 Other 'environmental' factors should, however, be considered. It may be possible to reduce labour turnover by attending to what Frederick Herzberg considered to be 'hygiene' factors in the environment (these are sources of worker dissatisfaction – as opposed to sources of positive satisfaction, or 'motivation' factors).

(a) The organisation will have to offer satisfactory (or at least competitive) wages and benefits, with fair differentials, and incentives. If it can also offer job security, through sound corporate planning, this is also an advantage.

(b) It will have to ensure that hours and conditions of work are in compliance with legal standards and best practice. Health and safety at least should be a priority.

(c) Jobs should be designed to offer, as far as possible, variety and discretion to those who desire them.

(d) Recruitment and selection procedures should ensure that the right calibre of worker is put into any given job. Some workers will be able to handle monotony, pressure, responsibility, lack of discretion etc better than others. The organisation should also ensure that its recruitment material does not make claims which will not be confirmed by the recruits' experience.

(e) Induction should be creatively used to introduce employees to the organisation. Training should be systematically planned to be on-going, effective and motivating. Career progression should be open to all employees, and clearly planned and communicated.

(f) Supervision and management style should be effective and appropriate to the nature of the task, the technology, the environment and the individuals concerned. If the leader is inadequate, lacks informal authority, is 'psychologically distant' from his team or over-autocratic, employees may be dissatisfied. In particular, management should ensure that plans, progress, and other feedback information is regularly communicated to employees.

Exercise

Do you think that organisational culture has a role to play in personnel strategy?

Solution

Hints. Possibly yes, if the approach by many large companies is anything to go by. In service organisations, the quality of the service depends on the individuals providing the service. If they are well motivated, committed and enthusiastic the service will be better. An appropriate organisational culture might encourage the 'right' behaviour.

---

5. CONCLUSION

5.1 Financial managers have duties relating both to their technical specialism and to the wider management issues of the organisation as a whole.

5.2 A manager's job involves acting a number of roles, depending on the situation, but a manager can play interpersonal, informational and divisional roles.

5.3 In service industries, and hence in the public sector, the majority of an organisation's costs are likely to be those relating to wages.

5.4 Personnel management is thus a crucial feature of resource management.

TEST YOUR KNOWLEDGE
The numbers in brackets refer to paragraphs of this chapter

1   What are the main issues which have to be considered in financial management? (1.7)

2   List the duties of financial managers. (2.2)

3   What types of behaviour are described by the Blake and Mouton grids? (3.6)

4   Distinguish between hygiene and motivator factors. (3.11, 3.15)

5   What might be contained in a manpower plan? (4.6)

Now try question 13 at the end of the text

Chapter 14

AUDIT AS A MANAGEMENT TOOL

This chapter covers the following topics.

1. Audit as a management tool
2. Audit efficiency and effectiveness in good management
3. Internal audit as an internal consultancy process

---

1. AUDIT AS A MANAGEMENT TOOL

1.1 Internal audit is seen as an independent appraisal function within an organisation, for the review of activities, as a service to all levels of management. It is a management control tool which measures, evaluates and reports on the effectiveness of internal control and efficient use of resources within an organisation.

1.2 The work of the internal audit will include studies of the performance of the organisation which examine whether the organisation is achieving the:

(a) *economy:* the achievement of a given result with the least expenditure;

(b) *efficiency:* the idea of converting resources into a desired product or service in the most advantageous ratio of resources to product;

(c) *effectiveness:* which brings into account the goals and objectives which the activity being audited is intended to meet;

(d) in the public sector, *equity*, discussed in paragraph 1.3 below.

1.3 *Equity* implies the extent to which the service has reached its appropriate target. A service can be delivered economically, efficiently and effectively, but may still be plagued by a low 'take up'. For example, it is felt that many social security benefits fail to reach their target recipients. These equity issues may be expressed as performance targets, as response rates to enquiries, completing a percentage of visits or repairs within a set time.

1.4 The actual results will require further investigation into the reasons why an indicator has shown to be different from the expected position. In education, the costs per student may vary between institutions and show a wide range of variation. This may be due to the mix of courses, the way they are taught, overhead costs for an institution spread over a number of sites.

Investigation of these variables and the expected cost implications can provide for a review of the operation and management of the institution. Reporting systems which can be used for this type of evaluation is an important factor in the audit process.

1.5 A consideration of the process of managing the organisation to secure an economic, effective and efficient operation of the organisation. The use of spreadsheet analysis to identify the control process can relate control objectives with performance.

Control objective	Expected control	Actual control	Evaluation and weaknesses	Comments

This can identify weaknesses in the system and be used to improve the control and reporting systems.

1.6 Clear reporting systems are needed to provide base information for a range of audits and evaluation exercises. This can cover audits on inventory balances, contract audits, internal audit to assure conformance with procedures and policies, data for external audits, value for money audits and meeting the requirements of government departments and other agencies.

1.7 *Internal audit* has historically been a checking process, reviewing data entry and control procedures, verification of payment systems and has been concerned with past procedures. The perception of the audit process as backward looking, compliance orientated, the 'spy in the cab tachograph', does not fit it well for a role in corporate management. As the audit function has itself come under scrutiny in the quality and cost of services, it has to demonstrate its worth to the organisation. The internal customers of the service are asked how they rate the clarity, understandability, practicality, simplicity and timeliness of the financial reports they receive. As financial responsibilities are devolved to cost centres, and these centres have to produce their own reports and establish control processes themselves, they may require a different service from the audit section.

1.8 The audit section itself may have to prepare for *contracting out* for competition in previously certain areas (eg in providing audits in a Trust Hospital). Strategic thinking and future planning has come to the audit section itself, the concern with customers, the cost and quality of services have to be considered, and the reasons for selecting their services marketed. Management buy outs have created independent audit services in some authorities.

1.9 In marketing the audit functions in relation to the management of the organisation, the development of *value for money audits* has been a major change in purpose of audits.

1.10 The Audit Code of Practice for Value for Money Audits sets out the auditors duties for commenting and advising on issues relating to management arrangements. These should include:

(a) systems of planning, controlling expenditure and allocating scarce resources;

(b) manpower management, including arrangements for training, rewarding and motivating employees;

(c) monitoring results against objectives and standards;

(d) whether policy objectives are set based on sufficient, relevant and reliable data, and critical underlying assumptions.

The auditor should be able not only to point out where and why the problems exist, but offer help in diagnosing potential problems and reviewing how improvements can be made.

1.11 Many auditing firms have developed into management consultants, and are used to provide advice on wider policy issues including the survival of the authorities in the light of the reforms of local government. The Audit Commission has also produced reports on management and management procedures in a number of areas, property and economic development.

1.12 The internal audit section in a local authority has also become involved in preparing value for money studies, in assisting in developing contract specifications and in contract audit. The audit function has become tied into meeting the policy objectives of the authority and not just about reporting procedures.

Direct service organisations

1.13 The establishment of Direct Service Organisations (DSOs) has meant a closer link between management and financial control. Contracting out of large parts of the authorities' services has required management of millions of pounds in some cases. The objectives in DSOs have been to:

(a) ensure value for money in the management of the service;
(b) assess consumer demand and service provision;
(c) apply commercial practices to the service;
(d) comply with legislation on compulsory competitive tendering;
(e) establish financial targets to recover costs and return on capital.

1.14 To achieve a successful tender the DSO must:

(a) remain competitive;
(b) be commercially efficient;
(c) monitor performance against targets;
(d) develop information systems;
(e) develop staff and management and finance skills.

1.15 The auditor can assist in achieving the management objectives by:

(a) providing an understanding of the DSOs financial service requirements;
(b) developing a range of appropriate services;
(c) providing cost effective advice and quality assurances;
(d) enforcing timely provision of reports and assistance.

1.16 The management of a DSO trading account requires different and better information than management of traditional budgets, when expenditure is the dominant variable and income of limited importance. Information is needed at cost centre level. A great deal of work was required to establish unit costs that were needed for the tender process. As experience is limited in running DSOs information systems are weak. The local managers require simplicity, speed and responsiveness. The centre being cautious having to follow procedure not usually having to be a quick response active and not being commercially orientated.

1.17   The reduction in central control and the freedom of the DSO to manage its own affairs has meant a challenge to internal audit. The DSO can choose its own auditors. The DSO operates a trading account and has responsibility for estimates, virements, can close its account. Managers 'own' payments and order systems and income. The DSO objectives are changing from being about cost reduction to being about competition and making a surplus (a profit). What happens to the surplus then becomes a management policy issue; should it be retained for capital replacement, returned to the general rate fund, used for profit sharing? As the DSO seeks profits it may even seek new business opportunities, and bid for work for other authorities.

1.18   This commercial base for DSOs may split the audit activities into being 'internal' to the DSO and the authority operating an 'external' overseeing role and applying legislative rules over the DSO operation.

1.19   The use of value for money audits across the DSOs may then be a way of relating the corporate objectives to the operational units, like a holding company to its divisions.

1.20   To use the value for money audits successfully the policy objectives have to be clearly specified and translated into measurable targets or indicators of performance. In reviewing the procedures for setting objectives the accuracy of the data, the comparative evaluation of alternatives can be obtained from audit reports. Policy may be based on zero based budgeting in which budget items are ranked for priority. Planning programming budgeting systems can be used to relate the elements of the operational aspects to higher level objectives.

1.21   Review process are encouraged to consider issues which have obvious pay back potential or provide good pilot demonstration projects. The focus should be on education and winning converts to the process which provides added value and effective procedures.

1.22   Procedures for ensuring proper control over scarce resources, using surplus land and buildings, control of cash flow, use of staff have been the areas identified by value for money audits. Reporting systems which test effectiveness and are concerned with outcomes as well as input costs have been important in the application of value for money.

1.23   The establishment of *best practice* in the management costs of services by the Audit Commission provides a bench mark for comparative reviews and audit guides for external audits of the provisions of authority services. Value for money has become a way of reviewing management and organisational behaviour, a process of reporting on the organisation's performance record as well as a technical audit function.

1.24 Review of economy and efficiency provide ways of improving the management's control of resources and establishing key performance measures for monitoring the performance of the organisation. By identifying cost reductions and improvement in performance at no extra costs, greater use can be made of limited resources. The audits can become an action plan to improve the operation of the authority.

1.25 Review of effectiveness can demonstrate if the programmes are achieving the policy objectives and whether policy objectives are clearly stated. Guidance can be provided for management on how to achieve objectives. Ways of reporting the success or failure in achieving objectives and setting up evaluative criteria can be investigated. Commentaries of the validity of the policy itself and possible changes in the way programmes are operated to achieve objectives may be made.

2. AUDIT EFFICIENCY AND EFFECTIVENESS IN GOOD MANAGEMENT

2.1 Audit reports should be acted upon.

(a) Corrective action can be taken when procedures are not being followed.

(b) Interviews and negotiations with senior officers can be conducted to assess improvements to procedures and availability of information.

(c) Value for money and performance review reports can be made to the Policy and Resources/ Performance Review Committee. Reports to the Chief Finance Officer and the Chief Officers Board can inform senior management of how well the organisation is being run.

2.2 The information from the audit can then be reported:

(a) to the Finance Committee on how (what procedures are followed) the resources are being used;

(b) to the Policy and Subject Committees on how (what is being achieved) the policy is working.

The Government Public Accounts Committee reports have been critical of policies having no real resource underpinning and achieving what would have happened anyway (regional policy) or having little impact on the problem (inner city policy). The basis of some privatisation deals have been thought to have underestimated the asset values of the bodies being sold and overestimated the subsidies required to attract a buyer; this has been the case in the sale of Rover to British Aerospace and the sale of bus companies.

2.3 It may be difficult to report on *policies* which cross the boundaries between departments or functions, or across different ministries or quasi-government agencies and across budget headings and estimates. The other difficulty is measuring the outcomes and effectiveness of policy within a changing set of social and economic conditions, as with inner city policy for example.

(a) The outcomes may be ineffective; but

(b) the control procedures, bidding, submitting tenders, following up pay and grant allocations and evaluation may be efficient. The efficiency of the procedures may be at fault in that the application and financial allocation systems are complex and for ever changing. On the other hand the efficiency of reporting and monitoring may show the way that the ineffectiveness is demonstrated.

2.4 Having simple systems and getting the implementers of the policy involved in the monitoring from the start is important for everyone to learn, especially when the policy approach is new, Care in the Community and involves different organisations, health, local authorities, voluntary sector and the private sector.

2.5 The training of staff and the development of technical audit and computing skills has to be supplemented with training in policy analysis and an understanding of the policy making process.

2.6 The objectives of producing financial reports are as follows.

(a) To meet legal obligations.

(b) To measure performance against objectives and resources used.

(c) To measure efficiency and effectiveness in the use of resources.

(d) To provide for future planning and resource allocation to bid for additional funding.

(e) To show that the organisation is viable and provides good quality services.

(f) To provide information to customers and interest groups about the working of the organisation.

2.7 The Code of Local Government Audit Practice lays down a number of duties for the auditor and provides for a wide range of audit activities from fraud to value for money.

A number of types of audit can be identified. These can be used for different management purposes.

(a) *Systems reliability audit* provides evidence of past control and internal and external process of audit to prevent fraud.

(b) *Attestation audit* of accounts provides an opinion on accuracy and fairness of a presented set of figures. These can cover published accounts, bids for grants and subsidies and internal trading accounts.

(c) *Fraud investigation* is aimed at proofing or disproving a suspected fraud.

(d) *Value for money* is an assessment of the economy, efficiency and effectiveness of an organisation or one of its functions. A development of value for money audit has become one of management consultancy and advice given on policy implementation. Provides advice on how to act in the future and through comparative studies demonstrates best practice.

(e) *Computer audit* detailed studies of the use of computer systems and the use of computer based audit techniques. Better computer use and application of computer systems and communications security of computer records.

(f) *Regulatory audit* testing and advising on compliance with statutory and internal regulations. This provides for a test of the legality of actions.

2.8 To guide and assist in the carrying out of the audit tasks discussed, the auditor needs to draw up a *strategic plan* to see that the assignments carried out meet the client's objectives.

In organising the audit work between clients or organisations the man day requirements of each of the elements of the work is often how the arrangements are shown. The objectives of the audit need to be clearly identified and arrangements made with those with the responsibilities of maintaining recording systems and making critical decisions involved in the detailed programming of the work.

2.9 In organising the work the auditor has to focus on financially material parts of the client's activities. The other area of general concern is where there is a risk of financial misstatement or poor value for money.

2.10 The auditor needs to use *statistical sampling techniques* to assess the level of evidence required for achieving a given level of materiality and risk. In planning the workload an assessment of materiality and risk gives the relative time one piece of work should take to another.

2.11 If internal control systems are relied upon to provide evidence of materiality then the control systems themselves have to be tested on an annual basis.

2.12 *Value for money* audits are not objectively provable and so statistical sampling techniques are less valid both in this area and in computer audit. Previous experience and judgement become important in organising the audit planning process.

2.13 The sensitivity of an area under discussions to management and politicians may be factors to take into consideration in planning the audit work.

2.14 The changes in local government services and the NHS mean that the internal audit function is liable to become a separate or even independent function and other companies will be able to bid for the work.

2.15 The Audit Commission now has responsibility for the Health Service, which has been encouraged to put its internal audit out to tender.

2.16 The existing internal audit teams may have to look at marketing their services to other authorities and so become involved with allocating resources and developing staff calendars and costing the audit work. Making the best use of staff time and the training and development of staff have to be taken into consideration. As knowledge increases it will become easier to plan for problems that arise over sick leave, taking examinations, going on training or updating courses at a charge out rate of £30 to £40.

2.17 User's needs have to be considered in what material and how audit data is presented. The users of audit reports are as follows.

(a) The public as voter taxpayers
(b) The customer or client
(c) The management
(d) Suppliers
(e) Employees
(f) Government
(g) Comparable organisations
(h) Competitors
(i) Lenders
(j) Donors
(k) Sponsors
(l) Investors
(m) Pressure groups

The evaluation and analysis of audit data then becomes necessary to make it a management function rather than just a checking function. Different users will ask different 'questions' of the material.

2.18 *Value for money* studies might indicate that a wide range of management problems can be part of a management audit. These can be related to the main features of the management arrangements in the authority.

(a) *Process systems*   *Problems*

   (i)   Financial: Poor management of resources
                        Financial assets underused
                        Lack of finance to provide future level of services

   (ii) Management processes: Service managers unable to react to customers' needs
                        No plan to deal with DSO and contract management
                        Management authority located at too high a level

   (iii) Communications: Uncertainty over objectives for the authority and the service
                        Poor public communication
                        No surveys of consumer needs/satisfaction

   (iv) Information technology: Expensive systems not being fully used
                        IT strategy not related to service delivery
                        Limited training in use of IT
                        Areas still untouched by IT having to use manual methods to compete with IT

(b) *Organisation and people*   *Problems*

(i)   Organisation structure: Central support services seen as separate from delivery of services

No clear line of control over contract activities and division of contractor client responsibility

High costs of audit service

(ii)   Staffing: High turnover

Lack of qualified staff

Conflict of interests, staff not motivated because of uncertain prospects

(iii)   People management: No staff development or training plan

Performance related pay seems to provide little in the way of reward and a great deal of resentment

New contracts of employment have not been related to job descriptions

The staff are the last to know about changes in policy, but they have to inform the service users

(c) *Direction and leadership*   *Problems*

(i)   Senior management: Too many immediate problems with dealing with change

Replacement of community charge

Contracting out to white collar staff

Reorganisation of internal structure of the authority

Not planning for future changes

Have low morale. Have to explain changes to members, and implement policies with which they disagree or do not understand

(ii)   Members: Unable to lead because they do not know where they are going

2.19 The Audit Commission identifies a number of key factors which they relate to the management process.

(a) To understand customers
(b) Respond to the electorate
(c) Have consistent achievable objectives
(d) Clear lines of responsibility
(e) Main motivate people
(f) Communicate effectively
(g) Monitor results
(h) Adapt to change

All these relate to the management process, financial management, policy planning and performance review.

2.20 The Audit Commission has developed a *quality exchange* which provides information on how authorities have adopted to innovation and are achieving quality standards.

2.21 Value for money studies can provide a starting point for the diagnosis of management problem and how well the performance indicators are being used. Leadership, people management and changing the culture of the organisation may well be key factors in managing change and in the financial health of the authority. An organisational fitness test can be used to assess if the management features are in good health, average, requirement treatment or have signs of terminal illness. Actions can be taken according to what is demonstrated by the test, not all of the features surveyed will be expected to show the same level of health.

2.22 The questions asked in reviewing the process of management will have subjective answers in many cases and will require negotiation with the people involved as well as advice on performance review systems or establishing corporate goals. The ratings given by staff can be compared with those of the auditors to show how the perceptions are related and how strengths and weaknesses are alleviated. At times of change communications may be seen as a problem by the external auditor but not by the senior management, and this may be related to people management.

3. INTERNAL AUDIT AS AN INTERNAL CONSULTANCY PROCESS

3.1 The functions of internal audit can be divided into:

(a) responsibility to ensure that adequate internal controls exist within the financial systems;

(b) responsibility for producing audits under legislative powers on annual reports;

(c) services to client departments and members to provide:

(i) value for money audits;
(ii) advice on management information systems;
(iii) audit of unofficial funds;
(iv) quality service programme review;
(v) consultancy work.

3.2 The internal audit section needs to develop its services as a consultant to the authority rather than accepting that it is the *only* supplier of internal audit available. Under proposals to extend compulsory competitive tendering, audit would be included as part of the tender. Other areas include:

(a) financial planning;
(b) exchequer services;
(c) cash collection;
(d) payroll administration;
(e) accountancy services;
(f) investment management.

The proposals for competitive tendering also cover computing services of which 80% are to be available for tendering, including information systems strategy and systems operation.

3.3 In considering how the audit section can be prepared for competition and act as an internal consultancy it needs to demonstrate its independence, and to prepare its own strategic and business plans.

The management audit

3.4 To prepare the strategic plan first an analysis of the position of the existing organisation and how well it is prepare to become competitive. This can be done through a management audit, which is a 'comprehensive, critical appraisal of the organisation's structure management practices and methods, ... its objectives are to motivate management to take action which will lead to increased efficiency and profitability of the organisation' (British Institute of Management).

SWOT analysis of an audit department

3.5 To prepare for the management audit, a review of the strengths, weaknesses, opportunities and threats (SWOT) analysis of the section and its environment.

(a) *Strengths*

The section has a good range of professionally qualified staff at all levels in the organisation. A comprehensive training programme covers professional development and non professional training in report writing, presentation skills. The section has recently invested in IT hardware and has its own computer experts developing in house software for information systems. It has a great deal of expertise in servicing the council and has good relations with client departments.

Management of the section has been based on clear objectives, planning and measuring work performance.

Work has been won for the direct service organisations.

(b) *Weaknesses*

Accountancy has been seen as the way management has cut costs and staffing so it is seen as an uncaring activity by remaining staff.

Resources can be tied up in a major audit programme such as dealing with unofficial funds. Central services represent a high cost to the section (25% of direct costs).

The section is inexperienced in having to compete or justify its costs to clients.

An uncertain future for local government makes it vulnerable to developing a plan to serve the authority.

(c) *Opportunities*

The changes going on could mean that the section has a change in focus, that specific audit services are offered (eg value for money audits, computer audit).

Manage in-house services.

Contract for work with the health authorities, other local authorities and small business, educational institutions.

(d) *Threats*

The environment of the public sector has been changing with privatisation, compulsory competitive tendering, proposed restructuring of local government, an emphasis on costs and market values.

New legislation is taking some functions away, adding new ones, creating partnerships with the private sector which is changing the nature of the work to be done.

Potential private sector takeover of contract work.

Direct service organisation audits.

The problems of *cost allocation* of central support services, administration and meeting legal requirements to provide audits for the authority, make it difficult to compete with the private sector.

The loss of internal audit functions in education has shown what can happen when services become independent of the authority.

The contracted functions will want to show they are responding to the market by selecting private auditors for the work, even though private firms may not give the best deal.

That limitations on staffing levels, working conditions, purchase of information technology will hold back the responsiveness of the section to client demands.

3.6 Various strategic options are available and can be evaluated against the likely position of the section.

(a) *Do nothing*

The section can operate as it does until the situation is more certain. This course of action could build on the strengths of the section and deal with some of the weaknesses in the short term with little increased costs or change in staffing. The action taken would be mainly an image and public relations exercise and marketing of what is already done. The threats could be dealt with as other changes occur such as negotiating on the section's share of the central support costs along with other users.

(b) *Withdrawal*

The section would withdraw from some areas of work, like dealing with unofficial funds, or school audits. This would release some staff and resources. The resources could then be used for money consultancy type value for money audits. Staff retraining and a more aggressive stance could help change the image.

(c) *Consolidation*

Once those areas of work which give good returns on staff usage have been identified to restructure operations. Redirect staff and resources to the successful areas of expertise. Take on agency work for other authorities in the areas of special work, in management audit and value for money studies.

(d) *Product and market development*

Systems auditing and *computer audit* can be offered to service managers and to opted out services. This may mean staff retraining or recruitment. The section should market its expertise and track record to other local authorities, other public bodies, the private sector, to take on some work for the private sector as a subcontractor. The section could act as an organising agency or buy in additional staff. This requires a change in culture. The section operate as a trading organisation as part of the local authority, separate from the authority through management buy out, or go into partnership or merger with a private sector company.

(e) *Diversification*

The product and market development option would require diversification and a change to the operation of the section's functions which would be best achieved outside the local authority. This independence from the local authority could be achieved through a company owned by the authority, or through a management buy out. These changes would mean a new management structure, and a responsibility for appointing, training, paying staff. A sufficient quantity of work would be required from the very beginning to cover costs of the staff, buildings and computer systems. As a commercial organisation, services could be contracted out (such as payroll, or packages brought in which could be offered as a service to other small organisations). The changing cost base would mean that the central support costs would no longer apply and services could be priced more commercially. As a consultancy function then the separate unit would have to compete for the authority work that it now does.

(f) *Implementation*

The implementation process would require getting staff agreement for the changes, and establishing a commercial culture. A new structure and working arrangements would be required and new staff contracts drawn up. Methods of financing the independent organisation would need to be investigated in detail and the required levels of work and cash flow to maintain the organisation, in staff numbers, training, computers could have to be calculated against the expected market for the services being offered. A plan and indicators of performance would be required to establish a plan for the organisation.

3.7 The development of a strategic plan will have to deal with these issues and select a way of dealing with the impending changes in the local government systems. To survive it seems that the Audit Service will have to become more independent, see itself as a trading activity, develop service level agreements with the DSOs and act in a wider consultancy role. A possible strategic plan could be for a county council, with a staff of forty and a budget of £500,000.

Strategic plan for an internal audit service division

3.8 Given the above analysis what follows is the strategic plan for the Internal Audit Services Division. The aim of the plan is to find the best strategic fit by capitalising on the Division's strengths and overcoming its weaknesses. At the same time opportunities need to be exploited and threats reduced.

3.9   *Short to medium term (1 to 3 years)*

   (a)   Consolidate on the Division's current position by continuing to improve:

      (i)   Relationships with clients officers – by being proactive and assisting managers in improving their service delivery and reducing their costs.

      (ii)   The quality and range of services offered by the division through training, the optimal reallocation of resources, the use of audit software and planning and performance monitoring.

   (b)   Undertake to charge for the audit of unofficial funds so that this service becomes self financing.

   (c)   Involve client departments in the planning of audit work over and above that required by the Treasurer's Section 151 responsibility. In this way the Division will be seen as a helper rather than a hindrance and specific work can be targeted more effectively.

   (d)   Target further education Colleges and DSOs for specific promotion of the Division and to be adequately prepared for the independence of colleges in 1993.

   (e)   Implement service level agreements and develop a charging system that reflects the costs of the division and is commercially acceptable.

   (f)   Introduce a new management information system that will monitor work performance and also the recovery of costs.

   (g)   To improve reporting procedures to members and managers so that they are aware of the work of the Division.

   (h)   To develop VFM and consultancy services so that they represent a significant proportion of the Division's activities, ie to reduce the Division's dependence on statutory duties.

3.10   *Long term (1 to 5 years)*

   (a)   To have successfully retained all further education college and DSO audits.

   (b)   To have started to undertake work for other local authorities. Significantly:

      (i)   to undertake three District Council computer audits;

      (ii)   to undertake three District Council contract audits;

      (iii)   to be respected within the county boundary of Nottinghamshire for the provision of consultancy services (especially management information) and VFM audits and be actively perusing such work with at least five district councils.

   (c)   To move to the position of a quasi-trading organisation, so that the divisional structure is such that it is prepared for compulsory competition if the abolition of the County Councils should arise.

Exercise

Why do you think equity is a necessary yardstick of the success of public sector services?

Solution

Hints. Basically, it is an acknowledgement of the fact that public sector organisations often have multiple goals, and that they are funded by the taxpayer for the collective good. As an example, the government might wish to ensure that there was equality of opportunity in education, which would mean certain common standards. If the take-up of educational opportunities was distributed toward one particular class, the service would not be meeting its aims, however efficiently and effectively it is delivered.

---

4. CONCLUSION

4.1 Internal audit is an internal appraisal function within an organisation, for the review of all activities to service the management.

4.2 It is the case that audit services are being contracted out to private sector firms.

4.3 The audit function can identify good management practices. Value for money audits are a way of reviewing organisational behaviour.

4.4 The design of reporting systems may not facilitate the understanding of the success.

TEST YOUR KNOWLEDGE
The numbers in brackets refer to paragraphs of this chapter

1 What are the aims of internal audit? (1.2, 1.3)

2 How can the auditor assist DSOs? (1.15)

3 What different types of audit can be understood? (2.7)

4 What strategies could there be for an internal audit department failed to complete? (3.6).

Now try question 14 at the end of the text

Chapter 15

OPTION CHOICE AND QUALITY MANAGEMENT

This chapter covers the following topics.

1. Quality management
2. Total quality management (TQM)
3. Quality standards
4. Quality measurement
5. Quality circles

---

1. QUALITY MANAGEMENT

1.1 Genichie Taguchi *(The System of Experimental Design)* has advocated that 'robust' products result from quality which is 'designed in', rather than 'controlled from without'. Robustness in organisations can be achieved through building up close knit teams, 'quality circles', close to the work face. In a robust quality environment, quality is everyone's responsibility; 'quality control', imposed through intervention, is replaced by 'quality assurance', a shared responsibility to getting it right first time.

1.2 Quality is a relative term that can mean all things to all people. Of all the definitions, it is Juran's simple notion of 'fitness for purpose or use', that is a common starting point. This has also a legal basis (Sale of Goods Act) in that goods purchased should demonstrate being fit for purpose. The definition can be expanded as in British Standards 477B 1987 which stated '... the totality of features and characteristics of a product or service that bear on its ability to satisfy stated or implied needs'. BS 5750 has expanded the limit of quality to include the quality of the management processes by which services and products are delivered.

1.3 Two general roles can be identified in the quality relationship, the 'supplier' and the 'client'. It is the ability of the supplier of the product or service to meet the client's needs and expectations, without waste, unscheduled delay or unnecessary effort, that constitutes a working definition of quality.

1.4 The systematic approach to quality attainment can then be seen to have three components:

(a) quality assurance;
(b) quality monitoring;
(c) quality review.

Advocates of total quality management (TQM) see all working relationships as following the supplier/client pattern, with quality being assured only when clients' needs are met.

1.5   In essence, total quality management recognises what the quality gurus such as Deming and Juran have been advocating since the 1950s: quality does not happen by accident – it has to be planned. Management is responsible for 80% of quality problems, and poor management wastes resources, in the end the customer has to pay.

1.6   As Deming has said:

'Everyone doing his best is not the answer. It is first necessary that people know what to do. Drastic changes are required. The first step in the process is to learn how to change. Long term commitment to new learning and new philosophy is required of any management that seeks transformation.'   (W E Deming *Out of Crisis* 1986)

1.7   All approaches to quality management emphasise the importance of the customer and the commitment of top management to achieving quality. No absolute measures exist but achieving *British Standard 5750* is seen as a benchmark. Other European and American standards systems can be obtained as a seal of approval.

1.8   Quality has to be organisation-wide concerning, all functions and levels. The highest quality for the price and specification should be achieved with maximum efficiency. The management style, organisation structure, and culture all have to come together around the concept of quality.

1.9   In terms of quality assurance, the quality group should ensure that all relationships and processes within the production process or delivery of a service are managed at the point of delivery, to be 'right first time'. The task is to identify and promulgate good practice.

1.10   The 'quality system' would be completed by establishing a management of structure that develops and puts good practice into operation. A small quality management team could be set up with the following tasks.

(a)   To secure commitment of staff to the quality aims.
(b)   To urge attention to detail in all aspects of the organisation.
(c)   To administer the monitoring programme.
(d)   To disseminate information about quality.
(e)   To review the assurance and monitoring system.

The 'quality system' costs time and money to make sure the background work is done so that the customers get what they want.

2.   TOTAL QUALITY MANAGEMENT (TQM)

2.1   Total quality management (TQM) is a management technique, derived from Japanese companies, which focuses on the belief that 'total quality is essential to survival in a global market'.

Building upon American concepts introduced into Japan in the 1950s, the Japanese recognised that customers do not just want technical quality, but also suitability of the product features for their needs and price, and on the quality of the organisation which provides the product or service.

2.2 Quality in the public sector and in higher education has been based on monitoring, peer review, Her Majesty's Inspectorate and on groups providing the delivery of the service. All parts of the service may not be subject to the same monitoring, the administration for example concerned with student admissions. The TQM system replaces this through a prevention based approach.

2.3 The basic principle of TQM is that the cost of preventing mistakes is less than the cost of correcting them once they occur. The aim should therefore be to get things right first time consistently.

> 'Every mistake, every delay and misunderstanding, directly costs a company money through wasted time and effort, including time taken in pacifying customers. Whilst this cost is important, the impact of poor customer service in terms of lost potential for future sales has also to be taken into account.'
>
> (Robin Bellis-Jones and Max Hard of Develin and Partners,
> in an article on TQM in *Management Accounting* May 1989)

2.4 There are several different TQM programmes, all aimed at identifying and then reducing/ eliminating causes of wasted time and effort. One such programme is called Qualified Total Quality (QTQ). In QTQ, a work group is asked to analyse its activities and classify these into three groups:

(a) *core activities*, which are the reason for the existence of the work group and which add value to the business;

(b) *support activities* which support core activities but do not themselves add value; and

(c) *discretionary activities* such as checking, progress chasing, dealing with complaints etc, which are all symptoms of failure within the organisation.

2.5 An article by Robin Bellis-Jones and Max Hard provides an example of an engineering company, with a group of 400 product engineers, which needed to reduce product lead times from about 4 years to 18 months to compete more efficiently with major foreign rivals. The company introduced computer assisted design equipment, but found that it was having to employ more engineers. A QTQ exercise revealed that the engineers were only spending about 12% of their time on core activities and the rest on support and discretionary activities. By looking hard at the efficiency of support activities and at ways of reducing discretionary activities, the group was able to increase time spent on core activities to 41%. The business need of quicker product lead times was achieved, without having to increase headcount.

2.6 Two approaches to controlling quality and quality costs are as follows.

   (a) *Approach 1:* minimise total quality costs by budgeting for a level of quality which minimises prevention costs plus inspection costs on the one hand and internal and external failure costs on the other.

   (b) *Approach 2:* aim for zero rejects and 100% quality. The desired standard of production is contained within the product specification and every unit produced ought to achieve this standard; in other words, there ought to be no defects. Zero-defect targets are one aspect of Japanese management philosophy. However, the actual level of defects must be recorded and reported, even if the quality costs are not measured.

2.7 Both approaches show a concern for quality and quality standard control. They both accept the need to incur quality costs: with a zero defect target, there must be costs incurred in preventing defects and testing output. However, there is a fundamental difference of view in the sense that approach 1 accepts some level of defects and approach 2 takes the view that *all* defects are undesirable.

> Eventually, as modern manufacturing systems are introduced and Just In Time systems are employed, Approach 1 is likely to result in the conclusion that the costs of failure are so high (because they hold up production) that the only acceptable quality standard is a zero defect limit (Approach 2).

Quality in the public sector

2.8 In the public sector, police work was examined. Officers were asked to keep diaries of their activities and it was found that officers spent only 20% of their time on *core* activities of dealing with crime. Time was taken up with producing reports, appearing in court and non crime issues. The response was to bring in more civilian staff to take over the administration and reporting.

2.9 In the service sector, the supplier-client relationships may be:

   (a) *direct* (tutor to student, and all students should have their needs and expectations met 100% of the time);

   (b) the client may be difficult to define, as a *number* of stakeholders can be identified;

   (c) the product itself is consumed as 'education' and used by the student for a range of purposes (eg pass examinations, get a job, enter a profession);

   (d) education is believed to be of wider social and economic benefit.

2.10 The stakeholders can be seen to include the following in higher education.

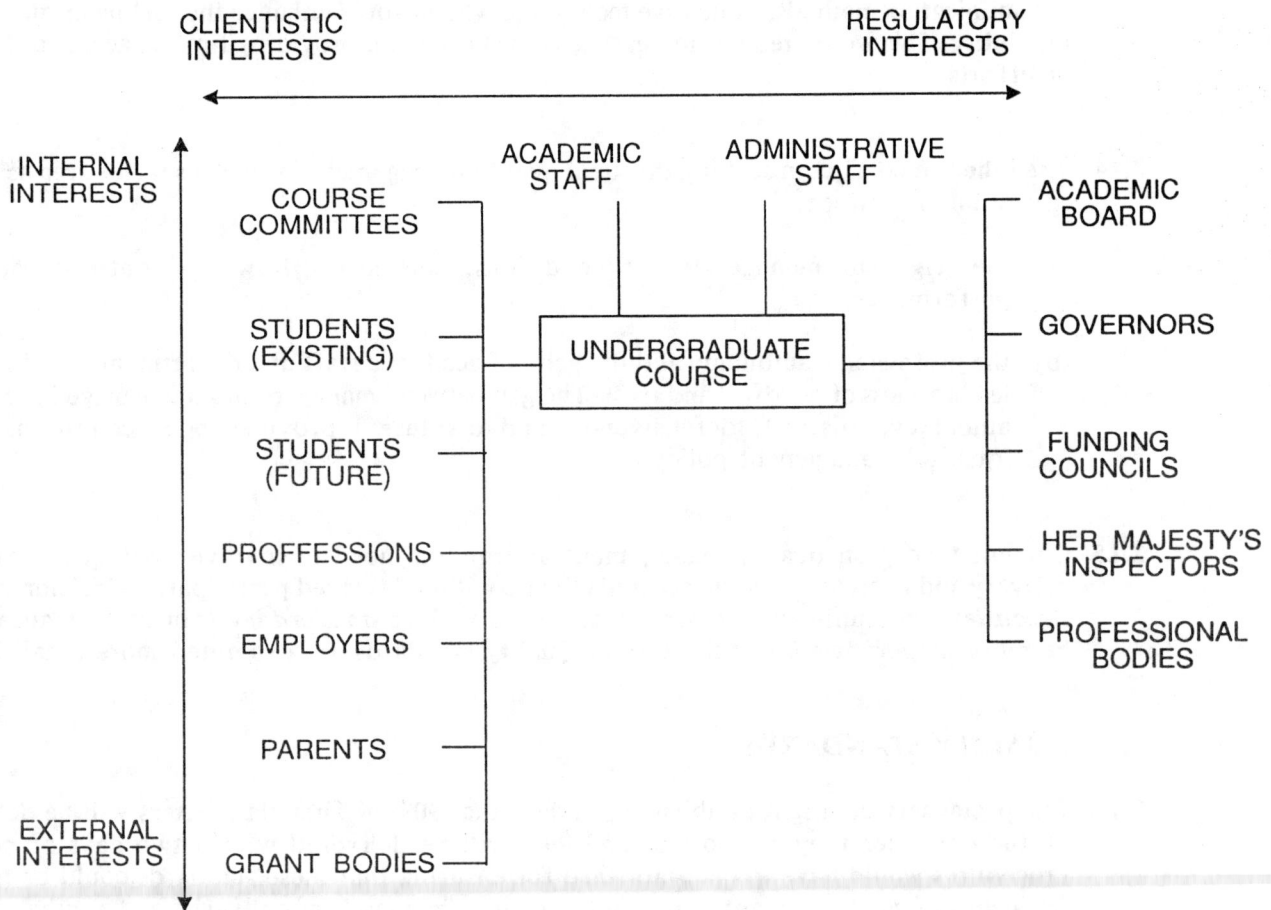

```
                   CLIENTISTIC                    REGULATORY
                    INTERESTS                      INTERESTS

                   ◄──────────────────────────────────────►

                              ACADEMIC     ADMINISTRATIVE
 INTERNAL ▲                    STAFF           STAFF
 INTERESTS │      COURSE                                    ─── ACADEMIC
           │   COMMITTEES ───┐        │           │             BOARD
           │                 │        │           │
           │    STUDENTS ────┐│    ┌─────────────────┐    ─── GOVERNORS
           │   (EXISTING)    ││    │  UNDERGRADUATE  │
           │                 ├┼────┤     COURSE      ├────
           │    STUDENTS ────┘│    └─────────────────┘    ─── FUNDING
           │    (FUTURE)      │                               COUNCILS
           │                  │
           │  PROFFESSIONS ───┤                           ─── HER MAJESTY'S
           │                  │                               INSPECTORS
           │                  │
           │   EMPLOYERS ─────┤                           ─── PROFESSIONAL
           │                  │                               BODIES
           │    PARENTS ──────┤
 EXTERNAL  │
 INTERESTS │  GRANT BODIES ───┘
           ▼
```

The range of stakeholder interests includes:

(a) establishing educational and financial standards of course provision;

(b) providing contracts at costs per student for a defined course and numbers of students on a course. The suppliers of the course, the staff, mainly academic staff and the support services which make it possible (eg librarians, electricians). The clients: the students? or future employers? or society as a whole?

2.11 To maintain standards, professional bodies like to limit access. The client's expectation is that not all will achieve the same degree classification.

2.12 The concepts of quality are being set by *regulatory bodies* who are replacing the 'tutor' supplier in setting standards. The client's interests may be representing the regulators (eg Academic Board/student and staff representation, employers as Governors, staff on professional bodies).

2.13 To achieve TQM, lecturers, managers, administrators, technicians and anyone involved in the operation of the course would be expected to create learning frameworks, documentation, communication methods, evaluative techniques which would enhance the feeling of quality and reliability. This would require increasing budget costs and providing time, space, coordination of efforts.

2.14 The inherent conflict in seeking this total quality management in such a service area as higher education is between:

(a) the 'right to manage' to set conditions, standards, draw up contracts, appraise performance;

(b) the professional autonomy and integrity of academic staff and departments, as this could lead to a loss of goodwill and trust. The gap between managers and the managed grows and autocracy, mistrust, defensiveness and disillusion provides poor conditions for a 'quality' management policy.

2.15 Current theory on quality management affirms the need to involve staff at all levels of delivery and to create a people centred climate within devolved participative decision making structures. The administrative control systems to achieve *standard levels* of performance might be more inappropriate in this setting. Quality standards are examined more detail below.

3. QUALITY STANDARDS

3.1 The postal service might establish a standard that 90% of first class letters will be delivered on the day after they are posted, and 99% will be delivered within two days of posting. Procedures would have to be established for ensuring that these standards could be met (eg frequency of collections, automated letter sorting, frequency of deliveries and number of staff employed etc). Actual performance could be monitored, perhaps by taking samples from time to time of letters that are posted and delivered. If the quality standard is not being achieved, the management of the postal service could take control action (eg employ more postmen or advertise again the use of postcodes) or reduce the standard of quality of the service being provided.

Quality control and inspection

3.2 The position of the quality control and inspection department within an organisation may vary. In manufacturing industries, quality control is often seen as a manufacturing responsibility based on the inspection of output by 'quality control' staff. The quality control manager might have a semi-independent position in the organisation, reporting details of rejected or defective items to the manufacturing manager, but not taking orders from him. Instead, the quality control manager might be accountable to the production director - to management at a senior level.

3.3 Inspection is only one aspect of quality control, however, and a distinction has to be made between *quality control* in its wider sense and *inspection*.

(a) *Quality control* is concerned with trying to make sure that a product is manufactured, or a service is provided, so as to meet certain design specifications. This involves setting controls for the process of manufacture or provision of a service. It is a 'technique' aimed at *preventing* the manufacture of defective items (or the provision of defective services).

(b) *Inspection* is concerned with looking at products that have been made, supplies which have been delivered and services that have been provided, to establish whether they have been up to specification. It is a technique of *identifying* when defective items are being manufactured at an excessive and unacceptable level.

Inspection is normally carried out at three main points:

(i)   receiving inspection - for raw materials and bought out components;
(ii) floor or process inspection; and
(iii) final inspection or testing.

3.4   Quality control therefore represents process planning and process control, whereas inspection deals with the identification of faulty output. There is a connection between them, and quality control staff ought to tell inspection staff:

(a) what needs inspecting;
(b) when it ought to be inspected; and
(c) how many items ought to be inspected.

3.5   Inspection management would decide *how* products or services ought to be inspected.

Where and when are quality control measures taken?

3.6   Quality control happens at various stages in the process of designing and providing a product or service.

(a) *Product design stage*
At the product design stage, quality control means trying to design a product or service so that its specifications provide a suitable balance between price and quality (of sales and delivery, as well as manufacture) which will make the product or service competitive. Quality is a characteristic which distinguishes the goods or services of one business from those of its competitors. However, higher quality will cost more and so a suitable balance has to be struck between quality and price. One technique for exercising quality control at the product design stage is *value analysis*. This is based on the idea that goods should be produced in the most economic way harmonious with value to the customer.

(b) *Production engineering stage*
Production engineering is the process of designing the methods for making a product (or service) to the design specification. It sets out to make production methods as efficient as possible, and to avoid the making of sub-standard items.

One aspect of quality control in production engineering is manufacturing tolerances. Production engineers must decide how much variation or 'tolerance' can be allowed in the manufacture of an item, before the item fails to meet its design specification. If tolerances are too lax, too many sub-standard products will be made. If tolerances are unnecessarily tight - an accuracy of plus or minus 0.005 cm when plus or minus 0.03 cm would be perfectly adequate - production costs will be higher than they need be. Surface finish is another area where production engineering might incur unnecessary costs by arranging for products to be 'over-finished'.

(c) *Quality assurance of goods inwards*
The quality of output depends on the quality of input materials, and so quality control should include procedures for acceptance inspection of goods inwards. Inspection methods, like inspection of finished goods within the organisation, will normally be based on statistical sampling techniques and the concept of an *acceptance quality level* (AQL). Another approach that can be used is to give each supplier a 'rating' for the quality of the goods they tend to supply, and give preference with purchase orders to well-rated suppliers. (This method is referred to as 'vendor rating').

(d) *Inspection of output*, perhaps at various stages in the production process. Inspection, based on sampling and other statistical techniques, will provide a continual check that the production process is under control. (This is sometimes called quality assurance.) The aim of inspection is not really to sort out the bad products from the good ones after the work has been done. The aim is to satisfy management that quality control in production is being maintained. More will be said about inspection methods later.

(e) *Monitoring customer complaints* with a view to deciding whether changes are needed in product design, product engineering or inspection methods.

Some sub-standard items will inevitably be produced. Inspection will identify some bad output, but other items will reach the customer. Customer quality complaints have to be dealt with, as part of the organisation's service. As far as quality control is concerned, complaints ought to be monitored, with a view to identifying quality weaknesses in product design, production engineering, production standards or the quality of raw materials in use.

How is quality performance measured?

3.7   If no defective items are allowed, and all output must be perfect, there would have to be 100% inspection. However, it is usual to accept that some defective output will be made and it is not the end of the world if they get through to the customer.

When some defectives are allowed to get through, the measurement of quality can be based on the inspection of *samples* of output (or goods inwards). This is known as *acceptance sampling*.

3.8   The inspection of samples rather than 100% testing of all items will keep inspection costs down, and smaller samples will be less costly to inspect than larger samples. The greater the confidence in the reliability of production methods and process control, the smaller the samples will be. For example, if a production process has a fairly high proportion of defectives, 10% of all output might be inspected; whereas if the process rarely goes out of control, the sample sizes for inspection might be 1% or less of output.

3.9   The acceptance quality level (AQL) is the maximum percentage of defectives that will be tolerated, on economic grounds, in the samples that are tested. If the AQL is 2%, say, this would mean that the organisation is taking the view that a maximum of 2% of output can be allowed to be defective, because the costs of reducing the proportion of defectives further would not be worth the costs of improved quality control. When defectives exceed the AQL, the quality-related costs will be too high, and improvements in quality would be called for.

Statistical quality control charts

3.10 Statistical quality control charts might be used to record and monitor the accuracy of the physical dimensions of products. The theory recognises that the exact dimensions may vary in a random manner due to the effects of chance. A typical control chart is shown below. The horizontal axis on the graph is time, the vertical axis is the physical dimension of the product in appropriate units. Above and below the level of the expected dimension of the product are the control limits. The graph shows inner warning limits and outer action limits although in many cases only one limit is used. The limits are set such a distance from the expected dimension that a value outside the limits is very unlikely to have occurred by chance and consequently the size of the deviation from the expected dimension indicates that something may have gone wrong with the manufacturing process. Normally, the values plotted on the chart would be the mean of a small sample taken at regular points in time.

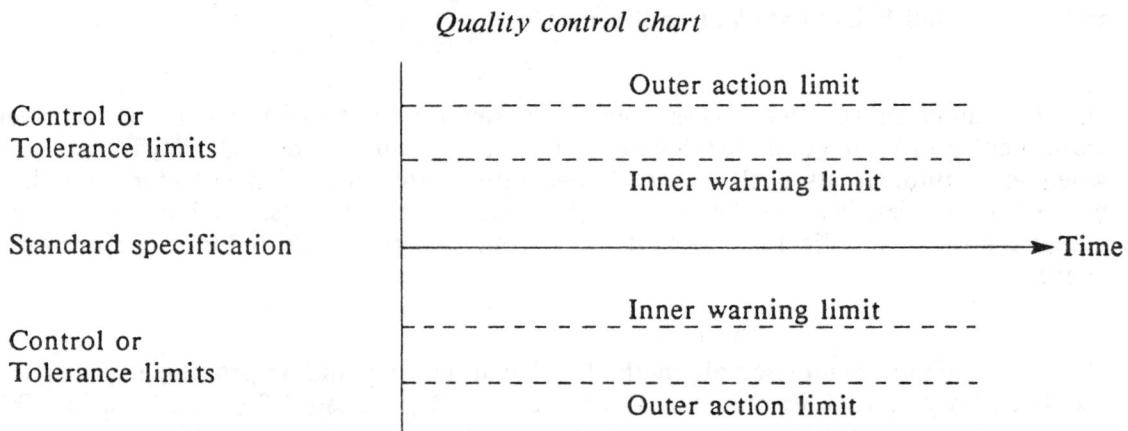

Quality control chart

	Outer action limit
Control or Tolerance limits	
	Inner warning limit
Standard specification	→ Time
	Inner warning limit
Control or Tolerance limits	
	Outer action limit

3.11 Samples of an output manufacturing process may be taken daily or even every hour, and faults in the manufacturing process which are revealed may be fairly simple to correct by adjusting the appropriate machinery. If output exceeds the control limits consistently, more urgent management action would be called for, because this would indicate:

(a) inefficiency in production, by labour or the machines;
(b) inadequacy in production methods;
(c) inadequate quality of raw materials and components; or
(d) excessively tight tolerances in the first place.

Quality assurance

3.12 The essentials of quality assurance are that the supplier guarantees the quality of his goods and allows the customers' inspectors access while the items are being manufactured. Usually agreed inspection procedures and quality control standards are worked out by customer and supplier between them, and checks are made to ensure that they are being adhered to.

(a) The main advantage to the customer is that he can almost eliminate goods inwards inspection and items can be directed straight to production. This can give large savings in cost and time in flow production assembly plant, and can facilitate JIT production.

(b) The advantage to the supplier is that he produces to the customers' requirement, therefore reducing rejects. Also the cost of returning reject material from the customer is saved.

3.13 Suppliers' quality assurance schemes are being used increasingly, particularly where extensive sub-contracting work is carried out, eg the motor industries.

3.14 Franchising activities may be based around a quality assurance provision with help from a central source on quality standards, and inspection of work in progress.

3.15 In the higher education service provision the use of external inspection and the Council for National Academic Awards has provided a level of quality assurance on setting up and reviewing courses and establishing rules for operating courses. External examiners are appointed to report to the CNAA and also to professional bodies on the quality of the outputs from the courses and evidence of the use of resources and developmental approaches taking place in courses. The loss and wastage from courses can be achieved through stringent entry requirements and having well briefed student applicants.

3.16 Quality assurance refers to the ways in which the relationship between clients and suppliers is 'patterned' in order to guarantee that needs and expectations are met. Quality is assured only when each tutor treats such clients (other tutors, students, administrators, employers, professional bodies) in a way that meets their needs and expectations. The implicit assumption is that the tutor (supplier) is able to discern accurately the needs and expectations of each client.

3.17 Quality assurance comprises all methods of maintaining and improving supplier client relationships and focuses on internal structures and processes of communication. These processes will cover subject documents, staff to staff communications, staff appraisals, use of employer or professional panels, bringing visiting experts; and all the elements which make up the course.

3.18 Quality monitoring is an important element of quality assurance. Monitoring is concerned with the external perception of the course and the accountability to the stakeholders. The view of the clients provides another view of how courses are run and how all the elements come together, the range of lecturers, working conditions, library, administration, marking and feedback to students. The collective view may be different from the view of the individuals input views who do not see the collective impact of the course only their own contribution. If the perceptions of the external monitors differs from the internal view then further work may be needed to communicate what is happening or improve the processes involved.

Quality control in the Employment Service

3.19 An article in the August 1992 issue of *Plus* magazine described the application of Total Quality Management in the Employment Service in the West Midlands. This was introduced after the regional director visited a Nissan factory where TQM or similar procedures were in operation. The regional director felt that the techniques of the manufacturing sector could be applied in the service sector.

3.20 The region used *statistical process control* to assess the degree to which management systems affected quality, and to explain this to officer managers.

3.21 Some of the changes are physical (eg open plan offices), some are cultural (a reduction in 'private offices'), others are technical.

    (a) Quality teams have been 'looking in painstaking detail at ways they could improve the rate of placing unemployed people into jobs, the speed with which a benefit claim is processed on to the computer and similar issues'.

    (b) Another example of the TQM approach to processes is an examination of the information requested on forms. This has enabled some unnecessary requests for information to be eliminated.

3.22 The article reported measurable improvements in performance. It is, however, important to note that TQM was not simply yet another technique bolted on top of existing management process but was accompanied by a *change in culture*, in that:

    (a) operators have more chance of influencing actual work processes;

    (b) the management style has changed from an autocratic one, to one where the manager is more of a team leader.

4. QUALITY MEASUREMENT

4.1 The quality assurance process requires that key performance indicators can be defined and that acceptable levels of performance can be determined and measured.

4.2 It is important that organisations can demonstrate their quality of performance by recognition through standards which show the right process and practices are adopted, or through consumer satisfaction (eg a repeat purchase).

4.3 In the new world of higher education it is necessary that 'we can demonstrate continuing and improving quality of our courses to those individuals and agencies whose judgements and decisions can affect out future survival, if we cannot we will assuredly begin to lose ground to our competitors'. This all depends on what is measured and what the clients see as relevant quality measures.

4.4 The measures have to be defined by the supplier as well as the client as it is the internal operation of quality assurance that will be most effective.

4.5 Quality measurements have come mainly from the private sector and from the manufacturing sector and need interpretation for the public and service sectors.

Customer care has become an issue, and the notions of skills and competencies related to attitudes and individual's behaviour have been taken up by the public sector. The 'production' 'non variable' output view from the manufacturing sector may be inappropriate to the interactive learning and development process over a three or four year period when the client may meet many 'actors' from the suppliers side.

4.6 The measurement in quality monitoring can cover inputs, processes and outputs. The Audit Commission have added the idea of outcomes as well, such as increasing students intrinsic capacity to learn, to be stimulated by the learning experience, which may be difficult to measure.

4.7 The types of factors which can be measured could include the following.

(a) *Input factors*

    (i)   Staff resources: individual academic/administrative
                                 group teaching team/course teams

    (ii) Student inputs: initial quality
                                 attendance
                                 participation
                                 contribution

    (iii) Access: minorities
                                 mature students
                                 overseas students
                                 European students
                                 transfer and credit accumulation
                                 franchising

    (iv) Learning facilities: rooms, lecture/tutorial/workshop
                                 environment
                                 library
                                 computing
                                 sport recreation
                                 students facilities - shops
                                 restaurants, bars

    (v) Research and development: institutional individual research
                                 consultancy links with industry and commerce
                                 course development/adaption
                                 new courses
                                 development of teaching methods and staff development

(b) *Process factors*

    (i)   Learning experiences: mix of activities

    (ii) Teaching experiences: range of teaching staff

    (iii) Placement: external learning experience

    (iv) Course administration: course committees, admin staff

    (v) Course management: day to day operation

    (vi) Assessment process: clear process of assessment

    (vii) Subject development: peer group review

(viii) Non academic support: public relations
marketing
communication

(c) *Output factors*

(i) Student performance: achievements
academic profiles
competencies
non academic contribution - membership course committees,
student union,
expeditions

(ii) Staff development: time available for learning new skills - computer aided
design
time for research consultancy
external examining
academic evaluation

(iii) Graduate employability: records of employment

(iv) Contact with professions
and business: teaching contracts

(v) Course reputation: quality criteria for course funding
repeat purchases
research grants
peer review

The measurement of all the factors can provide a profile of the organisation which can then be used for further investigation. A theme for carrying out an audit of performance in a particular year may be a way of measuring a particular activity, links with the wider community could be renewed and assessed. As 'companies' annual reports and financial audits can be used to demonstrate quality of performance.

4.8 Student satisfaction surveys and student centred feedback and profiling can provide detailed measurement of the immediate client interests. This is not a prevention approach but a learning approach. The opening learning organisation which is responsive to client needs is what can be aimed for, right than always getting it right.

5. QUALITY CIRCLES

5.1 Quality circles originated in America in the early 1960s and were further developed in Japan and have been used in Britain over the last ten years. They were used by Rolls Royce in 1978 but have been slow to be adopted. They have been used by such companies as Wedgewood and IBM.

5.2 The essential features of establishing a quality circle group are that:

(a) members join voluntarily;

(b) the group is kept small between five and ten members;

(c)   members are drawn from the same work situation;

(d)   the group select the topic to be tackled;

(e)   leadership is determined by the group;

(f)   training is provided on communication and problem solving skills;

(g)   quality control techniques and group process;

(h)   the group can make recommendations to management and where possible should be able to implement the agreed solution to the problem.

5.3   The acceptance of quality circles depends on the top management taking a participatory view of management, and being open and trusting with staff. Time has to be made available for the group to meet. Some training in how to conduct the group is necessary, and the role of any management representatives in the group, needs to be clearly defined. The group need to believe that the proposals they make or suggestions in working practices would be accepted by the management.

5.4   The issues being tackled in the groups are generally matters that cause small problems. They cover the redesign of forms used in the accounts department for stock control. The reorganising of the telephone directory so that time is saved in responding to calls. This is a matter that can relate to the whole organisation and may imply some costs and reorganisation of phone lines.

5.5   Quality circles can work well as part of an organisation development and training programme. This requires the organisational implications of quality circles to be considered in taking into account the interrelated nature of decisions for different sections and activities in the organisation. The group may be seen as a threat to the existing power structure in the organisation, to supervisory managers or to trade unions who lose the bargaining position they may hold.

5.6   Quality circles also take up time with a few hours set aside each week to work on the problem and make recommendations which may again require time to implement. To maintain group motivation and good group working relations over a three or four month period may be a challenge.

5.7   Quality circles tackle practical problems. The tackling of problems collectively means that ideas and technical issues can be worked on in an open and constructive way, with everyone benefiting. Issues of quality are particularly of interest.

5.8   To enable such an approach as quality circles to work, then the organisation has to be orientated to providing individuals with the opportunity to take part in developing the organisation. The performance of the organisation is an intrinsic reward for individual effort. This may be taking lots of barriers down and creating a people centred trusting organisation.

Exercise

What do you think are the costs of poor quality?

Solution

(a) Rectification costs (eg salaries, materials).
(b) Extra warehousing/storage costs, as the defective items have to be 'stored' somewhere.
(c) Complaints department.
(d) Loss of goodwill, repeat purchases etc.

---

6. CONCLUSION

6.1 Quality is a management philosophy that makes a priority of getting both products and processes right, which, in the long term are what an organisation needs for success.

6.2 There are some limits to the extent to which this philosophy can be transported wholesale to the service sector.

6.3 Quality control occurs at various stages in design and manufacture of products and services.

6.4 Successful application of techniques such as TQM require a change of culture. TQM is not a 'quick fix'.

TEST YOUR KNOWLEDGE
The numbers in brackets refer to paragraphs of this chapter

1   Define quality (1.2)

2   Describe two contrasting approaches to quality and cost control. (2.6)

3   What is quality control? (3.3)

4   What is a quality circle? (5.1)

Now try question 15 at the end of the text

Chapter 16

CREATIVITY, INNOVATION AND CONTROL

This chapter covers the following topics.

1. Creativity and innovation
2. Problem solving
3. Control of staff
4. Management education, training and development

---

1. CREATIVITY AND INNOVATION

1.1 *Creativity* is held to be a quality possessed in different degrees by different individuals. Broadly speaking, if a person is good at generating new ideas, and generates them frequently, then that person can be said to be creative.

1.2 Creativity, in organisational terms, can be useful for:

(a) spotting new ways of satisfying markets;
(b) devising new uses for existing products;
(c) developing ideas for new products;
(d) developing new ideas for administration;
(e) developing new work practices.

1.3 Successful innovation - which some authors argue is the elixir of corporate immortality - requires organisations to:

(a) encourage creativity (in that innovation shouldn't simply be a reaction to current conditions but a means of creating them);

(b) invest in research and development (including market research);

(c) implement the necessary personnel policies.

1.4 Examples of innovation are:

(a) Dell Computers, which innovated in the way in which the computers it sold were distributed and marketed;

(b) the Sony Walkman, a new product which created a new market.

1.5   Some industries require a constant flow of innovation in products in order to exist, even if innovation might simply mean the repackaging of the products.

    (a)   The fashion industry requires constant innovation.

    (b)   Consumer electronics companies need to innovate constantly in new products (eg digital compact cassette).

1.6   In some cases there is a dispute as to whether innovation is, or should be:

    (a)   technology-led ('let's find a way of selling this wonderful gadget'); or
    (b)   demand-led ('this is what customers might want').

Successful innovation requires attention to both product and market.

Encouraging innovation

1.7   To foster innovation requires a new(-ish) set of management attitudes. Some companies have departments in which 'creative' people (scientists, computer boffins, graphic designers etc) can be hidden away, so that their unconventional work practices do not infect the rest of the organisation.

1.8   Just as important, however, is bringing a new idea to market. Therefore the department responsible for innovation should not be isolated from production and marketing.

1.9   Some ways in which innovation can be encouraged are outlined below.

    (a)   Encourage self-reliance, initiative and a constructively critical approach to the way the organisation goes about its business.

    (b)   Thomas Attwood suggests the following steps for *creating an innovative culture* from one which has previously existed in a cosy, unthreatening world.

        (i)   Ensure management and staff know what innovation is and how it happens.
        (ii)   Ensure that senior managers welcome, and are seen to welcome, changes for the better.
        (iii)   Stimulate and motivate management and staff to think and act innovatively.
        (iv)   Understand people in the organisation and their needs.
        (v)   Recognise and encourage potential 'entrepreneurs'.

    (c)   An innovation strategy calls for a management policy of giving encouragement to innovative ideas. This will require:

        (i)   giving financial backing to innovation, by spending on R & D and market research and risking capital on new ideas;

        (ii)   giving employees the opportunity to work in an environment where the exchange of ideas for innovation can take place. Management style and organisation structure can help here:

        (1)   management can actively encourage employees and customers to put forward new ideas. Participation by subordinates in development decisions might encourage employees to become more involved with development projects and committed to their success;

        (2)   development teams can be set up and an organisation built up on project team-work;

  (iii)   where appropriate, recruitment policy should be directed towards appointing employees with the necessary skills for doing innovative work. Employees should be trained and kept up to date;

  (iv)   certain managers should be made responsible for obtaining information from outside the organisation about innovative ideas, and for communicating this information throughout the organisation;

  (v)   strategic planning should result in targets being set for innovation, and successful achievements by employees should if possible be rewarded.

(d) Creative ideas can come from anywhere and at any time, but if management wish to foster innovation they should try to provide an organisation structure in which innovative ideas are encouraged to emerge.

  (i)   Innovation requires creativity. Creativity may be encouraged in an individual or group by establishing a climate in which free expression of abilities is allowed. 'Hot water thought sessions' (brainstorming etc) could be used. The *role of the R & D department* will be significant in many organisations.

  (ii)   Creative ideas must then be rationally analysed (in 'cold water thought sessions') to decide whether they provide a viable (commercial etc) proposition.

  (iii)   A system of organisation must exist whereby a viable creative idea is converted into action through effective control procedures.

1.10 The innovation has to be accepted by all relevant areas of the organisation as being worthwhile and better than previous approaches or at lower cost. Gaining acceptance is sometimes a 'political process'.

1.11 For an innovation to be accepted:

(a) the innovation should meet users' needs;

(b) the innovation needs a champion in top management;

(c) the innovation must work, and can be implemented without major changes to existing activities;

(d) resources should be available to implement the changes required;

(e) the customers ought to be satisfied by the outcome of the changes;

(f) cooperation must be sought when introducing the innovation.

1.12 Resistance to innovation can result from the following.

(a) Previous experiences of unsuccessful innovations because:

(i)   they had not been fully thought through in technical or operational terms;
(ii)   more resources or training were needed than was made available;
(iii) the new methods were not any better than those they proposed to replace.

(b) The innovations were poorly communicated and not well endorsed by senior management.

(c) The innovation had little value.

(d) The scale of the innovation was such that it threatened the whole organisation with disruption and required massive, costly and long term adjustments to working arrangements.

1.13 Relocations or joint ventures are opportunities to introduce innovation. However the innovation might fail because of all the additional disruption.

1.14 The introduction of innovations should be a controlled process.

(a) There may be unintended or unexpected side effects, which are detrimental to the innovation or to the organisation as a whole.

(b) Personnel might be required to implement the innovation.

The balance of forces

1.15 There may be a number of factors affecting the success or otherwise of an innovation.

(a) People may not recognise a problem. If a problem is identified, the innovation can be presented as a solution. Perhaps this is an internal marketing exercise by the proponents of innovation.

(b) The ways in which the innovation can be implemented can be identified by:

(i)   looking at comparative situations;
(ii)   using rigorous analytical methods to interrogate the current situations;
(iii) identifying the gap between the current situation and the desired outcome to detect the ways in which this can be bridged.

1.16 It is possible to describe relationships between the *need* to innovate, the willingness to innovate and the feasibility of the innovation.

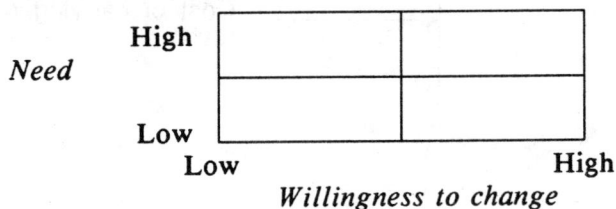

```
          High ┌──────────┬──────────┐
   Need        │          │          │
               ├──────────┼──────────┤
               │          │          │
           Low └──────────┴──────────┘
             Low                    High
               Willingness to change
```

Are the problems so bad, how willing are people to change?

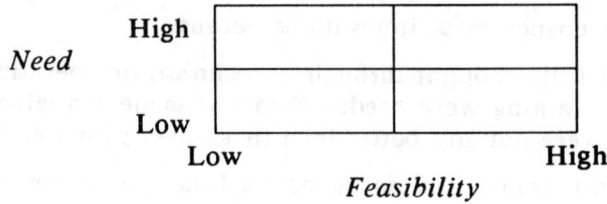

```
         High ┌──────────┬──────────┐
   Need        │          │          │
              ├──────────┼──────────┤
          Low  │          │          │
              └──────────┴──────────┘
              Low                  High
                    Feasibility
```

Which issues should be treated first? How likely is change to occur?

1.17 Forcefield analysis can be used to identify ways of dealing with an unsatisfactory situation. It is based on the idea that in any group or organisational situation there is an interplay of restraining and driving forces that keeps things as they are. Forcefield analysis maps these forces that are pushing toward the preferred state and the restraining forces, which are pushing back to the current state. They can then be presented in a chart.

Organisational situation: No system for performance review

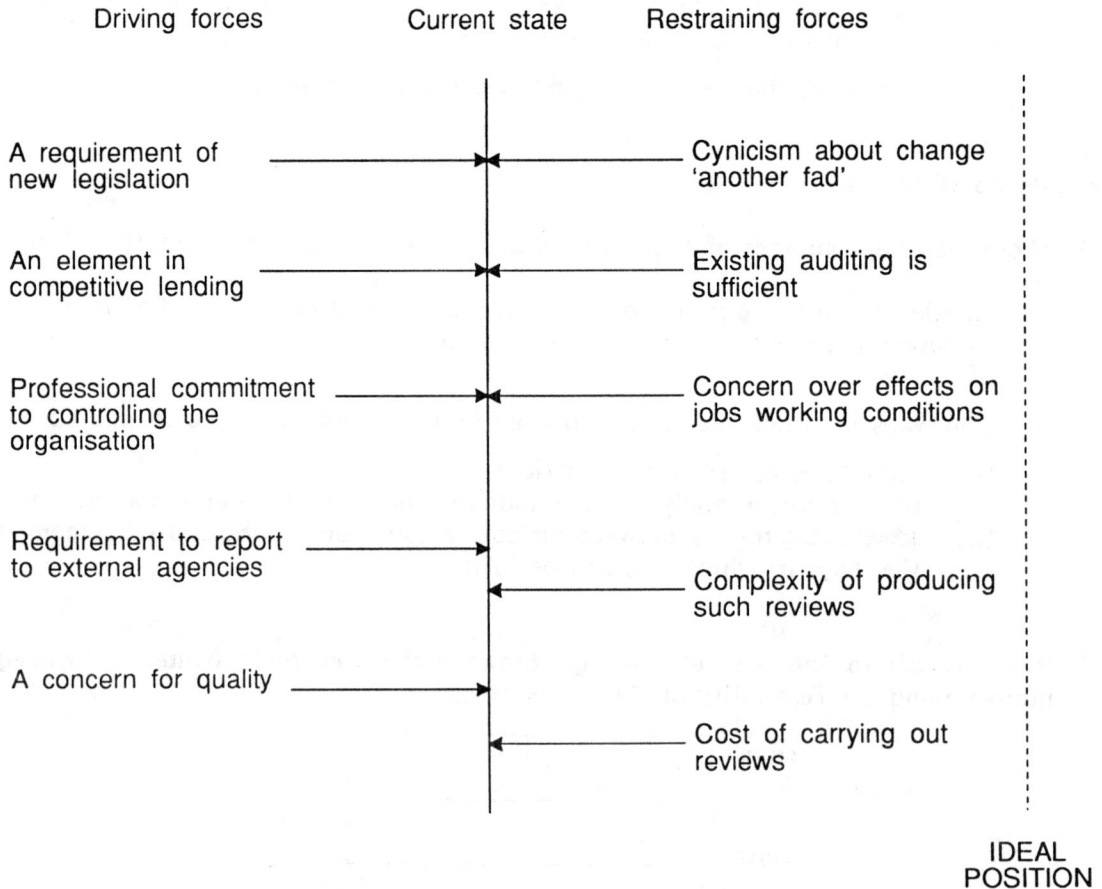

Driving forces	Current state	Restraining forces
A requirement of new legislation		Cynicism about change 'another fad'
An element in competitive lending		Existing auditing is sufficient
Professional commitment to controlling the organisation		Concern over effects on jobs working conditions
Requirement to report to external agencies		Complexity of producing such reviews
A concern for quality		Cost of carrying out reviews

IDEAL
POSITION

278

1.18 Once the driving and restraining forces have been identified, an action plan can be drawn up covering the following issues.

(a) People associated with the driving forces can be co-opted to educate opponents.
(b) Vested interests will have to be addressed directly.

1.19 How much coercion should be used?

(a) Some element of coercion may ultimately be necessary. It helps, for example, if the external auditor can be persuaded to suggest measures supported by the proponents of the innovation.

(b) Involving people in diagnosing problem situations (eg in quality circles), wins over 'hearts and minds'.

1.20 The fears of the resistors may be 'irrational', but because of rumour, ambiguity, poor communication, previous bad experiences, fears of redundancy and cost cutting, a leadership style of encouragement and improvement rather than one which dictates solutions and decisions, is needed.

1.21 To achieve innovation it is necessary to consider:

(a) education and communication;
(b) participation and involvement;
(c) facilitation support;
(d) negotiation and agreements;
(e) manipulation and co-option;
(f) coercion, implicit or explicit.

Factors (a) and (b) are desirable strategies as people are psychologically prepared in advance, and disruption will be minimised.

1.22 Innovation then becomes part of the management of change. In the public sector it is particularly related to the management and control of professional staff.

Organisational learning

1.23 If we combine the ideas that:

(a) an organisation is more than an arrangement of individuals but a social organism; with
(b) knowledge must be created to ensure continuous innovation;

we can say that organisations have to learn. Both technical and management skills are embodied in the ways people relate to each other in the organisation.

1.24 The learning organisation therefore:

(a) encourages continuous learning and knowledge generation at all levels;
(b) has the processes to move knowledge around the organisation;
(c) can transform knowledge into actual behaviour.

1.25 Peter Senge (in *The Fifth Discipline - The Art and Practice of the Learning Organisation*) argues that to create a learning organisation, individuals and groups should be encouraged to learn five disciplines.

(a) *Systems thinking*. This is the ability to see particular problems as part of a wider whole, and to devise appropriate solutions to them.

(b) *Personal learning and growth*. Individuals should be encouraged to acquire skills and knowledge.

(c) *Mental models*. These are deeply ingrained assumptions (perhaps of the Theory X/Theory Y type) which determined what individuals think about other individuals. This can be about the best way of managing people, about products (eg how are car looks more important than how comfortable it is to drive) or marketing (price is more important than quality).

Learning organisations can use a number of group techniques to make these models explicit, and to challenge them.

(d) There must be a shared vision, but not so forceful as to discourage organisational learning. It should not filter knowledge which undermines the vision.

(e) Team learning. Some tasks can only be done in groups. Teams, however, must be trained to learn, as there are factors in group dynamics which impede learning.

1.26 Organisational learning would seem to turn some of the ideas about *leadership* on their head, as it is about *group* communication and responsiveness. It also challenges some of the assumptions about creativity (eg that it resides only in the *individual*) that underpin one of the basic stereotypes of Western culture.

2. PROBLEM SOLVING

2.1 Rather than using analytic methods it may be useful to encourage individual and group creativity. The creative process has four stages.

(a) Preparation (researching for relevant information).
(b) Incubation (finding time to think about the issue, 'sleeping on it').
(c) Insight (different ways of presenting the problem).
(d) Verification (testing the insights to see whether worthwhile or feasible).

De Bono's technique of *lateral thinking* is one way of looking at problems outside the notional range. Sometimes it is important to define the problem in a new way. Tony Buzan *(Use your Head)* also looks at ways of drawing up 'mind maps' to find intuitive relationships of ideas and then refining and verifying them.

2.2 Brainstorming is a technique to encourage creativity through the free association of ideas in a group situation. A problem situation is set up then the group come up with as many ideas within a limited time period as possible. During the brainstorming session:

   (a) no criticism of ideas is allowed;

   (b) a free wheeling approach is taken (the wilder the idea, the better);

   (c) quantity of the ideas is regarded as more important than the quality;

   (d) combinations and variations of ideas are encouraged so that the ideas can be built into chains of inspiration.

   Variations include a *clean slate approach* (participants must start from scratch and make no assumptions about the existing situation).

2.3 From these freewheeling exercises, more practical responses can be developed. (Say a member of staff did not fit in. 'Send him on a cruise' might be the brainstormed response, if he is ill at ease. This can be translated into 'send him on a training course'.)

2.4 Techniques of evaluating alternative solutions can then be brought into play.

   (a) Evaluation criteria may be laid down to judge the solutions (eg the time, costs or disruption required to introduce the potential innovations).

   (b) Solutions can be weighted by how many of the goals are reached, and how important they are.

2.5 Weighting systems can be arbitrary. Some issues may be hard to quantify in this way. The outcome of such analysis may be that satisficing solutions are accepted rather than optimum or maximising ones (ie the safest, rather than the best solutions).

2.6 The greater degree of certainty the lower the risk. Risk is an assessment of the probability that a decision will be right or wrong, or somewhere in between, granted the certainties and uncertainties of the problem situation.

2.7 (a) Risk averse people avoid uncertain situations, and like problems to be quantified in a subjective way to reduce irrational analysis.

   (b) The risk seekers on the other hand see problems as opportunities and are willing to take chances if the outcomes are attractive.

2.8 A *decision tree* is a graphical portrait of the problem solving process. It shows how each alternative solution forks or branches to produce several possible outcomes.

16: CREATIVITY, INNOVATION AND CONTROL

Decisions	Response	Performance

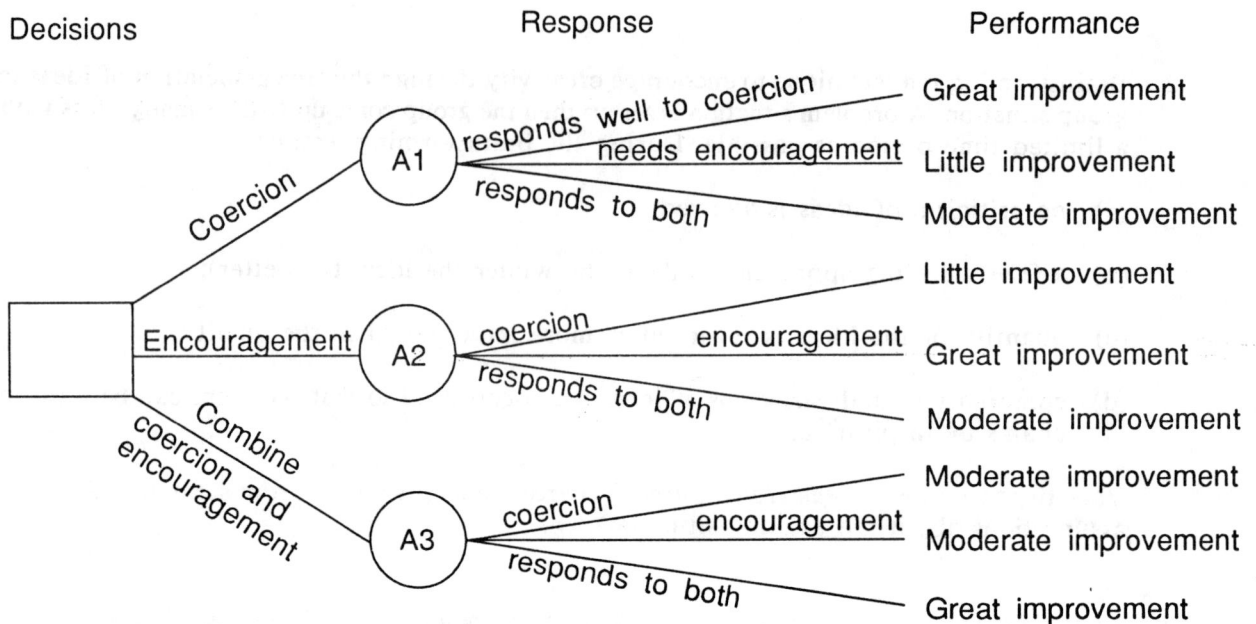

Decision free on use of coercion or encouragement to obtain change in working conditions.

A values can be given to each outcome (eg great improvement 5 points, moderate improvement 3 points, little improvement 1 point). A probable outcome for A1 is 9 points, for A2 9 points and for A3 is 11 points. A3 is the option then to choose.

2.9 Computer aided techniques can be used to model situations (eg input/output analysis, 'what if' questions, sensitivity analysis). These models depend on the quality of the data, and the appropriateness of the relationships outlined in the model.

2.10 Linear programming can produce optimum solutions to problems that require the allocation of a combination of limited resources as in economic location models.

2.11 Simulation and game theory can be used to simulate actual and possible conditions.

(a) Bringing together managers to work on problem solving in a simulated working situation can bring out solutions and develop competences which would be difficult to generate in the real world.

(b) Game theory can be used to develop competitive strategies and to see what would happen if certain choices are made.

3. CONTROL OF STAFF

3.1 Staff development and training play an important role in introducing new ideas and developing new working practices.

3.2   The organisation should then set up policies for the development of staff and the introduction of creative and innovative working. Training for the organisation's management of its professionally qualified staff should focus on the functions of management (that is, to plan, organise, coordinate, direct and control).

Planning

3.3   The planning required vis-à-vis professionally qualified staff should be part of the overall personnel planning exercise, from recruitment and training to how to plan for staff turnover and retirement.

3.4   A manpower plan should be constructed for the organisation to denote present and future manpower needs, given any planned changes such as growth, divestment, diversification etc. It will dictate how many staff should be recruited and how they should be trained, taking into account how long it is expected that training to become professionally qualified should take and what the likely dropout rate will be.

3.5   Planning for training is also important because without carefully constructed individual development programmes professionally qualified staff are likely to become out-of-date and/or to leave. Training and the promotion which goes with it are important motivational factors for staff whose qualification is a hard-won and rare commodity. If these are not provided it is likely that staff turnover will be relatively high, which must therefore also be taken into account.

3.6   Although professionally qualified staff are neither more nor less likely to retire early, the organisation must plan for staff losses through retirement. If it wants to be more sure of retaining staff then it is wise to have an attractive pension policy to entice them to stay.

These plans become even more vital if the organisation depends on the development of teamwork and long-term commitment from qualified staff - say in the aerospace industry where planning horizons are broad and technical expertise vital.

3.7   The planning of promotion and creating new managers by using staff development appraisals or job rotation is also important. Having staff on *short term* contracts and encouraging an exit culture has made succession planning easier in the public sector where security of employment had been previously guaranteed, and promotion was by 'Buggins' turn'.

Organising

3.8   As with any other staff the work of professionally qualified managers must be organised so that organisational objectives are met. However, organising can prove problematic since in effect such people have two roles - as professionals and as managers. They may see a dichotomy between *working* - implementing their own technical skills - and *attending* - watching over others using their skills (ie managing). Broadly speaking, the balance must be right.

(a) *Flexibility*. Although workflow must be organised so that individual and departmental task and job objectives and allocation are integrated, such organisation must be flexible enough to allow the professionally qualified staff to feel that they have some autonomy and are achieving a balance of professional and managerial work.

(b) *Training and development*, as we have seen, must be built into the organisation of staff so that both organisational and individual objectives are met.

(c) *Delegation* of authority can be problematic because, although managerial authority may be delegated, professional ethics often state that professional authority cannot be implemented by another person. This may mean that every professional in the hierarchy feels that he must minutely analyse the work of his subordinates to ensure that it meets his own professional standards. This can be time-consuming.

(d) *Responsibility*, in a professional and in a management sense, may mean two different things (linked with (c) above). In order to ensure professional standards it may be necessary to organise a review body which assesses whether the line professional staff have performed their work properly.

(e) Technical skills and management skills can be linked together in *hybrid posts* (eg a research chemist working six months in the laboratory and the next six months managing the production process in the German subsidiary, then selling the new products in the Far East for six months). This is particularly relevant when it comes to information technology.

3.9 Management responsibilities are being pushed lower down (eg to the ward sister to organise duty rotas, training, discipline and appraisals).

3.10 It is important to consider organisational development, the overall needs of the organisation as well as the section or individual in development training and development schemes.

Coordinating

3.11 Both within a professionally qualified manager's job and within the organisation as a whole there must be coordination between the functional context - getting the job done - and the professional context - doing the job properly. This will require formal communication channels as well as, possibly, elements of a matrix structure.

Directing

3.12 Professionally qualified staff, as with any other type, need to be motivated to produce satisfactory work and to remain with the organisation. They may be motivated by:

(a) having responsibility and discretion;

(b) being included in decision-making (consultation or participation);

(c) a clear promotion policy and good continuing training;

(d) good remuneration and terms and conditions of work;

(e) being treated as intelligent, self-starting and conscientious staff (a management style based on Theory X would alienate them);

(f) being clearly and fairly directed in accordance with stated policies. (Inconsistent management styles are likely to be as counter-productive with professionally-qualified staff as they are with others.)

3.13 Because it is probable that professionally qualified staff will be directed by other qualified staff, it is important that there should be mutual respect. Hence the leader should ideally be better qualified (say by being a fellow of the relevant institute rather than an associate), more highly skilled, and capable of doing all those tasks which subordinates are called upon to do.

Controlling

3.14 The output of professionally qualified staff needs to be reviewed and controlled in the light of original plans as much as any employee's work, but there can be difficulties if control is too tight and impinges on their professional integrity. They expect to be trusted to exercise self-direction and, to some extent, self-supervision.

3.15 This dilemma can be met by operating an agreed and defined staff appraisal system whose objectives are stated clearly. Although this may be viewed as a vehicle of control, it is also a useful way to identify training and other development needs of the professional staff and, linked to a job evaluation scheme, should be seen as an integral part of promotion planning.

3.16 With senior professional staff it may be preferable to exercise control more informally. This will allow the professionals to feel that they 'own' their own careers and are free to seek further training if they feel they need it.

3.17 It is possible to have across-the-board control of all professional staff by ensuring that each and every one of them attend technical updating training. This will mean that none is allowed to become out of date whilst, at the same time, none feels that he or she has been singled out.

3.18 The degree of control can depend on the context in which the organisation is operating. During a period of change it may be necessary to exert more control than at a time when operations are just 'ticking over'.

3.19 In the managerial framework, control procedures should be implemented with professionally qualified staff as with non-qualified people. In particular responsibility for a budget cannot be differentiated between the two types of employee.

The broad features of the management of managers might be summarised as follows:

Function	How it might be done
1 Plan and control the activities of other managers.	(a) Corporate planning (b) Budgeting, budgetary control (c) Performance measurement/appraisal (d) Accountability.
2 Direct and motivate other managers. *Note*. Motivating subordinate managers is necessary if their own subordinates in turn are to stand much chance of being motivated. Managers set an example for their staff.	(a) Delegation of authority or centralisation of decision-making authority. (b) Allowing subordinate managers decision-making discretion.
3 Organise the work of other managers. Co-ordinate their work.	(a) Suitable organisation structure (b) Good communication.
4 Fill managerial vacancies. Staff, recruit, guide and develop managers.	(a) Selection procedures (b) Management development and appraisal programmes (c) Training and education.

3.20   In the rest of this chapter, we shall concentrate on item (4). An organisation should have:

(a)   a capable management team, with a suitable blend of abilities and experience; and

(b)   a system for filling management positions when vacancies arise, either through:

(i)   promotion from within; or
(ii)   appointments of managers from 'outside'; or
(iii)   a mixture of (i) and (ii).

4.   MANAGEMENT EDUCATION, TRAINING AND DEVELOPMENT

4.1   You might subscribe to the trait theory of leadership, that some individuals are 'born' with the personal qualities to be a good manager, and others aren't. There might be some bits of truth in this view but very few individuals, if any, can walk into a management job and do it well without some guidance, experience or training.

4.2   In every organisation, there should be some arrangements or system whereby:

(a)   managers gain *experience*, which will enable them to do another more senior job in due course of time;

(b)   subordinate managers are given *guidance* and *counselling* by their bosses;

(c)   managers are given suitable *training* and *education* to develop their skills and knowledge.

If there is a planned programme for developing managers, it is called a *management development programme*.

The difference between management education, training and development

4.3   A useful distinction between management education, training and development was given in the report *The Making of British Managers*, prepared for the BIM and CBI in 1987 by Constable and McCormick. The report gave the following definitions.

(a)   *Education* 'is that process which results in formal qualifications up to and including post-graduate degrees.'

(b)   *Training* is 'the formal learning activities which may not lead to qualifications, and which may be received at any time in a working career.'

(c)   *Development* 'is broader again: job experience and learning from other managers, particularly one's immediate superior, are integral parts of the development process.'

Development will include features such as:

(i)   career planning for individual managers;
(ii)   job rotation;
(iii)   standing in for the boss while he is away on holiday;
(iv)   on-the-job training;
(v)   counselling, perhaps by means of regular appraisal reports;
(vi)   guidance from superiors or colleagues; and
(vii)   education and training.

4.4   Education is therefore an element of training, which is an aspect of development.

The relationship of education, training and development

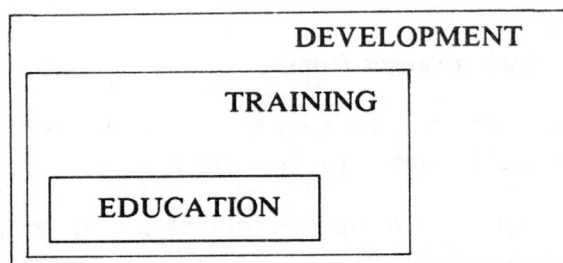

```
┌─────────────────────────────────────────┐
│              DEVELOPMENT                  │
│  ┌─────────────────────────────────────┐ │
│  │             TRAINING                 │ │
│  │  ┌──────────────────────┐           │ │
│  │  │      EDUCATION        │           │ │
│  │  └──────────────────────┘           │ │
│  └─────────────────────────────────────┘ │
└─────────────────────────────────────────┘
```

4.5   It is worth getting clear in your mind at the beginning why management education, training and development are needed.

(a)   Without training and development, managers are unlikely to be ready for promotion when the time comes, and they will not do their new job well until they have learnt by mistakes.

(b)   The selection of individuals for promotion is unlikely to be reliable, and the 'wrong people' might be selected for senior jobs. Individuals will rise to their level of incompetence!

(c)   Vacancies will often have to be filled by recruitment from outside the organisation, because not enough 'in-house' managers will be good enough or sufficiently ready for promotion.

(d)   An organisation should show an interest in the career development of its staff, so as to motivate them and encourage them to stay with the firm. Management development programmes are an important feature of being a good employer.

Management education

4.6   Education, for successful students, leads on to a formal qualification. For managers in the UK, these qualifications include:

(a)   undergraduate business and management degrees;

(b)   undergraduate degrees in related subjects such and Economics and Accountancy;

(c)   postgraduate business and management degrees (MBA course);

(d)   the postgraduate Diploma in Management Studies (DMS);

(e)   qualifications from professional institutes. Accountancy qualifications are the most common professional qualifications in the UK.

Management training

4.7   Formal training which does *not* lead on to a qualification consists mainly of:

(a)   post-experience management courses, provided by training companies or colleges and polytechnics;

(b)   in-company management training, using the company's own training staff and/or consultants brought in from outside.

4.8   In-company management training ranges from:

(a)   basic training for those without any formal education and training, such as induction courses for new recruits into junior management posts; to

(b)   continuing internal development programmes, for managers as they progress through their careers and up the seniority scale; to

(c)   senior general management programmes. Fairly senior managers need training too, to help their development to even more senior positions!

4.9   The report by Constable and McCormick, referred to earlier, found from a survey of UK employers that:

(a) most employers regard innate ability and experience as the two key ingredients of an effective manager. But education and training help, *especially in broadening the outlook of managers with only functional experience previously, and without experience of general management*;

(b) there was agreement that it would be both inappropriate and impossible to make management a controlled profession similar to accountancy and law. However, making a managerial career more similar to the professions and *having managers require specific competences appropriate to each stage of their career* were seen as beneficial.

A management charter initiative has been developed to provide a set of steps in management development and competencies, which are applicable everywhere.

An approach to skills training

4.10 Skills training is concerned with teaching a person how to do a particular job, or how to do it better. Functional managers, especially supervisors and junior managers, should be given skills training to help them to do their job better.

4.11 In addition to skills training, an organisation should provide training to potential managers or existing managers in management techniques and skills. It has already been suggested that employees might want promotion, but cannot be offered it yet, either because there are not enough vacancies and they must wait their turn, or because they are not yet good enough, or even because they might never be good enough for further advancement. Large organisations have the problem of:

(a) motivating their existing staff and keeping them where they might be expected to wait for further promotion; and

(b) providing training to ensure that sufficient staff are available to fill management positions capably when vacancies do arise. (In this respect, management training and development should be planned within the framework of the manpower plan).

4.12 Training follows on from recruitment and selection, and also appraisal of performance. Appraisal should identify the staff development needs of individuals.

(a) Potential managers can be given training in management skills, either on internal courses or on courses with external organisations such as business schools.

(b) Existing managers can be given training in new skills required for their existing job (eg the technological changes in organisations and the development of computer usage suggest the need for training in computer applications and software for management work).

(c) Existing managers can be given training in the skills required for higher, general management (eg with discussions of organisation policy, and lectures given by directors).

A programme for education and training

4.13 A successful programme for management education and training should involve both senior management and the individual managers who should expect to receive training.

Recommendations

Senior management		*Individual managers*	
1	Create an atmosphere within the organisation where continuing management training and development is the norm.	1	Actively want and seek training and development. 'Own' their own career.
2	Utilise appraisal procedures which encourage management training and development.	2	Recognise what new skills they require, and seek them out positively.
3	Encourage individual managers, especially by *making time available* for training.	3	Where appropriate, join a professional institute and seek to qualify as a professional member.
4	Provide support to local educational institutes (eg. colleges) to provide management education and training.		
5	Integrate in-house training courses into a wider system of management education and training. *Make the subject matter of in-house courses relevant to managers' needs.* Work closely with academic institutions and professional institutions to ensure that the 'right' programmes are provided.		

4.14 Designing appropriate in-house courses and encouraging some managers to obtain a professional qualification should be two key features of an education and training programme for managers. Combined masters qualification in management are being provided by companies and local authorities with associated education centres.

The time given to managers for education could be provided by:

(a) a full year off to study for a qualification, say;

(b) block release to attend study courses or revision courses;

(c) day release, perhaps to attend courses at a local college;

(d) reducing the workload on individuals, so that they don't have to work long hours and overtime, to give them time to attend evening classes or study at home.

Time off for studying should be paid for by the employer, who might also contribute towards the cost of text books and courses for professional examinations.

As resources become limited, staff are having to meet their own costs, and take up self development courses. The Open University has the largest business school with 25,000 students.

16: CREATIVITY, INNOVATION AND CONTROL

Management development

4.15 Management development is the process of improving the effectiveness of an individual manager by training him/her in the necessary skills and understanding of organisational goals. Although management development is in some respects a natural process, the term is generally used to refer to a conscious policy within an organisation to provide a programme of individual development. The techniques of management development include:

(a) formal education and training;
(b) on-the-job training;
(c) group learning sessions;
(d) conferences; and
(e) counselling.

4.16 The principle behind management development is that by giving an individual time to study the techniques of being a good manager, and by counselling him about his achievements in these respects, the individual will realise his full potential. The time required to bring a manager to this potential is *possibly* fairly short.

4.17 It is important to emphasise the planned nature of management development programmes. Consider the following as an illustration:

Management development programme

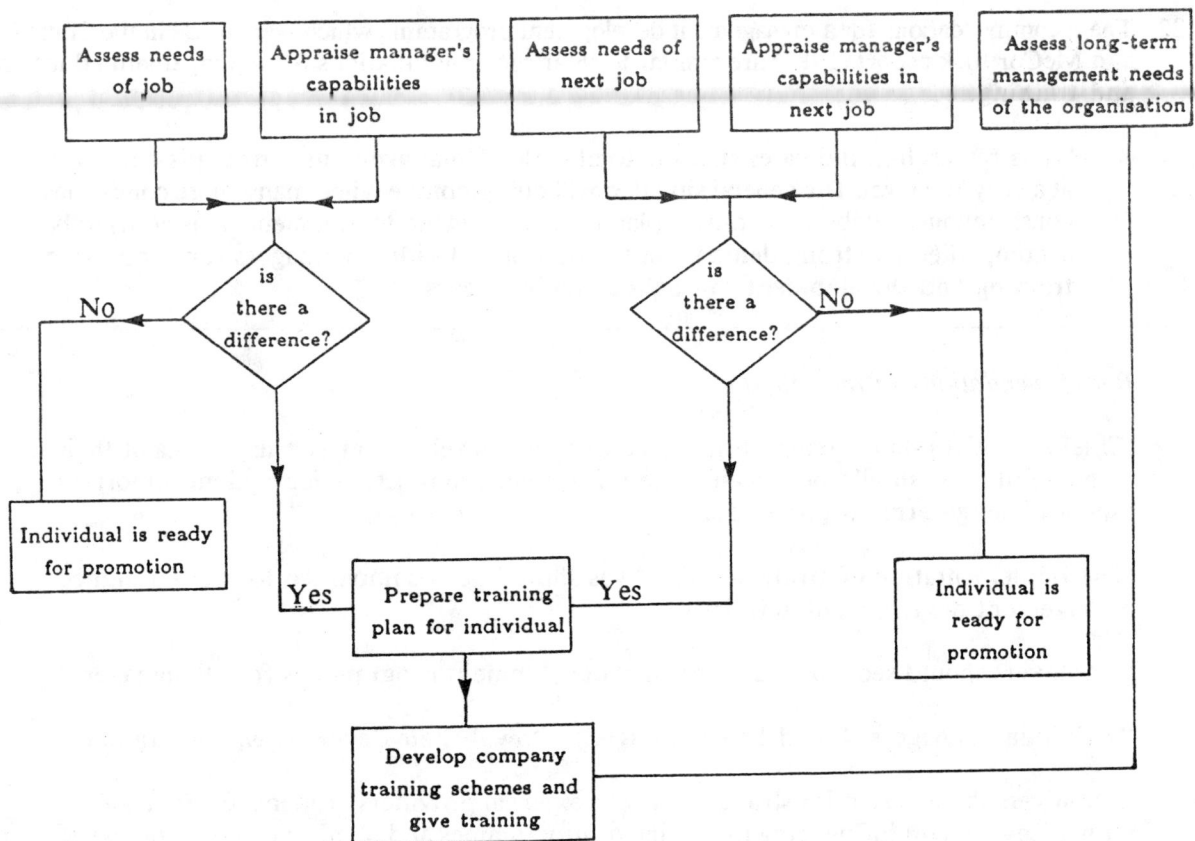

4.18 This diagram brings out the importance of *appraisal* in a system of development. Although we have been discussing the development of managers, staff appraisal is important for all grades of employees.

The plateaued manager

4.19 One particular problem of staff development has recently been discussed in the Harvard Business Review by Jay W Lorsch and Haruo Takagi.

4.20 Lorsch and Takagi looked at the problem of the *plateaued manager*. Long-serving managers may reach a plateau in an organisation, beyond which they recognise that they are unlikely to make progress. They may be faced with a further ten or fifteen years before retirement during which they will feel uncommitted and frustrated.

4.21 Lorsch and Takagi argue that this common problem can be converted into a benefit both for the organisation and for the manager concerned. Experienced executives who have spent a number of challenging 'mainstream' years in an organisation will identify with it and will care about the development of its next generation of professionals and managers. If they participate in the training of newer management staff they will benefit from a renewed sense of importance; meanwhile, the new generation will benefit from their experience and advice.

Recommendations for management development

4.22 The recommendations for a management development programme which were made in the Constable and McCormick report (1987) are similar to their recommendations for management education and training.

> 'This research ... indicates that the total scale of management training is currently at a very low level. The general situation will only improve when many more companies conscientiously embrace a positive plan for management development. This needs to be accompanied by strong demand on the part of individual managers for continuing training and development throughout their careers.'

Recommendations in the report

'Chief executives should see continuing management development as a major area of their responsibility. It should be a regular item for boardroom discussion and an important aspect of long-term corporate plans.'

'The implementation of strategic initiatives should be accompanied by well-designed management development activities.'

'Employers should seek to create personal development programmes for all managers.'

'Individual managers should be encouraged to 'own' their development programme.'

'Employers should establish strong links with external providers of management training with a view to both influencing the design of programmes and obtaining maximum use of expertise.'

4.23 It should also be added that a senior manager in the organisation – perhaps the personnel director – should be given the responsibility for implementing a planned management development programme, and the issue of management development within the organisation should be regularly discussed at board level.

Transition from functional to general management

4.24 There is one particular aspect of management development and training that organisations should look at closely – *the transition from functional to general management*. At some stage in his or her career, a manager will be promoted from a job which is concentrated mainly on functional expertise (eg knowledge of production techniques, personnel techniques, accountancy skills, marketing skills) into a job where the requirement is for broader and more general management skills – eg organising, staffing, controlling, dealing with other departments or organisations, long-term planning and so on.

4.25 The change in a manager's work caused by moving from a functional to a general management position can be seen by highlighting some of the important differences in the two types of role.

	Functional manager	General manager
Orientation	• task orientated – focus on the functional tasks in hand	• goal orientated – focus on achievement of organisational (and divisional) goals and objectives
Role	• organiser	• facilitator – co-ordinating interdepartmental activities; obtaining and allocating resources
Information	• defined sources • usually through formal channels	• poorly defined sources • often acquired by informal contacts
Goals	• short term	• long term

4.26 The transition from functional to general manager is usually accompanied by promotion to a more senior position in the management hierarchy and therefore the contrast in roles between functional and general management is also found between junior and middle/senior management. But this comparison must not be overstated; much depends on the structure of the organisation concerned. The traditional, functional structure tends to keep managers in functional roles until they reach very senior levels and sometimes for their entire careers.

4.27   A *divisional structure*, however, gives relatively junior managers experience of general management roles, usually as the chief executive of small business units. Organisational structure can therefore have a significant impact on the age and seniority of managers making the transition from functional to general management and therefore the extent of the difficulties it may create.

4.28   Recent research has brought to light the difficulties which managers face in changing from one role to another and these are often particularly acute when the change involves moving from a functional to a general management position. In addition to the normal problems of switching jobs, the manager taking up a general management post has to deal with an abrupt change in the skills needed to perform his role effectively.

Skills required of managers

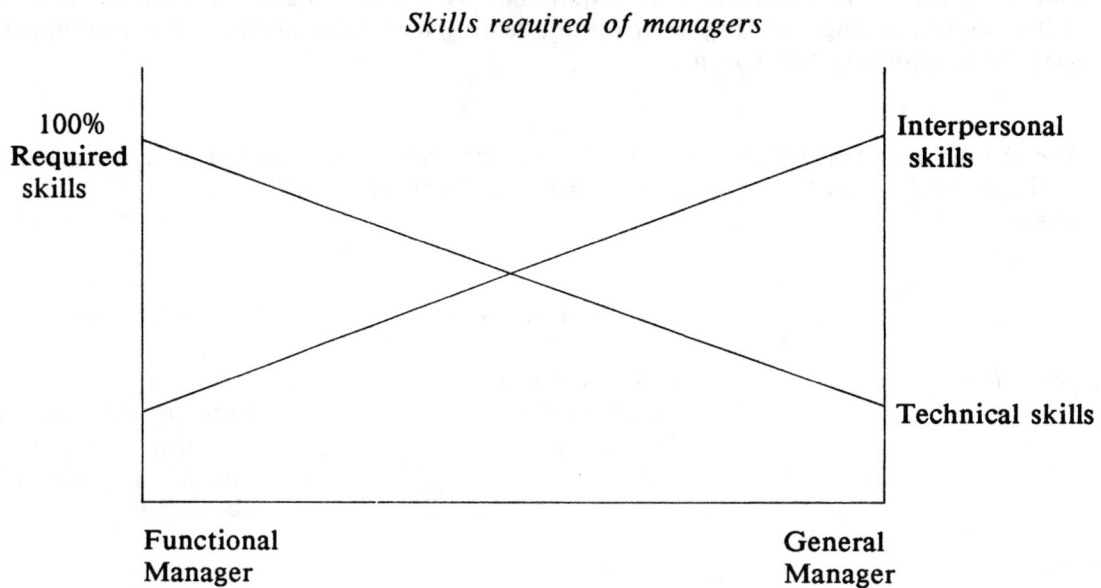

4.29   Technical skills are concerned with an ability to cope with large quantities of data and information and to select the appropriate key points to form the basis for decision-taking. Interpersonal skills involve inspiring, motivating, leading and controlling people to achieve goals which are often poorly defined. For the general manager, the latter are more important.

The transition curve

4.30   The transition from functional to general manager is a complex process and the time taken to complete the 'learning curve' varies depending on the degree of perceived change. Since a move from functional to general management is often, and correctly, viewed as a major change, transitions of this sort take longer than average to complete. The diagram below shows a typical transition curve.

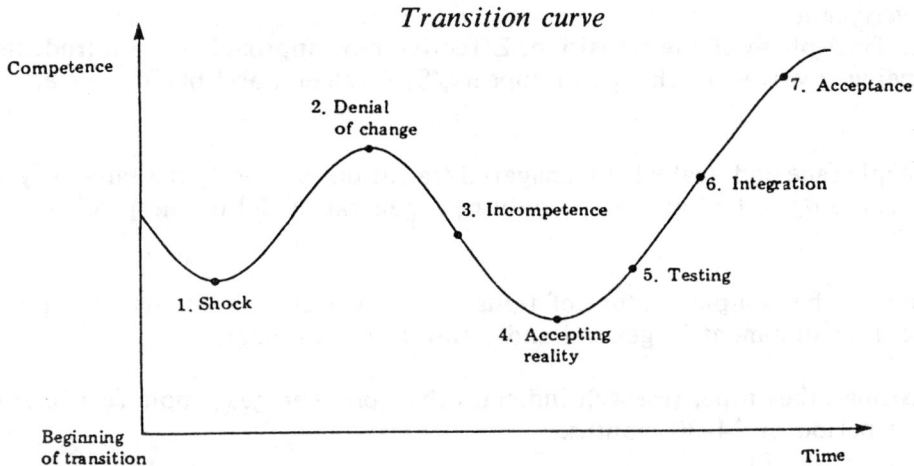

Transition curve

4.31 *Stage 1: immobilisation or shock*
A sense of feeling overwhelmed. This occurs because the reality of the new job does not match the person's expectations. The individual stops and tries to understand what is happening. Typical attitudes at this stage are 'did I really want this job?' and 'this isn't the job I expected'.

4.32 *Stage 2: denial of change*
There is a reversion to previously successful behaviour. This can be useful if it is temporary, but becomes a handicap if it goes on too long and inappropriate behaviour becomes dominant. Sometimes individuals do remain at this point on the curve indefinitely and this is what is described as the *Peter Principle* (promoted to the level of their incompetence). They perform badly because their behaviour is based on their past activities rather than their current ones.

4.33 *Stage 3: incompetence*
Awareness that change is necessary accompanied by frustration because the individual finds it difficult to cope with the new situation or relationships. A fall in performance level is common but, despite this, the phase is very important in the transition process since, without the realisation of change, people can never develop new attitudes and patterns of behaviour. Organisations which adopt a 'sink or swim' approach to transition actually hinder the process in that this phase is commonly regarded as the start of 'sinking'. Consequently, individuals are reluctant to share their current experience with others.

4.34 *Stage 4: accepting reality*
The reality of the new situation is accepted for the first time. Up to this point managers have been concerned with hanging on to past values, attitudes and behaviours. There is now a preparedness and willingness to experiment with change.

4.35 *Stage 5: testing*
Testing new behaviour and approaches. There is a lot of activity and energy as the testing progresses and mistakes are liable to be made. But the experimentation needs to be encouraged since only by doing this can effective approaches be found.

4.36 *Stage 6: integration*
This is a reflective period, in which individuals search for meaning in an attempt to understand all the activity, anger and frustration that went before.

4.37   *Stage 7: acceptance*
This is the final phase of the transition. Effective new approaches are introduced and the sense of being involved in change disappears. Self-esteem, and performance, rises.

4.38   No two people face and deal with managerial transition in exactly the same way and so the transition curve described above can only be a general model of the process.

4.39   Recognition of the complex nature of transition, however, has important implications for management development in general and training in particular.

   (a)   Transition takes time; research indicates that, on average, people feel in control only after a period of 24-30 months.

   (b)   Changes which involve considerable adaptation, such as moving from a functional to a general management position, take longer than the average.

   (c)   Because transition is often a lengthy process, management should avoid moving people from position to position too frequently.

   (d)   For succession planning and training to be successful, it needs to go beyond the point of entry to the new job.

   (e)   People in transition often have more severe entry problems than newcomers, since they are frequently not given a "breathing space" before being expected to perform adequately. This increases the pressures on them and may ultimately reduce their performance and that of the organisation as a whole.

4.40   To help with the transition from technical to general management, an organisation should have a *planned management development programme.*

   (a)   Individuals should be encouraged to acquire suitable educational qualifications for senior management. 'High-fliers' for example might be encouraged to study for an MBA or a DMS early on in their career. Top finance managers (eg. the finance director) ought to have an accountancy or similar qualification.

   (b)   Provide in-house training programmes for senior managers and individuals who are being groomed for senior management. Formal training in general management skills can be very helpful.

   (c)   Careful promotion procedures. Only managers with the potential to be a good senior manager should be promoted into a senior management position.

   (d)   A system of regular performance appraisal, in which individuals are interviewed by their boss (or their boss's boss) and counselled about:

      (i)   what they have done well;
      (ii)   what they have not done so well;
      (iii)   how to improve their performance in their current job;
      (iv)   how to develop their skills for a more senior job.

(e)   Provide suitable experience to managers for more senior positions. This can be done, as mentioned earlier, by means of:

   (i)   allowing subordinates to stand in for their boss whenever the boss is away;

   (ii)   using 'staff officer' positions to groom future 'high fliers'. More is said about these jobs later;

   (iii) job rotation;

   (iv)   using a divisionalised organisation structure to delegate general management responsibilities further down the management hierarchy. Divisional organisation can give managers experience of general management at a fairly early stage in their careers.

Exercise

Fishpaste Ltd is a business making adhesives. One of the employees, during the course of some research into adhesives, discovers a dryish glue that will not quite stick properly. It holds things in place, but two pieces of paper stuck together with this glue can be easily separated without damage to either. What do you do both with the tub of glue and the employee?

Solution

You could have simply ignored the product, on the grounds that a glue which does not stick things together is not a glue that is worth making or selling. This is one response.

Another response would be to discuss with the employee, and other employees, the possible use for such a glue. In this case, you might come up with a revolutionary idea - the 'Post-it' note.

---

5.   CONCLUSION

5.1   Some writers think that an ability to innovate successfully is a key to the survival of an organisation.

5.2   There are various ways of nurturing or encouraging creativity of employees. Sometimes, it might be a matter of management attitudes.

5.3   Innovation has its proponents and opponents and so getting it adopted might require offending vested interests.

5.4   A number of techniques exist to facilitate problem solving.

5.5   In service industries, the role of staff in delivering innovation is of paramount importance, so risk management and training is a necessary part of creating an innovative climate.

TEST YOUR KNOWLEDGE

The numbers in brackets refer to paragraphs of this chapter

1   What is forcefield analysis? (1.17)

2   What is brainstorming? (2.2 to 2.3)

3   Distinguish between education, training and development. (3.23)

4   Draw a diagram of a management development programme. (4.17)

5   What are the problems of changing from a functional to a general manager? (4.31 to 4.39)

Now try question 16 at the end of the text

Chapter 17

RENEWAL AND CHANGE MANAGEMENT

This chapter covers the following topics.

1. The environment of change
2. Managing change
3. Teams and team building

---

1. THE ENVIRONMENT OF CHANGE

1.1 Earlier chapters have discussed the environment in which the public sector operates, particularly the turbulence in the environment, caused by changes in:

(a) technology;

(b) political power distribution;

(c) the moves to quasi-markets;

(d) the slow empowerment of the consumer of public sector services (given some impetus by The Citizen's Charter);

(e) challenges to professional elites as allocators of resources.

1.2 However, the ultimate problem of implementing these changes is that the very people who are derided for their outdated attitudes are those who must subscribe to the changed culture. For example, those who object to change, in the light of strenuous *exhortation*, might be accused of being:

(a) behind the times;
(b) cosseted by outdated agreements and working practices;
(c) unimaginative;
(d) self-interested and obstructive.

1.3 In fact, the process of change can be summarised as:

(a) exhortation, pressure from outside bodies;
(b) decision to change;
(c) organisational restructuring, new management and personnel;
(d) new reporting systems;
(e) 'improvement' of service providers now uncertain of their role.

1.4   Sometimes the changed practices are almost forced upon people, with altered institutional arrangements, for example:

(a)   increased powers to parent-governors on school bodies;
(b)   opting-out rights for schools;
(c)   managers brought in to manage the organisation, not directly involved in service delivery.

In (a), it might be inferred from the quality of services actually delivered that the resources used are perhaps a waste of money.

1.5   At the same time, techniques of organisation development, training and so forth, are used to generate a change in culture.

1.6   In short, changes are both:

(a)   institutional and technical (eg new performance measures and contractual arrangements);
(b)   cultural (a new 'culture of service').

Resistance to change

1.7   Individuals might view the proposed changes with sullen resignation or with active hostility. Resistance, from the individual's point of view, has a number of causes.

(a)   The fear that the individual will be unable to cope.

(b)   The fear that managers do not understand how the job is done, and so there will be no frame of reference for the new conditions.

(c)   Insecurity at having to learn new habits.

(d)   Worries about economic security (loss of pay).

(e)   Worries about promotion prospects disappearing.

(f)   Fear of taking decisions, and being held responsible and accountable for them if they go down to a lower level.

1.8   Change may be resisted at the organisational level. In other words, the institutional arrangement and procedures may have their own dynamic - more than the total of individual fears - which inhibit change. This might arise for several reasons.

(a)   The organisation might be concerned with maintaining stability and predictability within existing structures and procedures. These provide for clearly defined tasks to be achieved within set rules. It may, in practice, be very difficult to adjust.

(b)   The organisation's resources are already committed to current activities, and there is neither time nor money for an intensive change program.

(c) If the proposed change requires massive resources and the abandoning of existing plant and planned expenditure to meet the changes, an organisation might be hesitant about introducing it.

(d) Agreed contracts with external organisations could be prejudiced by changing the operation of the organisation which could open up the organisation to loss of the contract or at worst legal action. Although setting up Executive Agencies has been seen as a way of achieving freedom and encouraging change the initial framework documents and agreed targets to be achieved may in the short run prove more limiting of opportunities, especially as the Treasury are wary of uncontrolled spending anyway.

(e) The changes proposed might threaten to the power or influence of certain decision making groups in the organisation. The contracting out of functions in local government, the local management of schools, separating providers and purchasers in the health service provide examples of this challenge to existing power structures.

1.9 In the public sector, changes in institutional arrangements are being introduced at the same time as changes in funding and performance measurement.

2. MANAGING CHANGE

2.1 One model of change was suggested by Kurt Lewin.

(a) Before the change, existing ways of behaviour are set in a particular mould (like a jelly).

(b) These must be unfrozen, so that ...

(c) ... they can be refrozen or remoulded into a new pattern (re-freezing in Lewin's jargon).

2.2 However, change might be a more complex issue, and one model is suggested by Peters and Waterman *(In search of Excellence)*.

2.3 Waterman developed the concept of the *renewal ring*. This brings together the 7Ss *(In Search of Excellence)* and the 7Cs around capability and shared values. We have already discussed the 7Ss and 7Cs. The diagram represents cylinders and pistons in an engine. The engine (organisational performance) works best when all the pistons are working in unison. The organisation has to build the skill competences and create the organisational culture to make the engine work. Applying the concepts of the renewal ring the organisation identify which of the pistons are not working effectively and so deal with the structure or the staff or reporting systems. This might be hard to do in practice as they are all interrelated.

The renewal ring

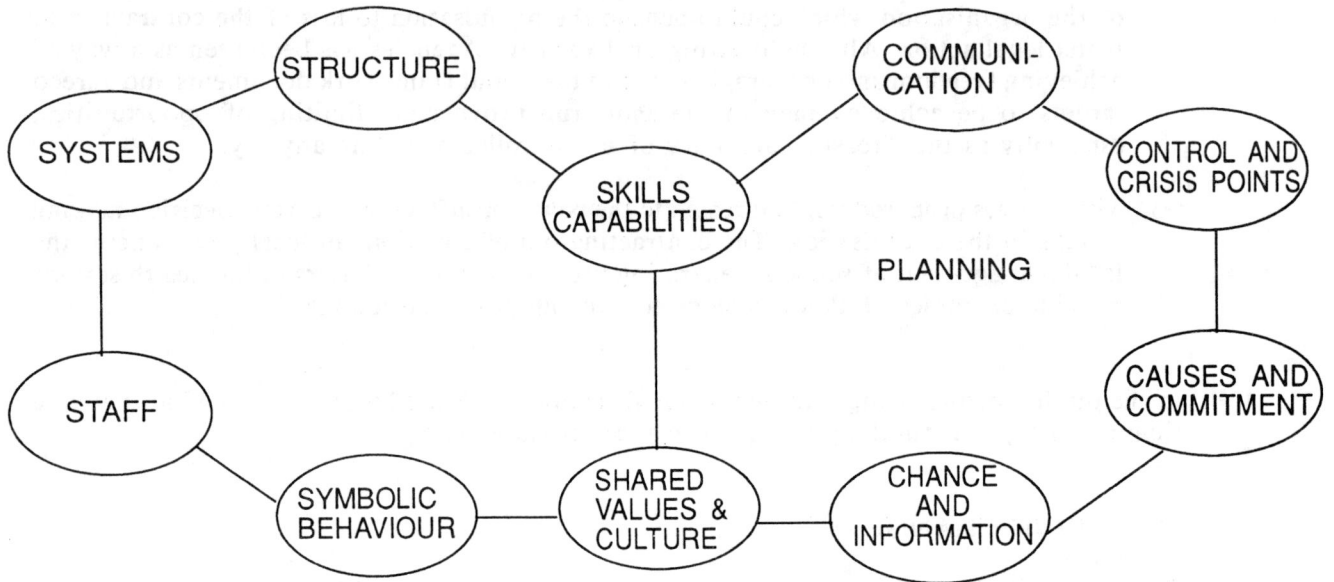

2.4   To recap, the elements which make up the 7Ss cycle are concerned with establishing shared values. The meaning of the elements are as follows.

(a) *Structure* (the organisation chart, who reports to whom, division of tasks).

(b) *Systems* (how things get done from day to day, formal and informal process and flows of information).

(c) *Symbolic behaviour* (evidence of what managers regard as important, the way they act in crises).

(d) *Shared values* (what the organisation stands for, how it behaves).

(e) *Strategy* (plan for allocating resources and maintaining competitive advantage, the strategy dimension becomes a framework in its own right).

(f) *Skills* (managerial, technical and personnel skills are all included).

(g) *Staff* (the right personnel, development of personnel).

2.5   Planning is the underlying concept to the 7C framework, and includes communication, elements of control, and is concerned with generating ideas; asking 'what if?'. These planning elements can be seen to be in conflict. Controls drive out innovation, communication can be limited and ideas and opportunities lost in the organisation. Grouping or 'chunking' elements of the process Waterman believes, helps to understand and manipulate the process.

(a) *Capability* (described as skills in the 7S framework, to build institutional skill).

(b) *Communication* (a way of reintegrating the subdivided tasks which give the organisation its purpose, planning makes explicit which should be talked about and sorted out).

(c) *Chance and information* (strategy is 'informed opportunism', to know when to duck or seize the opportunity).

(d) *Causes, commitment* (identifying a list of issues and having issue brokers who push them around so they become priorities).

(e) *Crisis points* (anticipation through 'what if' scenarios, can the organisation change course before the crisis hits - is it a matter of survival).

(f) *Control* (a set of targets which help steer the organisation and check on progress).

(g) *Culture* (planning reinforces what the organisation stands for, its vision and shared values).

2.6 The application of these ideas in the public sector has been actively pursued by the Audit Commission, Local Government Training Board and Institute of Local Government Studies.

Certain common themes recur across the public services in their development in public service management.

(a) Strategic management in setting objectives, determining priorities and clarifying policy.

(b) The devolution of management responsibility for implementing policy and accountability for that achievement.

(c) Review of policy effectiveness and of the efficiency of operations.

(d) Changes in organisational culture, setting a climate both for purposive direction and for responsiveness in action.

(e) A public service orientation which focuses on the public for whom the services are provided.

(f) Active staff management which mobilises through communication and develops potentially new patterns of organisation to meet new problems or to create new forms of service delivery.

(g) A 'learning organisation' which recognises the need for adaptation in a changing society.

2.7 Waterman provides a summary of his views on renewal which, in an uncertain environment, is a 'to do' list.

(a) Strategy and planning need to be 'informed opportunism'. In other words, a strategy should be developed which is responsive to the opportunities that might arise, and which is based on appropriate information to detect those opportunities.

(b) Information can be a source of strategic advantage.

(c) Always consider probabilities, and accept that all decisions have some element of 'gut feeling' or 'intuition' given that the future is unknowable.

(d) The 7S and 7C frameworks can be used to analyse the way the organisation is working.

2.8 Waterman sees that organisations should serve individuals and not the other way around.

'Dreams, not desperation, move organisations to the highest levels of performance. Our dream ought to be institutions that work for, not against, our needs. That is the hope, the power, the dream and the challenge is renewal.'

2.9 Most of the arguments about change or renewal management are about *people skills*, about acting as a coach, getting the best out of people, listening and reaching developing symbols of change.

2.10 A paper by the Ashridge Management Resource Group (*Management for the Future*) emphasises the skills of the management and the need for training and development. The future needs *flexible managers* who have potential to acquire new skills.

A flexible manager will have the following qualities.

(a) An active and analytical approach.
(b) Willingness to take risks.
(c) Strong personal goals, action oriented.
(d) Awareness of own strengths and weaknesses (so that others can compensate for them).
(e) Constructive outlook.
(f) Wide vision (of the job and of the organisation).
(g) Sensitivity to others.
(h) Distancing skills (ie see the wood for the trees, don't get over involved with detail).
(i) Ability to compromise.

2.11 Managing change appears to require flexibility, strong values and ability to be constructive. The development of a learning and a planning capability is key factors for the change managers, and organisations.

2.12 Actually implementing the changes is a serious managerial task in itself.

(a) Winning staff acquiesience.

(b) Ensuring that changes in culture espoused by senior management are communicated successfully at operational level.

(c) Meticulous planning of any dislocation (eg office moves).

(d) Appropriate training and reassurance.

(e) Realistic timescales, so that service provision does not suffer.

3. TEAMS AND TEAM BUILDING

3.1 Most organisations are not dependent on individuals but on groups or teams that are organised to complete a particular function or tasks in the organisation.

3.2 For the public sector in particular, the management and development of teams is vital to managing change and dealing with new opportunities.

3.3 Informal problem-solving teams, without too much operational direction from senior management, are seen as ways of tackling problems successfully.

Attributes of teams

3.4 Handy in *Understanding Organizations* defines a group as 'any collection of people who perceive themselves to be a group'. The point of this definition is the distinction it implies between a random collection of individuals and a 'group' of individuals who share a common sense of identity and belonging.

3.5 A group has certain attributes that a random 'crowd' does not possess.

(a) *A sense of identity.* Whether the group is formal or informal, its existence is recognised by its members: there are acknowledged boundaries to the group which define who is 'in' and who is 'out', who is 'us' and who is 'them'. People generally need to feel that they 'belong', that they share something with others and are of value to others.

(b) *Loyalty to the group, and acceptance within the group.* This generally expresses itself as *conformity* or the acceptance of the 'norms' of behaviour and attitude that bind the group together and exclude others from it.

(c) *Purpose and leadership.* Most groups have an expressed purpose, aim or set of objectives, whatever field they are in: most will, spontaneously or formally, choose individuals or sub-groups to lead them towards the fulfilment of those goals.

3.6 People in organisations will be drawn together into groups by:

(a) a preference for small groups, where closer relationships can develop;
(b) the need to belong and to make a contribution that will be noticed and appreciated;
(c) familiarity: a shared office, canteen etc;
(d) common rank, specialisms, objectives and interests;
(e) the attractiveness of a particular group activity (eg joining an interesting club);
(f) resources offered to groups (eg sports facilities);
(g) 'power' greater than the individuals alone could muster (eg trade union, pressure group).

3.7 *Formal* groups will have a formal structure; they will be consciously organised for a function allotted to them by the organisation, and for which they are held responsible - they are task oriented, and become *teams*.

(a) *Permanent* formal groups include standing committees, management teams (eg the board of directors) or specialist services (eg information technology support).

(b) *Temporary* formal groups include task forces, designed to work on a particular project, ad hoc committees etc.

Functions of teams

3.8 From the organisation's standpoint the functions of groups or teams include:

(a) performing tasks which require the collective skills of more than one person;

(b) creating a formal organisation by which management can control work, by defining responsibilities and delegating as appropriate;

(c) testing and ratifying decisions made outside the group;

(d) consulting or negotiating, especially to resolve disputes within the organisation;

(e) creating ideas (acting as a 'think tank');

(f) exchanging ideas, collecting and transmitting information;

(g) co-ordinating the work of different individuals or other groups;

(h) enquiring into what has happened in the past;

(i) motivating individuals to devote more energy and effort into achieving the organisation's goals.

3.9 There may be no strict division between these different functions. They will inevitably overlap in practice. But the effectiveness with which a group acts is likely to be greater if they are not attempting to cope with different functions simultaneously.

3.10 From the individual's standpoint teams also perform some important functions.

(a) They satisfy social needs for friendship and belonging.

(b) They help individuals in developing images of themselves (eg a person may need to see himself as a member of the corporate planning department or of the works snooker team).

(c) They enable individuals to help each other in matters which are not necessarily connected with the organisation's purpose (eg people at work may organise a baby-sitting circle).

(d) They enable individuals to share the burdens of any responsibility they may have in their work.

The formation of teams

3.11 Groups are not static. They mature and develop. Four stages in this development are commonly identified:

(a) forming
(b) storming
(c) norming
(d) performing.

3.12 During the first stage (*forming*) the team is just coming together, and may still be seen as a collection of individuals. Each individual wishes to impress his personality on the group, while its purpose, composition, and organisation are being established. The individuals will be trying to find out about each other, and about the aims and norms of the team. There will at this stage probably be a wariness about introducing new ideas. The objectives being pursued may as yet be unclear and a leader may not yet have emerged.

This settling down period is essential, but may be time wasting: the team as a unit will not be used to being autonomous, and will probably not be an efficient agent in the planning of its activities or the activities of others. It may resort to complex bureaucratic procedures to ensure that what it is doing is at least something which will not get its members into trouble.

3.13 The second stage is called *storming* because it frequently involves more or less open conflict between team members. There may be changes agreed in the original objectives, procedures and norms established for the group. If the team is developing successfully this may be a fruitful phase as more realistic targets are set and trust between the group members increases.

3.14 The third stage (*norming*) is a period of settling down. There will be agreements about work sharing, individual requirements and expectations of output. The enthusiasm and brain-storming of the second stage may be less apparent, but norms and procedures may evolve which enable methodical working to be introduced and maintained.

3.15 Once the fourth stage (*performing*) has been reached the team sets to work to execute its task. Even at earlier stages some performance will have been achieved but the fourth stage marks the point where the difficulties of growth and development no longer hinder the group's objectives.

3.16 It would be misleading to suggest that these four stages always follow in a clearly defined progression, or that the development of a group must be a slow and complicated process. Particularly where the task to be performed is urgent, or where team members are highly motivated, the fourth stage will be reached very quickly while the earlier stages will be hard to distinguish.

Group norms

3.17 A work group establishes 'norms' or acceptable levels and methods of behaviour, to which all members of the group are expected to conform. This team attitude will have a negative effect on an organisation if it sets unreasonably low production norms (anyone producing more is made the social outcast of the group).

3.18 The general nature of group pressure is to require the individual to share in the team's identity, and individuals may react to group norms, customs etc with:

(a) compliance ('toeing the line' without real commitment);
(b) internalisation (full acceptance and identification); or
(c) counter conformity (rejecting the group and/or its norms).

3.19 Pressure is strongest on the individual when:

(a) the issue is not clear cut;
(b) the individual lacks support for his or her own attitude or behaviour; and
(c) the individual is exposed to other members of the group for a length of time.

3.20 This 'consensus' power is often demonstrated in the ways in which work teams manipulate output.

Roethlisberger and Dickson quote employees who were told by their colleagues that if an operation turned out more than x units in a day 'they'll just raise the rate and ask you to do more for the same money'. The same discouragement was offered an individual who had a suggestion to improve work methods. Of course, this discouragement might reflect actual management practice.

3.21 From the findings that an individual's opinions can be changed or swayed by group consensus, it may be argued that it would be more effective, and probably also easier in practice, to change group norms than to change individual norms. Motivation should therefore involve the work group as a whole, because changes agreed by a group are likely to be more effective and longer lasting.

Team cohesion and competition

3.22 In an experiment reported by Deutsch (1949), psychology students were given puzzles and human relation problems to work at in discussion groups. Some groups ('co-operative' ones) were told that the grade each individual got at the end of the course would depend on the performance of his group. Other groups ('competitive' ones) were told that each student would receive a grade according to his own contributions.

3.23 No significant differences were found between the two kinds of group in the amount of interest and involvement in the tasks, or in the amount of learning. But the co-operative groups, compared with the competitive ones, had greater productivity per unit time, better quality of product and discussion, greater co-ordination of effort and sub-division of activity, more diversity in amount of contribution per member, more attentiveness to fellow members and more friendliness during discussion.

Sherif and Sherif

3.24 Another experiment, conducted in 1949 by Sherif and Sherif, set out to investigate how groups are formed, and how relationships between groups are created. The experimenters also tried to create friction between their teams of schoolboys. The results suggested that *inter-group competition may have a positive effect on team cohesion and performance.*

3.25 Within each competing group:

(a) members close ranks, and submerge their differences; loyalty and conformity are demanded;

(b) the 'climate' changes from informal and social to work and task-oriented; individual needs are subordinated to achievement;

(c) leadership moves from democratic to autocratic, with the group's acceptance;

(d) the group tends to become more structured and organised.

3.26 Between competing groups:

(a) the other group begins to be perceived as 'the enemy'; and
(b) inter-group communication decreases.

3.27 The 'winning' team, if there is one, will:

(a) retain its cohesion;
(b) relax into a complacent, playful state ('fat and happy');
(c) return to group maintenance, concern for members' needs etc; and
(d) be confirmed in its group 'self-concept' with little re-evaluation.

3.28 The losing group will:

(a) deny defeat if possible, or place the blame on the management, the system etc;

(b) lose its cohesion and splinter into conflict, as 'blame' is apportioned;

(c) be keyed-up, fighting mad ('lean and hungry');

(d) turn towards work-orientation to regroup - rather than members' needs, group maintenance etc;

(e) tend to learn by revaluating its perceptions of itself and the other group. It is more likely to become a cohesive and effective unit once the 'loss' has been accepted.

3.29 All members of a team will act in unison if the group's existence or patterns of behaviour are threatened from outside. Cohesion is naturally assumed to be the result of communication, agreement and mutual trust - but in the face of a 'common enemy' (competition, crisis or emergency) cohesion and productivity benefit.

3.30 In an ideal functioning team:

(a) each individual gets the support of the team, a sense of identity and belonging which encourages loyalty and hard work on the group's behalf;

(b) skills, information and ideas are 'pooled' or shared, so that the team's capabilities are greater than those of the individuals;

(c) new ideas can be tested, reactions taken into account and persuasive skills brought into play in group discussion for decision-making and problem-solving;

(d) each individual is encouraged to participate and contribute and thus becomes personally involved in and committed to the team's activities;

(e) goodwill, trust and respect can be built up between individuals, so that communication is encouraged and potential problems more easily overcome.

3.31 Unfortunately, team working is rarely such an undiluted success. There are certain constraints involved in working with others.

(a) Awareness of group norms and the desire to be acceptable to the group may restrict individual personality and flair. This may perhaps create pressure or a sense of 'schizophrenia' for the individual concerned who can't 'be himself' in a team situation.

(b) Conflicting roles and relationships (where an individual is a member of more than one group) can cause difficulties in communicating effectively, especially if sub-groups or cliques are formed in conflict with others.

(c) The effective functioning of the team is dependent upon each of its members, and will suffer if one member:

(i) dislikes or distrusts another;
(ii) is so dominant that others cannot participate; or
(iii) is so timid that the value of his ideas is lost; or
(iv) is so negative in attitude that constructive communication is rendered impossible.

(d) Rigid leadership and procedures may strangle initiative and creativity in individuals.

(e) Differences of opinion and political conflicts of interest are always likely and if all policies and decisions are to be determined by consultation and agreement within the team, decisions may never be reached and action never taken.

'Group think'

3.32 It is possible for groups to be *too* cohesive, too all-absorbing. Handy notes that 'ultra-cohesive groups can be dangerous because in the organisational context the group must serve the organisation, not itself.'

If a group is completely absorbed with its own maintenance, members and priorities, it can become dangerously blinkered to what is going on around it, and may confidently forge ahead in a completely wrong direction. I L Janis describes this as 'group think'.

3.33 The cosy consensus of the group prevents consideration of alternatives, constructive criticism or conflict. Symptoms of 'group think' include:

(a) sense of invulnerability (blindness to the risk involved in 'pet' strategies);
(b) rationalisations for inconsistent facts;
(c) moral blindness ('might is right');
(d) tendency to stereotype 'outsiders' and 'enemies';
(e) strong group pressure to quell dissent;

    (f)   self-censorship by members (not 'rocking the boat');

    (g)   perception of unanimity (filtering out divergent views);

    (h)   mutual support and solidarity to 'guard' the decision.

3.34   Victims of group think, which is rife at the top and centre of organisations, take great risks in their decisions, fail to recognise failure, and are highly resistant to unpalatable information. Such groups must:

    (a)   actively encourage self-criticism;

    (b)   welcome outside ideas and evaluation; and

    (c)   respond positively to conflicting evidence.

Creating an effective team

3.35   The management problem is how to create an effective, efficient work team. If managers can motivate groups (and individuals) to work harder and better to achieve organisational goals, the sense of pride in their own competence might create job satisfaction through belonging to the team and performing its tasks.

3.36   Handy takes a contingency approach to the problem of team effectiveness which, he argues, is constructed as follows.

Handy's approach to groups

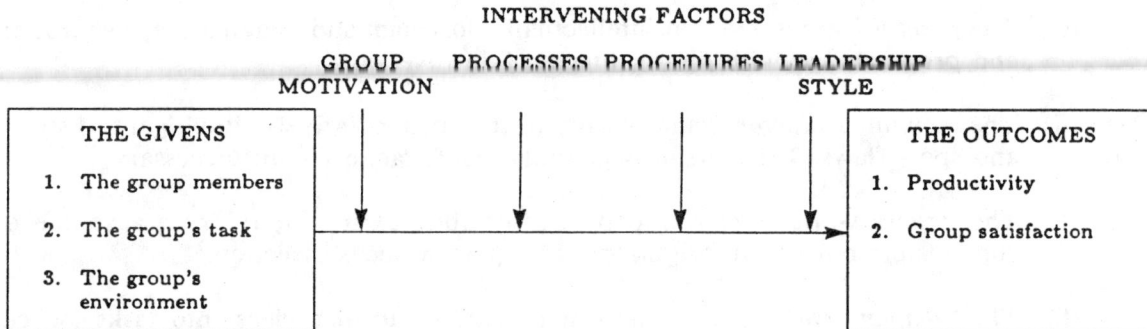

INTERVENING FACTORS

GROUP   PROCESSES PROCEDURES LEADERSHIP
MOTIVATION   STYLE

THE GIVENS	THE OUTCOMES
1. The group members	1. Productivity
2. The group's task	2. Group satisfaction
3. The group's environment	

These factors are important, and are worth learning carefully. Management can operate on both 'givens' and 'intervening factors' to affect the 'outcomes'.

Group members

3.37   The personalities and characteristics of the individual members of the team, and the personal goals of these members, will help to determine the group's personality and goals. An individual is likely to be influenced more strongly by a small group than by a large group in which he may feel like a small fish in a large pond, and therefore unable to participate effectively in team decisions.

3.38 It has been suggested that the effectiveness of a team depends on the blend of the individual skills and abilities of its members. A project team might be most effective if it contains:

(a) a person of originality and ideas;

(b) a 'get-up-and-go' person with considerable energy, enthusiasm and drive;

(c) a quiet, logical thinker, who ponders carefully and criticises the ideas of others;

(d) a plodder, who is happy to do the humdrum routine work;

(e) a conciliator, who is adept at negotiating compromises or a consensus of thought between other members of the group.

3.39 Belbin, in a study of business-game teams at Carnegie Institute of Technology in 1981, discovered that a differentiation of influence among team members (agreement that some members were more influential than others) resulted in higher morale and better performance. Belbin's picture (which many managers have found a useful guide to team working) of the most effective character-mix in a team involves eight necessary roles which should ideally be balanced and evenly 'spread' in the team.

(a) The *chairman* presides and co-ordinates and will be balanced, disciplined and good at working through others.

(b) The *shaper* is highly strung, dominant, extrovert, passionate about the task itself, and a spur to action.

(c) The *plant* is introverted, but intellectually dominant and imaginative, a source of ideas and proposals but with disadvantages of introversion.

(d) The *monitor-evaluator* is analytically (rather than creatively) intelligent, dissects ideas and spots flaws. This person is possibly aloof, tactless - but necessary.

(e) The *resource-investigator* is popular, sociable, extrovert, relaxed, a source of new contacts etc but not an originator. This person needs direction.

(f) The *company worker* is a practical organiser, turning ideas into tasks (scheduling, planning etc). Trustworthy and efficient, this person is not excited (or exciting, often), not a leader, but an administrator.

(g) The *team worker* is most concerned with team maintenance: supportive, understanding, diplomatic and popular but uncompetitive and noticed only in absence.

(h) The *finisher* chivvies the team to meet deadlines, attend to details etc. Urgency and follow-through are important, though the person is not always popular.

The group's task

3.40 The nature of the task must have some bearing on how a group should be managed. If a job must be done urgently, it is often necessary to dictate how things should be done, rather than to encourage a participatory style of working. Jobs which are routine, unimportant and undemanding will be insufficient to motivate either individuals or the group as a whole. If individuals in the team want authoritarian leadership, they are also likely to want clearly defined targets.

Environment

3.41   The team's environment relates to factors such as the physical surroundings at work and to inter-group relations. An open-plan office, in which the members of the group are closely situated, is more conducive to cohesion than a situation in which individuals are partitioned into separate offices, or geographically distant from each other. Team attitudes will also be affected, as described previously, by the relationship with other teams, which may be friendly, neutral or hostile.

Intervening factors

3.42   Of the 'intervening factors', motivation and leadership have already been discussed in separate chapters of this text. With regard to processes and procedures, research indicates that a team which tackles its work systematically will be more effective than one which lives from hand to mouth, and muddles through.

Outcomes

3.43   High productivity may be achieved if work is so arranged that satisfaction of individuals' needs coincides with high output. Where teams are, for example, allowed to set their own improvement goals and methods and to measure their own progress towards those goals, it has been observed (by Peters and Waterman among others) that they regularly *exceed* their targets.

3.44   Individuals may bring their own 'hidden agendas' to groups for satisfaction - goals which may have nothing to do with the declared aims of the team - such as protection of a sub-group, impressing the boss, inter-personal rivalry etc.

A contingency theory of team leadership

3.45   Perhaps the leading advocate of contingency theory is F E Fiedler. In an early work (1960) he studied the relationship between style of leadership and the effectiveness of the work group. Two styles of leadership were identified.

(a)   *Psychologically distant managers* (PDMs) who maintain distance from their subordinates by:

   (i)   formalising the roles and relationships between themselves and their superiors and subordinates;

   (ii)   being withdrawn and reserved in their inter-personal relationships within the organisation;

   (iii)   preferring formal consultation methods rather than seeking opinions of their staff informally.

(b)   *Psychologically close managers* (PCMs) who:

   (i)   do not seek to formalise roles and relationships with superiors and subordinates;

(ii) are more concerned to maintain good human relationships at work than to ensure that tasks are carried out efficiently;

(iii) prefer informal contacts to regular formal staff meetings.

3.46 It is perhaps not surprising that in his 1960 study Fiedler concluded that the most effective work groups were led by psychologically distant managers and not by psychologically close managers. The explanation for this appeared to be that a manager cannot properly control and discipline subordinates if he is too close to them emotionally. Moreover, PDMs were observed to be primarily task-oriented.

3.47 Fiedler went on to develop his contingency theory in *A Theory of Leadership Effectiveness*. He suggested that the effectiveness of a work team depended basically on two factors:

(a) the relationship between the leader and his group; and
(b) the nature of the work or tasks done by the group.

3.48 He concluded that:

(a) a structured (or psychologically distant) style works best when the 'situation' is either very favourable, or very unfavourable to the leader;

(b) a supportive (or psychologically close) style works best when the 'situation' is moderately favourable to the leader.

3.49 A situation is 'favourable' to the leader when:

(a) the leader is liked and trusted by the team;
(b) the tasks of the team are clearly defined;
(c) the power of the leader to reward and punish with organisation backing is high.

3.50 Fiedler's analysis can be described by a three-dimensional cube:

(a) the first dimension represents the level of respect and trust for the leader amongst subordinates;

(b) a second dimension is the degree to which the tasks of the group are clearly defined; and

(c) a third dimension is the degree to which the leader has power and authority to reward or punish subordinates.

Fiedler's contingency analysis of groups

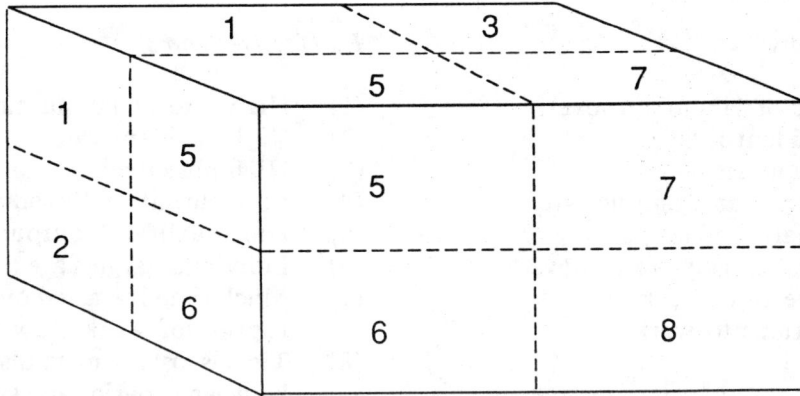

The blocks 1-8 (4 is hidden from view) show the eight possibilities. Block 3 illustrates high authority, high respect and a clearly defined task.

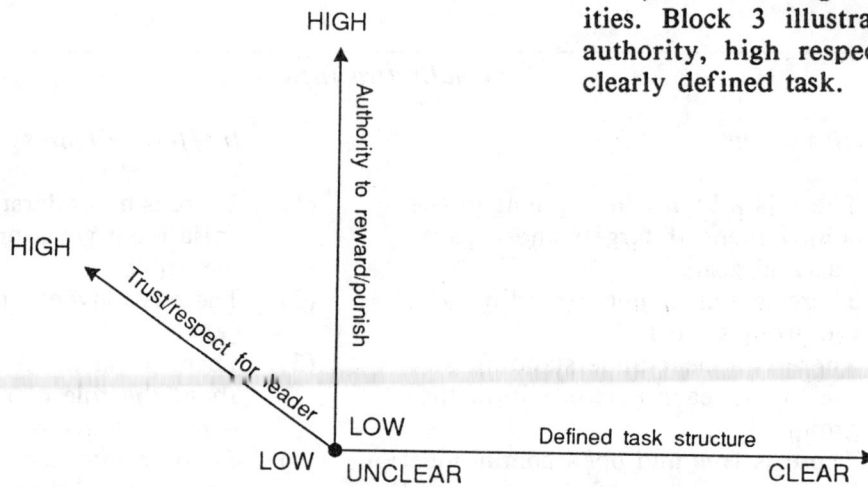

(a) When the situation is very favourable for the leader, he or she can afford to concentrate on the task, and be a task-orientated, psychologically distant manager. The leader of a research team might be in this position.

(b) When the situation is only moderately favourable for the leader, he or she will need to show more concern for people - be a psychologically close manager.

(c) When the situation is unfavourable for the leader, he or she will need to be task-orientated, and a psychologically distant autocrat.

(d) Concern for task and concern for people should be balanced according to the needs of the situation, and the degree to which it favours the leader.

The characteristics of effective and ineffective work teams

3.51 If a manager is to try to improve the effectiveness of his work team he must be able to identify the different characteristics of an effective and an ineffective group.

Quantifiable factors

Effective teams

(1) Low rate of labour turnover
(2) Low accident rate
(3) Low absenteeism
(4) High output and productivity
(5) Good quality of output
(6) Individual targets are achieved
(7) There are few stoppages and interruptions to work

Ineffective teams

(1) High rate of labour turnover
(2) High accident rate
(3) High absenteeism
(4) Low output and productivity
(5) Poor quality of output
(6) Individual targets are not achieved
(7) Much time is wasted owing to disruption of work flow
(8) Time is lost owing to disagreements between superior and subordinates

---

Qualitative factors

Effective teams

(1) There is a high commitment to the achievement of targets and organisational goals
(2) There is a clear understanding of the group's work
(3) There is a clear understanding of the role of each person within the group
(4) There is free and open communication between members of the group and trust between members
(5) There is idea sharing
(6) The group is good at generating new ideas
(7) Group members try to help each other out by offering constructive criticisms and suggestions
(8) There is group problem-solving which gets to the root causes of the work problem
(9) There is an active interest in work decisions
(10) Group members seek a united consensus of opinion
(11) The members of the group want to develop their abilities in their work
(12) The group is sufficiently motivated to be able to carry on working in the absence of its leader

Ineffective teams

(1) There is no understanding of organisational goals or the role of the group
(2) There is a low commitment to targets
(3) There is confusion and uncertainty about the role of each person within the group
(4) There is mistrust between group members and suspicion of group's leader
(5) There is little idea sharing
(6) The group does not generate any good new ideas
(7) Group members make negative and hostile criticisms about each other's work
(8) Work problems are dealt with superficially, with attention paid to the symptoms but not the cause
(9) Decisions about work are accepted passively
(10) Group members hold strongly opposed views
(11) Group members find work boring and do it reluctantly
(12) The group needs its leader there to get work done

3.52 It will be helpful if you try to make a distinction in your mind between:

(a) what work teams can be organised to do (perform a task, control work, make decisions, ratify decisions, create ideas, exchange ideas and co-ordinate work etc); and

(b) the implication for management that since some groups develop certain characteristics and norms, it would be advisable to give some attention to the leadership of teams and to making norms and attitudes work in the organisation's favour (perhaps through participation in decision-making etc).

Disadvantages of groups as work units

3.53 It is worth noting, too, that for all its opportunities for exchanged ideas and knowledge, immediate feedback, 'brainstorming' etc, the 'group' as a work unit is not necessarily superior to the individual in terms of performance in all situations.

(a) Decision-making may be a cumbersome process where consensus has to be reached. However, it has been shown (rather surprisingly) that teams take *riskier* decisions than the individuals comprising them - perhaps because of the sense of shared responsibility.

(b) Group norms may work to lower the standard rate of unit production - though, again, individuals need groups psychologically; isolation can produce stress and hostile behaviour, and can impair performance just as surely as 'rate fixing'.

(c) Group cohesion may provide a position of strength - solidarity - from which to behave in hostile or deviant (from the organisation's point of view) ways.

(d) Groups have been shown to produce less ideas - though better evaluated - than the individuals of the group working separately. A group *will* often produce a better solution to a quiz than its best individual, since 'missing pieces' can be added to his performance.

Exercise

Andrew Charters is the manager of a group of six people. Although each of the six has a separate job and works to a large extent independently of the other five, they do spend about 30% of their time working together as a team. The team activity is important to the organisation.

Recently two members of the group, Shirley and Norman, received promotions and left the group.

Norman, the team's ideas man - who was also a shrewd politician - was replaced by Hilary, who has a deserved reputation as a good organiser and a meticulous administrator.

Shirley had a large number of contacts, many of whom were useful to the team and its activities: when the group were working as a team, Shirley could always be relied upon to ensure that their needs were well supplied.

Shirley was replaced by Graham who, so far, has contributed little to the team effort apart from (mainly justifiable) criticism of his colleagues' ideas. Graham is a very sound and competent worker.

How has the balance of personality changed?

Solution

Analysis of teams and group behaviour carried out by the Carnegie Institute suggests that a successful team will comprise individuals who are able to carry out the following roles.

(a) *Chairman* - this is Andrew's job.

(b) *Shaper* - who is a spur to action, and is very committed to the task.

(c) *Plant* - the team's creative intellectual, an ideas person. Part of this role might have been played by Norman.

(d) *Monitor-evaluator* - this person is the most analytical member of the team, and perhaps exposes the flaws in its current activities. Graham, Shirley's replacement, is the sort of personality to play such a role.

(e) *Resource-investigator* - is a source of new contacts, but not an original thinker. This role has been played by Shirley.

(f) *Company worker* - an efficient organiser turning ideas into tasks, an effective administrator. Hilary probably fits this role.

(g) *Team worker* - keeps the team together, smooths over conflict. Norman the 'shrewd politician' had probably played this role.

(h) *Finisher* - chivvies the team to meet deadlines, ensures follow through, ensures that lose ends are tidied up and things get done. Arguably, Hilary is playing this role, too.

Andrew has been asked for a 20% increase in the team's output, although it appears that if current trends are followed it will just meet its targets for the year. This is requested at the same time as the composition and balance of power in the team has changed.

The team has lost:

(a) its ideas person (Norman);

(b) the person who was able to keep the team supplied with resources and smoothed the team's progress through the wider world (Shirley);

but the team has gained:

(c) somebody who can evaluate critically how the team is performing (Graham, who is a sound and competent worker);

(d) a person who is a good organiser and administrator (Hilary).

4. CONCLUSION

4.1 Successful organisational change in the public sector, and in service industries generally, depends on converting those who deliver the service.

4.2 Change can be resisted on an individual level, for both rational or irrational reasons, and because the organisational structure and cultures means that change is hard.

4.3 Managing change, or renewal successfully, can be assisted if attention is paid to all the items on the renewal ring.

4.4 Flexibility and the ability to learn will be required of both individual managers, and the organisations they serve.

4.5 Attention should be paid to the way people work in teams.

TEST YOUR KNOWLEDGE
The numbers in brackets refer to paragraphs of this chapter

1 Can you identify phases of the introduction of change in public sector organisations? (1.3)

2 Describe causes of resistance to change. (1.7, 1.8)

3 Draw the renewal ring and briefly describe each element. (2.3, 2.4, 2.5)

4 What skills do you see the flexible manager requires? (2.10)

6 Teams should ideally contain a wide range of roles. Identify the roles required in a successful team. (3.39)

Now try questions 17 and 18 at the end of the text

PART E
ACCOUNTABILITY

Chapter 18

ACCOUNTABILITY AND ACCOUNTABLE MANAGEMENT

> **This chapter covers the following topics.**
>
> 1. What is accountability?
> 2. The role of accountable management
> 3. Freedom, responsiveness, accountability and responsibility

---

1. WHAT IS ACCOUNTABILITY?

1.1 The exercise of social and ethical responsibilities are seen to be part of the public domain. In the private sector it is held that profitability, market share and keeping costs low are more important than 'social responsibility'. The growth in 'consumerism' in America in the 1960s, issues of environmental pollution and the political impact of the 'Green' parties has made social responsibility a political issue and ultimately a commercial one, as companies endeavour to benefit from 'green consumerism'. The responses of the businesses sector have been a concern to show that:

(a) they are obeying the law (eg on use of toxic chemicals);

(b) their activities are environmentally friendly;

(c) they take their social responsibilities seriously. This may extend to providing special help to particular areas or sections of the community (through such organisations as Business in the Community, or the Two Percent Club).

1.2 Despite the efforts to demonstrate ethical and socially responsible behaviour, it is generally felt that *formal mechanisms* are required to hold organisations and individuals accountable for their actions in both the public and private sectors. Even so, the unhappy record of fraud trials and other public scandals demonstrate the difficulties of enforcing accountability.

1.3 Ultimately, a concern for ethics will be part of the culture of the organisation and embedded in its procedures.

1.4 The question of 'accountability' of managements and organisations is a vexed one. To what people or institutions should an organisation be accountable? In the public sector, this is not well defined. The elected councillors? Service consumers? Taxpayers? A wider perception of the public interest?

1.5   An organisation can be accountable by being open about its workings and achievements, and giving insights into its results. This is one of the reasons for schools publishing examination performance. However, in the public sector a problem might be that different interest groups use the results in different ways, or might be misunderstood (eg the results of the first 'standard assessment tests' for seven year olds produced statistically what one would expect from such a test, but they were used to attack teaching methods).

1.6   It may be difficult to find agreement on 'what or who to hold to account' with so many interpretations of what the inputs are, and their relative importance. How should the 'blame' should be apportioned between teachers, teacher training, education authorities, governors, parents, the Department of Education, previous Ministers, the Treasury, television and society in general?

1.7   Being answerable to the *public* or to the *taxpayer* may seem to be a way of ensuring accountability. There are a number of problems with ensuring this in the following cases.

   (a)   The public need to be informed and be able to make comparisons and exercise complex analytical judgements and some governments make a point of withholding information.

   (b)   The analysis of political decisions and the impact of government policies may only be made at election times. A particular issue may be difficult to isolate in a political manifesto, and many other factors may influence voters.

1.8   In a limited sense it is possible for organisations to be made accountable by law. For example, the law specifies certain minimum requirements for financial disclosure. However, this is accountability to provide, as it were, minimum protection against fraud, misappropriation of funds and so forth.

1.9   Similarly, the Board of Directors can be made accountable for the activities and behaviour of the organisation, to ensure that its rules and procedures are adhered to. However, while this might enforce minimum standards of behaviour, any sanctions can rarely be exercised.

1.10   'Acceptable behaviour' is defined in legislation and case law. British courts can be used to shape 'acceptable behaviour' by redefining common law, establishing precedents, by the interpretation of statutes and by judicial review of the actions of ministers and government bodies. *Judicial review* is the procedure whereby a citizen can challenge directly any act or decision of a minister, government official, or public body on the grounds that they have acted unlawfully or improperly. The role of the media and special interest groups continually challenge the balance of social, political and even scientific positions which underlie these judgements of acceptable behaviour.

1.11   European institutions can also enforce minimum standards on British institutions and practices.

   (a)   The European Court of Human Rights has had an impact on UK law with regard to subjects as diverse as telephone tapping and welfare.

   (b)   The European Court of Justice can be used to enforce adherence to European regulations.

(c) The European Commission can also take executive decisions (eg withholding regional grant aid to the UK if it is used merely as a substitute for UK government spending, rather than an addition to it.

1.12 Use of legal and EC remedies by citizens is expensive and time consuming. While a citizen might have suffered a 'wrong' at the hands of a public body, securing a remedy may not be worth the trouble. (If the matter in dispute is a point of principle concerning many people, a pressure group might fight on behalf of a particular individual.)

1.13 However, whilst there make organisations accountable to the law for breeches of probity, or justice, they do not provide simple remedies. Nor do they encourage good performance from public services.

The *Citizen's Charter*, and the various sub-charters it has spawned, might be a way of bridging this gap by specifying performance standards in the public sector that citizens have a right to expect, and remedies or compensation for failing to meet them.

This provides a useful halfway house, as a spur to motivation and a benchmark of performance.

2. THE ROLE OF ACCOUNTABLE MANAGEMENT

2.1 At one time, much of the public sector was immune from civil action (eg it was difficult to sue hospitals if environmental health standards were not observed in restaurants). Crown immunity, as it is called, has been removed from many parts of the public sector.

2.2 The existence of Parliamentary Select committees has brought the activities and performance of the public sector under greater scrutiny. The Audit Commission and National Audit office exist to ensure greater efficiency in public services.

2.3 The management of these newly-accountable bodies will have to adjust to practices which might have more in common with the private sector. A useful comparison can be made comparing the extent to which public sector and private sector bodies are accountable to 'outsiders'.

(a) Companies are accountable:

(i) to the Inland Revenue and Customs and Excise (to pay taxes);
(ii) to bodies (eg for product safety);
(iii) to shareholders (audit);
(iv) to clients and customers (products of merchantable quality);
(v) to suppliers (pay up in time);
(vi) to workers (contractual wage agreements, health and safety);
(vii) to regulatory bodies (especially for privatised utilities);
(viii) to tribunals and adjudicators.

2.4 In the public sector accountability may be seen to be more political. Public sector organisations are accountable:

(a) to elected members (of Parliament, local councillors);
(b) to Ombudsmen;
(c) to National Audit Office and the Auditor and Controller General;
(d) to Select Committees and Parliament;
(e) to Ministers;
(f) to professional standards bodies (eg British Medical Association).

2.5 Ways of enhancing a sense of accountability in public sector organisations include:

(a) professional ethics (which might encourage whistle-blowing for unethical behaviour);

(b) public relations techniques;

(c) benchmarks of performance (if results are published, the taxpayer can ensure they are met);

(d) attention by the media (makes decision makers more open to criticism);

(e) pressure on law makers to enact legislation to make the public sector more accountable.

2.6 It is argued that *professional* and *political* accountability in the public sector are being replaced with *managerial* accountability, with contracting out, local management and devolved freedom of management of services. This implies a greater freedom of action for the managers to achieve agreed objectives in their own way. These are discussed in more detail in the next chapter.

2.7 Establishing accountable management in the public sector can be seen from a number of viewpoints.

(a) *Those providing the financial resources*

   (i)   *Taxpayers:* individuals and corporations.

   (ii) *Investors:* individuals, pension funds, banks, insurance companies and business corporations.

   (iii) *Granters:* research institutes, government bodies providing monies through funding bodies to public, private and charitable organisations. This may extend to obtaining European funding for development schemes, training and social need.

   (iv) *Fee payers:* as part of the revenue of the organisations' charges are set for certain consumers. It is necessary to calculate expected earnings from fee payers and the level of subsidy to free users of the services.

(b) *Labour and materials*

   (i)   *Employees:* in the public sector the main expenditure goes on employing people, providing pensions.

   (ii) *Vendors:* the providers of materials being consumed. The public sector is a major purchaser of goods made in the private sector, or provided through contracts from military procurement, through contracted out services to stationery purchase.

(c) *Allocation of resources*

    (i) *Legislatures:* the government machinery which determines and controls expenditure and sets policy objectives and exercises controls on spending.

    (ii) *Management:* the chief executives and boards in the public sector have to meet set standards and targets. Freedom to operate more local management agreements have been introduced across the public sector with more decentralised management.

    (iii) *Local decision makers:* elected members, voluntary bodies, also decide to allocate resources to achieve their objectives.

(d) *Reviewers*

    (i) *Voters:* at national and local level who are the ultimate stakeholders in paying for and judging the 'value' of the services and money spent.

    (ii) *Watchdog bodies:* who act on behalf of the public to see fair play and that rules and procedures are followed. Audit Commission, Ombudsman, Equal opportunity.

    (iii) *Legal bodies:* through judicial review and the use of the courts, government's decisions are being questioned.

(e) *Measurement of performance*

    (i) *Comparative studies:* for evaluating costs and effectiveness, the relationships between strategy and budget and how the management compares.

    (ii) *Competition:* opening up the public sector introduces competitors against which performances can be assessed and management compared.

    (iii) *Value for money:* studies of effectiveness and management behaviour are becoming the way of establishing best practice in management between organisations.

    (iv) *Achievements:* the effectiveness can be carried outside the organisation to see what the outcomes in such issues as 'quality of life measurements', which can be used to review policy and use of resources.

2.8   As public sector organisations develop enabler or arranger roles then the judgement of the 'managers' in allocating resources becomes vital to the success of the organisation. Professional staff, local doctors and headteachers are now expected to take on accountable management roles, allocating and evaluating the use of resources and balancing the needs of a wide set of interests. Previously this would have been the job, say, of the local health authority, or local council.

3.   FREEDOM, RESPONSIVENESS, ACCOUNTABILITY AND RESPONSIBILITY

Stakeholder analysis

3.1   The 'stakeholder view' is a way of looking at an organisation's social responsibility which states that many different groups of people have a 'stake' in what the organisation does. From their various perspectives they have different objectives which they would like to see the organisation fulfil.

3.2   There are three broad types of stakeholder in an organisation, such as a company, as follows:

(a)   internal stakeholders (employees, management);
(b)   connected stakeholders (shareholders, customers, suppliers, financiers);
(c)   external stakeholders (the community, government, pressure groups).

These types are indicated in the diagram below.

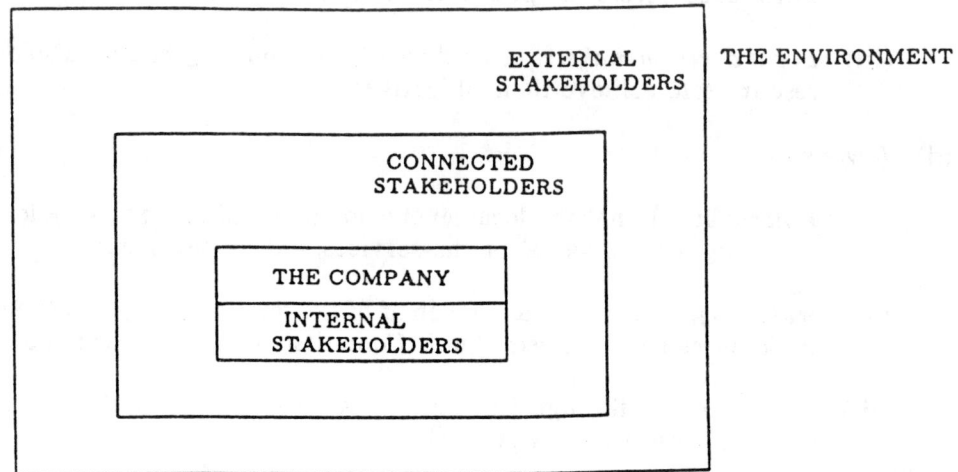

We shall consider each of them in turn.

3.3   *Internal stakeholders*
Because employees and management (which includes the Chairman and the Board of Directors) are so intimately connected with the company, their objectives are likely to have a strong and immediate influence on how it is run. The nominated or elected members in public organisations represent political interests. Officers' professional interests, on the other hand, may suggest different objectives.

3.4   *Connected stakeholders*
The objective of shareholders (eg making a profit) is often taken as the prime objective which the company's management seeks to fulfil. But clearly financiers such as banks have similar objectives which must be met (usually the payment of loan interest is a contractual obligation whilst the payment of dividends is not), whilst the customer's objectives, in a market-led company, must also be fulfilled if the company is to be successful. Other stakeholders directly 'connected' with the company are suppliers, trade unions and distributors. In the public sector, the consumers of the service (patients, school children, taxpayers) are connected stakeholders.

3.5   *External stakeholders*
These groups - the government, local authorities, pressure groups, the community at large, professional bodies - are likely to have quite diverse objectives and have a varying ability to ensure that the organisation meets them. Many diverse interests are involved in the external environment and they each look to achieve their own objectives which may not be related with each other.

3.6 How stakeholders relate to the management of the organisation depends very much on what type of stakeholder they are - internal, connected or external - and on the level in the management hierarchy at which they are able to apply pressure. Clearly a organisation's management will respond differently to the demands of, say, its shareholders or political masters and the community at large. This is because both the character of the relationship and the means by which the relationship is conducted depend on the relative bargaining power and philosophy of the stakeholder on the one hand and the organisation on the other.

3.7 The relationship may be characterised by a number of stances. Each party (stakeholder and organisation) may actively seek dominance or they may each adopt defensive roles. Ideally they should seek a balance of objectives but in turn this can mean that they may actively seek agreement or may merely react to circumstances as they arise. Hence the organisation and its employees/trade unions may have a relationship characterised by each party seeking dominance over the other, whilst with its customers the company may find itself reacting to the demands made of it by them. This shows that the ability to influence management does not necessarily arise from mere closeness to the organisation (employees are internal to the organisation but often the shareholders' and customers' objectives are more important).

3.8 The way in which the relationship between organisation and stakeholders is conducted again is a function of the relationship's character, the parties' relative bargaining strength and the philosophy underlying each party's objectives. This can be shown by means of a spectrum as follows.

	Stakeholders' bargaining strength				
Weak					Strong
Company's conduct of relation- ship	Command/ dictat by company	Consultation and consideration of stakeholders' views	Negotiation	Participation and acceptance of stakeholders' views	Democratic voting by stakeholders	Command/ dictat by stakeholders

Influence of stakeholders

3.9 Stakeholders can influence and constrain the management of the organisation at a number of different levels, which can be defined at the *strategic level* (the main mission and objectives of the company), the *planning level* (how those objectives are going to be met) and the *operations level* (how plans are put in practice day-to-day). But in addition management is constrained at every level by the legal environment in which it exists and the regulations with which it must comply. These can be said to arise from the objectives of the community at large and of the government, and can affect things such as employment rights, financial control and reporting, safety and environmental protection and the way in which competition is handled. The history and culture of the organisation can be important in determining how open the organisation is to the influence of the different stakeholders.

Strategic level

3.10 When deciding on a company's mission and objectives, and the strategies to be adopted in meeting them, the company's board will almost certainly be constrained primarily by the interests of the shareholders (profit) but also by those of the customers (price, variety, reliability) and of other financiers (interest and capital repayments, value of security, value of shares). But the extent to which management has discretion to make profits for shareholders is itself constrained by the demands of customers for value and of financiers for reducing risk to their investment. A balance must clearly be reached. The public sector has seen a shift towards central control, but services targeted to individual customers.

3.11 The organisation must comply with identifiable constraints such as its statutory duty to exercise 'stewardship' over its shareholders' assets, its contractual duty to pay interest on loans and its legal duties regarding employment and environment protection. These may come into conflict with other stakeholders' interests and even with the organisation's preferred strategy such as to be 'market-led' or 'quality led'.

3.12 Finally the organisation's strategy may be influenced by intangible constraints from the external stakeholders and the environment as a whole such as 'green' culture and concern for Third World development and good employment practices. The impact of changes in Europe will create another dimension to the role of external stakeholders.

Planning level

3.13 In order to achieve objectives and ultimately fulfil the company's mission, the management must make tactical plans. These will be influenced to a greater or lesser extent by stakeholders.

   (a) *Customers'* demands will dictate decisions for investment in new products, development of existing ones and setting-up of new outlets. They will also affect the standards adopted for quality control, and the extent to which they can be enticed away by competitors' products will affect the planned advertising spend.

   (b) *Suppliers'* and *distributors'* demands will affect the timing and amount of production, the amount of raw material and finished goods stock held and hence the financial planning which allows production to take place.

   (c) *Employees'* attitudes and objectives will greatly affect the organisation and co-ordination required to put production plans into effect. Construction of departments and work groups, job design, workflow and the amount of training undertaken will all be matters in which management will have to take the employees' stake into account. This may be particularly relevant when new technology or working practices are introduced.

   (d) *Specialised or professional employees* have two sets of priorities - their jobs, and the requirements of their professional bodies. The management must be careful not to bring these two into conflict, say by asking a qualified construction engineer to operate with untrained staff. The professional stakeholders may be very important in introducing changes into the organisation.

(e) *Trade unions* represent employees *en masse* and seek to ensure that pay, terms and conditions of employment, disciplinary and grievance procedures and employment protection policies are formulated with the employees in mind. Management will have to consider these and will have to involve unions in the planning process in order to preserve good industrial relations. The Social Charter if eventually adopted in the UK would increase the consultative role of unions.

(f) *Legislation, regulations and the community at large.* At the planning level management discretion can be contained by a great number of restrictions which are put in place to protect the community as a whole. Examples are planning restrictions on a construction company, pollution controls on a chemical works and disclosure requirements for a financial services group. New services provided by the local authority (eg 'Care in the Community', the Children's Act) will require different approaches from social service departments.

(g) *Financial stakeholders.* At the planning stage it will be essential to consider the financial stakeholders and the role they have in keeping the organisation viable.

Operations level

3.14 Clearly many of the constraints affecting management at the strategic and planning levels will also filter down to the running of day-to-day operations. Certainly consumers will affect production aims (size, quality, colour) and procedures (planning, stockholding, computerisation etc) when demand is variable (as in the fashion and high-tech industries). Health and safety legislation for employees and consumer protection legislation also mean that day-to-day operations must be constantly reviewed for compliance.

Management responsibilities

3.15 Management is be responsible not only to the organisation's owners (shareholders) but also to:

(a) employees;
(b) customers;
(c) suppliers;
(d) competitors;
(e) the local community; and
(f) the general public (and government).

Responsibilities to employees

3.16 An organisation's broad responsibilities to its employees are well set out by United Biscuits plc as follows:

To achieve the dynamic morale and team spirit based on mutual confidence without which a business cannot be successful, people have to be cared for during their working lives and in retirement. In return we expect from all our staff loyalty and commitment to the company. We respect the rights and innate worth of the individual. In addition to being financially rewarding, working life should provide as much job satisfaction as possible. The company encourages all employees to be trained and developed to achieve their full potential.

United Biscuits takes a responsible attitude towards employment legislation requirements and codes of practice, union activities and communications with staff.

We place the highest priority on promoting and preserving the health and safety of employees. Employees, for their part, have a clear duty to take every reasonable precaution to avoid injury to themselves, their colleagues and members of the public.

3.17 General principles have to be converted into practice, and should take the form of good pay and working conditions, and good training and development schemes. They should also extend into:

(a) recruitment policy;
(b) redundancy and retirement policies.

3.18 *Recruitment* of new staff should be done as carefully as possible, because if an organisation recruits an individual who turns out to be bad at the job the company has to ask the person to leave. Dismissals will be inevitable in any large organisation, but careful recruitment methods should manage to keep such demoralising incidents down to a small number.

Legislation on equal opportunities and employment for disabled people may have to be taken into consideration in recruitment policies.

3.19 With the establishment of short-term contracts and performance related pay, a new recruit might be given an individual contract. As job mobility increases, then pensions and health insurance schemes carried by the individual have to be dealt with.

3.20 Staff who are about to retire, after years of service with the organisation, should be provided for in their *retirement*.

(a) The organisation might have a good pension scheme. Employees might join private schemes instead.

(b) One of the problems for retired people is learning what to do with their leisure time. Some organisations provide training courses and discussion groups for employees who are coming up for retirement, to help them to plan their future time constructively.

(c) Trade unions may have schemes to help retired members.

3.21 Dealing with *redundancies* is a more difficult problem. Even for organisations which show an ethical sense of responsibility towards their employees, there may be occasions when parts of the business have to be closed down, and jobs lost. In such a situation, the organisation:

(a)   should try to redeploy as many staff as possible, without making them redundant;

(b)   where necessary, should provide retraining to give staff the skills to do their new job;

(c)   transfer to companies taking on public sector contracts may be possible (eg from a council's direct labour force to the payroll of a subcontracted company).

3.22   For those staff who *are* made redundant, the organisation should take steps to help them to get a job elsewhere. Measures could include:

(a)   counselling individuals to give them suggestions about what they might try to do;

(b)   providing retraining, or funds for training, in other skills which the employees could use in other organisations and industries;

(c)   arranging 'job fairs', by inviting other employers to come and display the jobs that they have on offer, and to discuss job opportunities with redundant employees;

(d)   providing good redundancy payments, which employees might be able to use to set up in business themselves or which at least should tide them over until they find employment again.

Responsibilities to customers

3.23   Ethical responsibilities towards customers are mainly those of providing a product or service of a quality that customers expect, and to deal honestly and fairly with customers.

3.24   The guidelines of United Biscuits plc again provide a good example of how these responsibilities might be expressed.

> UB's reputation for integrity is the foundation on which the mutual trust between the company and its customers is based. That relationship is the key to our trading success.
>
> Both employees and customers need to know that products sold by any of our operating companies will always meet their highest expectations. The integrity of our products is sacrosanct and implicit in the commitment is an absolute and uncompromising dedication to quality. We will never compromise on recipes or specification of products in order to save costs. Quality improvement must always be our goal.
>
> No employee may give money or any gift of significant value to a customer if it could reasonably be viewed as being done to gain a business advantage. Winning an order by violating this policy or by providing free or extra services, or unauthorised contract terms, is contrary to our trading policy.

Responsibilities to suppliers

3.25   The responsibilities of an organisation towards its suppliers are expressed mainly in terms of trading relationships.

(a) The organisation's size could give it considerable power as a buyer. One ethical guideline might be that the organisation shouldn't use its power unscrupulously (say to force the supplier to lower his prices under threat of withdrawing business).

(b) Suppliers might rely on getting prompt payment in accordance with the terms of trade negotiated with its customers. Another ethical guideline is that an organisation should not delay payments to suppliers beyond the agreed credit period.

(c) All information obtained from suppliers and potential suppliers should be kept confidential.

(d) All suppliers should be treated fairly, and this means:

   (i) giving potential new suppliers a chance to win some business; and also

   (ii) maintaining long-standing relationships that have been built up over the years with some suppliers. Long-established suppliers should not be replaced unless there is a significant commercial advantage for the organisation from such a move.

(e) Suppliers will be expected to comply with contract agreements and expect inspections and reviews of their operations. Contract specifications should not be changed without agreement.

Responsibilities to competitors

3.26 Some ethical responsibilities should exist towards competitors. In part, this means a commitment not to engage in industrial espionage, or other forms of 'sharp practice'.

Responsibilities towards the community

3.27 An organisation is a part of the community that it serves, and it should be responsible for:

   (a) upholding the social and ethical values of the community;

   (b) contributing towards the well-being of the community, eg by sponsoring local events and charities, or providing facilities for the community to use (eg sports fields);

   (c) responding constructively to complaints from local residents or politicians (eg about problems for local traffic caused by the organisation's delivery vehicles);

   (d) control of pollution and other environmental impacts of the production processes, and controlling disposal of waste.

3.28 In areas of economic or industrial decline, the public sector has set up enterprise bodies to help with establishing new businesses through provision of premises, retraining, advertising the area to inward investors. Government and European grants to areas where the coal and steel industries have been run down have helped in keeping communities together.

3.29 Investment in new communities have been used to regenerate run down areas through new towns and Urban Development Corporations in London Docklands and Merseyside. The movement of people and companies into an area can mean that communities have to be built up from incomers to an area.

Balancing the stockholders and freedom of action

3.30 In much of the public sector a balancing act is required. What are the best ways of treating a patient is a matter of professional judgements and choices. How *many* patients can be treated within budgets and the effective operation of the hospital may be a management decision (in consultation with medical staff). So clinical freedom of action is restricted by the availability of time, money and staff resources. At the wider level, the number of patients on waiting lists, the development of new hospitals and the demand for resources is a matter of political choice.

Exercise

How do you think the accountability of a facilities management firm which has taken over the running of computer services will differ from a direct service organisation?

Solution

Hints. The facilities management firm has an *additional* commercial accountability to its shareholders. Otherwise, if the DSO is kept at arm's length from the council, the accountability of each should be broadly similar.

---

4. CONCLUSION

4.1 Accountability in the public sector deals with management having to account for its actions to outside bodies, or interests.

4.2 Accountability in the public sector is harder to define than in the private sector, where ownership gives the ultimate right to make decisions.

TEST YOUR KNOWLEDGE
The numbers in brackets refer to paragraphs of this chapter

1 Why is a concept of legal accountability inadequate as the sole basis of accountability for the public sector? (1.13)

2 To what interests are public sector bodies accountable? (2.4, 2.6)

3 What are the roles of stakeholders in managing the organisation at strategic level? (3.10)

Now try question 19 at the end of the text

Chapter 19

POLITICAL, PROFESSIONAL AND MANAGERIAL ACCOUNTABILITY

This chapter covers the following topics.

1. The tensions between political, professional and managerial accountability
2. A typology of public sector accountability
3. Managerialism in the public sector

---

1. THE TENSIONS BETWEEN POLITICAL, PROFESSIONAL AND MANAGERIAL ACCOUNTABILITY

1.1 In the public sector, more than the private sector, tensions exist between political, professional and managerial accountability. This is caused by different values.

(a) The ideal choices suggested by in professional practice may conflict with the requirement to provide services at least cost.

(b) What are sound commercial reasons for an action may increase the cost to the state as communities are made unemployed and benefits have to be paid out. Applying a social accounting approach, in which the costs to society are subtracted from the benefit to the company, might have suggested a different decision.

1.2 As elected and mandated bodies acting under legislation, local authority councillors operate in a political arena. The legal decisions they make collectively as 'The Council' are based on measuring technical advice with political judgement. Decision-making is often slow, and may involve political gerrymandering (in supporting policies which favour one party interests). Undue influence may be exerted by some groups through the political parties.

1.3 The Community Charge was a method of local taxation designed to spread the payment to all adults who would be able to send clear signals to the local authorities on their spending. Because of the way Central Government controlled the expenditure of local government and have imposed charge capping, it has been central rather than local government which has been accountable for the Community Charge.

1.4 Local government finance will still be controlled from the centre with little local choice being exercised. Other changes on structure and the services provided by local government may mean even more central control over large spending areas like education, social services and the police. Accountability at the *political level* then may be different to attribute between central and local government politicians. Local government might take the flak for central government decisions. The point at which political decisions give way to technical decisions may also be difficult to identify, both between central government ministries and their regional offices and the local government officers and between local members and officers. In some estimations, the *officers* make ninety percent of the decisions.

1.5 Nevertheless, local councillors are being pushed into a managerial role, by being given the difficult decisions to make on policy and resources, and cuts in services. Appointments to senior staff positions are made by councillors. For some leaders and committee chairs, local government has become a full time activity.

1.6 Proposals from the Secretary of State for the Environment in a July 1991 White Paper *(The internal management of local authorities)* would give the elected councillors more power to manage the authority. The ideas in the discussion document include:

(a) a cabinet system to improve the setting of policy and strategic decision making;

(b) an elected mayor to run the authority.

1.7 This results from mistrust of the average councillor, and the controlling influence of party groups. This was reflected in the Widdecombe Report and Research on 'The Conduct of Local Authority Business'. The Widdecombe Report was concerned with political controls in local government.

Amongst its recommendations were:

(a) to increase the role of the chief executive;

(b) to use the chief executive's position to maintain a record of the councillors' interests and to control the information received by councillors.

A national code of conduct would be the model to keep councillors accountable under the Local Government Act 1989, s 20. These model codes are enforceable under the law.

1.8 The prohibition of officers from being councillors and the barring of council officers above a certain level from political activity have been introduced following Widdecombe's recommendations. An independent adjudicator has been appointed to adjudicate on exemptions on political restricted posts. It is recognised that some posts can be taken up by political activists as advisors to leading councillors. These political posts are limited in number and do not come under the control of the chief executive.

1.9 The recommendations of the Widdecombe report very much strengthened the role of the *chief executive*. The idea for establishing chief executives goes back to Maud and Mallaby studies of the 1960s on the operation and staffing of local government. The Bains report of 1972 (The Local Authorities: Management and Structure) provided the impetus for creating chief executives, chief officers' boards and tighter member control through fewer committees and a Central Policy and Review Committee. The corporate management ideas of the time have now been replaced with a concern for strategic management in the 1990s. The latest attempts at improving management are based upon having a central leadership figure for the authority, as an overall director and coordinator of activities.

1.10   The question arises about how 'political' such a leader needs to be to give the authority a clear lead. The current thinking would see a leader in some way elected and representative of local community views. Thus, this position becomes a political office.

1.11   Clashes do occur between the political and professional interests in local government. More power has been given to the finance directors, chief executives and legal officers of the council under recent legislation.

1.12   The departmental and service provision of local government has meant that managers - directors of services - have come up the professional and departmental hierarchies and are seen as professionals first and managers second. With the creation of direct service organisations, managers have been recruited from the *private* sector to improve public sector management. Whilst many senior officers take up management training opportunities, middle ranking officers require the training too. A management perspective added to the organisation of the work of many departments would mean a threat to existing working practices. The lack of strategic or business plans in the organisation and the absence of performance measures means basic management practices are missing.

1.13   The provision of in-house staff development and the links with MBA programmes in a few authorities is providing new dimensions to management development.

1.14   The proposals to extend contracting out to central services, legal departments, architects and other white collar services may well change management approaches to planning and running services.

1.15   Decentralisation of service provision, relating services to local communities and bringing together councillors and teams of officers from a range of disciplines to work together on a particular project, are all breaking down barriers between political, professional and managerial interests.

1.16   The creation of boards and task forces for 'urban challenge' projects is perhaps a model of creating a clear set of objectives, creating a strategy and financial plan and bringing together public, private and community interests in a small geographical area. A more 'managerial approach' is required to lead these bodies but it also has to encompass the *political and professional competencies* to achieve given ends by a set of agreed means.

1.17   These competencies can be divided into those concerned with 'doing' which are about techniques and work practices and 'being' which are about personal characteristics. The 'doing' skills and the 'being' skills have to be combined to create an *active* manager.

(a)   *'Doing' competencies*

(i)   Good technical specialist skills in own area
(ii)   Analytical skills and ability to think things through clearly
(iii)   Financial skills and understanding
(iv)   Marketing skills and techniques
(v)   Planning skills
(vi)   Project management skills and techniques

      (vii)   Information technology skills: how to acquire, select and understand the information needs

      (viii)   Decision-making skills, including how to sell ideas and gain consensus

      (ix)   Communicating

      (x)   Negotiating

      (xi)   Motivating

      (xii)   Listening (not doing all the talking)

      (xiii)   Involving people at all levels

      (xiv)   Counselling and appraisal skills

      (xv)   Delegation

(b) *'Being' competencies*

      (i)   Bright and intellectually robust

      (ii)   Mentally agile

      (iii)   Enthusiastic and energetic

      (iv)   Resilient and tough: willing to cope with conflict

      (v)   Confident

      (vi)   Strong will and motivation to achieve

      (vii)   Committed

      (viii) Honest with integrity

      (ix)   Flexible

      (x)   Decisive

      (xi)   Open-minded and open to change

      (xii)   Creative and imaginative

      (xiii) Sensitive to other views and to 'vibes'

      (xiv)   Desire to 'keep moving'

      (xv)   Proactive and preventative in approach: not reactive and curative

      (xvi) Willing to take responsibility

      (xvii) Prepared to delegate and to live with it

      (xviii) Approachable, 'open-door' policy

      (xix) Business-minded and commercially aware

      (xx)   Able to take an integrated view of the organisation and understand the impact of one's actions on the rest of the organisation

      (xxi) Internationally aware and sensitive to other cultures

2. A TYPOLOGY OF PUBLIC SECTOR ACCOUNTABILITY

2.1 Glynn has produced a typology of the concepts of accountability in the public sector *(Public Sector Financial Control and Accountability 1985)*.

(a) *Political accountability*

    (i)   *Constitutional accountability:* the parliamentary system.

    (ii) *Decentralised accountability:* devolution of control to agencies, local government.

    (iii) *Consultative accountability:* the involvement of interest groups and pressure groups.

(b) *Managerial accountability*

    (i)   *Commercial accountability:* public organisations which are financed by charging the consumer. Privatised state gas, water and electricity organisations have had to move across to full commercial trading.

      (ii)   *Resource accountability:* establishing budgetary control processes to improve efficiency and effectiveness.

      (iii)   *Professional accountability:* self regulation through professional bodies.

(c)   *Legal accountability*

      (i)   *Judicial accountability:* a review of executive action at the instigation of an aggrieved person.

      (ii)   *Quasi-judicial accountability:* the control of administrative discretion review tribunals.

      (iii)   *Procedural accountability:* a review of decisions by an external agency, an ombudsman or a regulatory body.

Constitutional accountability

2.2   The UK, unlike most other EC members has an unwritten constitution which depends on an acceptance of a rule of law based on a set of historical precedents. The constitution is constantly being challenged and procedures amended, most notably by the UK's obligations under the Treaty of Rome, the Single European Act, the agreements of the Maastricht Summit on a framework and timetable for European Political and Monetary Union and the incorporation of European law.

2.3   Efforts to create a set of citizens rights and to incorporate charters on human rights into UK law and a Bill of Rights have so far failed.

2.4   The doctrines of individual ministerial responsibility (a minister takes responsibility for all the activities of his or her department) and collective cabinet responsibility (all ministers share responsibility for cabinet decisions) have become less effective with the scale and complexity of modern decisions, and the existence of separate cabinet committees where decisions are taken, only to be ratified by the Cabinet.

2.5   Moreover, prime ministerial power, the executive machinery of the Cabinet Office, the use of political advisors and policy units, have been seen as an undermining of Ministers' powers, with the Chancellor of the Exchequer Lawson resigning in a dispute over advice to Prime Minister Thatcher. The concentration of power, and the limitations on the parliamentary and legal controls over the decision makers, calls into question the accountability of strong prime ministerial government.

2.6   Parliament is required to vote on the raising of taxes and for government spending which provides for the appropriations for expenditure and the Budget to raise the money. The government is also responsible for macro economic policy, membership of the European exchange rate mechanism, setting interest rates, international agreements on tariffs and trade and economic management.

2.7   The role of Select Committees in monitoring government activities has increased with annual reports to Parliament. The Treasury and Civil Service Committee have reviews of government expenditure plans. More user friendly 'Blue books' on government expenditure and policy are available. The Select Committees are limited in the areas that can be investigated. They cover a few topics and they may be more about expert opinion rather than investigatory or interrogative inquiries. Civil servants are limited to what they can say under the Osmotherley rules, and the Secrets Act and rules of evidence.

2.8   The *Comptroller and Auditor General* is responsible to Parliament, reports to the Public Accounts Committee of Members and is the watchdog over government expenditure. The National Audit Office carries out value for money studies and reports to the Public Accounts Committee. Recent studies have covered the sale of Rover Group to British Aerospace, the sale of water authorities, inner city policy, regional aid policy. All of these have been critical of the way in which the activities have been conducted and the use of government funds. Other parliamentary select committees look into areas such as the NHS, or energy (eg the recent investigation into the pit closure programme).

2.9   Management information systems for ministers have been established as a way of setting objectives and measuring performance of government departments, and these have been extended to the Agencies now carrying out government services.

2.10   This links *accountability* with *resource management and control* by having stated objectives.

2.11   The exercise of decision-making power is sometimes delegated. Parliament, which has the sole power to authorise the raising of taxes, sometimes delegates money-raising power in legislation. Examples of delegated powers are as follows.

    (a)   Under UK constitutional arrangements, Parliament delegates to local authorities the right to fund local expenditure through local taxation (eg council tax). That being said, the bulk of local government finance is still provided by central government. Local authorities, then, are perhaps, more accountable to central government than they are to their electorates.

    (b)   Some legislation includes a provision for statutory instruments in which certain powers are delegated by Parliament to ministers.

    (c)   Decentralised accountability includes hospital trusts.

    (d)   Some services which previously were accountable to local authorities are now accountable to 'consumers' (eg opted-out schools).

    (e)   Other bodies set up by legislation also have expenditure powers, but are ultimately accountable to Parliament. These include bodies such as the following.

       (i)   The Arts Council
       (ii)   The National Rivers Authority
       (iii)   The Housing Corporation
       (iv)   The Countryside Commission
       (v)   The Commission for Racial Equality
       (vi)   The Health Education Council.

Some of these are regulatory bodies, whereas other exist to promote services. These organisations have to account for the money they spend, as do government ministries, and might be regularly paid for by the audit commission.

2.12 Controls over these organisations are maintained by the legislation underpinning their existence, and short term contracts given to personnel.

2.13 The relationship between central government and these agencies is laid down by a sponsoring ministry and the Treasury in a framework document setting out the ground rules.

2.14 In short, a role of stewardship is necessary for the control of the organisation's finances. This will be revealed by the audit process, by budgetary and information control systems, and by the appointment, perhaps, of accounting staff.

Consultative accountability

2.15 Government agencies or quangos provide advice to government, and also implement policy. They are responsible to Parliament, and sometimes their advice is required on the framing of new legislation. The Highlands and Island Development Board, Development Corporations, Sports Council, Countryside Commission provide examples of these bodies.

2.16 Interest groups are also consulted. An example is the National Farmers Union which works closely with the Ministry of Agriculture, Fisheries and Food.

2.17 Professional organisations, like CIPFA, are consulted on government proposals and take part in studies and research exercises on issues relevant to professional expertise. Participation in such exercises is voluntary for both partners of course.

Commercial accountability

2.18 The government may take the role of banker or holding company. The organisation is expected to produce given returns on capital employed or to break even on earnings. This has been evident in nationalised industries. British Rail investment projects have to reach a commercial rate of return.

2.19 In preparing organisations for privatisation, the government has had to develop transitional accounting arrangements for the bodies to be privatised.

2.20 In contracting out health and local authority services, a more commercial view of accountability has been introduced. Levels of returns have been set to establish a surplus and make comparisons with the commercial sector. The operation of services are also looking at ways of *income generation* (eg the use of advertising, sponsorships or letting space in hospitals for shops, hairdressers, banks and restaurants).

Resource accountability (economy, efficiency and effectiveness)

2.21 The *Audit Commission* has established audit practices and has used 'value for money' audits to establish best practice to improve efficiency against performance standards. Comparative studies are required to show how an authority performs in relation to like authorities on an annual basis. As new programmes of expenditure are introduced the Audit commission is working with organisations to develop best practice.

Professional accountability

2.22 The UK's system of local government depends on a full time bureaucracy. In some areas, this has spanned a number of professional organisations to which members belong. Membership of the professional body requires completing recognised periods of training and completion of examinations. This maintains standards of qualified members of the profession. The professional bodies provide journals, to keep members up to date, and courses. Achievement of the qualification might be necessary for career advancement. An example include CIPFA, of course, but also other organisations such as the Institute of Housing.

2.23 With contracting out and fragmentation of services, the *professional base* of local government may well come to be replaced by a *managerial base*. Alternatively, specifically managerial skills might be built into the professional qualification.

2.24 All the staff are responsible to the council and should abide by council procedures and council decisions. Actions are taken in the name of the council (except under certain legislation, such as sectioning under the Mental Health Act if carried out by social workers, when action is required quickly).

2.25 The traditional view is that the councillor makes the policy and the officers carry it out. Because of the size and professional ability and complexity of day to day decisions, detailed policy formulation is sometimes, in practice, delegated to officers as well.

2.26 If this is the case, and officers have control and knowledge about day to day events, it is they who are responsible for most of the actions of the council. The council, perhaps like Parliament, will end up largely as a rubber stamp for executive decisions.

3. MANAGERIALISM IN THE PUBLIC SECTOR

3.1 'Managerialism' in the public sector has a long history going back to the 1930s, when proposals were made to improve the efficiency of government services and local governments. Reports on the management and structure of central government (Fulton 1968), of local government (Bains 1972) and of the health service (Griffiths 1983), have all identified a concept of accountable management.

3.2 The Fulton Committee (1968) view was that individual civil servants must accept responsibility for and be answerable for the resources they control, and their performance measured as objectively as possible. Accountable management requires the identification of discrete cost centres, or, as expressed by Fulton, *accountable units of management*. Organisations would be broken down as far as possible into units or commands to which specific resources would be allocated and managers would be held accountable, using some objective standard of performance for results. This requires establishing acceptable and measurable performance targets. For civil servants, it may also require a clear separation of political ministerial *policy-setting objectives* and *management-operational* objectives in delivering services.

3.3   The models set out by Fulton has been the basis for applying management by objective principles into government services and the public sector generally. The type of objectives being set can relate to commercial or resource objectives (eg in setting staff costs per service unit, by setting returns on investments or assets). Performance targets may be set and resources allocated accordingly, with local managers given freedom to determine the means.

3.4   Establishing procedures for setting objectives and putting in place performance measurement has been a slow process and has required a change in culture in the civil service and other parts of the public sector.

3.5   To implement accountable management a number of conditions have to be met.

(a)   *Units* of management, where the resources used and the results achieved can be distinguished from those of the organisation as a whole, must be identified. This involves developing the necessary financial accounting concepts and conventions.

(b)   Unambiguous, measurable and constant objectives for performance should be set.

(c)   Information systems, which can identify the decision makers in service delivery and resource allocation. Analytical frameworks have to be designed so that actual performance against target objectives over time, between organisations, across different approaches and within a 'political' time frame can be assessed.

(d)   It has to be possible to delegate freedom to managers to manage money and manpower as seems to them to be most efficient and effective in achieving their objectives. Responsibility without power is unfair. Accountable management is about freedom to manage as well as having systems of control and review.

(e)   It should be possible at the end of the day to assess the effectiveness of the management in achieving the desired outcomes or achieving some element of 'added value'.

3.6   Structural reforms in the 1970s established super-ministries (eg Department of the Environment) which would be better and setting objectives *across* a policy field and coordinate services. A number of bodies were hived off to be run as managed units with clear objectives (eg being the Property Services Agency, Manpower Services Commission).

3.7   The 1979 Conservative Government took more positive action to implement accountable management into government services and the public sector. The introduction of private sector managers to review the workings of government created the Efficiency Unit headed by Derek Rayner (from Marks and Spencer). Rayner's studies identified cost savings and improvements in working arrangements across a wide range of services and functions, in some 130 scrutiny exercises).

3.8   The Efficiency Unit became part of the cabinet and the new head was Robin Ibbs (from ICI) whose report 'Improving Management in Government: the Next Steps' proposed setting up agencies - executive units that deliver a service for government. Rather than being 'clerks' a reporting point in the machinery of the civil service and the Whitehall power culture, heads of agencies would be independent executives with freedom to manage resources. They would operate in a contractual relationship with Ministers to provide agreed services and functions, with an agreed 'price' from the Treasury being established for performing these functions. A similar system operates in some Scandinavian countries.

3.9 The notion of contractual relationships (to provide a specified service at an agreed price, of an agreed quality) is now pervasive in the public sector.

3.10 The other implications of these changes in relationships is about the position of the political accountability of the 'Next Steps agencies'. The chief executives are responsible to a minister, to the Treasury and the Civil Service department as well as answerable as the 'accounting officer' to the *Public Accounts Committee* of the House of Commons, and the scrutiny of the *National Audit Office*.

3.11 Public bodies have also been 'sold off', privatised or bought out by the management. These organisations now running at arms length from the government have to demonstrate that they are as efficient and effective as private sector competitors.

3.12 These changes in the provision of services and the structure and management objectives in the public sector can also be seen in local government and the health service.

3.13 The Griffiths Report (The National Health Service Management Inquiry 1983) proposed that a clear accountable structure should be created in the Health Service so that the links between ministerial and operational decisions could be clearly identified. The creation of unit general managers, the linking of management to both cost control and a wide view of making the best use of resources (including land, buildings, manpower), meant that below board level managers in the health service were no different to managers in Sainsburys. The reforms which have followed in the health service have taken into account such approaches as performance related pay for health managers.

3.14 As with reform in the civil service, the need to establish new ways of working, changing the culture and managing the change to new ways of doing things has been expensive and painful. More control over resources have been devolved to the lowest possible levels. As you might have inferred from the list of conditions for establishing accountable management in the public sector, the setting of performance measures, and the creation of accounting and information systems are both problematic. The effectiveness of the new management in achieving better patient care or providing better health care as a result of efficiency will be difficult to judge.

3.15 The Bains Report *(The Local Authorities: Management and Structure 1972)* also proposed a streamlining of the decision making process in local government with a central *Policy and Resources Committee*, which would oversee performance, review manpower and resource issues. The appointment of a chief executive and establishing chief officers' teams were proposed to more corporate working and accountability. Approaches to management (eg corporate management, programming, planning budgeting, matrix structures and creating across the organisation accountability for the impact of services) were all linked with Bains.

3.16 The structural reorganisation in local government in 1974 meant that many new authorities adopted the organisation forms advocated by Bains. The dominance of *professional* interests, combined with local *political* accountability, restricted the impact of accountable *management* until the reforms of the 1980s. The reform of local government structure and a review of the internal management of local authorities is under way at the moment, and one of the principles for the reform is to create more efficient and effective service delivery.

3.17 The Audit Commission has been the main advocate of establishing performance standards, of carrying out value for money studies, proposed ways of reducing costs of services.

3.18 Compulsory competitive tendering in local government, contracting out services in health authorities and contracting out in the civil service departments have all had an impact on management performance, and opening up the public sector to competition. Comparative performance review from the Audit Commission and competitive tendering have required these organisations to be clear about the level and quality of service required and relate objectives to costs. That most contracts have been won *in-house*, in the compulsory competitive tendering process, has shown that management can achieve these types of accountable objectives given an incentive.

3.19 The role of local government has been changing. Some functions being taken away from local government (waste disposal and management), while other functions have been given delegated budget powers or have been hived off to central government control. In managing the local authority, conflicts may arise because of the roles it is expected to perform, and the range of stakeholders or interests to whom it is responsible. The political process sets the purpose for management, the pressure groups and local protest are a necessary condition of providing a service to customers and meeting the citizens' and voters' perceptions. The management has a responsibility to achieve equity as well as economy effectiveness and efficiency. Performance has to be measured in political terms. The allocation and rationing of resources is thus a key issue in local government.

3.20 Local governments can be any or all of the following.

(a) A direct provider of a service.

(b) A contract authority who pay for the service.

(c) A regulatory body who licence and control activities who oversee planning, environmental health, building standards and control licensing.

(d) A commercial enterprise in providing functions which are charged.

(e) A public service in providing parks, museums, theatres, roads, lighting infrastructure which are public goods.

(f) A representative body, attracting inward investment, tourists and obtaining for the area as much government funding as possible.

(g) A body which represents the voters' and citizens' interests in the local area, in allocating resources and meeting local needs.

Each of these roles may imply a different set of objectives for management and therefore different measures of accountability.

3.21 The attributes of the accountable manager in the public sector may again be related to set of competencies. The accountable manager must be able:

(a) to take a broad and unfettered view as possible and to recognise the range of actions available to the local authority from direct provision through influence;

(b) to deal with uncertainty and frustration;

(c) to influence and convince other people to take action;

(d) to look out for opportunities, to innovate and to improve the working of the organisation;

(e) to manage contracts and deliver high quality services through others;

(f) to operate in a political system which requires a balancing act between a number of interests;

(g) to use the art of persuasion across multi-disciplinary teams and across organisations;

(h) to develop skills in contract management, financial analysis of organisational objectives;

(i) to have a capacity for learning and developing new ways of working;

(j) to be able to cope with uncertainty, as the public sector is still undergoing change and is very unstable.

Exercise

Assume that, once you have earned your CIPFA qualification, you work as a chief financial officer of a local council. What 'accountabilities' will you work under?

Solution

(a) Professional accountability (as you are a member of a professional accountancy body, which has a professional code).

(b) Political accountability to the council.

(c) Accountability to central government for resources.

---

4. CONCLUSION

4.1 Political accountability means accountability to parties or segments of the electorate, or to a political party.

4.2 Professional accountability implies prime allegiance to professional standards and bodies, and a commitment to the service, irrespective of resource constraints.

4.3 Managerial accountability means a prime allegiance to the objectives of the organisation and its efficient operation.

4.4 There has been a shift in the public sector towards *managerial* accountability. For example, the internal management of the NHS is run by management as opposed to medical professionals, and there is a separation between the executive and policy-making machinery of the NHS.

TEST YOUR KNOWLEDGE
The numbers in brackets refer to paragraphs of this chapter

1 Why are there tensions in the public sector between political, professional and managerial accountability? (1.1, 1.4)

2 Describe Glynn's three categories of accountability. (2.1)

3 What are the conditions for accountable management? (3.5)

Now try question 20 at the end of the text

Chapter 20

ETHICS AND THE CONSUMER
IN THE PUBLIC SERVICE

This chapter covers the following topics.

1. The nature of ethical judgements
2. Delegation, authority and responsibility
3. Consumers of public services

---

1. THE NATURE OF ETHICAL JUDGEMENTS

1.1 Underpinning the provision of public services and other social arrangements go the ideas of freedom, of equality, and of fraternity in the distribution of a society's resources. The political philosopher, Rawls, holds that the first virtue of social institutions is *justice*, which has a role analogous to truth in other systems of thought. In other words, a theory however elegant or economical must be rejected or revised if it is *untrue*; likewise, laws and institutions, no matter how efficient and well arranged, must be reformed or abolished if they are *unjust*. Each person possesses inviolable rights founded on justice, which even a welfare state as a whole cannot override. An integrated theory of justice incorporates the ideas of freedom, equality, and fraternity in some kind of balance.

1.2 An example of the difficulty in striking this balance is in the allocation of health resources.

(a) Health care is clustered in certain locations, making it harder for some people to obtain treatment than others with similar needs.

(b) Acute medicine obviously saves lives, and is, according to one view, the preferred option of the average health service professional. Preventative medicine has fewer tangible results - its results are measured abstractly in trends and statistics, not in the drama of the operating theatre.

Consequently, deciding, as in (b), between acute and preventive medicine or, as in (a) as to where health care resources should be sited, is a political decision: where should the authority for making it be sited? How can the justice of resource allocation decisions be assessed?

1.3 Rawls has developed a *social contract theory* of justice. Rawls started with an original position that societies are formed by the agreement of free individuals. (In practice, of course, we are born into a society, and educated into a language and culture, but Rawls is constructing a 'model'.) These individuals, who are ignorant of their own abilities and disabilities in relation to the other individuals, establish a system of justice based on fair agreement.

(a) Justice is fairness in that there is a basic equality in the assignments of rights and duties in society.

(b) Inequality is tolerated if it can be shown that everybody benefits from it.

1.4 Rawls also sets out two principles of justice.

(a) *Liberty principle:* each person is to have an equal right to the most extensive total system of equal basic liberties compatible with a similar system of liberty for all. This safeguards every person's basic liberties.

(b) *Difference principle:* social and economic inequalities are to be arranged so that they are both:

(i) to the greatest benefit of the least advantaged; and

(ii) attached to offices and positions open to all under conditions of fair equality of opportunity.

This ensures that there is maximum help to the socially disadvantaged compatible with general social welfare.

1.5 The tendency to equality reduces the gap between the rich and the poor: the advantages gained by the more able or more fortunate are regarded as *common assets* and so those with the fewest advantages or aptitudes also benefit from them.

1.6 In health care, the question of equity is related to *who defines the needs*, and *who has the authority* over resource allocation. Some issues are easy: everyone benefits from improved water quality and waste disposal, and the control of contagious diseases. Other ethical judgements depend on skill and knowledge and the availability of *resources* for health treatment. Medical professionals have had to make these decisions; now it is accountants who allocate resources.

1.7 The *public domain* enables citizens to participate and take responsibility for the government of the community. To be able to participate, citizens have to be supported by institutions which express justice. Citizens might be prevented or discouraged from taking part because of inadequate education, poor health care, unemployment, low wages and poor living conditions.

1.8 *Autonomy* defines the capacity for citizens to express their mind and advance their ideals. *Civitas* expresses the civic virtues of cooperation and friendship which are the requirement for autonomy. The interdependence of autonomy and cooperation can go to form the moral and social ties which help to integrate a society and make it into a community. The provision of many collective goods has provided the basis for autonomy and participation. Community local self government is set out in the European Charter on Local Self Government, and has basic considerations of citizenship and fraternity embedded in it.

1.9   Other thinkers (eg R Nozick, *Anarchy, State and Utopia* 1974) argue that the individual has *inalienable* rights of possession of property and skill, which cannot be invaded by the public domain. Narrow limits should be set for the arena of public choice (to include only: law and order, enforcement of contract and defence). The freedom of individual choice and the allocation of resources through free competition in the market place has come to challenge the restrictions and failures of the public domain to serve the individual's self interest. The view that individual self interest can be determined by professionals and bureaucrats in the state service, by restricting choice and rationing services through a centralised system, is seen as a nonsense.

1.10   When a service cannot be transferred easily and quickly to the market place, then according to this view, quasi-markets have to be created to achieve some freedom of choice. Participation of user groups in the provision of the services is one approach (eg giving power to tenants associations, for tenants to choose a landlord, devolving decision making to the school governors). Creating purchaser and provider relationships in the health service, enabling doctors to choose where they buy the services for their patients is another way. These structures to allocate and access resources contain ethical judgement about fairness and justice in the use of resources.

1.11   A duality of purpose exists in the public domain in enabling citizens to express a *collective choice* which emerges through elected members operating in the general interest; and the provision of services to the customer, an individual whose interests are being served. A person as a *citizen* might want low taxes and for people to be free, but as a *customer* 'Ms/Mr public' wants a safe city, well lit and paved, policed, a good environment, good quality public transport.

1.12   Ethical judgements then have to balance collective and individual interests. It is necessary to be aware of how those interests are presented, and the consequences of choosing how to balance them. Fairness will depend upon values and attitudes which become part of the common practice of organisations and large institutions, and are reflected in political and professional codes of behaviour. The shift to individual autonomy shows that the 'political interests' often defend the individual autonomy against the *professional's* views of the collective interest.

1.13   The language of these arguments become complex. In education, do we consider the interests of all our children taken in totality, or individuals developing at their own pace? What about the rights of parents, employers and society in determining how much of the society's total resources are allocated, and how they are spent?

1.14   Ethics and attitudes change over time and differ from one society to the next. It may take time to bring about change. The Disabled Persons Act has set statutory requirements on employers for fifty years but has been able to be ignored. Equal opportunity and racial discrimination are both issues to which organisations and individuals have had scant regard.

Social attitudes and ethics

1.15   It is possible to note some value shifts in the culture of the UK.

(a)   There is a growing belief in preserving and improving the quality of life by reducing working hours, reversing the spread of pollution, developing leisure activities etc.

(b)   Pressures on organisations to consider the environment are particularly strong because most environmental damage is irreversible, and some is fatal to humans and wildlife.

(c)   Many pressure groups have been organised in recent years to protect social minorities and under-privileged groups. Legislation has been passed in an attempt to prevent racial discrimination and discrimination against women and disabled people.

(d)   There has possibly been some erosion in respect for authority, the role of the police and the courts (eg non-payment of poll tax). If authority is seen to be arbitrary or incompetent (eg miscarriages of justice) then it will be taken less seriously.

1.16   The ethical environment refers to justice, respect for the law and a moral code. The conduct of an organisation, its management and employees will be measured against ethical standards by the customers, suppliers and other members of the public with whom they deal.

Ethical problems facing managers

1.17   Managers have a duty (in most enterprises) to aim for profit. At the same time, modern ethical standards impose a duty to guard, preserve and enhance the value of the enterprise for the good of all touched by it, including the general public. Large organisations tend to be more often held to account over this than small ones.

1.18   The types of ethical problem a manager may meet with in practice are very numerous. A few of them are suggested in the following paragraphs.

1.19   In the area of *products and production*, managers have responsibility to ensure that the public and their own employees are protected from danger. Attempts to increase profitability by cutting costs may lead to dangerous working conditions or to inadequate safety standards in products. In the United States, product liability litigation is so common that this legal threat may be a more effective deterrent than general ethical standards. The Consumer Protection Act 1987 is beginning to ensure that ethical standards are similarly 'enforced' in the UK.

1.20   The pharmaceutical industry is one where this problem is particularly acute. On the one hand managers may be influenced by a genuine desire to benefit the community by developing new drugs which at the same time will lead to profits. On the other hand, they must not skimp their research on possible side-effects in rushing to launch the new product. In the UK, the Consumer Protection Act 1987 attempts to recognise this dilemma. Drugs companies are not held liable for side-effects which could not have been foreseen by scientific knowledge as it existed at the time the drug was developed - the 'development risk' defence.

1.21   Another ethical problem concerns *payments* by companies to officials (particularly officials in foreign countries) who have power to help or hinder the payers' operations. In *The ethics of corporate conduct* Clarence Walton refers to the fine distinctions which exist in this area.

(a)   *Extortion.* Foreign officials have been known to threaten companies with the complete closure of their local operations unless suitable payments are made.

(b) *Bribery*. This refers to payments for services to which a company is not legally entitled. There are some fine distinctions to be drawn; for example, some managers regard political contributions as bribery.

(c) *Grease money*. Multinational companies are sometimes unable to obtain services to which they are legally entitled because of deliberate stalling by local officials. Cash payments to the right people may then be enough to oil the machinery of bureaucracy.

(d) *Gifts*. In some cultures (such as Japan) gifts are regarded as an essential part of civilised negotiation, even in circumstances where to Western eyes they might appear ethically dubious. Managers operating in such a culture may feel at liberty to adopt the local customs.

Examples of social and ethical objectives

1.22 However, companies are not passive in the social and ethical environment. Many organisations pursue a variety of social and ethical objectives. The following list is not comprehensive.

(a) For employees:

    (i) a minimum wage, perhaps with adequate differentials for skilled labour;

    (ii) job security (over and above the protection afforded to employees by government legislation);

    (iii) good conditions of work (above the legal minima);

    (iv) job satisfaction.

(b) For customers:

    (i) to provide a product of a certain quality at a reasonable price;

    (ii) to make products that should last a certain number of years (eg. for consumer durable goods).

(c) For suppliers, to offer regular orders in return for reliable delivery and good service.

(d) For shareholders, to remain independent and resist takeover offers.

(e) For society as a whole:

    (i) to control pollution, noise and smell;

    (ii) to provide financial assistance to charities, sports and community activities;

    (iii) to co-operate with government authorities in identifying and preventing health hazards in the products sold.

1.23 As far as it is possible, social and ethical objectives should be expressed quantitatively, so that actual results can be monitored to ensure that the targets are achieved. This is often easier said than done - more often, they are expressed in the organisation's mission statement which is rarely a quantified amount.

The social responsibility of organisations and managers

1.24 It will be apparent from the preceding paragraphs that not only does the environment have a significant influence on the structure and behaviour of organisations, but also the organisation will have some influence on its environment.

1.25 Since organisations have an effect on their environment, it is arguable that they should act in a way which shows social awareness and responsibility.

1.26 Social responsibility is expected from all types of organisation, be they businesses, governments, universities and colleges, the church, charities etc.

(a) Local government is expected to provide services to the local community, and to preserve or improve the character of that community, but at an acceptable cost to the ratepayers.

(b) Businesses are expected to provide goods and services, which reflect the needs of users and society as a whole. These needs may not be in harmony - arguably, the development of the Concorde aeroplane and supersonic passenger travel did not contribute to the public interest, and caused considerable inconvenience to residents near airports who suffer from excessive aircraft noise. A business should also be expected to anticipate the future needs of society; an example of socially useful products might be energy-saving devices and alternative sources of power.

Pollution control is a particularly important example of social responsibility by industrial organisations, and some progress has been made in the development of commercial processes for re-cycling waste material. British Coal attempts to restore the environment by planting on old slag heaps.

(c) Universities and schools are expected to produce students whose abilities and qualifications will prove beneficial to society. One view of education, by no means universally shared, is that greater emphasis should be placed on vocational training for students.

(d) In some cases, legislation may be required to enforce social need, for example to regulate the materials used to make crash helmets for motor cyclists, or to regulate safety standards in motor cars and furniture. Ideally, however, organisations should avoid the need for legislation by taking earlier self-regulating action.

Management as a profession

1.27 If it is accepted that the managers of organisations should have certain social and ethical responsibilities, the next question is 'should there by a formal code of behaviour for managers, and if so, who should issue such a code?'

1.28 A code of social and ethical behaviour might be issued:

(a) by a professional or management institution; or
(b) by an organisation, as a guide for its own managers and employees.

1.29 Professional bodies such as those for accountants, lawyers and doctors issue and enforce a code of ethical conduct for their members. Breaches of the code are punishable, *in extremis*, by expulsion from the profession.

1.30 There is a view that, in a broader sense, management is a profession too, and managers of all organisations ought to share a common code of professional ethics. One such code in the UK has been issued by the British Institute of Management (BIM).

The BIM's Code of Conduct

1.31 A *Code of conduct* (and supporting *Guides to good management practice*) is published by the British Institute of Management and gives guidance on the ethical and professional standards required of BIM members.

1.32 According to the *Code* managers should:

(a) comply with the law;
(b) respect the customs and practices of any country in which they work as managers;
(c) not misuse their authority or office for personal or other gains.

1.33 The supporting *Guides* lay down a number of professional ethics.

(a) In pursuing their personal ambitions, managers shall take account of the interests of others.

(b) Managers should never maliciously injure the professional reputation or career prospects of others, nor the business of others.

(c) Managers should make immediate and full declaration of any personal interests which may conflict with the interests of the organisation.

(d) Managers should be concerned in the working environment for the health, safety and well-being of all, especially those for whom they are responsible.

(e) Managers should respect the confidentiality of any information if so requested by customers and suppliers.

(f) Managers should neither offer nor accept any gift, favour or hospitality intended as, or having the effect of, bribery and corruption.

(g) Managers should ensure that all public communications are true and not misleading.

1.34 The need for this kind of ethical guidance may not be immediately obvious. You might think that adequate legislation exists to prevent any abuse of their position by managers. But professional standards go beyond compliance with the law to ensure that not even an appearance of unethical conduct is given. 'The law is a floor. Ethical business conduct should normally exist at a level well above the minimum required by law.'

1.35 It is not clear to what extent ethics will determine the decisions of management. An international survey reported in 1983 found that even with a published code of ethics, the business executive is still more likely to make the expedient rather than the moral decision. The problem, it appears, is 'group think' - a result of companies, especially multi-nationals, creating their own morality. A group of managers, especially when working closely together on an important project, tends to come to a consensus view of the world which may not always be the same as the views held by outsiders or be in accordance with society's normal codes of morality.

1.36 Political expediency may mean that ministers' or councillors' interests are not declared or apparent in a particular decision and that they are acting unjustly. Self interest and self protection may mean that individuals and groups take particular decisions.

2. DELEGATION, AUTHORITY AND RESPONSIBILITY

2.1 As organisations are delegating actions to lower levels, then the commensurate levels of responsibility have to be allocated to individuals to perform the tasks in an ethical way.

Authority, responsibility and delegation

2.2 It is easy to confuse these three concepts since they are all to do with the allocation of power within an organisation. We shall begin therefore by defining and discussing each of them in turn.

Authority

2.3 *Organisational authority* refers to the scope and amount of discretion given to a person to make decisions, by virtue of the position he or she holds in the organisation. The authority and power structure of an organisation defines:

(a) the part which each member of the organisation is expected to perform; and
(b) the relationship between the members

so that their concerted efforts should be effective in achieving the purpose of the organisation.

2.4 A person's (or office's) *authority* can come from a variety of sources, including from above (supervisors) or below (subordinates).

(a) Top-down authority is associated with formal organisations and is *organisational authority* or *position power*.

(b) Bottom-up authority comes from subordinates, and may be related to an individual's personal qualities or social rank. It is not generally associated with formal organisations although it can be argued that it exists in a democratic trade union.

Responsibility

2.5   *Responsibility* refers to the liability of a person to be called to account for his/her actions and results. A subordinate may have a responsibility for which he will be called to account by his superior; a board of directors may have a responsibility to its shareholders; and a government in a democracy has a responsibility to the electorate. Responsibility is therefore the obligation to do something; in an organisation, it is the duty of an official to carry out his assigned tasks.

2.6   Unlike authority, responsibility cannot be delegated. Where a supervisor delegates authority to his subordinate, he remains responsible for ensuring that the work gets done, albeit by the subordinate rather than by himself personally. The superior will exact responsibility from the subordinate for the authority delegated but he will remain responsible himself too.

2.7   With responsibility, we must associate *accountability*. Managers are accountable for their actions to their superiors in the organisation and are obliged to report to superiors how well they have exercised their responsibility and the use of delegated authority.

Delegation

2.8   *Delegation of authority* occurs in an organisation where a superior gives to a subordinate the discretion to make decisions within a certain sphere of influence. This can only occur if the superior initially possesses the authority to delegate; a subordinate cannot be given organisational authority to make decisions unless it would otherwise be the superior's right to make those decisions himself. Delegation of authority thus refers to the process by which a superior gives a subordinate the authority to carry out an aspect of the superior's job. Without delegation, a formal organisation could not exist.

2.9   In a formal organisation, the source of all authority (eg shareholders) delegates authority to a subordinate or representative (eg the board of directors) but retains some of the authority itself (eg shareholders retain certain authority, as established by company law and the Articles of Association of the company).

       The subordinate in turn delegates some authority to its own subordinates (eg individual executive directors) whilst retaining some exclusively for its own discretion. The process of delegation is repeated, stage by stage (or scale by scale) down a chain of command to the lowest level of subordinates given delegated authority.

2.10   The command structure of authority may be shown by an *organisation chart*, or it may be documented in schedules or manuals. It may be easily appreciated that authority, responsibility and delegation are critical aspects of an organisation structure, and are significant factors in determining the efficiency with which an organisation operates.

Authority and power

2.11   If an organisation is to function as a co-operative system of individuals, some people must have authority or power over others. Authority and power flow *downwards* through the formal organisation.

(a) Authority is the right to do something; in an organisation it is the right of a manager to require a subordinate to do something in order to achieve the goals of the organisation. Managerial authority thus consists of:

    (i)   making decisions within the scope of one's own managerial authority;
    (ii)   assigning tasks to subordinates;
    (iii) expecting and requiring satisfactory performance of these tasks by subordinates.

(b) Power is distinct from authority, but is often associated with it. Whereas authority is the *right* to do something, power is the *ability* to do it.

2.12 Three aspects of authority developed by Hicks and Gullet *(Management)* are as follows.

(a) *Responsibility and accountability* are coupled with managerial authority. When a manager is given the *authority* to do something, it is automatically presupposed that he has the ability to do it and the facilities that he needs, and that the desired results will be achieved.

The manager is *responsible* for the actual results achieved, and he is held *accountable* because information about his achievements will be fed back to his superiors, and they can then call him to account to explain his performance.

(b) *Authority is subjective.* Amitai Etzioni made a study of authority and motivation in differing environments. He found that the way in which authority and power are exercised will differ according to the environment, relationships and type of subordinates. Thus the way a prison warder, or even a shopfloor supervisor, exercises authority to get subordinates to do what he wants will be different from the way in which the director of a public company or the managing partner of an audit firm will exercise theirs. It will differ again in the case of the captain of the rugby team, or a parish priest. In general, at the bottom end of the management hierarchy, authority must be exercised with more coercion whilst at the top end of the hierarchy authority is more discreet and immediate subordinates more self-motivated.

(c) *Sources of authority.* The authority of a manager might come from one or more sources.

    (i)   *Top-down authority* refers to the authority conferred on a *manager* because of the position he holds in the organisation's hierarchy and the extent to which authority has been delegated. It is the official authority 'traditionally' associated with management, which goes down the scalar chain. In most organisations, top-down authority goes hand-in-hand with departmentalisation and the division of work, so that a senior manager in department A cannot tell a junior manager in department B what to do, because his authority does not cross department or sectional boundaries.

    (ii)   *Bottom-up authority* refers to the authority conferred on a *leader* from the people at lower levels in the organisation. Elected leaders, such as politicians and many trade union officials, have such authority, which they will be expected to exercise in the interests of the electors/union members.

    (iii) *Rank.* In some organisations, such as the armed forces, rank is a clear expression of authority and orders gain credibility because they come from someone of higher rank.

    (iv) *Personal authority or charisma.* Some managers acquire authority through their personal charisma, and as a consequence are capable of influencing the behaviour of others.

(v)   *Tradition*. Some individuals acquire authority by tradition. In old established family firms, the elder members of the family might continue to be obeyed and held in respect, even after they have officially retired.

Delegation of authority

2.13   It is generally recognised that in any large complex organisation, management must delegate some authority because:

(a)   there are physical and mental limitations to the possible workload of any individual or group in authority;

(b)   routine or less important decisions are passed 'down the line' to subordinates, and the superior is free to concentrate on the more important aspects of the work (eg planning), which only he is competent (and paid) to do;

(c)   the increasing size and complexity of organisations calls for specialisation, both managerial and technical. This is the principle of division of work.

However, by delegating authority to subordinates, the superior takes on the extra tasks of calling the subordinates to account for their decisions and performance, and also of co-ordinating the efforts of different subordinates.

2.14   To be truly effective, the process of delegation should consist of four stages.

(a)   The expected *performance levels* (the expected results) of the subordinate should be clearly specified (to determine the required results). These should be fully understood and accepted by the subordinate.

(b)   Tasks should be *assigned* to the subordinate who should agree to do them.

(c)   *Resources* should be allocated to the subordinate to enable him to carry out his tasks at the expected level of performance, and *authority* should be delegated to enable the subordinate to do this job.

(d)   *Responsibility* should be exacted from the subordinate by the superior for results obtained (because ultimate responsibility remains with the superior).

2.15   The subordinate's ability and experience must be borne in mind when allocating tasks and responsibilities, since it is highly damaging to allocate tasks beyond a subordinate's capabilities both for the organisation and for the employee, who may suffer severe 'role overload' or stress. In addition frequent contact must be maintained between the boss and subordinate to review the progress made and to discuss constructive criticism. *Feedback* is essential for control, and also as part of the learning process.

2.16   A subordinate may have written or unwritten authority to do his job. Written authority is preferable because it removes room for doubt and argument. Authority may also be general or specific:

(a)   it is general if the subordinate is given authority to make any decisions with regard to a certain (specified) area of the operations - he is put in charge;

(b) it is specific if the subordinate has authority to make certain limited and identified decisions within that area of operations. General authority gives the subordinate greater discretion and flexibility.

Principles of delegation

2.17 There are certain principles of delegation, recommended by classical theorists, and many of them are still relevant in the context of formal organisation structure. These are as follows.

(a) Authority (and power) and responsibility (and accountability) must be properly balanced within an organisation; there must be parity between authority and responsibility:

  (i)   a manager who is not held accountable for any of his authority or power may well exercise his authority in a capricious way. It is a common human trait to wish to maximise power and minimise accountability;

  (ii) a manager who is held accountable for aspects of performance which he has no power or authority to control is in an impossible position.

(b) Responsibility cannot be delegated. A subordinate should be responsible to his superior for achievements within delegated authority, but the superior in his turn remains responsible to his own boss for the achievements of his subordinates.

(c) There should be delegation of authority according to the results required; a subordinate must be given sufficient authority to do all that is expected of him.

(d) Once authority has been delegated, a superior should not expect his subordinate to refer decisions back up the chain of command to him for confirmation (or ratification) provided that the decision is within the subordinate's scope of delegated authority.

(e) There must be no doubts about the boundaries of authority because where doubts exist, decision-making will be weak, confused and possibly contradictory (if boundaries of authority overlap). Classical theorists such as Fayol therefore argued that the chain of command must be clearly specified in terms of who holds what authority and who is accountable to whom and for what. Information flow does not have to be restricted to passing up and down the chain, but authority should.

(f) The greater the clarity of:

  (i)   the functions given to each department;
  (ii)   the activities and authority of each department;
  (iii) the ways in which departments are meant to inter-act and co-operate

  the greater will be the ability of individuals with authority in each department to contribute towards the achievement of the organisation's goals.

(g) Classical theorists such as Fayol argued in favour of the principle of *unity of command*. Each individual should report to only one superior so as to avoid conflicts created by dual command. A subordinate who reports to a single boss will accept responsibility more readily, because there will be no stress or confusion created by having two bosses with conflicting demands. The principle of unity of command is not accepted by supporters of organisation structures which include matrix management or inter-disciplinary project teams, however.

2.18 When authority is delegated, the relationship between subordinate and superior is critically important. Drucker has argued that although authority is passed down to subordinates, the relationship between subordinates and superiors, and their responsibilities, have three dimensions.

(a) Every manager has the task of contributing towards what his or her superior's section must do to achieve its objectives.

(b) Every manager has a responsibility towards the organisation as a whole, and must define the activities of his or her own unit so as to contribute towards achieving the organisation's objectives.

(c) Every manager has a responsibility towards his or her subordinates (to make sure they know what is expected of them, to help them set their own objectives, to help them attain their objectives, to offer counsel and advice etc).

2.19 It is interesting to ask why, in a formal organisation built up in the 'classical' hierarchical manner, there should be so many levels of management. After all, the purpose of management is to see that the work of the organisation gets done, and the only managers who supervise 'actual work' directly are the 'front-line' or 'first line' supervisors.

2.20 If a first line supervisor has a superior, the work of the superior must derive from the supervisor. Drucker noted that 'the managers on the firing line have the basic management jobs – the ones on whose performance everything else ultimately rests. Seen this way, the jobs of higher management are derivative and, in the last analysis, are aimed at helping the firing line manager do his job. Viewed structurally and organically, it is the firing line manager in whom all authority and responsibility centre; only what he cannot do himself passes up to higher management'.

2.21 Yet authority is passed down or delegated through the formal organisation; it is not passed up from supervisors to senior managers. Although the front-line supervisor manages the 'real' work, the authority to do so comes from higher up.

(a) A front-line supervisor only has authority over his part of the work of the organisation and cannot issue instructions to another part. For example, the manager of the Oldham branch of a clearing bank cannot issue instructions to employees in the Huddersfield branch. Senior managers are required to co-ordinate the work of subordinates by having authority over a wider area of work, right up to the chief executive and board of directors.

(b) Front line supervisors make short-term day-to-day decisions and have no time for longer-term plans and decisions. Longer-term decisions are kept within the authority of more senior managers.

Problems of delegation

2.22 In practice many managers are reluctant to delegate and attempt to do many routine matters themselves in addition to their more important duties. Amongst the reasons for this reluctance one can commonly identify the following.

(a)   Low confidence and trust in the abilities of the subordinates - the suspicion that 'if you want it done well, you have to do it yourself'.

(b)   The burden of responsibility and accountability for the mistakes of subordinates, aggravated by (a) above.

(c)   A desire to 'stay in touch' with the department or team - both in terms of workload and staff - particularly if the manager does not feel 'at home' in a management role, and/or misses aspects of the subordinate job, camaraderie etc.

(d)   An unwillingness to admit that subordinates have developed to the extent that they could perform some of the manager's duties. The manager may feel threatened by this sense of 'redundancy'.

(e)   Poor control and communication systems in the organisation, so that the manager feels he has to do everything himself if he is to retain real control and responsibility for a task, and if he wants to know what is going on.

(f)   An organisational culture that has failed to reward or recognise effective delegation by superiors, so that the manager may not realise that delegation is positively regarded (rather than seen as a 'shirking' of responsibility).

(g)   Lack of understanding of what delegation involves - *not* giving subordinates total control, making the manager himself redundant etc.

2.23   Handy *(Understanding Organisations)* writes of a 'trust dilemma' in a superior-subordinate relationship, in which the sum of trust + control is a constant amount:

$$T + C = Y$$

where T = the trust the superior has in the subordinate, and the trust which the subordinate feels the superior has in him or her;
C = the degree of control exercised by the superior over the subordinate;
Y = a constant, unchanging value.

Any increase in C, that is the superior retains more 'control' or authority, will mean that the subordinate will immediately recognise that he is being trusted less. If the superior wishes to show more trust in the subordinate, he can only do so by reducing control (C), that is by delegating more authority.

2.24   To overcome the reluctance of managers to delegate, the following is necessary.

(a)   Provide a system of selecting subordinates who will be capable of handling delegated authority in a responsible way. If subordinates are of the right 'quality', superiors will be prepared to trust them more.

(b)   Have a system of open communications, in which the superior and subordinates freely interchange ideas and information. If the subordinate is given all the information he needs to do his job, and if the superior is aware of what the subordinate is doing:

(i)   the subordinate will make better-informed decisions;
(ii)   the superior will not 'panic' because he does not know what is going on.

Although open lines of communication are important, they should not be used by the superior to command the subordinate in a matter where authority has been delegated to the subordinate; communication links must not be used by superiors as a means of reclaiming authority.

(c)   Ensure that a system of control is established. Superiors are reluctant to delegate authority because they retain absolute responsibility for the performance of their subordinates. If an efficient control system is in operation, responsibility and accountability will be monitored at all levels of the management hierarchy, and the 'dangers' of relinquishing authority and control to subordinates are significantly lessened.

(d)   Reward effective delegation by superiors and the efficient assumption of authority by subordinates. Rewards may be given in terms of pay, promotion, status, 'official' approval etc.

When to delegate

2.25   A manager should be coached, if necessary, about the particular instances in which he should or should not delegate. He or she will have to consider the following.

(a)   Is the *acceptance* of subordinates required (for morale, relationships, ease of implementation of the decision etc)? If so, the manager would be advised at least to consult them. If acceptance is the primary need and the decision itself is largely routine, such as in the case of canteen arrangements, office decor etc, then the manager should delegate.

(b)   Is the *quality* of the decision is most important, and acceptance less so? Many financial decisions may be of this type, and authority should be retained by the superior, who alone may be capable of making them. If acceptance and quality are equally important, eg for changes in work methods or the introduction of new technology, consultation is advisable.

(c)   Is the *expertise or experience* of subordinates is relevant or necessary to the task, or will enhance the quality of the decision? If a manager is required to perform a task which is not within his or her own specialised knowledge, he or she should delegate to the appropriate person: the office manager may delegate repair and maintenance of machinery to an operations supervisor, perhaps.

(d)   Being as objective as possible, does the manager trust the competence and reliability of subordinates? As Handy notes, there is bound to be a dilemma here, but the manager is accountable for his or her own area of authority, and should not delegate if he or she *genuinely* lacks confidence in the team (in which case, there are other problems to solve).

(e)   Does the task of decision-making requires tact and confidentiality or, on the other hand, maximum exposure and assimilation by employees? Disciplinary action, for example, should not be delegated (say, to a peer of the individual concerned), whereas tasks involving new procedures to which employees will have to get accustomed should be delegated as soon as possible.

2.26   In instances where *reference upwards* in the scalar chain to the manager's own superior may be necessary, the manager should consider:

(a) whether the decision is *relevant* to the superior: will it have any impact on his area of responsibility, such as strategy, staffing, or the departmental budget?;

(b) whether the superior has *authority* or *information* relevant to the decision that the manager does not possess (eg authority over issues which affect other departments or interdepartmental relations, or information only available at senior levels);

(c) the *political climate* of the organisation: will the superior expect to be consulted, and resent any attempt to make the decision without his authority? Are there, on the other hand, useful 'points' to be scored for showing initiative and independence (especially if the decision is a success)?

2.27 The general structure and accepted practices of the organisation will partly decide the extent to which a manager will delegate decisions to subordinates, or refer them to his superior: eg. if the corporate culture favours participation, group decision-making, a consultative style of management etc.

Systems of appeal and pooled authority

2.28 Further problems with delegation occur when:

(a) subordinates who must co-ordinate their activities cannot agree about how things should be done; or

(b) the collective authority of subordinates may be required to make a decision.

2.29 Disagreements will inevitably occur within any formal organisation. The general rule is that problems which cannot be solved at lower levels are referred upward through the organisation structure until the problem reaches an official with enough authority and power to solve the problem. The channel for appeals would be described by an organisation chart:

Organisation chart

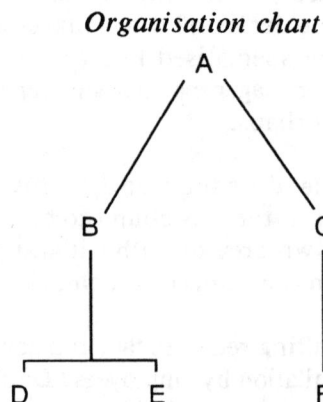

A disagreement between D and E could be settled by B, whereas a disagreement between D and F would need to be settled either by B and C together (using their pooled authority) or by appealing up the scalar chain to A.

2.30 Some organisations may have a special *appeals* procedure, with problems or grievances referred to an independent arbitrator. Pooled authority (or 'splintered' authority) refers to a situation in which two subordinates join together and use their collective authority to make a decision, instead of referring the matter up the chain of command to a superior. In the preceding 'organisation chain' B and C might pool their authority to make a decision affecting their common area of work, or affecting subordinates D, E and F, instead of referring their problem to A. Management conferences are an example of attempts to exchange ideas and reach collective decisions on the basis of pooled authority.

2.31 Tribunals may be used if the issue becomes something which cannot be settled internally, such as cases of sexual harassment, prejudice, unfair dismissal, discrimination is promotion. Trade unions or the Equal Opportunities Commission may help individuals fight cases in the courts.

2.32 If the actions taken by the organisation affect the consumers' or citizens' rights, then cases can be taken up by the Ombudsman (for local government) to review any possible maladministration and misuse of authority.

2.33 The Ombudsman and the Tribunal decisions can be a public condemnation of the particular action and can propose restitution to the individuals concerned. The aim is that the behaviour of those responsible within the organisation will change, or procedures will be developed to prevent it happening again.

Exercise

A company manufacturing baby food, in a very competitive market, has received in *private* a phone call saying that a very small sample of the jars currently in shops have been tampered with, and contain shards of broken glass. What would be the most ethical approach to deal with this problem? What do you think would be in the best interests of the company?

(a) Withdraw all goods from sale?
(b) Take out advertisements in newspapers?
(c) Ignore it, but offer compensation to people who claim injury, in return for their silence.

Solution

This is similar to a case in the USA, where the company withdrew *all* its products from sale, and better security procedures were installed at the factory. An advertising campaign was instituted to reach people who had purchased the product. This draconian approach earned the company public goodwill.

---

3. CONSUMERS OF PUBLIC SERVICES

3.1 In public sector services, the attitude has been that services are provided *to* the public rather than *for* the public. The emphasis has changed especially through compulsory competitive tendering to a concern with:

(a) the cost of the service;
(b) quality of service;
(c) putting value on the public as customers;
(d) responsiveness to the customer's needs.

3.2   The first steps in involving the customer are to open up the organisation to customer communication, through customer panels, surveys, making senior staff meet the customer. Access to the authority building, the quality of the reception area, the friendliness of the staff and the link to professional advice can all help involve customers in the service. Westminster City Council's *One Stop Advice Centre* is a model of the kind with an attractive reception centre, telephones, photocopying, meeting rooms available and professional staff on duty to respond to customers' requests. The aim at Westminster is to create a number of these centres across the borough. The authorities have created neighbourhood offices to provide easier access for customer, like Walsall, Tower Hamlets, and Islington.

3.3   As well as improving points of access, it is necessary to provide written communications and pamphlets which are easy to understand. Information can be made available to see the services available and provide guidance for customers on the availability of services. Some boroughs, mindful of ethnic diversity, print written material in several languages so as not to disadvantage those with a hesitant command of English.

3.4   Annual reports, summaries of the authorities' expenditure and performance can be made available to the public as shareholders would be informed. Leaflets supplied with the local tax demands are one way of doing this. Another is to combine information on what has been done with simple surveys and comments about future proposals.

3.5   The performance review process should include a survey of the public's and customers' views. The information collected should be disseminated down the system to the street level workers, receptionists, telephone operators as the first line of contact with the public.

3.6   In considering what information to collect and how to obtain it, the first thing to do is to ask people.

    (a)   People can tell you:

        (i)   their priorities and preferences - can score/rank choices;
        (ii)   describe the kind of services they want;
        (iii)   give views on what services they know of;
        (iv)   assess the quality of the services;
        (v)   restate their experiences of using the services;
        (vi)   assess the benefits they receive;
        (vii) give views on the image of the authority.

    (b)   The public concerned include:

        (i)   existing customers;
        (ii)   potential customers;
        (iii)   all those who live, work, study and visit the area;
        (iv)   local taxpayers;
        (v)   the electorate and their representatives.

Once the information is obtained then the analysis can be used to set targets and budgets for services, to redesign service delivery, to set up performance reviews and reporting systems. The image of the organisation as being a listening/caring authority and building on positive attitudes to the service can be important in developing customer confidence.

3.7 Public image and responsiveness are important, and good use of local media to provide good news stories and develop positive public relations is an important step in building customer confidence. Responsiveness to telephone and written communications, complaints procedures and dealing with grievances can also positively affect people's views of the authority if successfully delivered.

3.8 Front line staff have to be given responsibility and power for improving the service and not expected central direction. Communication across the organisation, newssheets, bulletins, open meetings are as important as the external image building. The goals of the authority and how they relate to service provision can be demonstrated through action plans and inspiring examples.

3.9 Changing the culture of the organisation is important as the role of local authorities in particular moves to that of a facilitator or enabler, acting on the customer's behalf rather than a provider. A concept of the quality 'staircase' shows how the organisation culture needs to change.

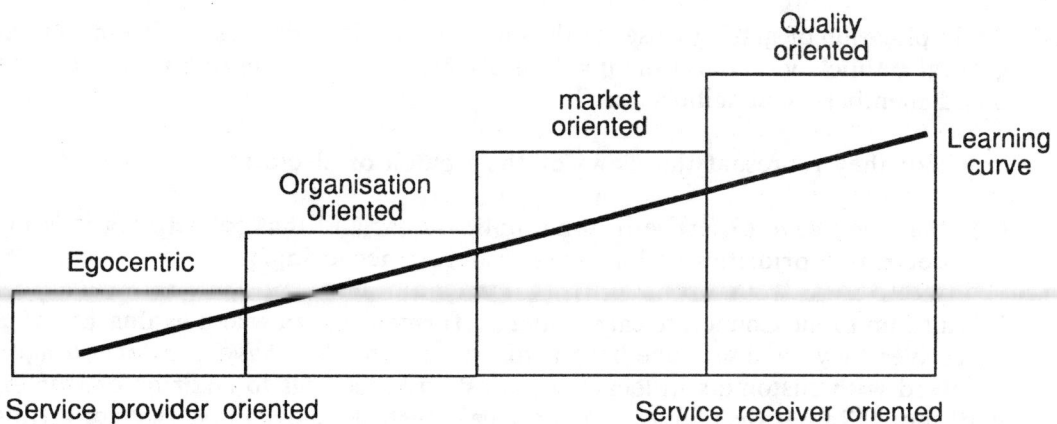

3.10 The organisation has to be a *learning organisation* that is willing to take the next steps to quality orientation, rather than have grand plans that do not work.

(a) Review the organisation's current practice, to establish goals to improve service provision and open the organisation to respond to customers.

(b) Through a market led approach, using surveys, questionnaires, panel responses, try out different ways of running a survey.

(c) Comparative reviews of how the job is done in other authorities may be a useful way of involving employees in adapting innovations.

(d) The quality oriented level may mean restructuring of the organisation and creating new values and attitudes. This may involve changing rewards and sanctions, changing managers' behaviour, getting people to talk and act in a different manner. This will involve training and creating an atmosphere which accepts change and can handle the changes, the organisation needs to be 'prepared' for these cultural changes.

3.11 Training needs to be designed to demonstrate how to do things in the right way to secure service to the customers:

    (a) a concern with 'a public service orientation';
    (b) with a focus on output not inputs;
    (c) developing creativity and innovation;
    (d) developing listening and communication skills;
    (e) encouraging delegation and involvement;
    (f) emphasising flexibility and responsiveness.

3.12 Ideas for training could include:

    (a) role play simulations customer/staff relations;
    (b) using videos to show good/bad practice;
    (c) listening and communicating exercises;
    (d) mini surveys of the public;
    (e) observing and discussing how services are provided;
    (f) induction training on how the authority works.

3.13 An implication of getting closer to the customer is that this perspective might clash with the general public's views and the position of the peoples representatives, local councillors or board members. Councillors feel:

    (a) that they represent the views of their patch or electorate;

    (b) that they have expertise in some policy areas and that collectively it is up to them to determine priorities and allocate resources accordingly.

It is also up to the Council to carry out a performance review and evaluation of how well the objectives they have set have been achieved. Councillors have been encouraged to become involved with customers in local 'surgeries' and meetings to chairing consumer panels and workshops. Rather than being a threat, local constituencies can be used for setting up service centres and focusing responses through the councillors. Councillors' political positions can be improved through becoming *closer to the customer* themselves.

3.14 The diagram demonstrated the views of the National Consumer Council on how users can evaluate services. This may provide a way of developing criteria to assure the users that services do come up to standard.

Consumer criteria for evaluating services

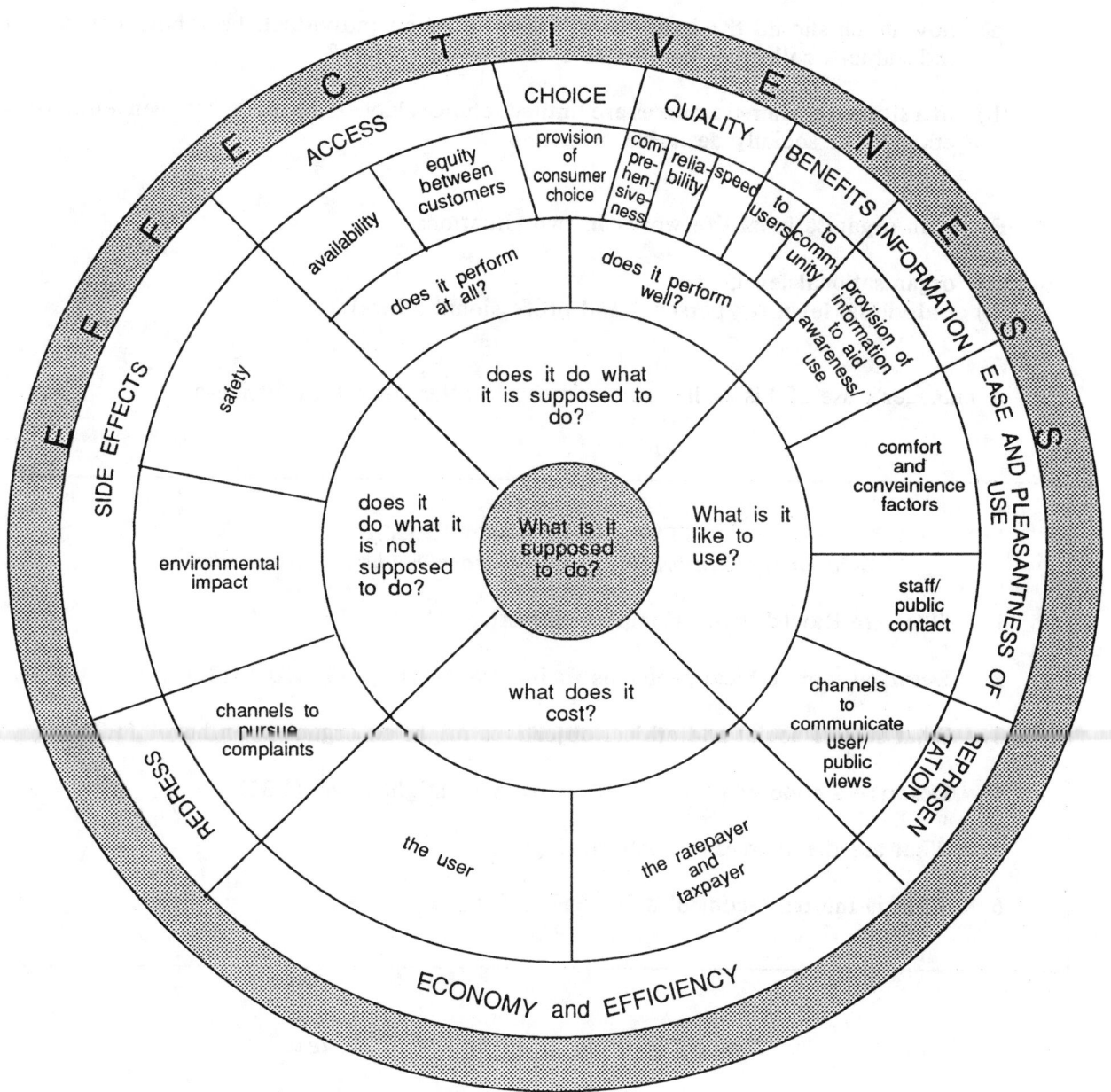

'The Service Wheel'

The NCC developed this framework to help ask all the important consumer questions about a service's performance: the actual questions to be asked will differ according to the nature of the service.

4. CONCLUSION

4.1 The public sector has two sets of ethical issues to consider:

(a) how much should the individual's interests, as an individual, be subordinated to the individual's collective interest as a member of society?

(b) in a situation where resources are limited, choices have to be made between a number of ethically or socially desirable priorities.

4.2 Ethics in organisational life works in two situations:

(a) organisational level;
(b) individual level (eg personal and professional ethics).

4.3 A manager's use of his or her authority is a matter for ethical concern.

TEST YOUR KNOWLEDGE
The numbers in brackets refer to paragraphs of this chapter

1 What are Rawls's two principles of justice? (1.4)

2 Describe some ethical problems facing managers. (1.19, 1.20, 1.21)

3 What sort of social and ethical objectives might an organisation have? (1.22)

4 Describe a code of ethics which a manager might have. (1.33)

5 What are the sources of authority? (2.12)

6 What is the trust-control dilemma? (2.23)

Now try question 21 at the end of the text

ILLUSTRATIVE QUESTIONS
AND
SUGGESTED SOLUTIONS

ILLUSTRATIVE QUESTIONS

1 DEFINITION OF MANAGEMENT

Why may the definition 'Management is getting things done through people' be inadequate?

2 MANAGEMENT IDEAS

Comment on the contribution of the classical and scientific schools of management to the development of organisational and managerial theory and practice.

3 CORPORATE MANAGEMENT

The concept of corporate management is generally accepted within the public sector but in practice often has limited application.

Describe corporate management and discuss this statement.

4 KLEE'S DIVISIONALISATION

Klee is interested in *divisionalisation*. Define this term, and describe why organisations make use of divisionalised structures.

5 ORGANISATION STRUCTURE

Identify the principal factors that might influence the structure of an organisation.

6 CULTURE AND 'EXCELLENCE'

Since the publication of *In Search of Excellence*, the concept of 'culture; has become very fashionable. What exactly is meant by the term 'culture' when applied to an organisation? How can the 'culture' of an organisation be so designed as to promote 'excellence'?

7 COMMUNICATION

The efficiency of your department is being impaired because two members of your staff seem to be unable to communicate properly with each other. What are the barriers to effective personal communication that you would investigate, and what are the remedies you would seek to apply in an attempt to solve the problem?

8 STRATEGY PREPARATION

You are a member of a working party discussing preparing a strategy for the Treasury division. Discussions get sidetracked on what is meant by strategies and how they relate to work schedules. You are asked to produce a set of definitions and show how the strategic plans fit with operating schedules.

9   MANAGERIAL ATTITUDES IN DIFFERENT COUNTRIES

You are required to describe and explain *four* features of the social or environmental climate which may cause differences in managerial attitudes in various countries.

10   NATIONALISED AND SEMI-STATE BUSINESSES

The mixed economies of industrialised and less developed countries have large commercial enterprises that are either partly (semi-state) or fully (nationalised) state owned.

What policy, planning and operating difficulties may be faced by nationalised or semi-state business enterprises (in any mixed economy) when they are instructed to act in a more profit-orientated and market-sensitive manner than hitherto?

11   RATIONAL DECISION-MAKING

Can decision-making be an entirely rational process? In what ways is decision-making limited by inadequate information and by the style of management in an organisation?

12   STRATEGIC MANAGEMENT

The process of strategic management can be defined as comprising strategic analysis, strategic choice and strategic implementation.

Describe each of these three stages, and comment on their inter-relationship.

13   PERSONNEL PROBLEMS

One of the activities of a local authority is headed by a manager responsible for approximately forty professionally-qualified staff, plus ancillary workers. Section heads look after groups of between three and six staff. The previous manager had an abrasive personality; he closely observed the performance, weaknesses and strengths of each member of staff, commented on them, and was unpopular with them and his superiors. The activities were efficient and highly regarded. Staff used to take part in many discretionary activities such as involvement with the public, and voluntary unpaid overtime.

A year ago a new manager, business school trained, was appointed. He promoted two section heads to be assistant managers, one for contact with the public, the other for administration, responsible for a new system of weekly performance reports and briefing meetings.

25% of the staff have left and the rest have gradually ceased all their discretionary activities. There is now a policy of positive non-co-operation.

You are required to analyse the situation, explain it on the basis of theory and suggest four reasons why it might have arisen.

14   MANAGEMENT AUDIT

Write brief notes on the management audit.

15 QUALITY CONTROL

Describe and comment on some of the techniques of quality control used within manufacturing or service industries. Why has quality management emerged in recent years as an issue of major strategic importance within the enterprise?

16 CHANGE AND IT

An organisation is proposing to introduce computerisation to improve customer care and to establish a quality audit. The organisation is a unit of a recently created Government Agency employing three hundred staff in five local offices. It has a poor reputation for dealing with clients and high administrative costs compared with similar units of the Agency. One problem faced by the unit is twenty percent annual turnover of counter office and clerical staff.

Required

(a) Draw up a forcefield analysis of the possible forces for and against introducing computerisation and new technology.

(b) Identify the attitudes which will have to be dealt with in the introduction of computerisation.

(c) Make recommendations in a summary report to senior management on how staff can be prepared for the impending introduction of computerisation and what can be done to improve the unit's performance.

17 ANYBOROUGH COUNCIL: REORGANISATION AND REDUNDANCY

You are a recently appointed member of the management team in the chief executive's office of Anyborough Council. Over the past few years - prior to your arrival - Anyborough has experienced radical changes in almost all of its departments and there has been some extensive upheaval. Most of the changes were badly handled and often caused bitter conflict amongst the workforce, including strikes. Relations between management and the trade unions are still extremely strained and you have noticed that a great deal of suspicion remains amongst the staff.

The one area of Anyborough Council which has not experienced much change has been the housing maintenance section. The housing maintenance section is a sub-division of the housing department. The section consists of 37 members of staff of whom five are operations supervisors looking after the skilled maintenance workers. The operations side consists of about 300 skilled building trade craftsmen and about 50 unskilled workers. The whole section is currently situated in a depot close to the centre of Anyborough. The chief executive officer, who personally 'head-hunted' you, has notified you that the changes are coming to the housing maintenance section and has asked you to handle the problem. He has suggested that he wants it handled as smoothly as possible and you are therefore in overall charge of the operation. Rumours are already circulating and tension is beginning to build up. Most of the rumours are incorrect for concrete decisions are yet to be taken. There is, for example, no real appreciation as yet as to the likely effects of compulsory competitive tendering (whereby the Council are required by the government to invite tenders on a range of activities from its own departments, other local authorities and public sector companies to ensure the cost effectiveness of its services). However, the rumours are having an adverse effect on staff morale.

The following programme of tentative change is put forward from committee for consideration and is essentially what is required. It is intended that the programme will commence in six months time and will be completed thereafter in two months. You do have some margin of control over the changes although you will have to convince the housing committee of any changes to the programme that you make. The areas on which no change can be made are indicated below; the other areas are negotiable.

(a) The central depot which is currently the home of the housing maintenance section will be vacated and made available for town centre redevelopment. The decision cannot be changed.

(b) The administrative staff will move to another building, which is older and less desirable than the present premises and is situated some five miles away. This decision is final and cannot be changed. It will involve extra travelling for most employees.

(c) The operations side of the housing maintenance section will be moved to two separate sites in the centre of the council housing estates. The workforce will be divided roughly in half, as will the supervisory staff. Again this will involve extra travel for most employees.

(d) The move will involve the immediate loss of five administrative posts and the creation of three new posts under a new job category entitled 'technological assistant'. The new posts will be necessary for the introduction and maintenance of a sophisticated computer based 'management information system'.

(e) There is a strong possibility of a considerable loss of work on the operations side which may subsequently lead to redundancies. This potential loss of jobs will largely be the result of competitive tendering. This is a 'grey' area with so much interdependent factors that it is not possible to forecast its outcome with any certainty.

(f) You budget will be increased in line with inflation as agreed at a recent Council meeting. However, the chief executive officer has already warned you that the chairman of the housing committee will seek savings in the region of 10% about half way through the year. How these economies will be made is not yet known but they must be expected to have effects upon the workforce.

(g) There is some possibility of surplus labour being absorbed in other departments of the Council. However, the problem here is one of compatible skills.

Required

(a) Make specific proposals on the immediate steps you intend taking prior to the changes commencing.

(b) Outline the manner in which you see the changes taking place and how you will handle them.

(c) What alterations to the proposals would you advise?

18 TEAM LEADERSHIP

George Gillespie is a team leader. Sometimes he makes decisions unilaterally. At other times he will not decide unless he has the consensus of his entire team. It is never clear on which basis he decides to act. As a result, the members of his team are often confused and demoralised. How would you help him?

19 STAKEHOLDERS

Stakeholder analysis identifies individuals, groups and organisations who have some kind of influence in the enterprise, and who may exercise some degree of influence over the management of its affairs.

Give some examples of such stakeholders, and comment on how their aims, activities or effects may constrain the exercise of managerial authority and discretion within the enterprise.

20 PUBLIC ACCOUNTABILITY

Public accountability is an essential part of any democratic political system. Discuss, with reference to any public sector organisation with which you are familiar.

21 EXTERNAL ENVIRONMENT AND SOCIAL RESPONSIBILITY

(a) How would an understanding of the economic and social history of the surrounding community be relevant to the organisation and management of a commercial enterprise?

(b) The senior management of your company has expressed the opinion that there should be a social responsibility of managers. What do you understand by this and could you expect this view to be translated into policies and procedures within the organisation?

SUGGESTED SOLUTIONS

1 DEFINITION OF MANAGEMENT

The quotation, which appears a common sense rule of thumb, contains a number of assumptions about managerial work.

First of all, it implies that management is about tasks, before people. Getting things done through people implies a priority of the task of human relationships. At the back of this statement can be found a conceptual network linking:

(a) scientific management - which analysed the work in preference to the worker;
(b) a distribution of knowledge in which the worker has none, and the manager has all;
(c) an ignorance of the non-task functions of management;
(d) an emphasis on authoritarian decision-making.

The statement is too vague however, to allow further detailed analysis. Getting things done through people might also include manipulating the internal politics of the organisation so as to obtain resources. A number of theories of management and leadership would cause it to be disputed. The statement is not necessarily wrong, but insufficient.

Mintzberg emphasises a number of management roles, from interpersonal roles (eg ceremonial), informational roles (in which the manager is a source and conduit of information) and decisional roles. This does not mean that planning and controlling are not management functions as a whole, but they are only one aspect of a manager's work.

In some corporations, it is possible to detect a different emphasis. Rather than getting things done through people, it is sometimes asserted, in contrast, that management is 'the creation of situations where people can get things done.' This is a concentration on the social relations underpinning some management techniques, as expressed by the human relations school. more notably, it is often asserted that one of the Japanese manager's main functions is the maintenance of group relations. As business is less contractual, the social role is important. Rather than defining the task first, and setting people in motion like so many machines to carry it out, the idea is to provide the right sort of environment in which people can flourish. This might have the effect of changing the nature of the task itself.

Behind this philosophy lies the more complex world of Mintzberg and the human relations school. It may be that group management is part of getting things done through people. Although there is little justification for assuming, optimistically, that happier workers are more productive, it might be the case that happier workers might be more creative in their approach to problem solving, customer care, quality and so forth.

Finally, the statement perhaps conflates what managers *ought* to do with what they *actually* do in practice. Many managers are not task orientated, or the detailed supervision and direction of tasks is not a management function. If tasks are delegated, the manager perhaps is only interested in the successful end-result. The manager will review the progress of a number of different tasks at the same time, but this is not necessarily a directive role.

Getting the task done as a concept also excludes the idea of keeping things ticking over. Although this does not sound terribly dynamic, a manager's role, especially in bureaucracies, is to ensure that the organisation's tasks are unimpeded, that resources are there, and that the department has the appropriate information.

The quotation also ignores the extent to which political activity may take up a lot of a manager's time, whether this be to gain resources for the department, or promote its power as an end in themselves, or as a springboard for the manager's career.

2 MANAGEMENT IDEAS

The early theorists who put forward ways of understanding organisations were mainly practising managers - such a Henri Fayol (1841 - 1925) and F W Taylor (1856 - 1915). They analysed their own experience in management to produce a set of what they saw as 'principles' applicable in a wide variety of situations.

The label given to this body of theory is the *Classical* or *Scientific Management* approach. It is essentially prescriptive (it attempts to suggest what is good - or even best - for organisations).

The classical approach to management was primarily concerned with the structure and activities of the *formal* organisation. Effective organisation was seen to be mainly dependent on factors such as the division of work, the establishment of a rational hierarchy of authority, span of control and unity of command.

The practical application of Taylor's 'scientific management' approach was the use of work study techniques to break work down into its smallest and simplest component parts, and the selection and training of workers to perform a single task in the most efficient way.

Scientific management's four basic principles were:

(a)   the development of a true science of work; the scientific principle is that every work problem can be analysed, and laws can then be applied to its solution;

(b)   the scientific selection and development of workers; workers should be trained to do jobs for which they have a natural aptitude;

(c)   bringing together the scientifically selected and trained men with the scientific techniques of work, in order to maximise productivity;

(d)   the constant co-operation between management and workers.

In addition to scientific management, the classical school also produced the first analytical principles of the functions of management in organisations. The principles of division of work, matching authority with responsibility, fair discipline, the scalar chain of command, fair pay and so on were described and where appropriate 'rules' or 'laws' of organisation were suggested.

Fayol in particular was responsible for formulating these principles. Amongst them he included the following.

(a)   *Division of work*, or specialisation, is to produce more and obtain better results.

(b)   *Authority and responsibility.* Fayol distinguished between a manager's official authority (deriving from his office) and personal authority (deriving from his experience, moral worth and intelligence).

(c)   *Discipline.* A fair disciplinary system, with penalties judiciously applied by worthy superiors, can be a chief strength of an organisation.

(d)   *Unity of command.* For any action, a subordinate should receive orders from one boss only.

(e)   *Unity of direction.* There should be one head and one plan for each activity. Unity of direction relates to the organisation itself.

(f)   The interest of one employee or group of employees should not prevail over the general interest of the organisation.

(g)   *Remuneration* of personnel should be fair, satisfying both employer and employee alike.

(h)   *Scalar chain*: the scalar chain is the term used to describe the chain of superiors from lowest to highest rank. Formal communication is up and down the lines of authority, for example E to D to C to B to A. If, however, communication between different branches of the chain is necessary (D to H) the use of a 'gangplank' of horizontal communication saves time and is likely to be more accurate.

(i)   *Stability of tenure of personnel.* 'It has often been recorded that a mediocre manager who stays is infinitely preferable to outstanding managers who merely come and go'.

(j)   *Esprit de corps.* Personnel must not be split up. 'In union, there is strength.' Verbal communication is preferable to written communication which is frequently abused, causing friction between departments.

(k)   *Initiative.* 'It is essential to encourage and develop this capacity to the full'.

(l)   *Centralisation.* Although he did not use the term 'centralisation' of authority, Fayol argued that circumstances would dictate whether overall efficiency would be optimised by concentrating or by dispersing authority.

Fayol considered the main elements of management to be planning, organising, commanding, co-ordinating and controlling.

The contribution of the classical school was to bring rational thought and an interest in practical research into the problems of organisations. The scientific management approach to problem solving still has widespread application today, and the use of operational research techniques and management models stems from the pioneering work of this early school. The classical views of formal organisation are widely applicable in bureaucracies.

The 'negative contributions' or drawbacks to the classical school were that, firstly, the classical principles of management seem to favour rigid, unflexible and bureaucratic systems and, secondly, scientific management, when applied without concern for workers, had the effect of reducing workers to cogs in a machine.

3   CORPORATE MANAGEMENT

A corporate outlook, where the benefits to individuals and the community as a whole are of primary importance, has today generally replaced the traditional approach of public sector organisations where a limited range of specific services were formerly provided. To be efficient and effective an organisation with a corporate approach requires corporate management to formulate objectives and policy and to ensure they are achieved in practice and with the planned results.

The major resources are finance, manpower, land and of course time. These are in limited supply and therefore must be used in the optimum way from the viewpoint of the total organisation.

Corporate management normally includes a policy committee, executive management team, joint committees and working groups. All have the task of considering matters from a wide viewpoint having the interests of community as their concern rather than only some groups or some services.

A major committee concerned with policy and resources is usually set up to consider objectives and priorities and to formulate, recommend, co-ordinate and control the implementation of an overall plan and to monitor and review performance, perhaps with the assistance of a policy review committee. Officer reports to these committees should be comprehensive and include background information, alternative reasoned and fully costed proposals and recommendations. Members of this Committee may also serve on specific service committees or they may be chairman of other committees or a combination of both, thus having specialist interests but when sitting on a policy committee their function is particularly to take a corporate view. The effectiveness of this may depend on the strength or weakness of individual officers or members. Even after careful consideration by this committee the council or board may not accept the recommendation.

The committee structure in some public bodies has encouraged the corporate view by uniting separate committees into wider-ranging ones, such as highways and planning, education and libraries combined. This enables a broader view of related services to be considered. However these combinations can sometimes bring disagreement when priorities of each aspect (still thought of as separate services) cannot all be met due to insufficient resources.

Many large public bodies have continued this committee unification in their staffing and have formed directorates. These have joined two or more former departments under one chief officer with deputies or assistants to specialise in particular functions. A practical disadvantage may be found in that the range is too wide and departments too large to operate well, especially where they remain in all essentials as separate units. Some organisations have appointed corporate planning groups or research and intelligence groups to assist in their corporate approach.

Specialist staff (such as solicitors and accountants) within say legal or finance departments may have responsibility and expertise for a particular group of services. Problems may arise in overlapping of duties or responsibility with other departmental staff. Some functions are centrally based (for example computer, work study, purchasing and supplies) thus concentrating expertise and providing advice to line departments and functions, but this may result in isolation.

The executive management team led by the chief executive officer or equivalent has a corporate identity and fulfills a positive role in corporate management. Each chief officer then has an awareness of problems of the body as a whole and of other departments. Most major decisions or discussions have an impact on more than one chief officer or department. In theory a chief officer may have to subordinate his own interests and views for the common good; however in practice this may not be so. Some chief officers may have insufficient interest or knowledge to discuss the problems of others.

Multi-disciplinary working groups of officers within an organisation may consider matters such as capital programmes thus using expertise in several departments to combine and produce unified analysis, reports or recommendations.

Some bodies have joint meetings with other organisations interested in similar activities, such as regional water authority/local authority, Health authority/county council/district council, electricity or gas boards/consumer or consultative committee, health or local authority/voluntary body. All these groups consider wider aspects of mutual concern but conflict in areas such as finance or priorities may arise.

Corporate management is generally considered to have led to some increases in effectiveness, but problems in application are evident and views differ as to the value of corporate management in practice.

4   KLEE'S DIVISIONALISATION

> *Tutorial note.* Divisionalisation is not the same as decentralisation. Divisional-isation is the process of splitting an organisation into separate cost and revenue centres. If this is accompanied by a policy of making each division responsible for its own performance then a decentralisation of authority will also have occurred. But in theory divisionalisation could occur without decentralisation of authority.

Divisionalisation is a step frequently taken by expanding businesses. Its purpose is usually to overcome some of the problems which commonly occur when growth takes place.

(a)   The increasing size and complexity of organisations calls for specialisation, both managerial and technical.

(b)   It becomes more difficult to exercise effective control as the number of individuals in the chain of command expands.

(c)   Growth is often accompanied by expansion into new products and markets. This is particularly true of companies which grow by acquiring other companies, often in very different lines of business. If a publishing company, say, takes over a computer software house, it may be that managers in the acquiring company are quite unsuited to managing the new business because they lack the appropriate technical and marketing expertise.

The advantages of divisionalisation are as follows.

(a)   It may promote staff motivation. It is difficult to develop a sense of 'belonging' to a large conglomerate, but employees and managers may identify more closely with a division. This is just an extension of the familiar idea that productivity can be improved by dividing up the work between small groups.

(b)   Greater control may be exercised over the profitability of the business as a whole. The establishment of separate profit centres means that the causes of any failure to reach profit targets can quickly be identified and traced to a particular division. If each division is responsible for its own income and expenditure it is possible to set targets for profitability and return on investment. This permits evaluation not only of the division itself, but also of its managers. Some businesses have used such schemes as the basis of profit-sharing arrangements and/or incentive bonuses for divisional managers.

(c)   Divisional managers may have a better knowledge than head office managers of local conditions affecting their area of work. With the benefit of such knowledge they should be capable of more informed decisions. In the event of incorrect decisions being taken, a local response may be more rapid than a reaction from head office.

(d)   It may provide benefits in managerial development. Managers who are responsible for running a division will gain experience that will benefit them as they move on to higher positions.

The disadvantages of divisionalisation are as follows.

(a)   It may encourage decisions which benefit a division but are not in the best interests of the organisation as a whole. One aspect of this problem is the temptation for divisional managers to take decisions which lead to short-term returns. This may have the effect of producing an appearance of impressive profits and return on investment, while being damaging to the division's long-term success.

(b) It often involves costs which could be avoided if the organisation were run as a single unit. For example:

(i) establishment overheads are likely to be higher in a divisionalised organisation;

(ii) there may be inefficiencies, such as arise when one division is paying its staff overtime to meet a heavy workload, at the same time as another division has idle staff;

(iii) the organisation may lose the benefits of bulk purchasing. It would be possible to get round this by purchasing all supplies centrally and distributing them to divisions but that would reduce divisional autonomy and lessen the value of divisional profit measures. It would also create problems of transfer pricing.

(c) This last point leads on to a more general problem. It is not only purchases which need to be allocated over divisions; all the organisation's resources must somehow be divided in the same way. If capital, for example, is in short supply it may be difficult to decide which divisions should have first call on it to finance their projects.

5 ORGANISATION STRUCTURE

Various factors which may influence organisational structure can be identified.

(a) *The arrangement of work*

For instance, work which can be based upon a routine is likely to be undertaken eventually by a specialised department, for example, a typing or word processing department.

(b) *Specialisation*

As in (a) above, employees with specialist - perhaps professional - skills may be organised into a single unit such as the tax office, quality control, research and development.

(c) *Overall size*

The overall size (and how this is actually measured, say by number of persons employed, units of output, capital) will influence the structure. This reflects itself in the number of people controlled, number of levels in the hierarchy, divisionalisation of skills and expertise, and definition of duties.

(d) *Environment*

Environmental influences in relation to the organisational purpose will influence the nature of the structure.

(e) *Regional dispersion*

Geographical or regional spreading of customers and/or suppliers will affect structure. This will in turn be reflected by the product. Low value products may be made near the point of use. This may require a widespread dispersal of production facilities. Importers such as coal users and oil refineries need to be near the coast.

(f) *Ownership*

Ownership can, of course, range from a sole trade to a multi-national with wide share ownership. Alternatively the organisation may be owned by local or central government. The structure should reflect the control exercised by the owners. Company employees report up to a board which is answerable to shareholders. Local authorities answer to electorates and operate through functional committees.

(g) *Technology*

Here Joan Woodward found a very close relationship between technology and organisation. Technology is dictated by objectives, products and methods. A specialist software house and a mass producer of cattle feed will have different skills and methods and hence different organisations.

Since all production systems differ in their degree of technical complexity, from one man jobbing to processes such as oil refining, the organisation will differ.

(h) *Co-ordination needs*

Where departmental operations are interdependent some co-ordinating unit will be needed, hence the use of the matrix system of organisation on multi-disciplinary projects such as the developing of new products, and in major projects, such as building a nuclear power station.

(i) *Planning*

Any decision taken in corporate planning will ultimately be reflected in the structure (for example diversification of product).

(j) *Senior management views*

Views held by senior managers tend to prevail, for example in favour of decentralisation rather than centralisation. In the same way, past decisions taken will influence structure, as when the organisation has developed through acquisition or merging.

Clearly decentralisation in whatever form will reflect skills. If a firm has the skills it can, if appropriate, decentralise its decision making process.

6   CULTURE AND 'EXCELLENCE'

Culture

Culture may be defined as the complex body of shared values and beliefs of an organisation.

Peters and Waterman, in their study (In Search of Excellence) found that the 'dominance and coherence of culture' was an essential feature of the 'excellent' companies they observed. A 'handful of guiding values' was more powerful than manuals, rule books, norms and controls formally imposed (and resisted). They commented: 'If companies do not have strong notions of themselves, as reflected in their values, stories, myths and legends, people's only security comes from where they live on the organisation chart.'

Handy sums up 'culture' as 'that's the way we do things round here'. For Schein, it is 'the pattern of basic assumptions that a given group has invented, discovered, or developed, in learning to cope with its problems of external adaption and internal integration, and that have worked well enough to be considered valid and, therefore, to be taught to new members as the correct way to perceive, think and feel in relation to these problems.'

All organisations will generate their own cultures, whether spontaneously, or under the guidance of positive managerial strategy. The culture will consist of:

(a) the basic, underlying assumptions which guide the behaviour of the individuals and groups in the organisation, e.g. customer orientation, or belief in quality, trust in the organisation to provide rewards, freedom to make decisions, freedom to make mistakes, the value of innovation and initiative at all levels etc;

(b) overt beliefs expressed by the organisation and its members, which can be used to condition (a) above. These beliefs and values may emerge as sayings, slogans, mottos etc such as 'we're getting there', 'the customer is always right', or 'the winning team'. They may emerge in a richer mythology - in jokes and stories about past successes , heroic failures or breakthroughs, legends about the 'early days', or about 'the time the boss...'. Organisations with strong cultures often centre themselves around almost legendary figures in their history. Management can encourage this by 'selling' a sense of the corporate 'mission', or by promoting the company's 'image'; it can reward the 'right' attitudes and punish (or simply not employ) those who aren't prepared to commit themselves to the culture;

(c) visible artifacts - the style of the offices or other premises, dress 'rules', display of 'trophies', the degree of informality between superiors and subordinates etc.

Promoting excellence

Peters and Waterman define 'excellent' as 'continuously innovative' - ie the whole culture is prepared to adapt to the needs of customers, the skills of competitors etc. Excellent companies 'experiment more, encourage more tries, and permit small failures'.

They identify various attributes of 'excellent' companies including the following.

1 *A bias for action* - ie experiment, try, *do* rather than overanalyse, focus on problems etc. The 'results first' approach means not asking 'What's standing in the way?' but 'What can we do *now*?'

2 *Closeness to the customer*. Customer-orientation and concern for quality at all levels can be an intense motivator, as well as a spur to innovation, because the workers' actions have measurable, even tangible, effects - a better product.

3 *Autonomy and entrepreneurship:* giving teams and individuals control over their improvement goals and methods, and encouraging stimulating competition and adventurism.

4 *Productivity through people* - ie 'turning people on' to their work and to organisational objectives, by positive reinforcement, 'reaffirming the heroic element' of the job, treating people decently; 'demanding extraordinary performance from the average man'.

5 *Simultaneous loose-tight properties* - ie autonomy, but control through central faith, guiding values, replacing manuals and rules.

The creation or reinforcement of all of these will depend on the culture of the organisation, and the extent to which it can be 'sold' to all the employees. Indeed, Peters and Waterman noted the success of companies with such 'strong' cultures that employees had to 'buy in or get out'. They argue that 'dominance and coherence of culture proved to be an essential quality of excellent companies.' Although they present a rather 'rosy' and unqualifiedly approving picture of their excellent companies, in pursuit of their central thesis, culture is becoming a real force in management thinking.

7   COMMUNICATION

Barriers

(a)   The employees might have different attitudes and perceptions arising out of the difference in their social and family background, educational background, political opinions, or age etc.

(b)   There might be inter-personal dislikes, rivalries or jealousies which prevent free and open communication between the two employees. The result might be that they tend to communicate with each other, incompletely and inefficiently, through a third person. This would be a slow, inefficient and unsatisfactory communication system.

(c)   The employees, intentionally or otherwise, might either try to communicate more information than the other can use, or transmit much irrelevant information.

(d)   The employees, intentionally or otherwise, might make important errors or omissions in information they provide, so that the recipient is unable to understand what he is being told.

(e)   Again, intentionally or otherwise, the employee receiving the information might simply not understand what he is being told. The use of technical jargon might be one problem, but slang and poor English are equally likely to cause communication problems.

There is a tendency for people receiving information to:

(i)   hear what they want to hear; and
(ii)   overlook or ignore what they don't want to hear.

(f)   Evaluation of the message's recipient, the use of non-verbal signs and the emotions of the giver of the message might create serious barriers to communication.

Remedies

(a)   The major problem might be the seemingly irreconcilable differences in background between people. The remedy to this problem lies in man-management.

(i)   One approach might be to encourage the person who feels 'inferior' or 'aggrieved' to lessen his sense of inferiority or grievance. Similarly, a person who feels 'superior' or 'contemptuous' of the other should be encouraged to treat the other person with more respect and regard.

(ii)   The two employees must be persuaded to recognise the problem and their own contribution towards it. When each individual in private discussion accepts his own personal failings in the matter, it might be possible to bring them into a joint discussion about their problems.

    (iii) In the early stages of finding a remedy, it might be necessary to encourage each individual separately. This might be done by:

        (1)   trying to get each individual to convey information to the other as unevaluated data so as to give the other a chance to make up his own mind;

        (2)   try to instil some 'warmth' and spontaneity into communications.

(b) The department manager can also take a more procedural approach to some of the difficulties. He might institute a new set of guidelines or rules for the information system within the department.

    (i)   Communications between employees must be in simple English, avoiding jargon which is unfamiliar to everyone and slang expressions.

    (ii)   The recipient of information should let the giver know what he has done or proposes to do about it, to check that he has understood the message correctly.

    (iii) The 'principle of redundancy' should be used for certain types of communication - a message should be repeated, preferably in two or more different ways, so that if it is not properly understood the first time, it will become more clear on repetition.

8   STRATEGY PREPARATION

Drawing up a strategy and defining goals requires establishing what the organisation is supposed to achieve, in other words its broad purpose or mission. The *mission statement* is a description of the organisation's services or products, the functions that it will perform, the clients or markets it will serve, and perhaps its values. The mission statement is seen as a navigational tool to help steer the organisation in its dealing with its external environment. Specific targets or goals describe where the organisation expects over a given period of time.

Goals and objectives specify targets that support an organisation's survival. They provide a focus for management's actions, and a means to measure the performance of the organisation. A *goals statement* will include a range of goals from broad general goals to specific achievable objectives or targets. The time period should be clearly stated and the goals quantified when at all possible. There are multiple goals. Not all goals are equally important, but more importantly, not all goals are compatible. Some have to be achieved first so that others can follow. Goals are arranged in a hierarchy and the time horizon for goals will vary. Goals can be used for external monitoring and internal management.

Goals should always specify:

(a) what is to be accomplished?
(b) where it should be done?
(c) when it should be accomplished?

Business or operational plans will be drawn up once the mission and goal statements have been written. These will create detailed schedules of the policies, procedures and budgets that are required in the achievement of the organisation's goals and its mission.

The *business plan* will cover the resources to be used, methods, process and procedures to be followed, tasks to be performed and expected standards, the sequence or steps to be followed. It will contain a reiteration of the goals to be achieved by the plan, deadlines, measurement of progress, the critical strategic factors to be dealt with and verification of goal attainment.

The business plan describes how the goals will be achieved (ie operating plan of the methods and procedures to be used), and who is to do the work. This may require network plans or project plans, to put into effect complex and overlapping development schemes promoted by different organisations.

9   MANAGERIAL ATTITUDES IN DIFFERENT COUNTRIES

The American writers Gonzalez and McMillan carried out a two-year study of management in Brazil, and suggested that 'American management experience abroad provides evidence that our uniquely American philosophy of management is not universally applicable but is a rather special case'.

This opens up the possibility that no general principles of management can really be arrived at, and that different principles will apply in different cultures. The success of Japanese management has highlighted the differences in management attitudes and culture between nations.

The 'social or environmental climate' of a country may be defined as 'all the social factors that affect the way people behave' (Rosemary Stewart) or the sum of all its environmental influences; the class structure, economy, political structure, legal framework, employee representation structure, education, culture, lifestyle and level of technology created by the socio-political and economic trends in the country's history.

Four features of this climate that may account for the differences in attitude between managers in different countries include the following.

(a)   *Class structure.* The class structure of a nation is likely to influence the way in which management and workforce perceive each other, and the way in which both regard their work. It is an accepted fact that in britain there is a greater perceived social distance between manager and worker, leading to greater formality in interpersonal relations and a greater stress in management attitudes on the traditional hierarchical aspects of organisation than is evident in Japan or in America, where informality and worker participation in management are far more developed. According to Rosemary stewart, 'the gap, or social distance, that exists between different levels in the organisation reflects both the class structure in the society as a whole and management's place in it'.

(b)   *The labour relations climate* - including governmental influences (such as employment law), regulation and the structure of worker representation/trade unionism. The attitudes of management to labour is reflected in how authority is exercised and how conditions of work and employee services are regarded. Governmental intervention may shape management policy in these areas: in Latin America, the government is a vital intermediary in industrial relations, and in the early days of industrialisation in Britain, many factory owners had to be forced by the Factory Acts to provide minimum conditions, pay and welfare for their employees, to stop child labour and so on. There are other influences; a paternalistic approach to the employment relationship might grow out of a feudal social structure (as in Japan) or out of a strong traditional class/family structure (as in Italy). A history of industrial disputes in a country may reinforce managerial stereotypes of the militant worker.

(c)   *The dominant values of the society.* Whether they arise from history, religion, politics of any other source, there will be certain mainstream cultural characteristics which will affect the manager himself and the conditions within which he operates. Where materialistic values are uppermost, in countries like America, the manager will have high status, which will be reflected in his attitudes to his work and to his subordinates. Japanese cultural values, such as concern for the individual, respect for seniority and the concept of *'wa'* or 'harmony', are closely bound up with the managerial practices of consensus decision-making, paternalism, *'nenko'* or lifetime employment.

(d) *Technological advancement.* The extent to which technology is an accepted part of the social structure will influence managers' attitudes to its implementation and advancement in the workplace, and possibly to change in general. Managerial attitudes to work patterns, pace of work, and place of work - with networking eroding the supremacy of the office as the administrative heart of the organisation - have to take into account the level of technology available and employed by the competition. Workers with new technology are considered to be 'knowledge' workers with necessary skills and experience; administrative staff in countries where information technology is less advanced are likely to be less highly regarded, and the few who may have gathered technology-based skills elevated.

(e) *The occupational/professional structure.* This will depend on how organised and highly regarded the occupations and professions are in a country. The medical and teaching professions may be very highly prized in some cultures, whereas in more materialistic cultures, financial professionals have the highest status. This will affect managers' attitudes to their own position in their society, and to their importance in the organisation. Accountants may run companies in Britain, where engineers or production designers are in senior positions in Germany.

10 NATIONALISED AND SEMI-STATE BUSINESSES

The UK government in the 1980s attempted to make nationalised industries act in a more profit-orientated and market-sensitive manner than in the past. This shift in requirement has created a variety of policy, planning and operating difficulties, which would presumably be experienced in any other country where the government tried to achieve a similar change.

Policy

In a nationalised industry, where profitability is not a prime consideration, the objectives and policies of the organisation will usually be directed towards:

(a) providing a certain level of service to everyone who wants it, especially in key industries such as transport, water supply, electricity, postal deliveries and, in the past in the UK, gas supplies and telephone services;

(b) supporting other government policies, for example, on employment and regional development, by providing jobs in economically-depressed regions of the country.

Profit orientation and market sensitivity undermine the predominance of public service considerations, and a difficulty that arises for the nationalised industry's management is to reassess the industry's objectives and policies.

(a) The overall objective of the industry might now be any of the following: profit maximisation, or profit maximisation subject to certain minimum service requirements, or to provide a service but with certain minimum requirements about efficiency of resource utilisation (as in the case of the National Health Service).

(b) The industry's management might be uncertain about whether the ultimate objective of the government is privatisation. Where privatisation is planned, the industry will need to be *more* market-sensitive than might otherwise be necessary.

(c) The industry's policy towards employment and regional development might be required to change. In the coal industry, for example, the greater profit-awareness in the 1980s resulted in widespread pit closures, even though this created high unemployment levels in economically depressed areas, which was counter to the government's longer term economic policy objective.

(d) Difficulties arise with employment policy, as suggested above, because the nationalised industry will be required to reassess its manning levels, and recruitment and promotion policies. Employees should expect market rates of pay for working in a profit-orientated industry, but at the same time security of employment and 'carrying' weak staff might no longer be acceptable.

(e) Policy decisions about the quality of service provided, or the range of services, become more complex, because the industry's management will have to reassess the standards of service it is currently providing. In the case of the public transport industry, for example, management might have to assess the wisdom of its policy for maintaining certain routes or lines. Profit orientation might dictate significant closures.

Planning

Policy difficulties lead on to planning difficulties, and the problems for planning cover areas such as capital investment decisions, disinvestment, pricing and manpower.

(a) Most nationalised industries make large-scale capital investments, on which the return might be earned over a long time-scale. Greater profit-orientation will probably result in pressure for a quicker payback, higher returns and risk-avoidance. Schemes which would have been financially acceptable when profit-orientation was less strong might be doubtful investments if the need to earn a good return is paramount. When returns are uncertain and 'risky', a profit-orientated approach would be more likely to result in decisions not to invest. A difficulty that this creates is that the consequence of decisions *not* to invest now might not become apparent until much later, and the adverse effects on service of profit-orientated decision-making might not yet be apparent in the UK.

(b) Planning decisions by nationalised industries cannot be taken without making allowances for government wishes and public pressure. Although a government might pay lip service to 'the market', it might also impose certain requirements on nationalised industries that prevent it from taking market orientated decisions. Public pressure is also likely to be much stronger in the case of planning decisions by a nationalised industry than in the case of a private company. Decisions to build a nuclear power station, close a railway line, build an open-cast coal mine and so on, are almost certain to meet strong time-consuming public resistance.

(c) Pricing decisions might be restricted by monopolies legislation or public resistance to price rises from a monopoly industry. If the industry's prices are currently 'too low', it could therefore be difficult to raise them.

(d) Planning to withdraw services, reduce service levels or disinvest, as mentioned earlier, will be difficult to make because of public expectations.

(e) Manpower planning will be plagued by difficulties of trying to establish a profit-orientated management. Many 'old' managers might have to give way to younger managers, many recruited externally, but pay levels will have to be high enough to attract staff of a suitable calibre.

Operating
Many planning difficulties also become operating difficulties.

(a) Manpower and employee relations will be a particularly difficult problem. Trade unions and employees might be reluctant to accept the new profit-orientated approach, with the result that there might be trade union opposition or employee resistance to changes. It will also be difficult to introduce performance-related pay structures, which are often associated with market-orientation.

(b) To improve profit-orientation, there must be a better management information and control system. The task of creating a management accounting system and the other information systems that are needed could be complex and lengthy.

(c) Change is difficult to implement. It is one thing to pay lip service to profits but it is more difficult to put intentions into practice. Attitudes and ways of doing things have to be altered, and changes might be slow.

11 RATIONAL DECISION-MAKING

Decision-making cannot be scientifically rational in the full sense due to incomplete information, the complex interrelation of variables and change.

To be as rational as possible given human abilities and the time pressures on the decision maker requires the following steps.

1 Set your objectives.
2 Rank order objectives.
3 Create as many alternatives as possible.
4 Take your first (most important) objective as a decision rule and eliminate all alternatives which cannot achieve this objective.
5 Take your new most important objective, etc, and continue this process until one alternative is left and this is your decision.

This is called *elimination by aspects* and is more realistic than maximising.

Decision making is limited in the following ways.

(a) External relations, for example with government, suppliers, unions, are a major problem.

(b) The management style may be one of satisficing or muddling through rather than of maximising or rationalising.

(c) The decision-making exercise may be influenced more by the politics of the organisation than the substance of the decision.

Major decisions with costly and risky long term consequences must be made using forecasts, estimates and judgements, and thus contain many uncertain elements. It is not possible to know all the alternative solutions to the decision problem, nor all the relative pros and cons of each alternative.

However the decision maker is said to be 'rational' because he or she knows the objectives and makes decisions systematically in order to achieve them. Using the 'rational' model the decision maker knows the objectives and in the light of a fixed scale of preferences chooses the alternative that promises the maximum gain.

The style of management in an organisation may limit the decision-making process and encourage alternative ways of making decisions, such as satisficing, elimination by aspects or intuitive.

Satisficing is widely regarded as being more realistic in practice than maximising, and is said to be quasirational. This way of making decisions recognises that the manager does not know the many objectives clearly enough to rank them and lacks knowledge, information and time to learn all about the various alternatives. The manager investigates alternatives until a solution that satisfies the objectives reasonably (or perhaps only minimally is found). Often the manager will adapt decisions from the present decision situation and only make small incremental changes.

The process of satisficing uses what is called 'bounded rationality'. The decision-maker accepts the limitations in terms of information, ability and time and attempts to find a satisfactory solution.

A variation of satisficing is the approach termed 'muddling-through' which makes decisions that move the organisation away from the present decisions in small incremental steps.

The style of management may be to make decisions using *intuition*, and not to employ a systematic approach. This is the opposite of the rational approach, but many managers feel that intuition is an essential part of decision making.

Moreover, in a large organisation, especially the public sector, a decision on one area of policy may affect the activities of several different departments, each of whom have their own broader agendas. A decision may not therefore be taken on its merits. Rather, a decision taker on a particular issue will be affected by the context of the negotiation. If one department or interest group has given way on one issue, it might seek its own way on another.

In summary, one can say that the greater the tendency towards certainty in the decision situation, the more effectively the rational approach can be used. Even where the rational approach is used the weighing of the many alternatives is at least partly intuitive. Where there is high time pressure and conflict within the organisation, managers will tend towards satisficing. Where there is high time pressure and high uncertainty in the decision situation managers will rely more on hunches, gut feelings and intuition.

12 STRATEGIC MANAGEMENT

The process of strategic management comprises strategic analysis, selection and implementation and seeks continuously to evaluate change and its opportunities in terms of established criteria. It is important to note that strategic *management* goes beyond strategic *planning* – it is a distinct mode of management which proceeds from analysis to implementation and shares the same functions – planning, organising, directing and controlling – as operations management. In companies the objective of strategic management is often stated to be increased earnings per share.

Strategic analysis

The first step in the process involves analysis of the situation in which the organisation finds itself. This means identifying the conditions prevailing in both the internal and external environment and the effects of these conditions on the organisation. The following matters will need to be addressed.

(a) *SWOT analysis* (internal strengths and weaknesses, external opportunities and threats).

(b) *Competition analysis* - competition in most markets has increased rapidly in recent years and this trend is set to continue. The organisation must analyse who its competitors are, how and why they are competing, and whether and how competition will increase.

(c) *Customer analysis.* In many markets the needs/demands of customers are becoming increasingly sophisticated and complex. As a result, the status of market research has been transplanted from the marketing function of operations management to become an important part of strategic analysis. The status of the organisation's goods and services in the eyes of the consumer in terms of quality is now seen as integral to the status of the organisation itself.

(d) *Cultural analysis.* The culture or 'feel' of an organisation is seen as being of critical strategic importance. An organisation which has an enterprising, innovative and unique culture will be attractive to investors, customers and employees. Culture must therefore be analysed to see what kind of message it is giving out about the organisation.

(e) *Social analysis.* This can be seen as part of customer analysis since it attempts to identify how the complexity of modern society impacts on the organisation and its customers. It will take into account demographic and economic changes, changes in attitudes in society (such as towards environmental issues) and changes in political attitudes (for example, the favourable light in which the Government views initiative).

Strategic analysis along these lines paves the way for strategic selection since it identifies the sorts of ways in which the organisation has competitive advantage and indicates how far away the organisation is from its critical mass (that is, the ideal position for making the most of itself).

Strategic selection

Having analysed where the organisation is, the next step for the strategic manager is to decide where it wants to go. This involves a process of strategic selection, which involves the following further steps.

(a) Define the company's *mission* or overall objective: this is often a financial aim - such as to increase the earnings per share ratio - but can sometimes be expressed in rather less precise terms, such as 'to achieve excellence, add value and improve the quality of life'.

(b) Derive the company's *objectives* from the mission: having a referable set of objectives enables management:

(i) to organise and explain the purpose and direction of the business in a small number of general statements about goals

(ii) to test the validity of these goals as a means of achieving the organisation's purpose

(iii) to predict behaviour

(iv) to appraise the validity of decisions about strategies and budgets (by assessing whether these are sufficient to achieve the stated objectives)

(v) to assess and control actual performance.

Objectives should enhance the medium and the long-term future of the company, and may be set for particular functional areas such as marketing, finance and profitability, production, sales, industrial relations, productivity and new development.

(c)   Develop *strategies* by which these objectives may be met. These can take the form of plans of increasing detail which indicate how the particular objective, say of increasing market share, can be fulfilled by marketing, advertising and sales strategies.

When formulating mission, objectives, strategies and plans the organisation will have to have regard to:

(a)   the results of the strategic analysis indicating the current position of the organisation

(b)   the availability of funds and resources in order to carry out the strategies adopted

(c)   the state of the external environment which will impose pressures on the organisation's achievement of its aims

(d)   the effect of its strategic selection on the structure of the organisation.

Strategic implementation

Having formulated strategies and plans it only remains to implement them. This will almost certainly involve changes to the way things are done if the process of strategic management has been followed through from first principles. Areas in which implementing strategies are likely to cause change are:

(a)   the organisation's structure (such as new subsidiaries, new reporting lines, redefined responsibilities);

(b)   the organisation's culture (there may have to be a move from bureaucracy towards a task culture if it has been identified that the organisation is in an unstable environment);

(c)   the quality of all outputs - this may well have to improve;

(d)   attitudes towards innovation, entrepreneurship and individualism;

(e)   the degree of control exercised over subordinates, given new emphasis on innovation;

(f)   personnel - the organisation needs to acquire the services of the right personnel to put strategies into practice.

Conclusion

We can see then that the stages of strategic management - analysis, selection and implementation - are part of a process in which each follows on from the other. They are integrated in the sense that the results of each stage will inform the others, and indeed strategic management is an ongoing process whereby analysis and strategies are updated by feedback from implementation.

13 PERSONNEL PROBLEMS

> *Tutorial note.* There seems to be a lot to do to answer this question. Note that you are required to analyse the situation (briefly), explain it in theory, and then suggest four reasons why it might have arisen in these particular circumstances.

The situation is one where staff have withdrawn their co-operation from management, following a change in manager for the activity concerned. Morale has reduced to the point where there is 25% per annum staff turnover. Remaining staff are totally demotivated.

In theory, explanations for this de-motivation and loss of morale may be found by reference to content theories of motivation such as that of Frederick Herzberg. According to his two factor theory, there are certain factors which create job satisfaction and are effective in motivating an individual to superior performance and effort. These factors are those which give the individual a sense of self-fulfilment and personal growth, including:

(a) status;
(b) recognition;
(c) being given responsibility;
(d) challenging work;
(e) growth in the job.

Although Herzberg ascribes the cause of job *dis*satisfaction to other 'hygiene' factors (of which quality of supervision is one), he notes that the absence or withdrawal (as in the current situation) of motivating factors causes a preoccupation with environmental factors, and may create dissatisfaction, which may be demonstrated in such ways as withdrawal of labour or co-operation.

Reasons why the current situation may have arisen include the following.

(a) Despite the previous manager's abrasive manner and unpopularity, he gave personal attention to all of his staff, noticing them as individuals, and performance under his management was efficient and highly regarded. The new manager does not appear to want direct contract with his staff in the same way.

(b) The new manager has come in from outside the authority, and from a different background, namely business school. The professional staff may resent his being brought in, in preference to their own promotion. There may also be a feeling that a new orientation towards their activities is being encouraged, with an implied rejection of their previous approach.

(c) The introduction of the system of weekly reports and meetings may have implied a lack of trust in staff. The increased element of control in the department also reduces the discretion and autonomy previously allowed to them as professionals. Their performance to date has, after all, given no cause for complaint, and the need for change may not be clear.

(d) The chain of command has been lengthened by the appointment of assistant managers. This may represent a loss of status to those not promoted. It widens the gap between the staff and the manager. Section heads now report to two people, in a kind of matrix structure, which may create a sense of role ambiguity and confusion. These factors may all have a demotivating effect.

14 MANAGEMENT AUDIT

The auditing process is concerned with the independent checking of performance after implementing various decisions. Organisations undertake such audits of certain functional areas, such as in accounting, marketing and personnel, in order to verify the accuracy of data or to appraise the quality of the functional performance. The management audit specifically represents a process of assessing the overall management system of an organisation, not just finance, with the purpose of evaluating its effectiveness and efficiency. The emphasis is on the quality of overall management, rather than individual management or functional performance.

The benefits to be derived from the undertaking of a management audit are summarised as follows.

(a) It permits senior management to evaluate the effectiveness of their overall organisational policies, and an overall evaluation of the total organisation effort.

(b) It allows for an evaluation of the relationship between functional areas rather than their specific internal activities, but identifies areas of particular difficulty which may require special attention.

(c) It provides for an additional check on the suitability of various policies, programmes and practices.

(d) It alerts all managers and employees in all functions, on matters of organisational expectations.

(e) It will help to assess the effectiveness of various management controls and the need for limiting or providing more information and highlights areas for improvement.

(f) It provides the basis of objective performance evaluations.

The management audit may involve a consideration of most or all of the following subjects: organisational structure, organisational climate, organisational environment; objectives, policies, programmes, practices and rules; control of revenue, expenditure and finance; control of operations, particularly with production, inventory, purchasing, quality, personnel and sales; review of suitability and effectiveness in setting of standards, reviewing of performance and securing corrective actions; abilities and effectiveness of board of directors and senior executive managers.

It should however be noted that the implementation of management audit is limited within the UK. Reasons suggested might be a lack of suitable standards of measurement, a lack of suitable auditors, the risk of curbing managerial initiatives, or existing control being adequate.

15 QUALITY CONTROL

In ordinary language, quality implies some degree of excellence or superiority. In an industrial context, it is defined in a much more functional way. Here, quality is more concerned with 'fitness for purpose', and quality control is about ensuring that products or services meet their planned level of quality, and conform to specifications.

Objectives

Quality control may be defined as the process of:

(a) establishing standards of quality for a product or service (related to organisational objectives, the organisation's image, and assessment of the obtainable market price for a quality product/service);

(b) establishing procedures or production methods which ought to ensure that these required standards of quality are met in a suitably high proportion of cases;

(c) monitoring actual quality;

(d) taking control action when actual quality falls below standard.

Quality control is concerned with trying to make sure that a product is manufactured, or a service is provided, so as to meet certain design specifications. This involves setting controls for the process of manufacture or providing a service. It is a 'technique' aimed at *preventing* the manufacture of defective items (or the provision of defective services).

Techniques

Quality control may take place at various stages of the production process, such as:

(a) product design (safety criteria built into designs for children's toys);

(b) production engineering (deciding on manufacturing 'tolerances' allowable before the item fails to meet its design specification);

(c) quality assurance of goods inwards (acceptance inspection of input materials, on a vendor rating system, or using an AQL (acceptance quality level));

(d) inspection of output – perhaps at various stages in the production process – quality assurance;

(e) monitoring customer complaints.

If no defective items are allowed, and all output must be perfect, there would have to be 100% inspection. However, it is usual to accept that some defective output will be made and it is not the end of the world if they get through to the customer.

When some defectives are allowed to get through, the measurement of quality can be based on the inspection of *samples* of output (or goods inwards), in other words *acceptance sampling*.

The inspection of samples rather than 100% testing of all items will keep inspection costs down, and smaller samples will be less costly to inspect than larger samples. The greater the confidence in the reliability of production methods and process control, the smaller the samples will be. For example, if a production process has a fairly high proportion of defectives, 10% of all output might be inspected; whereas if the process rarely goes out of control, the sample sizes for inspection might be 1% or less of output.

The acceptance quality level (AQL) is the maximum percentage of defectives that will be tolerated, on economic grounds, in the samples that are tested. If the AQL is 2%, say, this would mean that the organisation is taking the view that a maximum of 2% of output can be allowed to be defective, because the costs of reducing the proportion of defectives further would not be worth the costs of improved quality control. When defectives exceed the AQL, the quality-related costs will be too high, and improvements in quality would be called for.

Statistical quality control charts might be used to record and monitor the accuracy of the physical dimensions of products. The theory recognises that the exact dimensions may vary in a random manner due to the effects of chance. The graphs show inner warning limits and outer action limits although in many cases only one limit is used. The limits are set such a distance from the expected dimension that a value *outside* the limits is very unlikely to have occurred by chance, and consequently the size of the deviation indicates faults in the manufacturing process. Normally, the values plotted on the chart would be the mean of a small sample taken at regular times.

Management

In manufacturing industries, quality control is often seen as a manufacturing responsibility based on the inspection of output by 'quality control' staff. The quality control manager might have a semi-independent position in the organisation, reporting details of rejected or defective items to the manufacturing manager, but not taking orders from him. Instead, the quality control manager might be accountable to the production director - to management at a senior level.

The management of quality will include such tasks as:

(a)   the definition of 'quality' for the product/service, and of required standards: ideally, these will be built into the product specification at the design stage;

(b)   the identification of acceptable 'tolerances', in other words the variation from ideal standard;

(c)   maintaining required quality control systems, and quality standards, without incurring unacceptable added costs: this will involve a discretionary 'trade off' between quality and improvement costs.

In western companies, there has traditionally been a separation of the functions of product design/quality design/work methods, and operations. Beliefs about task specialisation, control objectivity and the exclusivity of the management function have separated production from inspection and control. This has unfortunately created poor attitudes on the shop floor towards control, as a system imposed 'from outside' by non-operational staff and as an implication of lack of trust in workers to maintain quality standards or to apply the control system with objectivity themselves.

Attitudes to quality control and the management of it have, however, been undergoing changes. Quality management has been realised to have both operational and strategic importance.

(a)   As the pace of change in the environment has increased, attention to quality, and a commitment to quality standards, has become a vital factor for organisational adaptation and survival. Increasing efforts have been made (as reported by Peters and Waterman in *In Search of Excellence)* to create a quality-orientated culture in the organisation, and to motivate employees to become quality-centred.

(b)   It is also being recognised that workers can be motivated *by* a positive approach to quality focus. Producing quality work is a tangible and perceivedly worthwhile objective. Also, where responsibility for quality checking has been given to the worker himself (encouraging self-supervision), job satisfaction may be increased: it is a kind of job enrichment, and also a sign of trust and respect, because imposed controls have been removed.

(c) Non aversive ways of implementing quality control have been devised (or adapted from the consensus, 'teamwork' methods of Japanese companies). Cultural orientation (the deep 'belief' in quality, filtered down to the operatives) and work group norms and influence can be enlisted. Inter-group competition to meet and beat quality standards, for example, might be encouraged. Quality circles - interdisciplinary analysis/discussion groups concerned with quality issues - may be set up, perhaps with responsibility for implementing improvements which they identify.

National and international markets are becoming increasingly competitive, and the *competitive advantage* given by the consumer's perception of a product or service as being high quality is increasingly recognised. The management of quality is therefore highly important, with the emphasis shifting to building in quality to the product from the start (especially in the design of a service, but also in the case of a physical product).

Improved quality is crucially dependent on the attitudes of both the workforce and the management towards quality management. This requires a strategic emphasis on both the *work group*, to which much responsibility can be devolved (through the use of quality circles and so on), thus freeing management for other quality control tasks, and the *individual*, who must be motivated by consultation and reward for improvements made.

16 CHANGE AND IT

(a) The analysis will have to consider something like the following issues.

For change	Against change
Increasing client dissatisfaction	Fear of changing how the work is done when the organisation has been hived off
New technology	Uncertainty over the use of computers
Senior management need to reduce costs	Little trust in managers' ability
Managers have to improve quality	Poor staff morale
More freedom for managers to make adequately decisions on staff on operating procedures	Front line staff are not trained or rewarded; have little freedom to use discretion; always under stress

(b) The attitudes can be identified for the managers and for the staff.

    (i)   Managers' attitudes will include:

        (1) adjusting to the new freedoms they have been given and not depend on following instructions from head office;

        (2) gaining the confidence of middle ranking staff who will have arranged for the introduction of the changes into the five area offices;

        (3) establishing team working and set up training programmes on computerisation for all the staff;

(4)   considering incentive or performance payment for improved working;

(5)   considering the needs of front line staff and reducing staff turnover through improving support for these staff, their working conditions;

The new computer technology should be up and running to assist staff and not be either a programme that does not happen and work piles up or the systems crash and cause disruption to working.

(ii)   Staff attitudes include:

(1)   holding on to habits and practices that are comfortable and reduce stress;

(2)   that jobs and pay will not be adversely affected by the changes;

(3)   uncertainty that managers can manage the changes required and that promises will be honoured;

(4)   low morale has to be dealt with and frontline staff included in the changes;

The changes will not work anyway because the problem is with the nature of the service, and nothing to do with using computers or setting up expensive quality audits when the real problems are not being dealt with, complex rules which are difficult to interpret, clients who are unable to understand the rules, working in poor conditions for low pay and no appreciation of the difficulties of doing the job.

(c)   A plan for dealing with the introduction of computerisation and quality audit.

(i)   It is important to find out how the organisation performs at present and to develop a feel for the culture of the organisation.

(ii)   This can be done by asking a series of questions, if appropriate these could be used in a questionnaire to some or all of the staff, like an organisational fitness test.

Some of the questions which may be asked:
(Rating: A good to C poor to E unacceptable)

Service delivery

(1)   How would you rate the effectiveness of the organisation in terms of the working environment?

(2)   The impression clients have in using the service.

(3)   Comparison with other similar units.

(4)   Comparison with other service organisations used by the public, banks, buildings societies.

(5)   How would you rate the efficiency of the organisation in terms of the cost of the service (some unit cost or cost comparison)

(6)   Meeting targets, working within budgets.

(7) Level of arrears of work or delays in responding to clients.

(8) The use of staff, absences, staff turnover, level of morale.

Communication

(9) How would you rate how well the organisation deals with internal and external communications in terms of:

- the communications between managers and staff
- the communications with the public (is adequate training provided)
- the communications with head office

Recommendations on preparing staff for the computerisation

(i) Review the nature of the computers and information system that is going to be used and see that it works and is robust enough for the staff who are going to use it.

(ii) Review any training courses or programmes available with the package.

(iii) The staff who are going to use the new system should be involved if possible with reviewing the system and evaluating its suitability for the job they have to do.

(iv) A scheme to provide clear communications about what is going to happen and when, with representatives of those using the scheme being involved will reduce rumour and some of the apprehension over the scheme.

(v) Agreement with the trade unions on training, pay scales and any possible transfer or redundancy of staff.

(vi) Have a clear programme for introducing the computerisation and the development of staff who are going to be involved.

(vii) Make sure adequate resources are available to cover a staff programme of training and familiarisation with the information technology concerned.

(viii) Create teams or set up quality circles to look at how the problems with the transfer to computerisation can be overcome.

(ix) Involve staff from all of the sub offices in the induction programme so they understand why information is needed and what is going to happen to it.

To improve the units performance

By demonstrating a commitment to a computerisation programme it will show the staff how the workload problem is to be tackled. The computerisation record system can be used to improve performance, and be related to rewards. With the new system it will be possible to review procedures for dealing with clients. By setting up quality circles a range of procedural issues could be looked into, with the solutions providing a way of increasing cooperation between staff. One problem will be to improve the working environment within resource constraints. As part of the change, targets can be set to show improved performance, the targets being agreed in the working teams. The level of recruitment and retention of staff needs to be dealt with to reduce labour turnover and improve morale, better pay and working conditions should help.

17 ANYBOROUGH COUNCIL: REORGANISATION AND REDUNDANCY

(a) *Specific proposals on steps to be taken prior to change*

  (i) *Draw up a plan.* This might be easier said than done, as there will be a whole variety of different activities which have to be coordinated.

  (ii) *Issue a series of statements* to the workforce as soon as possible, indicating what is likely to occur, as the existence of rumours is likely to be make matters worse. However, at this stage it is best not to be too specific, as it might make things hard to negotiate later.

It is important to untangle the various issues involved, as some will require different approaches.

  (i) The relocation itself must be planned, to minimise the inconvenience and to continue.

  (ii) The introduction of the new management information system needs to be planned in detail.

  (iii) Personnel issues need to be sorted out, particularly the relocation, the redundancies, and the impact of compulsory competitive tendering.

In fact both the redundancies and the relocation will have to handled with a certain degree of sensitivity. Both might require consultation with the relevant trade unions. There might be several representing different kinds of worker.

Each of the issues above will have its own dynamic, demands and objectives. The difficult part will be to integrate them together to ensure that normal service is not interrupted.

This is particularly necessary if the risk of strike action is to be avoided.

The following will be matters to consider when dealing with the personnel issues.

  (i) Publicise the likely changes, and indicate the options that are available.

  (ii) Enter into discussions with workers' representatives immediately.

  (iii) Matters to negotiate include the possibility of compulsory competitive tendering. Most of the unions will be well acquainted with the fact that this is government policy. The case is to assess whether the efficiency standards can be reached so that the existing workforce can be a competitor.

  (iv) On a more specific note, the minimum requirements of the plan do involve redundancy. This is something which the workers' representatives are certain to be interested in, to ensure that employees, many of whom might find it hard to find jobs elsewhere, are fairly treated.

  To ensure harmonious settlement of these items, the possibility of voluntary redundancies might first be considered. It is possible that many workers nearing retirement will take these terms.

However, there should be a back up in case not enough people resign *voluntarily*. Some can be found jobs elsewhere within the council, but these may not be of equal status. Alternatively, some members of staff might be happy to consider job share arrangements.

(v) *New offices.* There is unlikely to be any compensation for the redeployment, or staff might be given a one-off payment, especially for those who have to travel further, and spend more on bus or train fares, or petrol.

(vi) On a practical note, there should be a timetable for moving section by section. As far as possible, the work of the department should not be interrupted.

(b) *Implementing the changes*

Assuming that there are no personnel problems such as strikes or go-slows - and this is a big assumption - then the changes would be implemented in a phased way.

Some of the steps of implementing change are those mentioned above. The change agent has to ensure that he or she has won at least the consent, if enthusiasm is too much to hope for, of the people most affected by it.

This propaganda exercise is important. As the changes are more or less inevitable, there may not be a great deal that can be negotiated for. If they are presented to the work force as a fait accompli, the change agent can *still* offer the workforce some say by negotiating at the margin. Negotiable items can include extra allowances for travelling and so forth, and redundancy terms. These should be sorted out before the change is implemented. It would also help to have some further options already available.

The order in which the changes take place is most important.

(i) The new buildings should be in a state ready to receive their new occupants.

This does not mean that all the necessary refurbishment has been done. Rather, that the refurbishment exercise is in planned stages (eg one floor at a time), so groups of people can be transferred in batches. This has the advantage that any teething problems with the building can be sorted out early.

Obviously, matters such as telephone connections must be sorted out in advance.

(ii) The new sites must be set up to run the computer system. The changeover to the new system must also be planned. During the period, the three personnel selected to be administrative assistants can be sent on training courses individually. It is probably the case that new and old systems will have to run in parallel for some time. This will enable the change agent to give some sense of security for the short term. On the other hand, the other disruptions may mean that the system should be delayed.

(iii) The move should be planned so that, if compulsory competitive tendering is introduced, it is possible to 'mothball' the sites for some other use.

(iv) The possible introduction of compulsory competitive tendering does put all the changes in jeopardy, as it will have a much greater longer term impact. If there are to be so many redundancies, then the offices will be too large, and it will be an expensive and inefficient use of space.

(v)   The first people to be moved in should be those sections whose work requires the least contact with the work of other sections. This means that the normal day to day operations of the department are not impeded.

(vi) Special transitional procedures need to be introduced to cover the two sites for the two month period. These can include special mail deliveries or couriers.

(c)   *Alterations to proposals*

The basic flaw with the proposals as they now stand is that the issue of compulsory competitive tendering is so vague. This would have the greatest impact on the workings of the department, leading to large scale redundancies if the council's work force failed to win the contract.

A first proposal then, would be to try and obtain a commitment as to a particular time for its introduction.

Secondly, the workforce should be given time to prepare a bid. It is not perhaps appropriate to expect them to bid when they are in the throes of a move to a new site.

The timescale is almost certainly too short. Three months would be better.

The issue of funding must be sorted out in advance with the chair of the housing committee. This is bound to be affected by compulsory competitive tendering, which may have the effect of producing those reductions. There are bound to be some costs involved with the change for it to be effective.

To conclude, then, the change agent could advise the housing committee to put the whole project on ice until the issue of compulsory competitive tendering has been agreed, to avoid the expense of moving. There is also the additional expense of training people in the new computer system. This must be considered, too.

In the probable absence of their agreement, the change agent should get a commitment as to the level of financial resources, and approval of the plans outlined.

18   TEAM LEADERSHIP

First of all, we must diagnose the problem and its causes. The problem concerns George Gillespie's approach to decision making. It also suggests that his leadership style should be investigated since the warning signs of confusion and demoralisation of his team indicate that they don't know what to expect from him, and he lacks consistency.

The factors causing the problems may include the following:

(a)   George might never have had any formal training as regards decision-making or participation. As a result he is continually changing from one management style to another in order to find the one which feels best, ignoring the fact that no one style can be correct for all the various types of decisions he had to make.

(b)   He might not have a clear idea of the relative importance of the decisions he has to make. Some will be his sole preserve, others could be given to subordinates, others might involve consulting the whole section for a consensus opinion.

(c) George may be having difficulty in reconciling the need to be seen to be in charge of his team and a desire to involve his group in the decision-making process.

(d) George may not be suited to leadership.

To find out which factor (or factors) is the main cause of the problem, we would need to obtain the following information:

(a) the nature of the work allocated to the team;
(b) the importance of the decisions that have to be made by George and his team;
(c) the quality of his staff.

Fielder's model shows that:

(a) when the situation is favourable to the leader, he can concentrate on tasks and be a psychologically distant manager;

(b) when the situation is moderately favourable he will need to show more concern for people;

(c) when the situation is unfavourable, he will need to be task orientated and psychologically distant;

(d) concern for tasks and people should be balanced according to the need of the situation, and the degree to which it favours the leader.

George should be given a counselling interview and asked to discuss his approach to decision-making. It should be explained to him that he must learn to distinguish between decisions that he must take unilaterally and decisions which should be made by the group or by subordinates. The factors relevant to this distinction are the following.

(a) The importance of the decision. The cost of making a mistake should be considered and evaluated. Important decisions should be taken by George himself.

(b) The subject matter of the decision. Sometimes delegation or sharing is not possible because of either company policy in relation to confidentiality or the technical and complex nature of the decision.

(c) The amount of time available and the ability of his team to deal with such situations.

(d) The importance of his team's acceptance of the decision. With some decisions such acceptance is vital to successful implementation, and so the decisions should either involve or be taken by the team as a whole.

George may well benefit from a training course in the art of decision-making and teamwork. He would be told that the choice is not a simple one between unilateral decision or group consensus. The department can be involved in the process by:

(a) obtaining information for George so that he will be better equipped to make the right decision;

(b) offering opinions either as individuals or as a team for George to consider, although he would not be bound to follow any suggested course of action;

(c) making decisions George feels can be safely delegated. This should improve morale as employees feel more regularly involved;

(d) reaching a decision by consensus which George then endorses.

The situation should be reviewed after a period to see if a more consistent pattern of decision-making had evolved and staff morale improved while an acceptable standard of work had been maintained. If the problem persists, further training may be necessary.

19 STAKEHOLDERS

There are three broad types of stakeholder in an organisation, such as a company, as follows:

(a) internal stakeholders (employees, management);
(b) connected stakeholders (shareholders, customers, suppliers, financiers);
(c) external stakeholders (the community, government, pressure groups).

These types are indicated in the diagram below.

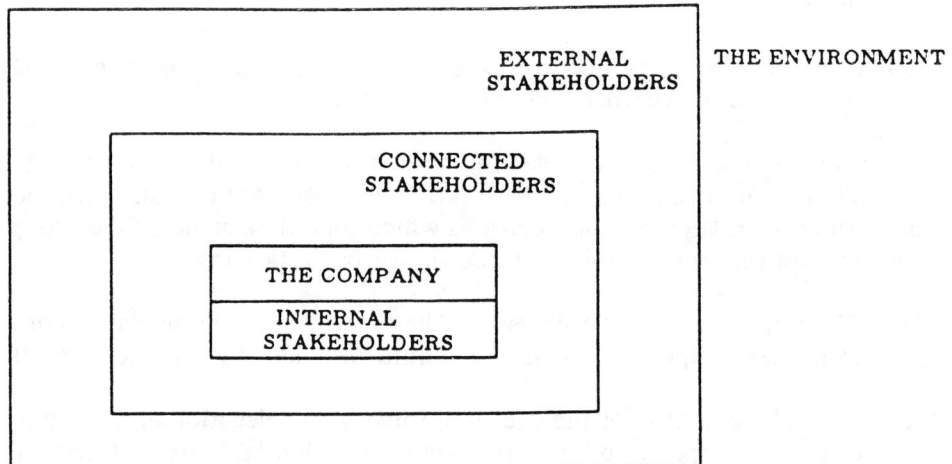

```
┌─────────────────────────────────────────────────────────┐
│                                EXTERNAL    THE ENVIRONMENT│
│                                STAKEHOLDERS               │
│   ┌───────────────────────────────────────────┐          │
│   │              CONNECTED                      │          │
│   │             STAKEHOLDERS                    │          │
│   │   ┌─────────────────────────────┐          │          │
│   │   │        THE COMPANY           │          │          │
│   │   ├─────────────────────────────┤          │          │
│   │   │        INTERNAL              │          │          │
│   │   │      STAKEHOLDERS            │          │          │
│   │   └─────────────────────────────┘          │          │
│   └───────────────────────────────────────────┘          │
└─────────────────────────────────────────────────────────┘
```

We shall consider each of them in turn.

(a) *Internal stakeholders*
     Because employees and management (which includes the Chairman and the Board of Directors) are so intimately connected with the company, their objectives are likely to have a strong and immediate influence on how it is run.

(b) *Connected stakeholders*
     The objectives of shareholders - which is generally that of making a profit - is often taken as the prime objective which the company's management seeks to fulfil. But clearly financiers such as banks have similar objectives which must be met (usually the payment of loan interest is a contractual obligation whilst the payment of dividends is not), whilst the customer's objectives, in a market-led company, must also be fulfilled if the company is to be successful. Other stakeholders directly 'connected' with the company are suppliers, trade unions and distributors.

SUGGESTED SOLUTIONS

(c) *External stakeholders*
These groups - the government, local authorities, pressure groups, the community at large, professional bodies - are likely to have quite diverse objectives and have a varying ability to ensure that the company meets them.

How stakeholders relate to the management of the company depends very much on what type of stakeholder they are - internal, connected or external - and on the level in the management hierarchy at which they are able to apply pressure. Clearly a company's management will respond differently to the demands of, say, its shareholders and the community at large. This is because both the character of the relationship and the means by which the relationship is conducted depend on the relative bargaining power and philosophy of the stakeholder on the one hand and the company on the other. Enterprises are open systems, and so there is inevitably a conflict of expectations between internal and external stakeholders.

Stakeholders can influence and constrain management of the company at a number of different levels, which can be defined at the strategic level (the main mission and objectives of the company), the planning level (how those objectives are going to be met) and the operations level (how plans are put in practice day-to-day). But in addition management is constrained at every level by the legal environment in which it exists and the regulations with which it must comply. These can be said to arise from the objectives of the community at large and of the government, and can affect such things as employment rights, financial control and reporting, safety and environmental protection and the way in which competition is handled.

Let us now look at how stakeholders constrain management at different levels.

(a) *Strategic level*

When deciding on the company's mission and objectives, and the strategies to be adopted in meeting them, the company's board will almost certainly be constrained primarily by the interests of the shareholders (profit) but also by those of the customers (price, variety, reliability) and of other financiers (interest and capital repayments, value of security, value of shares). But the extent to which management has discretion to make profits for shareholders is itself constrained by the demands of customers for value and of financiers for reducing risk to their investment. A balance must clearly be reached.

The company must comply with identifiable constraints such as its statutory duty to exercise 'stewardship' over its shareholders' assets, its contractual duty to pay interest on loans and its legal duties regarding employment and environment protection. These may come into conflict with other stakeholders' interests and even with the company's preferred strategy such as to be 'market-led'.

Finally the company's strategy may be influenced by intangible constraints from the external stakeholders and the environment as a whole such as 'green' culture and concern for Third World development and good employment practices.

(b) *Planning level*

In order to achieve objectives and ultimately fulfil the company's mission, the management must make tactical plans. These will be influenced to a greater or lesser extent by stakeholders.

(i) *Customers'* demands will dictate decisions for investment in new products, development of existing ones and setting-up of new outlets. They will also affect the standards adopted for quality control, and the extent to which they can be enticed away by competitors' products will affect the planned advertising spend.

(ii) *Suppliers'* and *distributors'* demands will affect the timing and amount of production, the amount of raw material and finished goods stock held and hence the financial planning which allows production to take place.

(iii) *Employees'* attitudes and objectives will greatly affect the organisation and co-ordination required to put production plans into effect. Construction of departments and work groups, job design, workflow and the amount of training undertaken will all be matters in which management will have to take the employees' stake into account.

(iv) *Specialised or professional employees* have two sets of priorities - their jobs, and the requirements of their professional bodies. The management must be careful not to bring these two into conflict, say by asking a qualified construction engineer to operate with untrained staff.

(v) *Trade unions* represent employees *en masse* and seek to ensure that pay, terms and conditions of employment, disciplinary and grievance procedures and employment protection policies are formulated with the employees in mind. Management will have to consider these and will have to involve unions in the planning process in order to preserve good industrial relations.

(vi) *Legislation, regulations and the community at large.* At the planning level management discretion can be constrained by a great number of restrictions which are put in place to protect the community as a whole. Examples are planning restrictions on a construction company, pollution controls on a chemical works and disclosure requirements for a financial services group.

(c) *Operations level*

Clearly many of the constraints affecting management at the strategic and planning levels will also filter down to the running of day-to-day operations. Certainly consumers will affect production aims (size, quality, colour) and procedures (planning, stockholding, computerisation) when demand is variable (as in the fashion and high-tech industries). Health and safety legislation for employees and consumer protection legislation also mean that day-to-day operations must be constantly reviewed for compliance.

20   PUBLIC ACCOUNTABILITY

Public accountability means that persons charged with determining, drafting and carrying out policy, in central government or in particular public sector organisations, should be required to explain their actions to their electorate.

The persons accountable may have been directly elected, such as MPs or councillors, or may have been appointed by persons directly elected, such as members of a Regional Health Authority.

The electorate or the 'constituents' is a composite group that includes taxpayers (and possibly community charge payers), press, clients, customers and employees.

To be accountable means to have a liability to reveal, justify and explain. Public accountability calls for openly declared facts and open debate of them. Judgement may then be made by taxpayers, users etc. Some power must lie in the hands of the questioners. External audit, efficiency studies and performance measurement all help to improve public accountability.

Accountability is a broad topic and different types of public accountability may be identified:

(a) Political accountability which involves two aspects.

  (i)   Constitutional accountability found in the UK in both parliament and local councils;
  (ii) Consultative accountability involving the requirement to confer with interested parties, for instance a district health authority consulting with its community health council.

(b) Legal accountability which may be broken down into three levels.

  (i)   Judicial accountability, a requirement to act within the law. Persons aggrieved, such as a local authority ratepayer, may demand a judicial review of executive action taken;
  (ii) Quasi-judicial, for instance the accountability of an administrative unit such as a tribunal;
  (iii) Procedural accountability, such as a review of procedures, and the application of rules, by an external body such as an ombudsman.

(c) Managerial accountability. The responsibility of managers and senior officials for the use of resources and for the making of professional judgements and recommendations.

In the public sector the term 'acting in the public interest' is often used to justify actions and decisions, but there is no precise agreement as to what is meant when the term is used.

Public accountability is about the responsibility relationship between persons inside and people outside the organisation. One important way to discharge the responsibility is to provide regular financial and related information, and annual accounts well presented and explained. All forms of public accountability should protect the individual from secret, arbitrary and unfair actions.

21 EXTERNAL ENVIRONMENT AND SOCIAL RESPONSIBILITY

(a) In the terminology of systems theory, an organisation is an 'open' system which interacts with its environment; in other words, the environment will have an influence on the way the 'system' works, and the 'system' or organisation will also in its turn affect aspects of the environment.

The economic history of the surrounding community helps to provide an understanding of the current economic, social and cultural, legal and political environment. This point may be illustrated with several examples:

  (i)   A history of growth or contraction in the community's system of education will vary the 'pool' of skilled labour available for recruitment, and the organisation's requirements for training etc.

  (ii) If there is an economic history in the community of low growth and low productivity, management will need to account for this in their forward planning. The type of products for which there will be a substantial market demand will also depend on the past and current economic situation.

  (iii) The economic history of a community will help to explain its financial systems; for example, what are the institutions which exist to provide investment capital, and how might an organisation make use of them to raise extra funds?

(iv) The history of price inflation in a community will be relevant to explaining the current state of markets in which the organisation operates.

(v) The community history of industrial relations may help to explain current employee attitudes within the organisation. Even within a single country, some regions may be more 'militant' in their support for trade unions than in others. Multinational organisations may prefer to invest in a country with a history of good industrial relations than in one where strikes and disruptions have been a frequent part of the economic scene.

(vi) The development of the tax system of the community will be relevant to an understanding of consumer demand (eg resistance to indirect taxation, such as VAT or excise duty or a purchase tax), employee motivation (eg high direct taxation may mean that there is little incentive to work harder for more pay) and the organisation's profitability (eg the rate of taxation on company profits).

(vii) The social history of the community will help to explain the strength of certain attitudes and beliefs held by the community at large, for example towards ecology, the desirability of a career in industry etc.

(b) The nature of social responsibility will depend on the type of organisation. A commercial organisation may exist to achieve a satisfactory return on its shareholders' capital, but it is widely believed that even in commerce a social responsibility exists and that managers should accept this responsibility as their own.

The improvement of the environment is an obvious example of such social responsibility: reducing pollution, preserving the landscape, re-cultivating derelict land etc. Products should meet certain standards of comfort, safety or utility without the need for legislation.

There are practical difficulties in converting social responsibility into a practical aspect of management:

(i) Social and ethical targets must be set by senior managers in the organisation.

(ii) Individual managers should be given delegated authority not only to achieve operating efficiency and better profits, but also to achieve social targets.

(iii) Managers should be held individually responsible for the achievement of social as well as commercial results.

(iv) To hold managers accountable, performance standards need to be established by which their success in terms of social responsibility can be measured.

7 'C's, 43
7 'S's, 40

Accountability, 323, 325, 336
 - public sector, 339
Adaptive organisation, 109, 121
Adhocracy, 123
Agendas, 36
Allen, 65
Ambiguous figure system, 112
Appraisal, 238
Arbitration, 117
Argyris, 92
Audit Commission, 56, 116, 126, 188, 244
 - and local government, 248
Australia, 150
Authority, 356

Bains Report, 60, 136
Barratt and Downs, 48
Behaviouralist school, 64
Belbin, 312
Benefits Agency, 212
Blake's grid, 198
Brainstorming, 281
BS 5750, 259
Bureaucracy, 21, 105
Business performance, 66

Care in the Community, 153
Centralisation, 82
Chain of command, 65
Change, 94, 112, 147, 299, 301
Chief executive, 188
Child, 65
Citizen's Charter, 47
Civil Service College, 23
Classical approach, 64, 72
Classical theories, 26
Club culture, 104
Committee system, 112
Comparative management, 154
Competencies of management, 45, 224, 338
Competitive tendering, 169
Conflicts, 116
Consumerism, 149, 365
Contingency approach, 32, 122, 200
Creativity, 274
Critical strategic factors, 205
Cultural differences, 160
Culture(s) of management, 39, 94
Cultures/structures debate, 102

Decentralisation, 46, 82
Decision making process
 - rational model, 182
 - partisan mutual adjustment model, 193
Decision roles, 36
Decision tree, 281
Delegation, 356, 357, 360
Departmentation, 81
Direct Service Organisations (DSOs), 125, 246
Divisionalisation, 86
Divisions, 67
Drucker, 16, 29, 66, 78, 85

EC, 148, 159, 324
Economic development units, 125
Economy, 244
Effectiveness, 223, 244
Efficiency, 223, 244
Efficient organisational structure, 64
Enabling authority, 126
Environment, 32, 140, 147, 204
 - internal and external, 140
Environmental audits, 148
Equity, 244
Ethics, 351
Excellence, 97
Executive Agencies, 38, 135
Expectancy theory, 227

Farmer-Richman model, 155
Fayol, 26, 66
Federal decentralisation, 86
Finance management in the public sector, 20, 215, 217
Finance specialists, 215
Flat organisation, 69
Forcefield analysis, 278
Formal organisation, 64
Formal planning, 138
Freewheeling opportunism, 138
Functional authority, 79
Functional decentralisation, 87
Functional departments, 78
Functional organisation, 73, 81
Functions of management, 26

Gang plank, 65
General manager concept, 190, 293
Goals, 133, 134, 144
Gods of management, 39
Graicunas, 68
Green issues, 147

Group creativity, 280
Group excellence, 101
Group learning, 237
Group norms, 307
Group think, 310

Hawthorne experiments, 29
Herzberg, 29, 225
Hierarchy, 65
Human relations, 28
Human resource management, 230
Hygiene factors, 225

Implementation of strategic plans, 207
Inefficient organisation structure, 64
Informal organisation, 63
Informal planning, 138
Information roles, 36
Information-based organisations, 167
Innovation, 275
Internal audit, 245, 253
Internal trading accounts, 172
International comparisons, 154
Interpersonal roles, 36

Job description, 233
Job enlargement, 226
Job enrichment, 226
Job rotation, 227
Justice, 350

KOW model, 157

Labour turnover, 240
Leadership, 47, 99, 191
 - styles, 192
Learning organisation, 279
Lewin, 29
Likert, 17, 196
Line management, 71, 77
Local authorities' roles
 - as enabler, 125
 - competitor, 169
 - regulator, 55, 126

McGregor, 16
Management, 16, 69
 - as profession, 354
 - competences, 45, 204
 - education, 296
 - responsibilities, 331
Management by objectives (MBO), 29, 87
Management Charter Initiative, 45
Manager as 'teacher', 48
Manager's roles, 36, 221
Managerialism in the public sector, 343
Manpower plan, 232
Market organisation, 81
Marketing, 78
Matrix management, 78
Matrix organisation, 88
Matrix structure, 73
Mayo, 29
Mechanistic management, 21
Mechanistic system, 111
Mintzberg, 36, 222
Mission statement, 41, 103, 133
Motivation, 18, 100, 224
Motivator factors, 225

National Health Service, 60, 82, 88, 95, 113, 164
Neighbourhood offices, 83
Network technology, 120
Networking, 35, 119
New Zealand, 151

Ombudsmen, 56, 149
Open system, 142
Operations managers, 77
Organic structure, 111
Organisation, 53
 - design, 75
 - development, 128
Organisational fitness test, 3
Organisational style, 108
Organismic structure, 111

Participatory view, 21
Partisan mutual adjustment (model of decision making), 183
Partnership (between organisations), 127
Patient-focused organisation, 82
Performance indicators, 142, 151, 212
Person culture, 106
Personnel planning, 231
Peters and Waterman, 40
Policy, 179

Polytechnics, 110
Position audit, 205
Post entrepreneurial organisation, 121
Power, 17, 187
  - club culture, 106
Pressures for uniformity, 32
Private sector comparisons and models, 46, 141
Private sector links, 55
Problem solving, 280
Product organisation, 81
Project teams, 89
Promotion (of staff), 240
Public relations, 72, 78
Public sector management, since 1982, 23, 46

Quality circles, 271
Quality control, 264, 266, 268
Quality management, 259
Quality measurement, 269

Rational model of decision making, 99, 182
Recruitment, 233
Regulatory organisations, 55, 56
Renewal, 299
Research and development, 72, 80
Role culture (or bureaucracy), 105

Scalar chain, 65
Scientific management, 28
Service level agreements, 173
Skills training, 289
Sources of power, 187
Span of control, 67
Stable environments, 32
Staff appraisal, 239
Staff management, 71, 77, 204, 282

Stakeholders, 327
Standards, 142
Stewart, 36
Strategic management, 59
Strategic planning, 135, 137, 165
Structure, 63, 205
Sub-optimality, 83
Support functions, 77
SWOT, 137, 206
Systems approach, 31, 199

T groups, 237
Tall organisation, 69
Task culture, 105
Teams, 92, 305
Teamwork, 92
Technology, 120, 148, 165
Territory, 59
Theory X, 16, 196
Theory Y, 16, 196
Theory Z, 16
Total quality management (TQM), 260
Training, 235, 286
Trust/control of dilemma, 362
Turbulence, 164

Unity of command, 88
Unstable environments, 32
Urwick, 68

Value for money audits, 245
Values, 45
Voluntary organisations, 126

Widdicombe Committee, 188

FURTHER READING

You may like to test your grasp of Organisational Management by tackling short questions in multiple choice format. BPP publish the *Password* series of books, each of which incorporates a large collection of multiple choice questions with solutions, comments and marking guides. The *Password* title relevant to Organisational Management is called *Organisation and Management*. This is priced at £6.95 and contains over 300 questions.

To order your Password book, ring our credit card hotline on 081-740 6808. Alternatively, send this page to our Freepost address or fax it to us on 081-740 1184.

To: BPP Publishing Ltd, FREEPOST, London W12 8BR   **Tel: 081-740 6808**
                                                          Fax: 081-740 1184

Forenames (Mr / Ms): _____

Surname: _____

Address: _____

_____

Post code: _____

Please send me the following books: *Quantity*   *Price*   *Total*

Password *Organisation and Management*   £6.95

Please include postage & packing:

UK: £1.50 for first plus £0.50 for each extra book   ....

Overseas: £3.00 for first plus £1.50 for each extra book   ....

I enclose a cheque for £_____ or charge to Access/Visa

Card number   [ ][ ][ ][ ][ ][ ][ ][ ][ ][ ][ ][ ][ ][ ][ ][ ]

Expiry date _____   Signature _____

On the reverse of this page there is a Review Form, which you can send in to us (at the Freepost address above) with comments and suggestions on the Text you have just finished. Your feedback really does make a difference: it helps us to make the next edition that bit better.

Name: _____

How have you used this Text?

Home study (book only) ☐   With 'correspondence' package ☐

On a course: college_____ ☐   Other _____

How did you obtain this Text?

From us by mail order ☐   From us by phone ☐

From a bookshop ☐   From your college ☐

Where did you hear about BPP Texts?

At bookshop ☐   Recommended by lecturer ☐

Recommended by friend ☐   Mailshot from BPP ☐

Advertisement in _____ ☐   Other _____

Your comments and suggestions would be appreciated on the following areas.

Syllabus coverage

Illustrative questions

Errors (please specify, and refer to a page number)

Presentation

Other